TUTANKHAMUN'S ARMIES

Artist's reconstruction of Akhenaten's year 12 reception of foreign tribute, based on scenes from the tombs of Meryre II and Huya at Amarna. After Clara Siemens, *Koenig Echnaton in El-Amarna*.

TUTANKHAMUN'S ARMIES

BATTLE AND CONQUEST DURING ANCIENT EGYPT'S LATE EIGHTEENTH DYNASTY

JOHN COLEMAN DARNELL
COLLEEN MANASSA

BICENTENNIAL
1807
WILEY
2007
BICENTENNIAL

John Wiley & Sons, Inc.

For general information about our other products and services, please contact our Cus-
tomer Care Department within the United States at (800) 762-2974, outside the United
States at (317) 572-3993 or fax (317) 572-4002.

Wiley also publishes its books in a variety of electronic formats. Some content that appears
in print may not be available in electronic books. For more information about Wiley products, visit our web site at www.wiley.com.

Library of Congress Cataloging-in-Publication Data:

Darnell, John Coleman, date.
    Tutankhamun's armies : battle and conquest during ancient Egypt's late
eighteenth dynasty / John Coleman Darnell and Colleen Manassa.
        p.   cm.
    Includes bibliographic references.
    ISBN: 978-0-471-74358-3 (alk. paper)
    1. Egypt—History, Military. 2. Egypt—History—Eighteenth dynasty,
ca. 1570–1320 B.C. 3. Military history, Ancient. I. Manassa, Colleen. II. Title.
DT81.D36 2007
932′.014—dc22

                                                                2006022117

Printed in the United States of America

10 9 8 7 6 5 4 3 2 1

To Charles and Cornelia Manassa
and John Susan Walker

CONTENTS

ATLAS

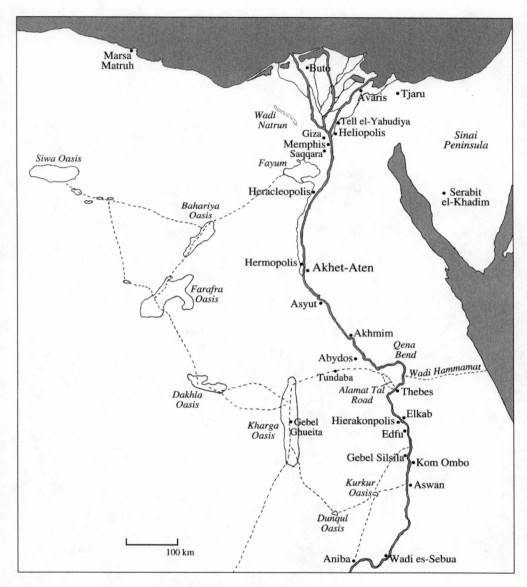

The Nile Valley and its desert hinterlands.

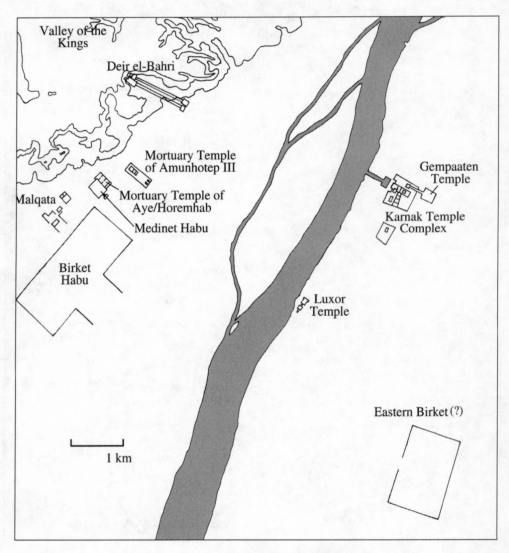

The important sites of New Kingdom Thebes.

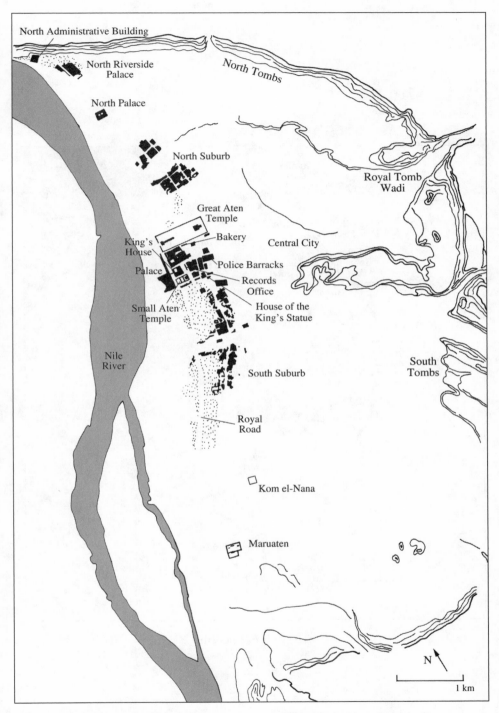

The city of Akhet-aten. After Freed, Markowitz, and D'Auria, eds. *Pharaohs of the Sun*, 15 (with additions).

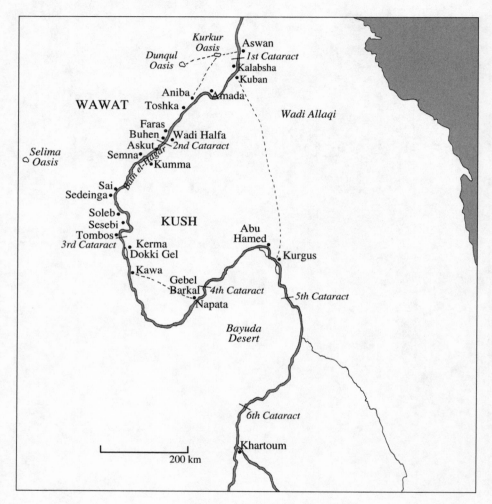

The Nubian Nile Valley.

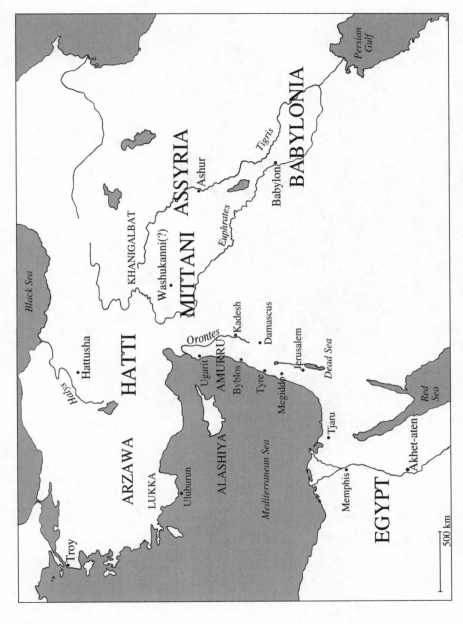

The great powers of the ancient Near East. After Cohen and Westbrook, eds., *Amarna Diplomacy*, xii (with additions).

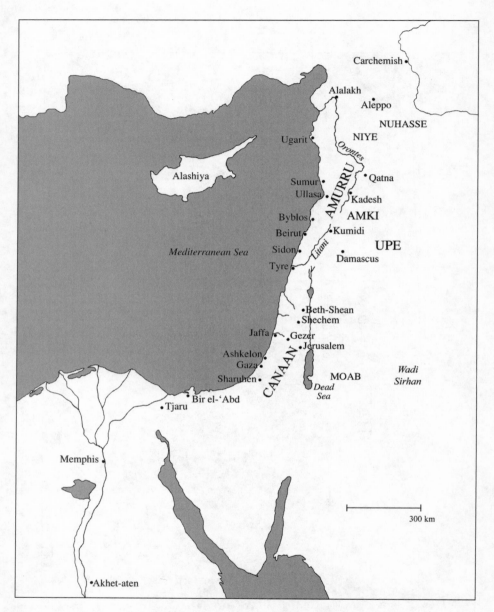

Syria-Palestine in the late Eighteenth Dynasty.

ACKNOWLEDGMENTS

We would like to thank Stephen S. Power, senior editor at John Wiley & Sons, for the opportunity to publish on a topic that has captured our interest for many years. Our appreciation extends to Naomi Rothwell, who first sought us out for this project, John Simko, the senior production editor, and William Drennan, who copyedited the manuscript. This book would not have been possible without the diligence of Maureen Draicchio, administrative assistant at the Department of Near Eastern Languages and Civilizations at Yale University.

In a number of ways, this book presents a preliminary overview of a number of forthcoming scholarly works by John Coleman Darnell. Although we have tried to provide the necessary bibliographic background to all major points in the volume, we also attempted to keep the notes to a reasonable size and a modest number and often did not provide the same level of documentation that we hope to provide in future publications. Nevertheless, those familiar with the literature on Amarna Period Egypt and those who in the future will familiarize themselves with these works will see clearly throughout the volume our debt to earlier works on the period. Here we would like specifically to signal the importance of publications by Cyril Aldred, Jan Assmann, Marc Gabolde, Erik Hornung, Raymond Johnson, Barry Kemp, William Moran, William Murnane, and Donald Redford.

Many of the concepts appearing in the present volume were developed during the course of lecture classes and text seminars taught by John at Yale University, and he would like to thank all the students who participated in these classes over the past eight years. For ten years, John was an epigrapher and senior epigrapher with the Epigraphic Survey of the Oriental Institute of the University of Chicago, working in Luxor, Egypt. At least half of this time was occupied in recording and editing the scenes and inscriptions of Tutankhamun, Horemhab, Seti I, and others in Amunhotep III's Colonnade Hall at Luxor Temple. During this time he not only honed the skills he would need for his later work with rock inscriptions in the Western Desert, but also acquired an intimate knowledge of one of the masterpieces of Tutankhamun's reign: the Opet Procession cycle in Luxor's Colonnade Hall. John would like to thank all the members of the Epigraphic Survey with whom he worked over the years, including former field directors Lanny Bell and Peter Dorman. John would particularly like to thank Deborah Darnell, Richard Jasnow, and Raymond Johnson (now field director of the Epigraphic Survey) for fruitful discussions about Egyptological—and particularly Amarna—topics.

No inconsiderable portion of the present publication also derives from the ongoing work of the Theban Desert Road Survey and the Yale Toshka Desert Survey in the Western Desert. Although it is not possible to thank everyone who has contributed to this project over the years, we would like to thank Deborah Darnell and all the members of the Egyptian Antiquities Organization and the Supreme Council for Antiquities, including former directors Dr. Gaballa Ali Gaballa, Dr. Ali Hassan, Dr. Abd el-Halim Nur El-Din, Dr. Mohammed Bakr, and the current General Director of the Supreme Council, Dr. Zahi Hawass. Dr. Bahai Issawy, Mohammed es-Saghir, Sabri Abd el-Aziz, Attia Radwan, Mohammed el-Bialy, Ali el-Asfar, Adel Kelany, Abd el-Hakim Haddad, and Mr. Mohy all assisted with our work in Thebes and Aswan. These and many others we have thanked in our publications and season reports, and express our utmost gratitude here.

Charles and Cornelia Manassa commented on a draft of the book and provided several insightful suggestions on how to present the material. Colleen would also like to thank Ruth Kimmel, the Kimmel family, and Greg Stone for their enthusiasm about our project.

The William K. and Marilyn M. Simpson Endowment for Egyptology at Yale University covered the reproduction costs for some of the images. We appreciate the help of Nicola Harrington at the Griffith Institute, Oxford University, and Tobin Hartnell and John Larsen at the Oriental Institute of the University of Chicago in acquiring photographs and illustrations. Images from the Ägyptisches Museum und Papyrussammlung and the Vorderasiatisches Museum in Berlin were acquired through the efficient Web site of the Art Resource.

NOTE TO THE READER

No consistent spelling of ancient Egyptian names and toponyms exists. Since the ancient Egyptian scripts did not overtly indicate voweling, the use of particular spellings is typically determined by either convention or the spelling of some words in Coptic, the last stage of the Egyptian language, which is written in Greek letters and includes vowel sounds. Some scholars prefer to use Greek versions of Egyptian names (e.g., Amenophis vs. Amunhotep), but the names used in the present work represent normalized versions of the hieroglyphic spellings. To distinguish between the name of the pharaoh Akhenaten ("He who is effective for the Aten") and his capital city, Akhetaten ("Horizon of the Aten"), the latter is spelled with a hyphen: "Akhet-aten."

For places outside of Egypt, we have tried to avoid using the names of modern nation-states, since their borders do not correspond to the boundaries of ancient states. For example, the term "Syria-Palestine" is used to encompass all or part of the modern countries of Palestine, Israel, Jordan, Lebanon, and Syria. Broader terms, such as western Asia, can include the Hittite homeland of Anatolia and the region of Mesopotamia.

The translations of Egyptian texts presented in this work are those of the authors, unless otherwise stated in the notes. Text placed between brackets indicates restorations when the original text is damaged, while parentheses provide explanations of names or terms.

CHRONOLOGY

Amunhotep II	1427–1400
Thutmose IV	1400–1390
Amunhotep III	1390–1352
Amunhotep IV/Akhenaten	**1352–1336**
Neferneferuaten	**1337–1334 (?)**
Smenkhkare	**1334–1333 (?)**
Tutankhamun	**1332–1322**
Aye	**1322–1319**
Horemhab	**1319–1292**

19th Dynasty

Ramesses I	1292–1291
Seti I	1290–1279
Ramesses II	1279–1213
Merneptah	1213–1203

20th Dynasty

Ramesses III	1184–1153

Third Intermediate Period: Dynasties 21–25	1069–664 B.C.E.
Late Period: Dynasties 26–30	664–332 B.C.E.
Ptolemaic Period	332–30 B.C.E.
Roman and Byzantine periods	30 B.C.E.–A.D. 641

Source: Adapted from Ian Shaw, ed., *Oxford History of Ancient Egypt* (Oxford, U.K.: Oxford University Press, 2000), 479–482.

1

❖❖❖❖❖❖❖❖

LAND OF DESERT
AND NILE

The two stallions strained against their yokes, hooves pounding the earth and plumed headdresses bobbing as they galloped ahead. The leather-tired wheels of the light chariot hurtled over the rocky terrain as the king, reins tied tightly behind his waist, drew back the bowstring to launch another arrow into the enemy hordes. The royal chariot charged into a seething scene of absolute mayhem, a towering mound of flailing limbs, terrified enemies trampling their fallen comrades to escape from the oncoming pharaoh and his chariot warriors. Around the king, his infantry waded through the wounded and dying, thrusting with their daggers and spears, pausing only to sever the right hands of the dead enemy soldiers as records of their kills. Egyptian victory was inevitable. Or so the pharaoh Tutankhamun would have us imagine his military exploits . . . but what was the reality of war in the time of Tutankhamun?

On November 26, 1922, Egyptologist Howard Carter looked through the small opening he had just made in the wall sealing the tomb of an ancient Egyptian pharaoh and gazed upon the mortuary treasure of Tutankhamun[1] (see figure 1). Among the fabulously bejeweled and beautifully crafted tomb furnishings were the pharaoh's implements of war—chariots, bows, arrows, daggers, a leather cuirass, and other martial equipment, both ceremonial and more mundanely practical. Carter's discovery of the tomb of Tutankhamun catapulted an otherwise obscure pharaoh into international fame, and gave impetus to yet another of the world's recurring cycles of Egyptomania, yet it failed to add significantly to the meager fragments of historical information for Tutankhamun's reign. The famous gold mask of the "boy king" may yet stare placidly across the millennia, but the reign

1

Figure 1. Asiatic battle scene from Tutankhamun's "Painted Box" (Egyptian Museum, Cairo, JdE 61467). Wearing the Blue Crown, the pharaoh Tutankhamun charges against a mass of Asiatic chariotry, where Egyptian soldiers are busy dispatching the enemies with spears and daggers. Symbols of pharaonic kingship and protection hover above the pharaoh, who is followed by fan-bearing officials in chariots. Courtesy of the Griffith Institute, Oxford University.

of Tutankhamun—like those of many who ruled before and after him—was not devoid of military conflict. In fact, the stability of ancient Egyptian civilization and the creation of the magnificent objects buried with Tutankhamun were the fruits of an often effective military strategy.[2]

Curiously, although Tutankhamun and his immediate predecessors and successors of the late Eighteenth and early Nineteenth dynasties engaged in a complicated and ultimately successful series of political machinations and military campaigns, the popular conception of Tutankhamun's age is one of religious obsession, nature worship, and even pacifism. This popular mythologizing arises from well-meaning but ultimately inaccurate attempts to explain the behavior of Tutankhamun's predecessor and father, Amunhotep IV/Akhenaten,[3] who set his personal imprint on the late Eighteenth Dynasty, an era long termed the "Amarna Period." Akhenaten, famous for his radical innovations in Egyptian religion, moved the administrative and religious centers of Egypt from Thebes (modern Luxor) and Memphis (near modern Cairo) to his new capital, Akhet-aten (near the village of el-Amarna in Middle Egypt). Through his activities at home and abroad, Akhenaten casts his somewhat misshapen shadow across the reigns of all of his Eighteenth Dynasty successors; even Horemhab, at the end of the dynasty, as forceful and important as he was in his own right, devoted no little time and energy to restoring temples that had suffered from Akhenaten's iconoclasm and to uprooting administrative corruption that appears to have flourished in the wake of Akhenaten's political and religious upheaval.

The reigns of Akhenaten's successors Ankh(et)kheperure, Smenkhkare, Tutankhamun, Aye, and to some extent even the reign of Horemhab are all subsumed under the designation "Amarna Period," an era that lasted from circa 1352 to 1295 B.C.E. The so-called religious revolution of Akhenaten, the splendid objects from Tutankhamun's tomb, the peculiarities of much of the art and architecture of the period, and the historical problems have all pushed the military history of the Amarna Period into the background. This ignoring of the seemingly mundane for the apparently esoteric is unfortunate, for the Amarna Period is a fascinating era for the study of military strategy and diplomatic maneuver, a time when great empires vied for power, minor polities sought to align and realign themselves to the greatest advantage, and mighty kings and wily princes went to all lengths to secure alliances and destroy their enemies. Diplomatic niceties meant that the pharaoh often commiserated with a city ruler while pushing the knife into the latter's back—a lack of direct conflict does not preclude a complex military history.

The lives of those engaged in the military affairs of Egypt—from the pharaoh and his chief generals and advisers down to the foot soldiers—were subject to the same polarizing forces that produced the unique character of pharaonic culture. The contrast of the flowing waters of the Nile and the often narrow surrounding margin of cultivation, with the forbidding rocks and sands of the vast deserts beyond, sets its imprint on all aspects of existence along the Nile Valley. By the beginning of the third millennium B.C.E., the deserts surrounding the Nile Valley had begun to approach their modern state of desiccation,[4] and the waters of the Nile and the oases of the Egyptian Western Desert had already become the foci for much of human activity in northeastern Africa.[5]

Certainly the Nile River and its annual inundation constituted the lifeblood of ancient Egypt—the chief source of water for irrigation and the origin of the black alluvial soil of Egypt's fields—but the now harsh deserts surrounding the Nile Valley also played an important role in the rise of Egyptian civilization. Geographically, the Egyptians divided their country between the lush Nile Valley, which they called *kemet* (the black land), a reference to the rich alluvial soil, and the desert, called *deshret* (the red land). This essentially east–west dichotomy running the length of the Nile Valley was balanced by a north–south division: Lower Egypt, encompassing the Nile Delta to the north, a broad region of fields, swamps, and river channels, and Upper Egypt, the Nile Valley south of Memphis, always a relatively narrow strip of cultivation bounded on the east and the west by desert cliffs. The opposition and balance between the desert regions and the cultivated lands, and those between Upper Egypt and Lower Egypt, together created much of the character of Egyptian culture and propelled many of the major events of Egyptian history.[6]

At the dawn of the Predynastic Period, in about 4500 B.C.E., over a millennium before Egypt possessed a single ruler and a centralized state, the cultures of Upper Egypt traded with other peoples who lived in the desert regions to the south and west, where seasonal lakes created an interesting blend of hunting, gathering, and pastoralism. This interaction between the inhabitants of the desert and those of the Upper Egyptian Nile Valley fueled the development of a complex and symbol-oriented culture that would become what we know as pharaonic Egypt.[7] Over time, the power centers of Upper Egypt became culticly and economically interrelated, even homogeneous.[8] The final form of a unified Egyptian state was melded in the crucible of interregional conflict from which one man, apparently the ruler of a coalition of the city-states of Hierakonpolis and Abydos, would emerge victorious. In approximately 3150 B.C.E., a ruler based at Abydos and possibly calling himself Horus Scorpion unified the three main centers of Upper Egyptian culture. Drawing on the centuries-old Upper Egyptian tradition of carving symbolic representations on the desert cliffs, the unifier of Upper Egypt commissioned what may well be Egypt's first historical document, an annotated depiction recording his military victory over his last rival in Upper Egypt.[9]

Less than two centuries later, Narmer completed the Upper Egyptian conquest of the Delta, a region that appears to have become a patchwork of city-states not unlike the contemporaneous political organization prevailing in the Middle East. The Egyptian love of dualism led the dominant Upper Egyptians to portray the conquest as the unification of an Upper Egyptian state and a corresponding Lower Egyptian state, even though predynastic Lower Egypt does not appear to have achieved the political and symbolic sophistication of Upper Egypt.[10] Narmer thus officially began the long history of pharaonic kingship, which would endure for the following three millennia. Modern divisions of Egypt's long history derive in large part from the Greco-Egyptian historian Manetho, who, utilizing earlier Egyptian king lists and other historical sources, divided the history of Egypt into dynasties grouped by city origin and family relationships.[11] Prior to the first millennium, three series of powerful dynasties ruled over a unified Upper and Lower Egypt: the Old Kingdom (Dynasties 4–6, 2686–2160 B.C.E.), Middle Kingdom (Dynasties 11–14, 2055–1650 B.C.E.), and New Kingdom (Dynasties 18–20, 1550–1069 B.C.E.).

These "kingdoms," times of centralization and powerful pharaohs, were interspersed with so-called intermediate periods, when the country fragmented into smaller political units. Beginning with the late Predynastic Period, Upper Egypt became the home of a particularly strong concept of centralized governmental authority, and during the various cycles of political weakness in the Egyptian Nile Valley, Upper Egypt was often the point of origin for the reestablishment of a powerful unified government. The period of disunity following the Old Kingdom—the First Intermediate Period (2160–2055 B.C.E.)—came to an end when a highly centralized and pugnacious Upper Egyptian kingdom centered at Thebes extended its authority along the entire Egyptian Nile Valley. The ensuing Middle Kingdom ushered in a four-hundred-year period of relative peace and stability, which ended with a weak Thirteenth Dynasty Egyptian administration first relinquishing control of the northeast Delta to local usurpers, and finally losing that same territory and more to an alliance of those Delta warlords, eastern Mediterranean traders, and foreign invaders from the northeast, the Hyksos.[12]

The Hyksos domination in the north coincided with the loss of Egyptian territories in the southern lands, usually termed Nubia, where the Kerma culture also established an independent kingdom. A powerful Theban-based Egyptian Seventeenth Dynasty, direct successor to the Thirteenth Dynasty, drove out the Hyksos rulers from the Delta and pushed the Kermans far south into Nubia, thereby reestablishing a unified Egypt and initiating the golden age of the New Kingdom. In some ways the New Kingdom is the ultimate and most wide-reaching expression of an Upper Egyptian concept of a militarily aggressive central administration, governed initially by Theban rulers whose ancestors were able to end two periods of disunity in the Nile Valley.

From the beginning of the New Kingdom, in iconic imagery, textual descriptions, and bloody reality, the Egyptian pharaoh became a true "warrior king." Pharaohs of the Eighteenth Dynasty in particular touted their mastery of weaponry and their skill in horsemanship, as well as their personal bravery in battle.[13] Claims of physical prowess were also balanced by assertions of mental acumen—not only was the pharaoh strong enough to kill the opposition, he also was clever enough to develop a strategy that would guarantee victory.[14] The emphatically militaristic ideology of pharaonic kingship in the New Kingdom is closely linked to changes in the nature of the Egyptian army. During the Second Intermediate Period, the Egyptian arsenal acquired two new weapons: the composite bow and the chariot. The composite bow enhanced the effectiveness of the two traditional branches of the Egyptian military, the infantry and the navy, and became the key weapon for the new Egyptian chariot corps. Furthermore, the greater diplomatic and military interaction of the Egyptians with more distant foreign groups, a direct outgrowth of the Second Intermediate Period, led to an increased use of auxiliary troops from Asia and Libya alongside the traditional employment of Nubian bowmen. The expansion of the three branches of the Egyptian military—infantry, chariotry, and navy—necessary for the battles against the Hyksos and the Kermans at the end of the Second Intermediate Period created one of the largest professional armies in the ancient Near East.

The reunification of Egypt and the rise of its highly militarized state at the beginning of the Eighteenth Dynasty combined with the memory of foreign invasion to fuel Egypt's aspirations to conquer territory to the south, modern-day southern Egypt and northern Sudan, and to the northeast, including the regions of Palestine, Trans-Jordan, and Syria. The pharaohs of the Amarna Period inherited a powerful Egyptian empire, the product of years of campaigning by pharaohs such as Thutmose I and

Thutmose III, who ruled the largest area of Egyptian hegemony in the history of the pharaonic state. Maintaining Egypt's extensive foreign territories required both military strength and diplomatic prowess to confront the problems posed by the very different cultures of Nubia and western Asia. The primarily tribal organization and increasingly mixed native and Egyptian cultures of Nubia and the complex and mutually distrustful city-states of Syria-Palestine necessitated two different forms of colonial administration in the southern and northern realms of Egypt's empire.

Nubia, the land stretching south from the Egyptian border at the administrative center and trade emporium of Aswan, was Egypt's primary source of gold as well as the gateway—by Nile and desert routes—to the trade goods of more southerly regions of Africa, including many of the products necessary for ancient Egyptian religious rituals. Throughout Egyptian history, Nubian political structure vacillated between centralized powers at war with Egypt, such as the Kerman kingdom of the early second millennium, and a colonial system ruled by Egypt.[15] The degree of Nubian independence reflected inversely the strength of pharaonic rule—during each of the highly centralized periods of Egyptian history—the Old, Middle, and New kingdoms—Egypt directly controlled large areas of Nubian territory. The intermediate periods of strife and decentralization within Egypt signaled a withdrawal of Egyptian garrisons and the abandonment of fortifications in Nubia, allowing the growth of independent Nubian states. Despite some of the internal Egyptian troubles during the reigns of Akhenaten and his successors, throughout the Amarna Period, Nubia remained an Egyptian colony with a Nubian "viceroy" and colonial administration. Monuments dating to the reign of Tutankhamun provide some of the most detailed and lively information about Egyptian and Nubian interactions from the entire New Kingdom. But even Egypt's strong colonial system was unable to prevent rebellions by nomadic tribes, which could threaten the all-important gold mining regions and necessitate swift Egyptian military action.

The Egyptian empire of the New Kingdom also extended beyond the northeastern border of the Nile Delta, into the region of Syria-Palestine, which, like all areas beyond the Sinai Peninsula, is often termed western Asia or simply Asia in Egyptological parlance. Much of the military history of the Eighteenth Dynasty is intimately related to Egypt's desire for greater control over the region of Syria-Palestine—won by force of arms under Thutmose I and Thutmose III, but often achieved by indirect means in the latter part of the Eighteenth Dynasty. The humiliation of the Second Intermediate Period fostered an aggressive Egyptian foreign policy, impatient to identify and neutralize any potential Asiatic threat as far as possible beyond the immediate eastern border of the Nile Delta. As the Eighteenth Dynasty progressed, the maintenance of buffer states in the northeast brought Egypt into contact and often conflict with the powerful kingdoms of the Near East and Asia Minor who might ultimately attempt an invasion of Egypt's northeastern holdings, if not perhaps the Nile Delta itself. The constantly shifting alliances between Egypt and these political entities of western Asia meant that the group posing the greatest threat to Egypt changed over time. The pharaohs of the early Eighteenth Dynasty led numerous campaigns against the kingdom of Mitanni, centered on the upper Euphrates. By the late Eighteenth Dynasty, however, Mitanni no longer posed a significant threat. The fierce military conflicts between Egypt and Mitanni instead became an alliance sealed by the marriage of Mitannian princesses to the Egyptian pharaoh, beginning with Thutmose IV and continuing with his successor Amunhotep III.

During the early Amarna Period a state of relative peace existed in the region of Syria-Palestine. However, the hostile role Mitanni once played gradually passed to the Hittite kingdom, centered at the city of Hattusas (modern Bogazköy) in Asia Minor. The strategy of the late Eighteenth Dynasty rulers toward the Hittites differed from the earlier pharaohs' direct attacks on Mitanni. Diplomatic maneuvering among Egypt, the Hittites, and the satellite states of the two powers during the reigns of Akhenaten and his successors often overshadows the evidence for military skirmishes. Much of this diplomacy took the form of a continuous stream of official written correspondence between the pharaohs of Egypt and the rulers of the major kingdoms and small city-states of Asia Minor and the Near East. While most of these ancient diplomatic letters are now lost, a large group of these missives was discovered at Akhenaten's capital city of Akhet-aten, from which find spot they derive their modern appellation the "Amarna Letters." Through these letters we may reconstruct the complex foreign policy of the late Eighteenth Dynasty toward the kingdoms that bordered on Egypt's northern territories.

In addition to political and military friction they experienced with the powerful and centralized kingdoms to the northeast, and occasional challenges to pharaonic authority in the increasingly Egyptianized lands to the south, the Egyptians of the Amarna Period also faced opposition from less urbanized groups on the borders of Egypt and her dependencies. The Libyans of the Egyptian Western Desert hovered about the fringes of pharaonic society and were both an integral part of life in the oases and an ever-present menace to Egyptian control thereof. Already by the time of

Amunhotep III, the northern coasts of Egypt and the Western Desert were also subject to piratical incursions of Mediterranean groups. Repelling raids by these mobile opponents demanded a set of strategies and tactics different from those the Egyptians employed in their more formal confrontations with the armies of Mitanni, the Hittites, and smaller groups in western Asia. Unlike the often wide-open battlefields of Syria-Palestine, with their set-piece battles on carefully chosen sites ideally suited to the use of massed chariotry, the rough terrain in the hinterlands of Egypt's borders probably relegated the chariotry to an at best subordinate role in many if not most expeditions against opponents such as the Libyans. Egyptian foot archers and infantry played a greater role in campaigns against those groups of "irregular" troops.

The ancient Egyptians did not simply seek imperial glory for its own glamour and prestige, but rather acquired much of their new imperial accolades in the search for internal security through establishment of colonial outposts and the fostering of buffer states beyond their borders. The term "empire" has rather extraordinary baggage for the modern world, and although the ancient empire par excellence is, of course, the Roman Empire, scholars have assigned the designation "empire" to a variety of political entities, ranging from geographically limited and relatively poorly documented city-states (e.g., the "empire" of Sargon) to conglomerations of large geographic extent and overwhelmingly elaborate and highly centralized bureaucracies (e.g., the Soviet empire).[16] The present publication will use the term "empire" when referring to New Kingdom Egypt, as composed of the pharaonic state of Egypt, her junior sister state Nubia, and her dependencies in Syria-Palestine.[17] Likewise we will also employ a mixture of imperial terminology, such as "province," "colony," and "viceroy," some of which derive from the Roman and British empires. The fact that the Egyptians tailored their diplomacy to the local situation, in light of the degree of integration of foreign territories within the Egyptian administration, indicates that the ancient Egyptian empire builders saw themselves not simply as expanding the static borders of Egypt proper, but also were well aware that they were dealing with a multiplicity of geographic, administrative, and cultural considerations, all of which mirror the actions of Rome and late-nineteenth/early-twentieth-century Great Britain.

In spite of the fact that New Kingdom Egypt appears to have adopted a pragmatic attitude toward the particular regions and circumstances of her empire, ideologically, all actions of aggression and acquisition outside of the traditional realm of Egypt could be termed *sewesekh tashu* (broadening the borders.)[18] In terms of Egyptian religious thought, Egypt is not only the model of the ordered world but also the most perfectly formed and well-functioning portion of the world. Just as creation exists as a bubble of order within the threatening abyss of chaos, so Egypt was surrounded by foreign groups, all of whom represented potentially dangerous and chaotic forces. By expanding Egyptian control over foreign lands, the territory of the ordered world was thereby enlarged. This can present some problems for the modern historian, because whatever may have been the mundane causes of any conflict, such a conflict would only acquire proper meaning for the ancient Egyptians when they could demonstrate that the struggle in some way produced an extension of the ordered cosmos—in the end, any and all physical or ideological expansion beyond the home territories of Egypt would for the ancient Egyptians be the acting out of "broadening the borders."

Whether recounted on a temple wall or on a private monument, the military records of the ancient Egyptians served a higher purpose—proof of the triumph of order over chaos. The ancient Egyptians lived in a cosmos governed by the universal duality of *maat* (order) versus *isfet* (chaos).[19] The preservation of maat, which included justice and all aspects of cosmic harmony, was the most basic ideological reason for warfare in ancient Egypt. Unlike our concept of objective history, all Egyptian historical texts—particularly military documents—served a theological purpose, whatever degree of historical accuracy they were intended to have. Furthermore, one must remember that most royal military texts and scenes decorated the exterior walls of temples, serving the dual role of historical record and symbolic protection of the sacred space from chaotic forces.[20] The religious aspects of their military records did not prevent the Egyptians from accurately reporting the events of the battles they chose to portray.[21] Occasionally, documents from Egypt's enemies also provide another point of view, enabling one to reconstruct Egyptian defeats that otherwise went unrecorded. Such outside evidence is most abundant during the Amarna Period, since letters written by rulers hostile to Egypt have survived. Although Egyptian military texts are often characterized as bombastic or purely propagandistic, when viewed properly within the perspective of their greater theological purpose, they may often yield considerable detail about historical events.

The reign of Tutankhamun was the final portion of a pivotal era in the realm of Egyptian military and diplomatic policies. The imperial vision of Thutmose I swept away the old Egyptian approach of limited borders and established far-flung limits of Egyptian influence in western Asia and Nubia. The warfare of his successors, particularly Thutmose III, later

evolved into intense diplomatic maneuvering, particularly under the pharaohs of the Amarna Period, who created a world in which major conflicts
between the powers were increasingly unlikely and undesirable, but one
in which lower-intensity military actions again became more prevalent.
Surprisingly, in spite of much that has been written, Tutankhamun and
the pharaohs of the Amarna Period did indeed engage in warfare—both
armed conflict and psychological warfare—and the outcome of those battles, as limited in scope as they might appear to modern eyes, nevertheless did, through the lens of the ancient Egyptian worldview, reveal an
ever-triumphant pharaoh standing atop the shattered remnants of his
chaotic foe.

2

·:·‡·:·‡·:·✦·:·‡·:·‡·:·

THE AMARNA
INTERLUDE

There are no rebels in your reign, since they have reached nonexistence. The chiefs [of . . . have fallen] to your power. Your battle cries are like a blasting flame in pursuit of every foreign country.

—Nubian viceroy's praise of Akhenaten[1]

The reign of Akhenaten was a turning point in Egyptian history, a moment when a highly idiosyncratic pharaoh could revel in the tremendous changes he had enacted on Egyptian society.[2] The multitude of gods revered for millennia were anathema to Akhenaten and his clergy, and a single deity, the Aten, became the object of royal worship—for the rest of Egypt, the triad of king, queen, and solar disk were the primary focus of all religious activity. The art, architecture, and even daily life in Akhenaten's new capital must have been a shocking experience for many of Akhet-aten's inhabitants. Although Akhenaten is sometimes characterized as a pacifist and a monotheist, both designations are simplistically false. Akhenaten did not shun martial pomp, but surrounded himself with a well-armed bodyguard heavily supplemented with foreign soldiers. Soldiers not only accompanied their monarch in his daily routine, but also were sent out to battle foreign enemies.

The military events of the reign of Akhenaten and his successors are described in detail in the following chapters, while the present section explores some of the historical and religious enigmas of the Amarna Period, providing the proper background to the warfare of the time. As much of an anomaly as Akhenaten's rule might be, his religious "revolution" is a reflection of trends already at work during the reign of his father, Amun-hotep III. The "Pax Aegyptiaca" from which Akhenaten benefited was the result of hard-earned military success by the pharaohs of the early Eighteenth Dynasty. A proper understanding of the history of the early Eighteenth Dynasty, and an appreciation of the origin and development of Akhenaten's worldview, are necessary for understanding the military and diplomatic events of the Amarna Period.

The Founding of the New Kingdom

The founder of the New Kingdom and the first pharaoh of the Eighteenth Dynasty is Ahmose (1550–1525 B.C.E.), whose reign saw the expulsion of the Hyksos from the Delta and the reunification of Upper and Lower Egypt under the rule of a single pharaoh. However, the rulers of the late Seventeenth Dynasty and the first two kings of the Eighteenth Dynasty are in terms of family and foreign policy a unity. The pharaoh Senakh-tenre and his queen Tetisheri appear to have begun the final phase of the Seventeenth Dynasty, during which the old Middle Kingdom system of titles was abandoned at Thebes, the royal women came to wield consider-able temporal power, and Thebes initiated open hostilities against the Hyksos.[3] The aggressive policies of the Theban rulers, facilitated by their control over the extensive road networks in the Western Desert,[4] set in motion the events that would end the Second Intermediate Period. Senakhtenre's successor Seqenenre Tao II died in battle against the Hyksos,[5] but his successor Kamose[6] recaptured the Second Cataract in the south; in the north Kamose drove the Hyksos out of Middle Egypt, and ravaged their merchant fleet beneath the very walls of their capital, Avaris.[7] Perhaps Kamose, too, died in battle, and his successor Ahmose, a son of Seqenenre Tao II, was probably quite young when he acceded to the throne.

Thebes tarried a while in her push against the Hyksos, but when Ahmose finally felt that the time had come, he attacked Avaris directly. The reason for the Theban delay following Kamose's harrowing of Avaris and destruction of the Hyksos fleet was probably to allow the Hyksos economy to corrode. Kamose appears to have damaged Hyksos merchant shipping during his limited naval assault on Avaris (for more on the Hyksos trade empire, see page 138). Like the Spartans at the Battle of Aego-spotami (405 B.C.E.),[8] the Egyptians achieved more in relatively indirect action against the Hyksos economic base than they might have accomplished through a more direct military encounter with the main body of the Hyksos forces whose outcome might have been less certain.

Ahmose appears to have also understood that no enemy should be forced to fight to the death, for the desperate may well achieve what those who may safely flee would never dare.[9] After entering the ancient capital of Memphis, soon to become the northern administrative city and the arsenal of militant New Kingdom Egypt, Ahmose captured Tjaru, at the far eastern fringe of the Nile Delta. Having thereby prevented a Hyksos escape either up the Nile Valley into Middle Egypt or south into the Eastern Desert and the Red Sea littoral, and leaving open a narrow strip of land south of the Mediterranean coast—a corridor northeast of Avaris— Ahmose then turned west and marched on Avaris itself. Presented with a difficult fight at Avaris or flight across the northern Sinai into southern Palestine, the remnants of the Hyksos soon chose the latter option, and ensconced themselves in their final redoubt, the fortified town of Sharuhen in southern Palestine (probably modern Tell el-Ajjul).[10] After a siege of three years, Ahmose took the city, and the Hyksos disappear from history.

The destruction of the Hyksos as a military and economic power appears to have been the main and early-achieved goal of the late Seventeenth and early Eighteenth dynasties' military activity in the Egyptian Delta and in Syria-Palestine. What more Ahmose may have accomplished or planned in western Asia is unknown to us. For the reign of Amunhotep I, a son of Ahmose,[11] no definite evidence for Asiatic campaigning has emerged.[12] With the accession of the third king of the Eighteenth Dynasty, Egyptian foreign policy changes. Whereas Ahmose and Amunhotep I were of the family of the late Seventeenth Dynasty, Thutmose I and his chief queen were not royal before their accession;[13] Ahmose Nefertari, the wife and sister of the pharaoh Ahmose, often appears with them in depictions, giving Thutmose I and his queen a connection with the early Eighteenth Dynasty through iconography that they never had through blood.[14]

The first two rulers of the Eighteenth Dynasty shared not only the blood of the late Seventeenth Dynasty kings; like those rulers, they appear to have shared the Middle Kingdom's approach to Egypt's northern and southern frontiers. After the defeat of Kerma and the southern rebels, the early Eighteenth Dynasty was content to maintain a southern border roughly equivalent to that of the Middle Kingdom. In the north, following the expulsion of the Hyksos from Sharuhen, the first rulers of the Eighteenth Dynasty may have dispensed with even the *razzias* (plundering raids) of the Middle Kingdom.[15]

The founding of the New Kingdom was not only due to the leadership of the pharaoh, but also owed much to the bravery and initiative of individual soldiers in the Egyptian army. In fact, much of what we know about the wars of Kamose, Ahmose, Amunhotep I, and Thutmose I is contained in the autobiographical texts of marines buried at Elkab. One of the lengthiest and most detailed inscriptions belongs to a soldier who led a long and successful military career—Ahmose son of Ibana (his mother's name).[16] During the rule of the pharaoh Ahmose, the soldier Ahmose succeeded his father, Baba, who had fought for the king Seqenenre, and went north with the ruler to take part in the attack on the Hyksos capital, Avaris. He served on the ships *Savage Bull, Northerner,* and *Glorious Appearance in Memphis,* and followed on foot when the king rode out on his chariot (the reference to the chariot in his autobiography records the earliest thus far attested use of this vehicle by Egyptians). After the fall of Avaris, Ahmose son of Ibana accompanied the victorious Theban army in its siege of Sharuhen.

Ahmose son of Ibana also campaigned in Nubia under the kings Ahmose, Amunhotep I, and Thutmose I. Under Thutmose I, Ahmose son of Ibana must have reached the site of the Egyptian boundary stele at Hagar el-Merwa, between the Fourth and Fifth cataracts (about four hundred kilometers north of Khartoum, as the crow flies). Under the command of the same ruler, Ahmose son of Ibana fought the armies of Naharin (a name meaning "river land," at this time indicating the kingdom of Mitanni on the northern Euphrates) in far northern Syria, and saw the erection of the Egyptian victory stela on the Euphrates. This Egyptian soldier had stood at the northern and southern limits of the Egyptian Empire, which he would have seen as the edges of the ordered world.

Ahmose son of Ibana owed much of his wide-ranging experience to the pharaoh Thutmose I, who shared neither the blood of his predecessors nor their relatively introverted and restrained vision for Egypt's power. Thutmose I roused the sleeping colossus that was early New Kingdom Egypt and established the foreign geographic goals toward which all of his militarily active successors would literally aim and shoot. Thutmose I reinaugurated the Eighteenth Dynasty, and in terms of foreign policy, he was the true founder of the New Kingdom, establishing Egyptian influence beyond the Fourth Cataract at Kurgus in the far south, and setting up his victory stela on the Euphrates in the equally distant north.[17] In Nubia Thutmose I further developed Nubian administration as a mirror of Egypt's own. In Syria-Palestine he began what would become during the course of the Eighteenth Dynasty a series of destabilizing campaigns that created a series of local buffer states, cultivated and supported by Egypt in the face of stronger opponents who might someday menace Egypt and her interests. Egyptian-style government came to Nubia, and political fragmentation was the rule for Syria-Palestine.[18]

The rule of Thutmose I codifies the imperialist tendencies that distinguish the New Kingdom from the periods of Egyptian history both before and after. Thutmose I recasts the mold of pharaoh, but does so within the context of a royal office more than a thousand years old. The reigns of the rest of the Eighteenth Dynasty pharaohs, particularly the kings of the Amarna Period, benefit from the military conquests of Thutmose I and the newly created identity of the warrior pharaoh.

Eighteenth Dynasty Kingship

Egyptian pharaohs were representatives of the gods on earth and in certain cases strove to reign as divine beings during their own lifetimes.[19] The pharaoh sat at the pinnacle of every aspect of Egyptian society—he was the political, religious, and military leader of the Egyptian Nile Valley and its hinterlands and dependencies. In theological terms, the pharaoh also held power over all foreign territories and their inhabitants, and the ultimate goal of the Egyptian ruler was to expand the ordered world. To combat the chaotic elements of the universe, the pharaoh could construct temples, commission civil engineering projects, or go to war. Depending on the historical situation during a particular reign, a pharaoh might succeed in many such projects.

In the beginning, the Egyptian king was the earthly manifestation of the cosmic deity Horus. Even before the unification of Upper and Lower Egypt, the kings of the protokingdoms in the south took the title "Horus" to represent their authority.[20] As the pharaonic state developed, further royal titles became part of the official titulary.[21] By the late Old Kingdom, each pharaoh possessed a complete five-part titulary expressing his dual mortal and divine royal nature.[22] Although each ruler had a unique set of names, throughout the Old Kingdom the personalities of the individual rulers remain for the most part hidden behind the hieratic mask of their office. The Old Kingdom pharaoh officiates at great ceremonies that renew both his power and that of the cosmos. His importance is his place in cyclical time; his true significance in the artistic and literary imagery of the Old Kingdom was not that he engaged in a series of different activities along a line of progression, but rather that his activities came ever back to the same point in the revolving spiral of religious festivals. He sits as god on earth, the essentially static core of an ever-repeating series of ritualized activities.

On the other hand, from the late Old Kingdom through the First Intermediate Period, private autobiographical inscriptions place increasing emphasis on personal skill.[23] A pride in personal achievement emerged in texts, resulting in a corresponding increase in historical detail, particularly in the inscriptions of district governors of Upper Egypt. The king lagged somewhat behind, however, and only at the dawn of the Middle Kingdom does a true royal personality emerge from royal inscriptions, the king adopting the often grandiloquently bombastic and self-confident style of private texts.[24] The new genre placed emphasis on the personal ability of the ruler, both physical and mental, and provided the groundwork for what would develop into the "royal novel."[25] Such royal texts remained stereotyped, following a formulaic development and retaining an emphasis on the importance of the office of king; nevertheless, the new royal "autobiographical" texts related no small amount of information regarding the personal and historic achievements of the king as an individual.

During the Middle Kingdom, perhaps as an offshoot of the increasingly historical and physically active ruler, texts—especially those of a more truly literary nature—depict the king as vicar of the supreme deity, the tired and worried good shepherd of Egypt.[26] Under the Thirteenth Dynasty, the supreme deity supports the ruler, who appears as a semidivine human both elected and supported by the divine ruler of the cosmos.[27] At the time of the late Seventeenth and early Eighteenth dynasties, all of these trends appear, enlarged, with an emphasis on the unique "historical" achievements of the ruler. With the military compositions of Kamose the true New Kingdom image of the king appears, and the personal and historic achievements of the king match the personal activity of a deity. The divinity of the office of king did not diminish, but the image of the king moved from a static regality to that of an active participant and motivator of history.[28] No longer confined to the potent but personally restrictive world of the cosmic festival, the New Kingdom pharaoh needed ever enlarging venues for repetitive manifestation and personal innovation in his revelation and affirmation of royal power. The changing expressions of kingship during the Eighteenth Dynasty have their roots in the founding of pharaonic rule.

Already during the Protodynastic Period (ca. 3200 B.C.E.), the king repeatedly played his role in great religious festivals that marked renewal of the cosmos. The first known ruler of the unified kingdom of Upper and Lower Egypt, Narmer, presided over a religious festival that included not only the ritual slaughter of sacrificial animals but also potentially the execution of human enemies.[29] This festival represented the king's rule over the natural world as well as foreign lands, and in the course of the festivities Narmer reaffirmed his assumption of royal regalia and power. The ultimate goal of this elaborate festival was the maintenance of the proper relationship between the king and the gods, and thereby the balance of order and justice, both summed up in the Egyptian word maat.

Adding to the already ancient and repetitive religious cycles in which each ruler took up his appointed place, the military exploits of the rulers of the late Seventeenth Dynasty and the early Eighteenth Dynasty provided a means by which the ruler could play out his role of god on earth. Not only does the New Kingdom ruler continue to function as officiant at religious celebrations, but also his own actions become the mirror of divine action—the ruler more openly shows himself as an actor in history and change, and by the reign of Amunhotep III (see below) he more ostentatiously presents himself as the representative of deity in the eternal and unchanging form of divinity in the ever-repeating cycle of the sacred year. For example, the historical document recounting the military success of the pharaoh Kamose against the Hyksos seldom mentions a deity directly within the historic section—the historically active and physically present king is in fact that divinity.[30] The individualistic and "self-made" private man of the First Intermediate Period autobiographical texts, hinted at in contemporaneous royal monuments, and already well present in the inscriptions of local rulers, asserts himself more strongly now in royal monuments at the dawn of the New Kingdom. At the same time, New Kingdom pharaohs begin to take on more permanently the role of divinity.

For rulers such as Thutmose I and Thutmose III, whose military exploits were truly epic without any need for embellishment, the wider world stage of the early New Kingdom provided ample opportunity for real and frequent manifestations of their "historic divinity." The desire to reenact events in the divine world could even influence the ways in which Egyptian pharaohs waged war. Ahmose son of Ibana describes how Thutmose I brought down the fleeing Nubian enemy leader by shooting him with an arrow in the chest; the pharaoh then hung the body of the dead Nubian upside down from the prow of his ship.[31] The inverted position of the enemy's body is a specific allusion to one of the Egyptians' greatest fears in the afterlife—the inversion of the damned, leading to the reversal of bodily functions, so that the cursed consume their own excrement and drink their own urine.[32] The damned Nubian ruler, condemned to his horrible fate, hangs from the prow of the ship, as though the royal vessel is about to sail over him, an allusion to another key religious symbol—the solar deity in his bark sailing over the back of the defeated chaos serpent Apep.[33] As Thutmose I sailed north to Egypt with his enemy hanging upside down from the prow of his ship, the pharaoh announced not only that his enemies were damned in the other world, but also that the foes of Egypt would share the same fate as the chaos serpent defeated by the sun god. In his victorious progress Thutmose I visibly acts the part of the sun god, while his Nubian enemy just as obviously takes on the role of the enemy of cosmic order, Apep.

Later in the Eighteenth Dynasty, Thutmose III announced the extraordinary nature of his own military activities by publicizing them through the monumental presentation of his almost totally unvarnished military campaign diaries at Karnak Temple.[34] Other New Kingdom rulers less burdened by real military necessities required other venues for the manifestation of their physical prowess, and already Amunhotep II, son of Thutmose III, combined the time-honored presence of the ruler in public ritual with the need to manifest his personal, physical power.[35] With Amunhotep II the concept of the ruler as divine athlete is preeminent, and Amunhotep II and others vaunt their accomplishments in equestrian pursuits and archery, among other sporting activities. In lieu of necessary military exploits, sporting pursuits allow for demonstration of divine royal prowess. Although ritual activities had been part of royal duties from the very dawn of pharaonic kingship, Eighteenth Dynasty rulers "personalized" some aspects thereof—leading a massed chariot charge or single-handedly propelling a vessel inevitably focused on the specific ruler and not so generally on abstract rulership.

Amunhotep III: The King as Solar Disk

The pharaohs of the latter Eighteenth Dynasty reaped the rewards of the military success of warrior kings of the early Eighteenth Dynasty. The tremendous wealth that flowed into the royal coffers and temple estates fueled what appears to have been a golden age of prosperity, stability, and cultural achievement. The long reign of Amunhotep III, the apogee of this period, witnessed an unprecedented celebration of the power and influence wielded by the Egyptian pharaoh.[36] Although Amunhotep III was able to commemorate at least one Nubian campaign,[37] the primarily peaceful nature of his reign led the pharaoh to new ways of expressing his royal authority.[38] The unique character of Amunhotep III's reign and his profound influence on the Amarna revolution are best seen in the events of his thirtieth year of rule. After millennia of development, Amunhotep III and his son Akhenaten attempted to reorient Egyptian religion and architecture on a vast scale, but their resulting creation was a colossus with feet of clay, which their successors and ultimately the early Ramesside rulers were forced to rebuild on a more stable footing.

A pharaoh who attained his thirtieth year on the throne could celebrate a great jubilee festival, known as the *heb-sed*, which renewed the vitality of the king and reaffirmed his rule.[39] The rituals and accoutrements of the heb-sed appear to form the basis of a cycle of Pre- and Protodynastic tableaux[40] and certainly are part of standard royal ceremony by the reign of Narmer (ca. 3050 B.C.E.).[41] Ideally the pharaoh celebrated the jubilee festival in the thirtieth year of his reign, with additional celebrations taking place more frequently thereafter. Some of the most detailed and spectacular information about a jubilee festival derives from the three jubilees of Amunhotep III in years thirty, thirty-four, and thirty-seven of his reign. Not only did Amunhotep III gather resources and personnel from all over Egypt, he also constructed an entire city to serve as the stage for this historic event.

The rulers of the early Eighteenth Dynasty transformed ritual into history through their physical and military manifestations of royal power. Now with Amunhotep III, history itself was about to become a series of ritual events. The king's display of his physical prowess in the mortal world led ultimately to a desire to display the religious and otherworldly power of the king while still within the world of the living. To achieve this goal, Amunhotep III sought out documents within the temple libraries that would tell him how to celebrate his jubilee festival in the same manner as the semidivine rulers of remote antiquity. Descriptions of the royal jubilee in the tomb of Kheruef, the chief royal steward of Amunhotep III, describe the results of the king's research:[42] "It was His Majesty who did this in accordance with the writings of old. Past generations of people since the time of the ancestors had never celebrated such rites of the jubilee. It was for the one appearing in truth, the Son of Amun (Amunhotep III), who enjoys the [legacy of his father], given life like Re forever, that it was decreed." Detailed reliefs in the tomb of Kheruef and other documents allow for a reconstruction of the key events of Amunhotep III's first and third jubilee; and physical remains of all three jubilees survive at the enormous festival city of Malqata, which Amunhotep III constructed at the southern end of the Theban West Bank.

The western bank of Thebes was the site of both the royal tombs in the Valley of the Kings, and the great mortuary temples in which the deceased pharaohs were worshipped as manifestations of the god Amun.[43] During the annual Beautiful Festival of the Valley, the statue of Amun from Karnak Temple would visit each of the royal mortuary temples on the West Bank,[44] the largest of which was the mortuary temple of Amunhotep III, built on an unprecedented scale. Although today the two seated colossi of Amunhotep III are the most visible evidence of the monumental scale of the building, when complete, the mud-brick pylons, open courts, and inner rooms of the mortuary complex covered an area larger even than that of Karnak Temple, which encompasses more than ninety acres.[45] The mortuary temple of Amunhotep III was only part of the pharaoh's construction program on the West Bank, however. At the site of Malqata, just south and west of his mortuary temple, Amunhotep III ordered the construction of his jubilee city. The mortuary temple and jubilee city of Amunhotep III were constructed to either side of an earlier temple to "Amun, Holy of Place," a site now known as Medinet Habu; the significance of the concentration of Amunhotep III's building activity in the region of Medinet Habu becomes apparent when seen in the light of his son's new capital city (see "The Location of Akhet-aten: The Home of the Ogdoad," pages 37–40).

Excavations at Malqata allow one to reconstruct the buildings' functions.[46] Malqata contained no less than four palaces, one of which was probably intended for Amunhotep's queen, Tiye; these palaces were decorated with brightly colored plaster paintings on the walls and ceilings.[47] A temple dedicated to the god Amun, to the north of the palaces, was built by the time of the second jubilee; in front of the temple was an open court and possible processional way leading to a large harbor. Additional buildings were residential and probably housed the large number of officials, priests, and support staff required for the jubilee festival.

"House of Rejoicing," the name of one of the palaces at Amunhotep III's new city at Malqata, emphasizes the solar nature of Amunhotep III's heb-sed festival, and the rituals celebrated at Malqata literally transformed the pharaoh into the sun god himself. The term "rejoicing" in the name of Malqata refers not only to the celebrations, but also to the action of the solar god—each time the sun rose, the Egyptians believed that "Re rejoiced in the horizon." This rejoicing could be further envisaged as a sexual union between the sun god and the horizon, *akhet*, the female counterpart and consort of the male solar disk.[48] Malqata could symbolize the horizon, and Amunhotep III, who took on the epithet "Dazzling Sun Disk," was able to rejoice therein as he celebrated his jubilee festival.[49] The result of the union of solar king and his palace horizon would be a rejuvenated king, an adult pharaonic sun child. The term for sun disk, *aten*, appearing in Amunhotep III's epithet "Dazzling Sun Disk," is the normal word in Egyptian texts for the visible manifestation of the sun god.[50] The importance Amunhotep III attached to that particular form of the sun god and his own transformation into the solar deity in the course of his jubilee festival presaged the religious "revolution" of his successor Akhenaten, who promoted the Aten to the most important—and indeed the only—deity of the Egyptian pantheon, with the exception of himself and his chief queen, Nefertiti.[51]

East of the jubilee city was one of the major features of the Malqata complex and the one most visible in the modern landscape—a great T-shaped harbor lake now known as the Birket Habu.[52] Although apparently never formally investigated in modern times, an East Bank counterpart to the Birket Habu once existed and appears as a large rectangle of debris mounds on the map of Thebes published by Napoleon's expedition to Egypt.[53] The eastern artificial lake was about the size of the original western lake, both dug for Amunhotep III's first jubilee. After the first jubilee festival, the western harbor was enlarged to a length of more than two kilometers, necessitating the dismantling of some of the earlier buildings at Malqata. The two lakes and the canals connecting them to the Nile figured prominently in what appear to have been the unique and archaic jubilee celebrations of Amunhotep III. According to texts in the tomb of Kheruef, the royal courtiers participating in the festivities hauled the towropes of actual vessels representing the boats of the day and the night sun, in which the pharaoh sailed:[54] "They were directed to the harbor of His Majesty to row in the bark of the king. They grasped the towropes of the evening bark and the prow rope of the morning bark, and they towed the barks at the great place. They stopped at the steps of the throne."

In Egyptian theology, Re traveled in the day bark from dawn until sunset and sailed in the night bark from sunset until dawn. In the western and eastern horizons, the day bark and the night bark met prow to prow and Re moved from one to the other.[55] In certain Netherworld Books recorded on the walls of the tombs of the Valley of the Kings, the solar barks also serve as the means by which the king's soul travels through the heavens and the underworld in his eternal afterlife. During his jubilee festival, Amunhotep III reenacted this journey of the sun god, sailing in the day and night barks on the Nile and in his artificial lakes, apparently transferring from one boat to the other, just as Re did in the heavens each day.[56] One might expect the king to travel in the day bark, acting as the visible sun disk, but more surprising is Amunhotep III's implied trip in the night bark, mirroring the sun's own nightly revivification in the bowels of the underworld. According to the Book of Amduat, in the fifth hour of the night, the sun god plunged into the primordial waters, out of which creation originally arose.[57] Each night, the sun god absorbed the chaotic power of the primordial waters, which engulfed the remnants—"flesh"—of the once-virile solar god. By subsuming the power of order, the power of chaos became the creative impetus for the new day. In staging his own solar regeneration on the waters of the Nile, Amunhotep III, the "Dazzling Sun Disk," appears to have signaled his own rebirth as a full deity on earth and also to have proclaimed the birth of a new solar regime for Egypt and her empire.

As Amunhotep III mimicked the daily peregrinations of Re, he also transformed into the solar falcon. In the jubilee scenes from the tomb of Kheruef, tail feathers protrude from the king's jubilee robe,[58] as if the king had literally sprouted the wings of the celestial deity. Like traveling in the day and the night barks, such physical transformations were normally only part of the king's Underworldly existence.[59] Amunhotep III's transformation also finds expression in a new artistic style introduced after the first jubilee festival.[60] The pudgy cheeks and enlarged eyes of royal iconography at this time suggest the features and proportions of a child, representing the literally reborn king.[61] The rituals enacted at Malqata ensured that Amunhotep III was not simply rejuvenated like previous rulers who celebrated jubilees, but that he also underwent the transformation and physical journey that no ruler should actually experience until after death.[62]

Another seemingly inexplicable element associated with Malqata is a long, cleared track leading from south of the main city into the western cliffs.[63] In the desert bay at the end of the track is a Coptic monastery; one interesting element of the monastery architecture was a carved pharaonic block showing a chariot,[64] perhaps deriving from Malqata proper or some otherwise vanished desert shrine or altar. Near the edge of the cultivation, not far from the beginning of the cleared track, Amunhotep III constructed a large mud-brick platform.[65] Various functions have been suggested for this enigmatic construction, and it may have served as the base for a police outpost that guarded the track leading into the western cliffs.[66] But what would police stationed at Malqata have been guarding? The bay would make an excellent necropolis for rock-cut tombs, and a few hieroglyphic symbols surviving in the bay, beneath the overlay of later Coptic inscriptions, suggest that some pharaonic "geologists" did visit the site.[67] The new city that Amunhotep III built at Malqata appears to have all the accoutrements of a complete settlement tacked onto the southern edge of western Thebes, including its own necropolis.

Throughout the jubilee festivals, and indeed at nearly every important event of Amunhotep III's reign, the pharaoh was accompanied by his chief wife, Tiye. Tiye wielded considerable influence, although she was not of royal blood.[68] On a scarab announcing his marriage to the Mitannian princess Gilukhepa, Amunhotep III emphasized the importance of his chief wife and provided the names of Tiye's parents. Tiye's father was Yuya, a chief officer in the Egyptian chariotry; her mother was Tuya, a priestess of the god Amun. Yuya and Tuya were some of the few nonroyal persons to be buried in the Valley of the Kings, and their burial further indicates their exalted status.[69]

Amunhotep III heaped greater and truly divine honors upon his queen. At Sedeinga in Nubia, Tiye's husband constructed a temple dedicated to the queen as an incarnation of the goddess Hathor.[70] The deification of Tiye during her lifetime mimics Amunhotep III's own transformation into a living god during his jubilee festivals.[71] In the temple of Sedeinga, Tiye possesses a title unattested for any previous queen—"great of fear, mistress of all lands."[72] The "fear" that Tiye inspires indicates her domination over the women of all foreign countries, just as her husband's awesome power cows all male foreigners. On a theological level, Tiye at Sedeinga is Sakhmet, the raging form of the goddess Hathor, who slakes her thirst for blood in the far south. In the tomb of Kheruef, Tiye sits behind her husband on a throne whose decoration embodies her status as queen universal. Beneath the arm of the throne, Tiye as a female sphinx tramples a female Nubian and Asiatic, while two further female enemies are bound to the struts that support the throne.[73]

Amunhotep III died after thirty-eight years of rule and was succeeded by a son, also named Amunhotep, later to change his name to Akhenaten, who had become crown prince after the death of his older brother Thutmose. At certain points in Egyptian history, a pharaoh would elevate a crown prince to the role of coregent, and both father and son would rule jointly.[74] Some have suggested that Amunhotep III and his son Amunhotep IV/Akhenaten ruled jointly for twelve years, while others believe their reigns overlapped by one or two years. The evidence for either a long or a short coregency is uncertain at best,[75] and most likely Akhenaten first ascended the throne upon the death of his father. Indeed, whether the coregency is real or not, Akhenaten's policies, both religious and political, continue and extend those of his father, Amunhotep III; and the queen mother Tiye, who outlived her husband by several years, continued to play an important role during the reign of her son.

Akhenaten: The Solar Disk as King

The pharaoh Akhenaten began his reign under the name Amunhotep, the fourth ruler of the Eighteenth Dynasty to bear that name. For the first five years of his reign, Amunhotep IV ruled from Thebes, although his new religious agenda was soon apparent. By regnal year six, Amunhotep IV, now calling himself Akhenaten, had moved to a new capital city in Middle Egypt, which would remain the center of the cult of the Aten until the end of Akhenaten's seventeen-year reign. Already before the final move to Akhet-aten, the new ruler had begun to promulgate the exclusive worship of the light of the sun as manifest in the glowing physical disk, the Aten.[76]

Akhenaten is perhaps best known as something he was not—a monotheist. Modern representations of Akhenaten as a prophet and worshipper of a sole deity stem from a misunderstanding of Egyptian religion in general and of Akhenaten's own version of solar worship in particular. Although Egyptian religion, with its abundance of deities, gives evidence of polytheism, the belief in a multiplicity of deities, this polytheism does not necessarily stress plurality of divinity; instead, New Kingdom Egyptian theological interpretation increasingly stresses a concept of divine unity. The many deities are the maximum differentiation in the ordered world of a primordial oneness; they are the balanced pairs of creation, the periodic table of divine elements—polytheism is not a constant cosmic state, but a particular stage or level of cosmic development. The ancient world gives evidence of two sorts of monotheism—a political monotheism ("our deity is better than your deity"), and a cosmological monotheism ("our deity is the only deity").[77] Akhenaten indeed appears to worship a single universal deity, the solar god Aten. Four basic features of Atenism lead to the conclusion that the Aten is alone because he exists at a time before the creation of the cloud of polytheistic deities. Aten is not the sole god because other deities do not exist, but because they do not *yet* exist—just as polytheistic deities are a manifestation of a period of cosmic development, so in Egyptian religion a monotheistic deity belongs to a time when the ordered cosmos was new and not yet differentiated.

Since the religious "revolution" of Akhenaten is *the* central focus of his reign, a proper comprehension of the main features of his new theology is essential to understanding all other events of his reign, including his military strategy and foreign policy. A careful examination of the texts, monuments, and artistic productions of Akhenaten's reign not only reveals the impetus behind his revolution and the reason for the construction and location of his capital city, but also ultimately provides the key to unlocking many of the mysteries of his reign.

Akhenaten at Thebes

During the first five years of his reign, Amunhotep IV instituted an extensive building program at the temple of Karnak.[78] The earlier buildings at the giant temple complex of Karnak were dedicated to Amun, his consort

Mut, and their child Khonsu. One of Amunhotep IV's few contributions to the great temple of Amun proper was the construction of a porch before the third pylon, decorated with monumental images of the pharaoh smiting his foes.[79] However, the four separate temples Amunhotep IV built as part of the great Karnak complex were dedicated to the solar gods Re-Horakhty and Aten. The earliest surviving reliefs commissioned by Amunhotep IV depict the falcon-headed god Re-Horakhty, the sun god syncretized with the deity "Horus of the Horizon," using the traditional artistic canon;[80] the primary overt theological innovation at this early stage is the addition of the epithet "who rejoices in the horizon" to the name of Re-Horakhty. However, these traditional representations soon give place to an entirely different depiction of the sun god—the disk itself.[81] The god Aten manifests himself as a solar disk, often appearing as a hemisphere in deeply sunk relief,[82] with a multitude of rays extending downward and ending in small human hands. Most often these hands hold signs of life to the noses of the royal family, but in a less-well-known scene, the hands of the Aten extend weapons to Akhenaten (see figure 2).[83] Although pacifism has sometimes been assumed to be one of the aspects of Aten-worship, no ancient Egyptian evidence—either textual or pictorial—supports this assumption, and in fact, Atenism could be just as militant as traditional Egyptian religion.

Amunhotep IV's architects and craftsmen completed his new solar temples in a surprisingly short time; working at a feverish pace, they introduced several new construction techniques.[84] Rather than constructing temples from massive blocks that required considerable time, planning, and logistical support to quarry, transport, and set in place, Akhenaten introduced an inexpensive bricklike form of stone architecture. Most of Akhenaten's temples were built with small stone blocks (roughly 52 by 26 by 24 centimeters) called *talatat* (a word probably derived from the Arabic for "three," a reference to their length of approximately three hands), each light enough for one man to carry. Adept as they were at moving massive stone blocks and statues, the Egyptians themselves recognized the relatively lilliputian proportions of Akhenaten's standard stone building blocks and termed the tiny talatat "bricks of stone."[85]

One of the major events recorded on the talatat from the Aten temples at Karnak is the celebration of Amunhotep IV's jubilee festival early in his reign, probably in year two (or perhaps year four), a festival in which the Aten appears also to have participated.[86] Since Amunhotep III died in his thirty-eighth regnal year, Amunhotep IV's heb-sed festival would correspond to the fortieth or forty-second year of his father's reign, either way an appropriate year for a jubilee. Amunhotep IV's incorporation of his

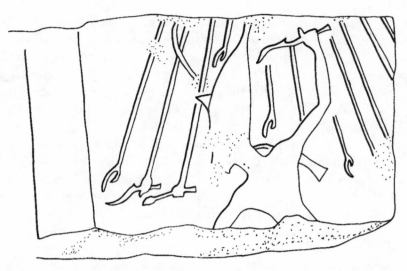

Figure 2. Akhenaten smites an enemy, while the Aten extends a mace and a scimitar. This relief, from a *talatat* block, was originally part of a scene depicting the facade of one of Akhenaten's temples at Karnak. After Traunecker, *JSSEA* 14 (1984): 61.

father's reign into his own was not unprecedented[87] and indicates how closely tied Amunhotep IV's religious agenda was to that of his father. By celebrating a jubilee so early in his reign, Amunhotep IV created continuity with Amunhotep III and set the stage for further development of his father's deification while on earth. Amunhotep IV's first heb-sed was a dated historical event, but the texts that accompany the jubilee indicate the simultaneous timelessness of the event. Each morning when the Aten rises, he grants his chosen vicar, Amunhotep IV, soon to become Akhenaten, yet another jubilee festival. As the daily events at Akhenaten's new capital reveal, Akhenaten transformed the progression of time into an endlessly repeated daily cycle, all focused on the Aten and the royal family. For Akhenaten, the celebration of his first heb-sed festival may never have ended.[88]

Four Features of Atenism

The succinct credo of Akhenaten's religion appears as the so-called didactic name of his sole deity, the Aten, which is enclosed within two cartouches, like the names of the king.[89] The cartouche, a ring of rope lashed together near the overlapping ends, represented the king's rule over the entire world—"all which the sun disk encircles."[90] The use of the royal cartouche for the name of the sun disk is peculiar to the religion of Akhenaten and expresses not only the intimate relationship between the king and his deity but also encapsulates the core of his solar theology. The first name of the Aten, in use possibly as late as Akhenaten's twelfth regnal year, was "The living one, Re-Horakhty who rejoices in the horizon in his identity of light, which is in the sun disk." The true nature of the Aten is not the physical manifestation of the solar disk, but the light emanating from that disk.[91] The visible light, the means of communication between the solar god and mankind, conceals the unique divinity of the Aten. The didactic names state the Aten's identity, further codified through hymns, such as the celebrated "Great Hymn,"[92] and teachings of Akhenaten himself.[93] Surviving texts leave much of Akhenaten's religion unexplained and only hint at the underlying theology of four of the most prominent features of Atenism: a new capital, a new artistic style, the proscription of other deities, and the importance of royal females in Amarna iconography. After examining each of these features and their reflection in texts, artistic production, and architecture, one may indeed find a single principle that connects and more importantly accounts for the four aspects of Atenism that distinguish it from Egyptian theology before and after the reign of Akhenaten.

Akhet-aten: A New Capital

During his fifth regnal year, Amunhotep IV enacted radical changes to both his own name and his place of residence. The pharaoh abandoned any affiliation with the god Amun and transformed his nomen to reflect his association with the solar disk—Akhenaten, "One who is effective for the Aten." At the same time, Akhenaten sought out a new capital for the worship of his all-encompassing deity. He found an ideal spot on the eastern bank of the Nile in Middle Egypt, a dramatic bay from which he could observe the sun rise each morning; the shape of the cliffs even resembled the Egyptian hieroglyph for "horizon" (⌂), contributing to—or at least providing an excellent topographical reflection of—the name Akhet-aten, "Horizon of the Aten." Akhenaten recorded the events of his discovery of the site and his intentions to construct a new city for the Aten in two sets of boundary stelae.[94] According to the first proclamation, the Aten himself instructed the pharaoh to found his new city at the site. Having gathered together all the civil and military officials, Akhenaten proclaimed:

> Behold the Aten! The Aten desires that one (the king) make monuments
> for him in an eternal and everlasting name. Now it is the Aten, my

father, who advised me about the "Horizon of the Aten" (Akhet-aten). No official advised me about it nor any other person in the entire land advised me about it, telling me [a plan] for making Akhet-aten in this place except for the Aten, my father.[95]

After the assembled officials praised the pharaoh and his solar orb for their wonderful plans for the new city, Akhenaten swore an oath to the Aten, setting forth the boundaries of the city, marked by the stelae themselves, and proclaiming his unwavering devotion to the plans of his divine father:

> It is in this place that I shall make Akhet-aten for the Aten, my father. I shall not make Akhet-aten for him south of it, north of it, west of it, or east of it. I shall not go beyond the southern stela of Akhet-aten toward the south, nor shall I go beyond the northern stela of Akhet-aten toward the north, to make Akhet-aten for him there. Nor shall I make it for him on the western side of Akhet-aten. It is on the eastern side of Akhet-aten that I shall make Akhet-aten for the Aten, my father, the place he himself made, surrounded for him with the mountain. Just as he shall be pleased with it, so shall I offer to him within it. This is it!
>
> The Great Royal Wife (Nefertiti) will not say to me, "Look, there is a good place for Akhet-aten in another place," and I will not listen to her. No official in my presence . . . will say to me: "Look, there is a good place for Akhet-aten in another place," and I will not listen to them.[96]

Akhenaten transplanted not only the new Aten cult to his new capital, but also the administrative and military infrastructure of Egypt, although other cities, such as Memphis, retained some important administrative functions.[97] Akhet-aten was laid out on a north–south axis along the edge of the great bay of cliffs, approximately ten kilometers long and six kilometers at its widest, which dominated the city.[98] The broad "Royal Road," approximately thirty meters wide through the Central City, linked the major sections of Akhet-aten.[99] At the northernmost extent of the city was an administrative building and the North Riverside Palace, which together formed the "North City." Only half a kilometer south of the North City was the North Palace, the residence of Merytaten, the eldest daughter of Akhenaten and Nefertiti. Three kilometers from the North City was the Central City, whose largest building was the Great Aten Temple, which contained the Gempaaten. Other major features of the Central City included a domestic palace (the "King's House") and an administrative palace linked by an elevated walkway over the Royal Road; south of the domestic palace was a small Aten temple, a miniature version of the Great Aten Temple. East of that complex were the primary administrative buildings of the city, including a library and archival buildings, and yet farther east of those were military structures (for more on the military features of Akhet-aten, see pages 191–196).

Between the North City and the Central City was the North Suburb, one of two main residential areas at Akhet-aten, which may have housed a population as large as twenty thousand to fifty thousand people.[100] South of the Central City were workshops, including the studio of the artist Thutmose where the famous bust of Nefertiti was discovered, and another residential area, which contained the houses of the most important officials of Akhet-aten. In the southern portion of the city were further cultic structures, such as the "garden" temple called the Maruaten, as well as palatial structures and an artificial lake. In the cliffs themselves were the three necropoleis of Akhet-aten—the royal tomb was deep in a wadi northeast of the Central City, while private individuals constructed their tombs in two concentrations in the eastern cliffs north and south of the main center of Akhet-aten.[101]

Each morning, the disk of the Aten rose above the eastern cliffs and illumined his newly constructed city, shining down upon his temples, their altars heaped with offerings. The temples of Akhet-aten did not have the traditional New Kingdom Egyptian form, in which a series of open courts led into a roofed and columned hall and increasingly dark and smaller chambers, culminating in the inner sanctuary. Instead, the Aten temples consisted primarily of open courts—even the doorways had broken lintels, so that sunlight could pour into every part of the temple.[102] These features were not invented by Akhenaten but inspired by the solar temples of Heliopolis,[103] where Akhenaten constructed at least one solar temple.[104] The temples at Akhet-aten did not contain a cult image of Aten, since the sun disk traveling across heaven each day was the ultimate cult image. The visible sun disk also obviated the need for festival processions, in which the cult statue, hidden within a portable bark shrine, was carried by priests.[105]

The "Amarna" Style of Art

Images of the royal family, their worship of the Aten, and scenes of other day-to-day activities at the new capital adorned the temples, tombs, and palaces of Akhet-aten. The artistic canon in effect at Akhet-aten—a style already present in Akhenaten's Theban constructions—differed greatly from traditional Egyptian representations.[106] Oddly proportioned bodies and elongated skulls combined with a unique sense of movement and feel for the momentary to express Akhenaten's new theology. But at least some aspects of the "Amarna" style of art have precedents in the type of representation introduced after the jubilee festival of Amunhotep III.

The art of the reign of Amunhotep III falls into three major phases, although fluid boundaries exist between these periods.[107] Initially Amunhotep III's artistic production is essentially a continuation of later Thutmoside art of the first part of the Eighteenth Dynasty. The second, "mature" style of Amunhotep III reveals a highly refined and polished style, two-dimensional art and bas-relief demonstrating a developed sense of proportion and fluidity of line. At about the time of the first jubilee, a third style appears, probably never entirely eclipsing the mature style, revealing pronounced and exaggerated forms of certain aspects of the royal physiognomy, particularly the face. Royal portraiture of the third phase shows the pharaoh's face with the proportions of that of a baby—large, almond-shaped eyes, small nose, and overall chubby features. This "baby" art foreshadows that of Akhenaten in the extreme alterations to the royal physique. This third-phase art of Amunhotep III also reveals a fascination with an almost baroque sense of adornment, and royal accoutrements—multiple uraei, sun disks, and streamers—add layer upon layer of solar imagery to the royal figure. These new features coincide with the living deification of Amunhotep III during his first jubilee celebration and show the king as the newborn sun on earth (see above). Amunhotep III has the face of the infant sun, he wears a multiplicity of solar adornments, and even the relief is cut so as to reveal most startlingly to the viewer the play of light and shadow, emphasizing the presence of the sun.[108]

In his initial artistic production, Amunhotep IV continues the mature second phase of Amunhotep III, but only for a short time. Within a couple of years, a new style of art appears, continuing and expanding upon the final "jubilee" style of Amunhotep III. During his hasty construction of temples at Karnak, Akhenaten revealed this first and most extreme, even caricaturish, form of his revolutionary artistic style, in which the figure of the king himself changes in a startling fashion.[109] The main peculiarities of royal physiognomy during the early phase of Amarna art are spindly extremities, thick thighs, pronounced buttocks and paunch, markedly effeminate breasts, long and drooping chin, and elongated skull. This new style suddenly reveals a further development of the third phase of Amunhotep III, now taken to an extreme and involving the proportions of the entire figure. The style is contagious, and rapidly spreads from Akhenaten to Nefertiti, his growing family, and ultimately the courtiers and residents of Amarna; not only do the Amarna courtiers adopt the physical characteristics of Akhenaten, but also they almost always appear in a bowing position, as if continually in awe of their ruler's divinity.[110]

In about regnal year eight, this more radical style softens and becomes somewhat less grotesque.[111] With the move of the court to Akhet-aten, the chief stone of Akhenaten's architectural and sculptural display ceased to be the rather coarse sandstone from the great quarries south of Thebes, such as Gebel Silsila, and became instead fine limestone from northern Egypt. Limestone allowed for a more subtle carving style and was less forgiving of haste and ineptitude in the quality of delineation of the figures and objects. The development of the latter phase of Akhenaten's mannerist art may have been due to several factors, such as the influence of Memphite artists, and the development of the important studio of the sculptor Thutmose at Akhet-aten, famous for the sculptor's models and other productions discovered during excavations at the site.[112] Although most of the odd physical features of the male and female body in early Amarna style, such as the distended belly, pendulous breasts, and elongated skull, persist in the second phase of Atenist art, the late phase of Amarna art exhibits a tightening of the sense of balance and proportion and produces figures that appear to have more of a firm skeletal substructure than in art prior to year eight. By the end of Akhenaten's reign, the grotesque features of the first years had blossomed into elegant and sophisticated representations of the royal family, while retaining all the peculiarities of Amarna art (see figure 3).

Proscription of Other Deities

One of the most notorious aspects of Akhenaten's reign from the perspective of the ancient Egyptians was the pogrom he instituted against the cults of many Egyptian deities, particularly that of the imperial god Amun. The proscription of Amun did not begin immediately, and Akhenaten ruled for his first four years with his original name Amunhotep, "Amun is content." During these early years, the Aten was still only one among many deities, although the solar disk was given more prominence than any other deity; as the tomb of Parennefer records: "the revenues of every (other) god are measured with grain measures, but for the Aten one measures in heaps."[113] At the time of the move to Akhet-aten and increasingly thereafter, the name and image of the god Amun were removed from temples, tombs, and other monuments.[114] The persecution of Amun's cult had its greatest effect at Thebes, the center of Amun worship, but the god's name was also hacked out of monuments throughout the Nile Valley, even far south, into Nubia. Akhenaten's proscription of other deities appears to have begun gradually and was applied inconsistently, but as time progressed, more elements of traditional Egyptian religion were attacked. On some

Figure 3. Akhenaten and Nefertiti play with their daughters as the Aten presents signs of life to the royal family (Ägyptisches Museum und Papyrussammlung, Berlin, 14145). Courtesy of the Bildarchiv Preussischer Kulturbesitz/Art Resource, NY.

monuments, even the word *netcheru* (gods) is erased so as not to offend the sole rule of the Aten over mankind.[115] The increasing intensity of Akhenaten's attack may be linked to the change in the name of the Aten that occurs between the ninth and twelfth years; in the second phase of the Aten's cartouches, the divine names "Re-Horakhty" and "Shu" disappear, and the cartouches contain the formula "The living one, Re, ruler of the two horizons, who rejoices in the horizon in his name of Re, the father, who returns as the sun disk."

While the erasing of divine names from monuments may not have affected most of the Egyptian population, Akhenaten's closure of the great Amun temples at Thebes and other temples throughout Egypt and Nubia impacted everyone's life. Temples in ancient Egypt were not simply places of worship, but also giant redistribution centers that regulated much of the Nile Valley's economy.[116] During the great annual festivals, the populace partook of thousands of loaves and cakes from temple bakeries and the meat from hundreds of slaughtered animals. Festivals were also work holi-days and governed the rhythm of life in Egypt as surely as the seasons. The closure of the temples meant the cancellation of these times of public worship and revelry, and the thousands of people affected would probably not have seen this curtailing of festivities in a positive light. Even within Akhet-aten, amulets and inscriptions referring to members of the tradi-tional Egyptian pantheon, particularly Bes and Taweret, have come to light, suggesting that Akhenaten's new religion did not fully replace the entrenched "private religion."[117] Time may have stopped at Akhet-aten, but at Thebes and elsewhere the year would have lengthened as it stretched out in a temporal desert, the festivals evaporated by the harsh rays of the jealous Aten.

The Importance of Women at Amarna

Because of the beautiful bust from Thutmose's workshop in Akhet-aten, now in Berlin, the great royal wife Nefertiti—already married to Akhen-aten at his accession—is one of the most recognizable individuals from ancient Egypt.[118] Her fame today is in many ways appropriate to her im-portance during Akhenaten's reign, for Nefertiti is as prominent in Amarna art as the pharaoh himself. Even Akhenaten's early monuments at Thebes demonstrate that Nefertiti's significance in his new cult was virtually equal to his own. One of the Atenist constructions at Karnak, the Temple of the Benben, was inscribed solely for Nefertiti, and no blocks from this temple preserve a depiction of Akhenaten.[119] Often in scenes from the Temple of the Benben, the image of Nefertiti—whose name is preceded by her new epithet Neferneferuaten, "Beautiful is the Perfection of Aten"— occurs alongside her eldest daughter, Merytaten, worshiping the great solar disk. Within this temple, Nefertiti appears performing rituals previously the prerogative of the pharaoh alone. In a scene decorating the prow of the queen's bark, Nefertiti even smites a female enemy (see figure 4).[120] Although Nefertiti's predecessor Tiye already appears in similar scenes as a sphinx trampling female enemies, Nefertiti's queenly smiting scene is oth-erwise unique for the pharaonic period.[121] Not only was the worship of the Aten compatible with the destruction of Egypt's enemies, Nefertiti's un-precedented participation in pharaonic activities even enabled her to adopt the same bellicose attributes and poses as her husband.

The royal couple had six daughters during their marriage: Merytaten (who would possibly later become pharaoh in her own right), Meketaten, Ankhesenpaaten (who became the wife of Tutankhamun and later changed

Figure 4. Nefertiti smites a female enemy beneath the rays of Aten (Museum of Fine Arts, Boston, 64.521). This scene decorated a depiction of the stern of the queen's bark, shown sailing along the Nile on a *talatat* from Hermopolis.

her name to Ankhesenamun), Neferneferuaten the Younger, Neferneferure, and Setepenre. In the "intimate" scenes of family life, Akhenaten and Nefertiti sit caressed by the rays of the Aten while they play with their numerous daughters. These "family portraits," possibly erected in shrines to the royal family in the homes of prominent individuals at Akhet-aten, never depict a male offspring of Akhenaten and Nefertiti.[122] Similarly, tableaux from the temples, tombs, and palaces of Akhet-aten show Akhenaten and Nefertiti accompanied by one or more of the daughters as they worship the solar orb.[123] This does not mean that Tutankhamun, then known as Tutankhaten, and probably a son of Akhenaten,[124] was ignored as a child or excluded from court life. Rather, the depictions of Akhenaten, Nefertiti, and their daughters are an expression of solar theology, as will be explained below.

Although Akhenaten—like at least most of the pharaohs who ruled before and after him—probably enjoyed a multiplicity of female consorts, only one other wife is known by name: Kiye.[125] Kiye remains an enigmatic figure, and like Akhenaten's ephemeral successor Smenkhkare, the discussions of Kiye's place at the Amarna court far outweigh the actual evidence. She does not appear ever to have held the title "great royal wife," but receives the epithet "greatly beloved wife of the king" or a designation rarely used for queens, "noble lady." The latter title has led some to suggest that she was a Mitannian princess—either Gilukhepa, previously married to Amunhotep III, or more likely Tadukhepa, married to Akhenaten.[126] Without further evidence, Kiye's identity—foreign or Egyptian—remains uncertain, as does her possible identification as Tutankhamun's mother.

Atenism: Re-creation of Creation

Why does Akhenaten move his capital? Why are Akhenaten and his family depicted in such a nontraditional and even grotesque fashion? Why does Akhenaten reject other deities? Why does he so frequently show himself surrounded by his wife and daughters? Although answers to these questions have been proposed, no current theory of Akhenaten's new solar religion provides a framework to explain all of the major features of Atenism.[127] Some have proposed that Akhenaten's religious revolution was a backlash against the powerful and allegedly corrupt priesthood of the god Amun, who controlled tremendous economic resources and supposedly infringed on the authority of the pharaoh.[128] While the temple estate of the god Amun possessed land and personnel far beyond Thebes, the New Kingdom clergy of Amun was dependent on the beneficence of the pharaoh—the priesthood of Amun was powerful because of, not in spite of, the authority of the pharaoh.[129] Simple hatred of Amun or his priesthood would also not explain the theological or artistic peculiarities of Akhenaten's solar religion. Others have suggested that Akhenaten suffered from a genetic disorder and that his representations are a reflection of his actual physical appearance.[130] Yet most disorders that would cause the deformations evident in Amarna art also result in sterility, and Akhenaten is known to have fathered at least six daughters and probably a son.

A proper appreciation of the religious changes begun with the jubilee festival of Amunhotep III sets one on the track to finding the underlying significance of the theological, architectural, and artistic changes of the third Amunhotep's son. In fact, a comparison of the location of Amunhotep III's new jubilee city, Malqata, with that of Akhenaten's new capital, Akhet-aten, suggests that both Amunhotep III and Akhenaten attempted to tap into the power of one particular account of Egyptian creation. Amunhotep III's jubilee theophany swept away the old Egyptian concept of the pharaoh as the balancing point between humanity and divinity and enabled the pharaoh to become wholly divine while still ruling on earth. Amunhotep III's reign was thus a difficult precedent for his successor. How could Akhenaten maintain his status as divinity on earth? The answer, as the four features of Akhenaten's religion ultimately reveal, is startling yet logical from the perspective of ancient Egyptian theology: as the official (and in his case actual) children of the god-on-earth Amunhotep III, Akhenaten and Nefertiti attempt to rule Egypt as the first male-female pair of creator deities, living as if each day were the first moment of creation, called *sep-tepy* in ancient Egyptian.[131]

The Location of Akhet-aten: The Home of the Ogdoad

The first seeming mystery of Akhenaten's theology is the location of its capital at an apparently remote area in Middle Egypt. The usual explanation is that the region belonged to no deity and was an otherwise undeveloped site. Indeed, in the first set of boundary stelae, Akhenaten claims that no divine cult had right of ownership over Akhet-aten:[132] "Behold, it is the pharaoh who found it, not being the property of a god, not being the property of a goddess, not being the property of a male ruler, not being the property of a female ruler, and not being the property of any people to do business of theirs with it." Akhenaten's statement indicates that he did not appropriate land from another divine cult, but it does not prove that Akhet-aten was not in some way related to nearby cities. In fact, Akhet-aten was not in the middle of nowhere, but only fifteen kilometers from the great city of Hermopolis, across the river and slightly north on the west bank, a religious center whose chief cults were dedicated to the god Thoth and the Ogdoad.

The Ogdoad, a group of eight deities, consisted of four male-female pairs who personified the basic elements of creation: darkness, primordial waters, infinite space, and hiddenness.[133] The four male elements of the Ogdoad often appear in human form with frog heads; their consort goddesses have the heads of serpents. The amphibian and reptilian forms of the Ogdoad identify them with the chaotic, primeval waters from which they emerged to fashion the world and into which they returned after starting the creative process. They were the first male-female pairs, the first divisions of the oneness at the beginning of time. Although ancient Egyptian texts preserve several creation accounts, they all shared one fundamental principle: the division of the primordial unity into a number of balanced pairs.

Worship of the Ogdoad was not limited to Hermopolis, the traditional birthplace of the eight creator deities. The founder of the Middle Kingdom, Montuhotep II, established a series of festivals connecting important religious sites around Thebes and binding together the major temples within the city of Thebes.[134] At about that time, the cult of the Ogdoad and a deity who may have begun as one of its members, the god Amun, becomes the official focus of Theban religion, transplanted from Hermopolis and joining the older Theban cult of Montu.[135] Over time, Medinet Habu became the cult center of the Ogdoad at Thebes, as we know primarily from later textual sources, especially of the Graeco-Roman period. The Egyptians called the site of Medinet Habu the "Mound of the Mothers and the Fathers," the burial mound of the four male-female pairs who were considered to be the mothers and the fathers of all creation. In the developed Ogdoad theology of the Graeco-Roman period, the birthplace of the Ogdoad was Hermopolis, and after creating the world, the eight deities receded into the primordial waters at Thebes, specifically at Medinet Habu. The creative powers of the Ogdoad, exercised during the creation of the world, remained latent at the sites of Hermopolis and Medinet Habu.

Today, the best-known monument at the site of Medinet Habu is the well-preserved mortuary temple of Ramesses III. Already an Eleventh Dynasty ruler constructed a small temple at the site of Medinet Habu.[136] During the Eighteenth Dynasty, Thutmose I may have built a small temple over the earlier monument, which Hatshepsut and Thutmose III then enlarged.[137] The constructions of Amunhotep III on the West Bank literally surround the Thutmoside temple and its environs at Medinet Habu—his mortuary temple lies to the north, while the great jubilee city of Malqata begins just to the south.[138] The great seated colossus of Amunhotep III and Tiye, which now towers over the central hall of the Cairo Museum, originally stood just outside the eastern gate of the later mortuary temple of Ramesses III at Medinet Habu.

Amunhotep III constructed his mortuary temple and jubilee city around Medinet Habu, the Theban home of the Ogdoad. Hermopolis was the original birthplace of the Ogdoad and its cult, and it is across the river from Hermopolis that Akhenaten built his grander complex of temples, palaces, administrative buildings, and necropoleis of Akhet-aten. Akhenaten appears to perpetuate many policies of Amunhotep III, specifically events during and following his father's first jubilee. To rejuvenate himself and return to the moment of creation, Amunhotep III went back to the place where the creator gods themselves were buried at Thebes. Akhenaten, in seeking a site for his city of Akhet-aten, went to the original place of the "first occasion" of creation, Hermopolis, and perpetuated this timeless moment throughout his reign in his new city.

Amunhotep III, his jubilee celebration, and his new city at Malqata form the precedent of much of Amunhotep IV/Akhenaten's building activity. Just as Amunhotep III made time stand still during his jubilee celebration, so did Akhenaten repeat that primordial moment each day in his chariot ride into and out of the city of Akhet-aten. Just as Amunhotep III became the solar deity as he journeyed from one harbor to the other in his jubilee city, changing between the day and night barks, so Akhenaten each morning rode in a gilded chariot into the city called "Horizon of Aten" as the human manifestation of the rising sun, and so each evening he rode out of the horizon just as the solar deity set.

At Akhet-aten, the daily journey of the sun disk and the corresponding daily activities of the royal family replaced all of the great annual festivals of Egypt.[139] The layout of Akhet-aten functioned as an enormous stage upon which Akhenaten and his family could enact this daily drama. Akhenaten, Nefertiti, and most of their daughters seem to have spent each night in the North Riverside Palace. Each morning they would mount their chariots and ride southward, being joined by the eldest daughter, Merytaten, at the North Palace as their chariots hurtled along the elevated Royal Road to the Central City. The centrality of the royal chariot ride to daily life at Amarna is apparent from its prominence in tomb decoration—nearly every private tomb at Amarna contains at least one image of the royal family in their chariots. A large armed military escort surrounds the royal family in these scenes, emphasizing the prominence of the army and the police at Amarna. The presence of the soldiers, however, is not necessarily entirely "militaristic," since the military played an important role in Egyptian festival processions before and after the reign of Akhenaten (see pages 204–209). Akhenaten's bodyguard not only protected him from physical harm but also helped to transform his daily chariot ride into a religious event.

Akhenaten and his family rode out of the northern "horizon" of Akhet-aten in their gilded solar chariots, just like the solar orb journeyed forth from the cliffs of the horizon each day.[140] The representations of Akhenaten and Nefertiti kissing while in the chariot further emphasize the solar associations of the royal couple—just like the sun god, they "rejoice" in the horizon, symbolizing the sexual union of Re and the horizon necessary for the re-creation of the world each dawn.[141] Both Malqata and Amarna were designed to function as stages on which the king could demonstrate his own divinity, and each contained not only palaces and temples, but also more mundane buildings for the civil and military administration. Furthermore, Amunhotep III may have planned a new royal tomb area in the desert cliffs behind Malqata, and Akhenaten chose to build his own sepulcher in the eastern cliffs opposite the Central City of Akhet-aten. Just as Amunhotep III transformed Thebes into a model of the cosmos,[142] Akhenaten would construct his own microcosm at Akhet-aten.

Even the name of Akhenaten's new city—"Horizon of the Aten"— reflects its connection with the constructions of Amunhotep III at Thebes and the initial constructions of Akhenaten himself. The name of a palace sanctuary of Amunhotep III at Thebes was *Hai-em-akhet-ni-aten* (One who rejoices in the Horizon of the Aten), perhaps originally located near the temple of Karnak.[143] In Akhenaten's early constructions, the name *Akhet-ni-aten* (Horizon of the Aten) is equated with the name of Thebes—the Southern City, the Horizon of the Aten prior to the completion of the new Akhet-aten in Middle Egypt.[144] The rationale behind the location of Akhet-aten is thus no longer a mystery—Akhenaten chose an abandoned area opposite the birthplace of the eight creator deities. Just as Amunhotep III built a large independent city and temple complex centered at Medinet Habu, the Theban home of the Ogdoad, so Akhenaten built an even larger city and temple complex at the original home of the Ogdoad.

Akhenaten as Creator Deity

Akhenaten's desire to reach back to the moment of creation also goes far in explaining the bizarre Amarna style of art. Just as the first male and female pairs in the creation cycle of Hermopolis have serpent and frog heads to show their closeness to the chaotic waters of creation from which they only so recently arose, so Akhenaten and Nefertiti retain physical attributes of their divine mother/father.[145] In the art of the age, Akhenaten and Nefertiti are androgynous, for they are the first male-female pairs, the Amarna counterparts of the Ogdoad deities. The thighs, belly, and buttocks of the Atenist rulers are those of fecundity and pregnancy, and the elongated skull is that of the newborn child only recently emerged through the birth canal. Even Akhenaten's oddly shaped navel resembles that of a woman after having given birth.[146] To enhance his identity as son of the sun, Akhenaten also had himself depicted as an actual child.[147] The portrayal of Akhenaten and Nefertiti as creator deities continues the "jubilee" style of art of Amunhotep III, which has the same purpose. Some statues depict Amunhotep III with a swollen belly, indicating his role as fertility god,[148] and his third phase of art initiates the "baby"-like features discussed above, the face of the creator at the birth of the cosmos.

Colossal statues from the Gempaaten temple at Karnak demonstrate the extremes to which Akhenaten would go to represent his own theological significance. One of these statues shows the pharaoh with what appears to be a nude body without male genitalia (see figure 5). Although the crown is damaged, the remains of the royal beard indicate that this is indeed a statue of Akhenaten and not his wife, Nefertiti. Rather than depicting the effects of some congenital abnormality or disease, these strange alterations to the normal human physique reveal a basic truth of Amarna religion—Akhenaten not only becomes a god on earth like his

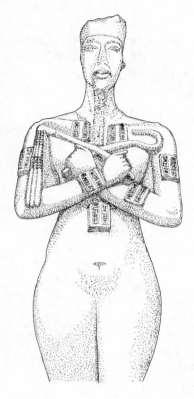

Figure 5. Colossal statue of Akhenaten (Egyptian Museum, Cairo). The pharaoh wears a partially broken white crown and holds a crook and a flail. His chest, arms, and midsection are decorated with cartouches of the Aten. Drawing by J. C. Darnell.

father, but also rules as a *creator* deity. The physical attributes of Akhenaten and Nefertiti normally identify the couple as the first differentiated male and female pair; in the Karnak colossus, Akhenaten is the embryonic androgyne, not yet the incomplete male he ultimately becomes. Details of other Amarna statuary and small objects from Akhet-aten indicate that Akhenaten and Nefertiti adopted the mythological roles of Shu (luminous space) and Tefnut (moisture),[149] the son and daughter of the creator deity Atum, the first differentiated male and female pair in the Heliopolitan account of creation.[150] In this creation account, Atum, Shu, and Tefnut play the role of the Ogdoad in the corresponding Hermpolitan tradition and begin the creative process by dividing the oneness of the primordial waters into balanced pairs—light/darkness, moisture/dryness, male/female. In Amarna religion, the creative forces earlier embodied by Atum and the Ogdoad are all encompassed in the theology of the Aten and his representatives on earth—Akhenaten and Nefertiti.

In addition to the Great Hymn to the Aten from the tomb of Aye, the inhabitants of Akhet-aten recorded in their tombs praises sung in honor of their revered pharaoh, Akhenaten. These eulogies repeatedly describe

Akhenaten "creating and raising" people, thereby referring not only to his promotion of previously low-ranking individuals, but also expressing a concept of theological significance.[151] These texts laud Akhenaten as various natural phenomena—air, light, and the Nile:

> Adoration of the lord of the Two Lands,
>   one who is effective for the Aten (*Akh-en-aten*);
>   fate who gives life, lord of commands;
>   light for every land, in whose season one lives;
>   inundation for everyone, through whose *ka*-spirit one is sated;
>   god who creates officials and fashions the commoners;
>   air for every nose, through whom one breathes.[152]

Such praise of the king has precedents in the Middle Kingdom, but the phraseology of those earlier texts indicates that the object of praise is the office of kingship rather than any particular incarnation thereof. When spoken by Akhenaten's courtiers, such epithets refer not to pharaonic kingship in the abstract, but to Akhenaten himself. A similar trend is evident in the relationship between Maat and Akhenaten—the king no longer simply rewards people for doing Maat, but under Akhenaten doing Maat is the same as acting according to the instructions of the king.[153] Akhenaten possesses the same intimate relationship with Maat as the solar god himself. In sum, Akhenaten abrogates to himself all of the prerogatives, epithets, and theological significance of the creator god, and his male child Shu, with Nefertiti taking the role of the latter's sister, Tefnut.

The Gods Have Not Yet Been Born

Akhenaten transforms the traditional artistic canon to portray himself and Nefertiti as the first male-female pair of deities. To harness the creative potential of the Ogdoad, Akhenaten moves his capital near their cult center at Hermopolis. But why does Akhenaten then attack the cult of Amun and other deities? Simply stated, if Akhenaten and Nefertiti represent the first offspring of the creator god, then no other gods yet exist.[154] Akhenaten himself has just emerged from the creator deity and can appear like the androgynous creator god. For his new theology to function, Akhenaten must deny the existence of other deities, which he does by hacking out their names and images and closing their temples. As with so many other aspects of Akhenaten's religion, moving back to the time of creation is a continuation of the policies of Amunhotep III. During his jubilee festival near the Theban cult center of the Ogdoad, Amunhotep III re-created primal time and ruled as the solar deity on earth. Akhenaten not only moves to a new city close to the original home of the Ogdoad, but he also rules almost from the beginning of his reign in a timeless repetition of the world at the moment of creation,[155] a time when other deities are not yet created. The apparent monotheism of Akhenaten's religion is the elevation of a cosmological stage—the creation of the world by the Aten—to the central focus of a theological system.[156]

The Female Light Powers

How does the prominence of Nefertiti and her daughters fit into Akhenaten's new theology? How is Akhenaten's role of creator deity enhanced by his daughters but not by a son? The answers lie in the Aten disk that dominates Akhenaten's religion. In Egyptian theology, each ray of the sun can be a goddess, a feminine manifestation of the solar deity. The word for light rays in ancient Egyptian, *setut*, is a grammatically feminine word; the arms of the Aten end in hands, which are another feminine element, since the Egyptian word for hand, *djeret*, is also grammatically feminine.[157] As the son of the sun, Akhenaten also possesses a multitude of feminine manifestations—Nefertiti and his daughters. The "family portraits" of Akhenaten and his daughters are at another level images of Akhenaten as the earthly manifestation of the solar disk and its arms. Just as the multitude of rays ending in hands represent feminine powers emanating from the Aten, so do Nefertiti and the royal daughters surround Akhenaten as his own feminine light powers (see figure 3). The princesses are at once further extensions of the feminine aspect of the first male-female division represented by Akhenaten and Nefertiti and projections of the light of Akhenaten himself.[158] If, however, a son appeared in these same representations, then Akhenaten would be acknowledging that creation really was continuing and yet another generation was born. A desire that creation remain "young" may explain the apparent invisibility of Tutankhaten, although from a block across the river from Akhet-aten at Hermopolis, he was a king's son during at least the latter portion of Akhenaten's reign (see below).

When Akhenaten and Nefertiti rode south on their chariots toward the Central City, they represented the anthropomorphic manifestations of the Aten and his rays. As the only divine offspring of the solar creator deity, the Aten, they "rejoiced" in the horizon of their own making. The chariot ride and daily offering to the Aten became the rituals that substituted for the great annual cycle of festivals at Thebes and other cities of Egypt. Akhet-aten became Egypt in microcosm, locked perpetually in a daily celebration of the re-creation of the world. Theologically, time was caught in a tight loop, and the royal couple ruled as gods on earth, mimicking the daily course of the only other existing deity: the Aten. The pharaoh was wholly divine, and Egypt became a theocracy in a very real—and for the Egyptians ultimately frightening—sense. Akhenaten's radical new theology held dominion for a little over a decade after his move to Akhet-aten, but ultimately his political and religious changes were doomed to failure. After his death, his successors appear to have found it impossible to maintain the fiction of the world at its moment of creation, Akhenaten's (vain)-glorious experiment at literally creating a new world.

Ankh(et)kheperure Neferneferuaten and Smenkhkare: The Ephemeral Kings

"Egyptologists know that the notoriety of the Amarna age is matched only by its obscurity."[159] This statement is particularly applicable to the reigns of Akhenaten's immediate successors, shadowy figures for whom some of the only surviving evidence is a series of names and epithets recorded on small objects from Akhet-aten and the tomb of Tutankhamun. Few historical texts or monuments help to clarify the situation, and one is left carefully examining a series of permutations of royal titularies. The disappearance or death of several members of the Amarna court between years twelve and fourteen of Akhenaten's reign further muddles matters. While some of these "disappearances" might be due to the adoption of new identities, a plague might have had some role in their deaths.[160] The identities of the rulers who follow Akhenaten often involve difficult and confusing evidence, but they are also important for understanding the political and religious transitions in the post–Amarna Period, particularly the actions of Tutankhamun.

In the tomb of Meryre II at Amarna, a scene sketched in ink depicts a royal figure accompanied by the chief royal wife, Merytaten, eldest daughter of Akhenaten.[161] The king bears the names "King of Upper and Lower Egypt, Ankhkheperure" (Living are the manifestations of Re) and "Son of Re, Smenkhkare Djeserkheperure" (Beneficent is the spirit of Re and holy are the forms of Re). The "Son of Re" name (the nomen) was the name the pharaoh was given at birth, although epithets, such as those representing the city of his coronation, could be added. The "King of Upper and Lower Egypt" name (the praenomen) represented the pharaoh's rule over the

South and the North. The names of the pharaoh Smenkhkare on several objects and his depiction alongside Merytaten are thus far the only evidence for this ephemeral ruler, whose exact identity remains a topic of debate.[162] The name Ankhkheperure, however, is more common, albeit virtually ignored in more popular publications. The clue to Smenkhkare's identity in fact lies in the permutations of the name Ankhkheperure and its association with other known figures at the Amarna court.

Smenkhkare's praenomen, Ankhkheperure, appears—also as a prenomen—in conjunction with another name, Neferneferuaten (Beautiful is the perfection of Aten), the latter an epithet Nefertiti adopted before Akhenaten's sixth regnal year.[163] During year twelve Neferneferuaten Nefertiti disappeared, and at the same time, a new royal name appears at Amarna: Ankh(et)kheperure Neferneferuaten.[164]

Neferneferuaten appears as Nefertiti's epithet and then becomes the nomen of a ruler with the praenomen Ankhkheperure. When the name Ankh(et)kheperure first appears, it has both masculine (Ankhkheperure) and feminine (Ankhetkheperure) versions.[165] At the North Riverside Palace of Amarna, the name (damaged but restorable as) "Ankhetkheperure beloved of Neferkheperure (Akhenaten) Neferneferuaten 'effective for her husband'" appears alongside the name and image of Akhenaten. Some of the funerary equipment of the ruler Ankh(et)kheperure Neferneferuaten became the property of Tutankhamun, and those objects reveal the use of the epithet "effective for her husband" and a number of feminine epithets associated with the name, such as "may she live forever." Apparently this Ankhetkheperure, linked to Nefertiti through the nomen Neferneferuaten and with Akhenaten through the epithets of both praenomen and nomen, was a woman ruling as a king, a female pharaoh. In fact, the monuments of the earlier female pharaoh Hatshepsut show a similar fluctuation of masculine and feminine forms—Hatshepsut's statues can depict her as a man or a woman, relief decoration shows her primarily as a male, and her inscriptions usually employ the feminine gender.[166]

Other attestations of the combined name dispense with references to Akhenaten, taking the form "Ankhkheperure beloved of Aten (Meryaten), Neferneferuaten, ruler." The name Ankhkheperure as praenomen is therefore associated with the name Neferneferuaten in two versions of a royal titulary—one version relating the ruler to Akhenaten, and another version relating the ruler to the Aten, this latter version insisting that Ankhkheperure Neferneferuaten is the ruler. The epithet Mery-aten, "Beloved of Aten," is similar to the name of the eldest daughter of Akhenaton and Nefertiti: Merytaten.

Inscriptions on two coffers from the tomb of Tutankhamun refer to "the King of Upper and Lower Egypt Ankhkheperure, beloved of Neferkheperure (Akhenaten), Son of Re Neferneferuaten beloved of Waenre (Akhenaten)," followed by the name of the great royal wife, Merytaten.[167] Is this evidence of a ruler with a chief wife or is Ankhkheperure Neferneferuaten the "pharaonic," coregent name of Merytaten? An unfortunately poorly preserved stela, now in London, appears originally to have depicted Akhenaten seated on the left, with Nefertiti standing behind him.[168] To the right, facing left and bowing slightly to the royal couple, were the little daughter Ankhesenpaaten, following a larger princess, almost certainly the eldest daughter, Merytaten. At a later stage the name of the eldest princess was erased, and the name of the king Ankhkheperure Neferneferuaten with feminine epithets inserted. Does this mean that Merytaten became that enigmatic, probably female pharaoh with the transgendered titulary?

Additionally, the name Ankhkheperure—the masculine form of the praenomen of Ankh(et)kheperure Neferneferuaten—forms a further titulary, still the praenomen, with the nomen Smenkhkare. On a calcite jar, the names of Akhenaten are juxtaposed with these names of Smenkhkare.[169] Except for the depiction in the tomb of Meryre II, other attestations of Smenkhkare, such as signet rings with his cartouches, are even less substantial than the monuments of the apparent female pharaoh Ankh(et)khperure Neferneferuaten.

Does the person of Nefertiti lie behind one or more of these titularies? Did she become a copharaoh with Akhenaten, survive him to rule alone, and then assign the title of chief royal wife to her eldest daughter, Merytaten?[170] Egypt presents more than one ruler whose titulary appears in three different versions, altered to mirror political changes through the reign.[171] Was Ankhkheperure Neferneferuaten Mery-aten in fact the daughter Merytaten ruling as pharaoh? If so, did she slightly later relinquish her rank and part of her name to a male named Smenkhkare? Or are all of the titularies incorporating Ankh(et)kheperure the names of three different people? Some diplomatic correspondence between Egypt and Syria-Palestine places particular emphasis on Merytaten, which would be appropriate to a newly appointed coregent,[172] and one may suggest that the initial Ankh(et)kheperure titularies belong to Merytaten as coregent with Akhenaten and then as sole ruler.[173] Shortly thereafter, Merytaten might have resigned her pharaonic status in favor of the ephemeral Smenkhkare.[174]

In the tomb of Pairy at Thebes (TT 139), a hieratic graffito written by a man Pawah is dated to year three of a ruler Ankhkheperure Mery-aten and Neferneferuaten Mery-[aten], the second version of the titulary of the mysterious ruler.[175] In this inscription, a temple of Ankhkheperure on the West Bank of Thebes is mentioned in passing; the location of this temple in the "domain of Amun" indicates that Ankhkheperure—whoever he or she may have been—did not adhere strictly to the religion of Akhenaten and attempted some reconciliation with the cult of Amun. Some of the funerary objects of Ankh(et)kheperure reused in the burial of Tutankhamun are also of an "orthodox" nature, and thus paradoxically Ankhkheperure appears to have distanced himself/herself from the exclusive cult of Aten even as he/she sought to associate his/her very names with Akhenaten and Nefertiti. The surviving evidence may not allow for certainty at this point, but one may observe—and this is perhaps the most important thing—that change was in the air at the end of the reign of Akhenaten, but the rulers of that time (if indeed Ankh(et)kheperure were not in fact one person with three titularies) were reluctant to abandon the names of Akhenaten and Nefertiti, even as they appear to have abandoned the disk worship of that illustrious pair.

A series of changes in titulary appears to lead from Nefertiti to Smenkhkare. The name Nefertiti appears first alone and then around the cusp of Akhenaten's regnal years five and six with the adjunct Neferneferuaten. This adjunct, without the original name Nefertiti, continues as the nomen of the royal name Ankh(et)kheperure Neferneferuaten. This name, occurring in masculine and feminine forms, appears first with epithets relating the person to Akhenaten and later in a form relating the enigmatic ruler to the Aten alone. This ruler, who significantly also adopted the epithet Mery-aten to the praenomen, is probably Merytaten, ruling as coregent with her father, Akhenaten, before assuming sole rule after his death. Eventually the name Neferneferuaten disappears, but the praenomen Ankhkheperure, in its masculine form, persists as the praenomen of Smenkhkare, the male ruler to whom Merytaten may have relinquished her kingly titles to assume her more traditional queenly role. Modern speculation and enthusiastic interest in the Amarna Period can lead one to forget how obscure much of this period truly is. The identity of the person or persons who bore the prenomen Ankh(et)kheperure is the darkest perhaps of the murky corners of the Amarna Period, starkly dark in contrast to the brilliant paintings and sun-drenched solar courts of Akhet-aten.

Tutankhamun: The Boy King

More than three millennia after his death, Tutankhamun acquired a fame, which had he ever actually achieved it in life, he had surely lost by the end of the reign of Horemhab. Prior to Howard Carter's historic discovery, only sparse details were known of Tutankhamun's reign. Objects within the tomb as well as more recent discoveries have illuminated previously unknown facets of the young king's tenure as pharaoh. Yet many questions remain; even the parents of Tutankhamun are not explicitly named in any ancient Egyptian document.

The best evidence for Tutankhamun's existence prior to his coronation as pharaoh is a block from Hermopolis, across the Nile from Akhet-aten, bearing this inscription: "beloved son of the king of his own body, Tutankh-aten."[176] Based on the name of the prince Tutankh*aten*, "Living image of the Aten," the unnamed royal father is almost certainly Akhenaten.[177] Although on later monuments Tutankhamun refers to Amunhotep III as his father, this need not be taken literally. Since Tutankhamun was about nineteen or twenty years of age at his death and ruled for nine years, one would have to assume a long coregency between Amunhotep III and Akhenaten for the former to be the father of Tutankhamun.[178] In a desire to erase the memory of his actual father, or at least to distance himself from Akhenaten, Tutankhamun related himself directly to his more remote predecessor and probable grandfather. Nowhere do we learn the name of Tutankhamun's mother, although a scene in the royal tomb at Akhet-aten showing a woman's death in childbirth has been interpreted as the demise of Kiye after giving birth to Tutankhamun.[179]

We know nothing of Tutankhamun's childhood prior to his coronation at about age nine.[180] During the second year of his reign, Tutankh*aten* changed his name to Tutankh*amun*, confirming his break with the religion of his father and the restoration of the cult of Amun;[181] similarly, Tutankh-amun's wife, Ankhesenpa*aten*, a daughter of Akhenaten and Nefertiti, changed her name to Ankhesen*amun*. The complete titulary of the phar-aoh could express his political and military goals, and Tutankhamun's tit-ulary casts the young ruler as restorer of proper order and pacifier of the neglected deities.[182] At the same time Tutankhamun adopted his full array of royal names, he abandoned Akhet-aten and restored the cultural and administrative prerogatives of Thebes and Memphis.[183]

Tutankhamun also lost little time in erasing the memory of his im-mediate predecessors, Merytaten/Ankh(et)kheprure Neferneferuaten and Smenkhkare. Tutankhamun legitimized his own rule by delegitimizing the entire Amarna interlude and expressing himself as the first proper succes-sor of Amunhotep III. This process presented a problem for Tutankhamun, since one of the chief ways an Egyptian pharaoh could prove his right to the throne was the proper burial of his father and predecessor. Since Amunhotep III was already properly interred in his tomb in the West Valley of the Valley of the Kings, Tutankhamun reburied his actual father, but at the same time vilified his memory by erasing Akhenaten's names from the burial equipment.

The result of Tutankhamun's compromise between filial duty and political expediency is another enduring puzzle of the Amarna Period—the enigmatic burial in the tomb King's Valley (KV) 55.[184] The tomb contained the remains of a gilded wooden shrine originally belonging to Amunhotep III's queen Tiye, prepared by Akhenaten for her original burial at Amarna. The tomb KV 55 also contained a badly damaged coffin, originally made for Kiye but modified in both iconography and text to serve the burial of a male ruler, apparently Akhenaten. Erased cartouches obscure the identity of the coffin's final occupant, and the poor preservation of the skeleton prevents definite conclusions about the body's sex and age.

Apparently Akhenaten had buried his mother, Tiye, in the royal tomb at Amarna and in turn Merytaten as Ankhetkheperure Neferneferuaten buried her father, Akhenaten, within the same hypogeum in the royal wadi at Amarna. Just as Hatshepsut's burial of her father, Thutmose I, was a major element in her attempt to legitimize her abnormal reign, so the reburial of Thutmose I by Thutmose III both legitimized the latter's rule and served to negate any hint of proper succession for the earlier reign of Hatshepsut. Similarly, Tutankhamun appears to have moved simultaneously the burials of Tiye and Akhenaten to Thebes to erase any hint of legitimacy for the reign of Ankh(et)kheperure Neferneferuaten. The occupant of the coffin in KV 55 was probably Akhenaten, buried with some of Tiye's paraphernalia as well, the old queen herself perhaps interred in the burial of her husband, Amunhotep III. A number of the burial goods of Tutankhamun appear to come from the burial of a female pharaoh, further evidence of the *damnatio memoriae* Ankh(et)kheperure, possibly his sister Merytaten, suffered during the reign of Tutankhamun. By reburying his grandmother Tiye, Tutankhamun also appropriated one of the duties of his own father and thereby went some way toward subsuming the religious duties of the reign of the heretic king.

The most significant political event of Tutankhamun's reign was the attempt to restore Egypt's religious institutions to their pre-Akhenaten state. The location of Ankh(et)kheperure's mortuary temple in the "domain of Amun" suggests that Tutankhamun's shadowy predecessor might have already abandoned the more extreme elements of Atenism, but Tutankhamun's restoration effort is better known due to the survival of a monument known as the "Restoration Stela." The text begins by vilifying the

ineffectiveness of Tutankhamun's immediate predecessors and the deplor-
able state of Egypt's temples. Nowhere does the name of Akhenaten
appear, and much of the text dwells on the psychological effects of the
Atenist "heresy"—the gods of Egypt no longer hearkened to people's
prayers:

> At the time when His Majesty was crowned as king, the temples of the
> gods and goddesses beginning in Elephantine and ending at the marshes
> of the Delta [. . .] had fallen into ruin. Their shrines had fallen into decay,
> having become mounds and teeming with weeds. Their sanctuaries were
> like that which did not exist. Their domains were footpaths. The land
> was in distress; the gods had abandoned this land.
>
> If an army was sent to Djahi (Syria-Palestine), in order to widen the
> boundaries of Egypt, they could not succeed. If one petitioned to a god in
> order take counsel from him, he did not come at all. If one prayed to a
> goddess likewise, she did not come at all.[185]

After his coronation, Tutankhamun responded to the Amarna crisis by
"taking counsel with his heart, searching out every occasion of excellence,
and seeking the effectiveness of his father, Amun."[186] After these deliber-
ations, the Restoration Stela lists the specific endowments Tutankhamun
made to divine cults throughout the country. For the god Amun, who
bore the brunt of the proscriptions of Akhenaten, and the god Ptah, chief
deity of Memphis, Tutankhamun added to the number of carrying poles
used to transport the divine images during religious processions; although
not explicit within the text, the increased number of carrying poles also
implies larger barks and more priests to man the poles.[187] Tutankhamun
further commanded that new divine statues be made out of the finest electrum and other precious minerals and that new processional barks be constructed out of the best cedar from Lebanon and decorated with gold and
silver. All of the priests, singers, dancers, and servants of the temples were
restored to their former positions and granted a specific decree of royal
protection, because by serving the gods, the temple staff was ultimately responsible for the protection of the land of Egypt. The temples also benefited from Tutankhamun's military activities, or at least those of his chief
generals, since the Restoration Stela reports that prisoners of war filled the
temples as servants. In sum, the Restoration Stela states that Tutankhamun
"has made great all the works of the temples, doubled, tripled, and quadru-
pled!"[188] The results of Tutankhamun's restoration program were prosperity at home, military success abroad, and most importantly the return of
Egypt's pantheon.[189]

The reign of Tutankhamun was the first of several in which much
effort was required to restore the depredations of the disk-worshippers

throughout Egypt. In addition to renewing the monuments of earlier pharaohs and restoring the names and images of Amun and other deities,
Tutankhamun commissioned temples and decorations of his own, the surviving examples of which are primarily in Thebes and Nubia.[190] The Theban monuments of the boy king include, but are not limited to, statuary
at the temples of Karnak and Luxor[191] and the extensive near-completion
of the decorative program of the Colonnade Hall of Amunhotep III at
Luxor Temple.[192] A small temple on the West Bank called the "Temple of
Nebkheperure in Thebes" was either built by Tutankhamun or constructed
for him by Aye.[193]

The death of Tutankhamun at about age nineteen led to a crisis in
succession,[194] since the king's only probable offspring were two stillborn
children, buried in minuscule coffins in the tomb of their father. At some
point during his reign, Tutankhamun may have appointed his general
Horemhab as heir (see below). However, Tutankhamun's widow, Ankhesenamun, was apparently not content to marry any eligible member of the
Egyptian court. Neither did Ankhesenamun attempt to rule independently
like her sister Merytaten/Ankhetkheperure Neferneferuaten. Instead, the
queen did something unprecedented: she wrote to the king of the Hittites,
the military rival of Egypt, and requested that a Hittite prince be sent to
marry her and become king of Egypt (for details of this episode, see pages
184–186). The foreign prince does not appear to have reached Egypt, and
the pharaonic regalia passed to one of Tutankhamun's top officials.

After Tutankhamun: Aye

Aye had experienced a long and varied career before ascending the throne
at an advanced age, probably near his seventieth year (see figure 6).[195]
Prior to becoming pharaoh, Aye held the important titles "fan-bearer on
the right of the king," "master of the horse" (i.e., commander of the chariotry), and "god's father." The title "god's father" was originally held by
members of the royal family, and in the case of Yuya, father of Amunhotep III's chief queen, Tiye, marks the holder's position as father-in-law of
the "god," Pharaoh Amunhotep III. In other cases, the holder of the title
was a royal adviser and may have played a role in the crown prince's education.[196] Aye and his family possessed strong ties to the city of Akhmim
in Middle Egypt,[197] which was also the birthplace of Yuya. The sum of
indirect evidence suggests that Yuya may be the father of Aye, in which
case Aye was the brother of Tiye, the brother-in-law of Amunhotep III,[198]
and a cousin of Akhenaten.

Figure 6. Gold leaf fragment from the Valley of the Kings. The pharaoh Aye shoots arrows into a metal target decorated with images of bound prisoners—or perhaps living ones. A Nubian and an Asiatic bow before the king's chariot and raise their arms in praise. A fan-bearer, wearing a heart-shaped military apron, and a dog run behind Aye. After Davis, *Tombs of Harmhabi and Touatankhamanou*, 127.

Even if Aye were not related to the royal family, both he and his wife shared a close relationship with Akhenaten and Nefertiti, Aye's wife, Tiye, holding the title "nurse of Neferneferuaten Nefertiti."[199] Like other Amarna officials, Aye and Tiye commemorate the royal couple awarding them with golden *shebiu* collars,[200] and the Great Hymn to the Aten appears only in Aye's tomb. Upon the death of Akhenaten and during the tenure of his short-reigned successors, Aye seems to have retained his position at court, particularly his title "god's father," and he continued to exert influence on the young pharaoh Tutankhamun. An exceptional depiction from the tomb of Sennedjem at Akhmim shows Aye riding in a chariot with Tutankhamun.[201] Otherwise only divinities stand alongside the pharaoh in his chariot, and the tomb scene emphasizes Aye's extraordinary role as guardian of the semidivine boy king. In another scene, on a piece of gold leaf from the Valley of the Kings, Tutankhamun smites foreign enemies while Aye stands behind the pharaoh, carrying the royal fan.[202] With images such as these, one easily imagines Aye as a scheming courtier using his influence and experience to manipulate the adolescent Tutankhamun, but we actually know nothing about Aye's behavior toward Tutankhamun until the boy king's death.

In the burial chamber of Tutankhamun's tomb, Aye appears in the role of the *sem* priest who conducts the funerary rites for the deceased pharaoh, a role only appropriate to the rightful heir to the throne. The depiction of Aye performing Tutankhamun's burial rituals is also irregular for royal tomb decoration, since it represents a single historical event, rather than the continual regeneration of the king's spirit through its integration into the solar cycle, which is the focus of nearly all of the tomb decorations in the Valley of the Kings.[203] After asserting his rights to kingship by burying Tutankhamun, and strengthening his position as heir through his choice of wall decorations in the tomb, Aye enjoyed but four years upon the pharaonic throne, and had little time to commission monuments or conduct military campaigns. Just north of Medinet Habu, Aye began to construct for himself a mortuary temple that Horemhab would later usurp and expand. The respect Aye shows toward Tutankhamun in the latter's burial chamber may have found further expression in Aye's completion of Tutankhamun's own temple constructions.

The titulary Aye assumed upon his coronation associated the aging courtier with the reigns of his predecessor and the earlier Amarna pharaohs. His praenomen Kheperkheperure, "Manifesting are the manifestations of Re," is similar to those of Akhenaten (Neferkheperure, "Beautiful are the manifestations of Re") and Tutankhamun (Nebkheperure, "Re is the Lord of Manifestations"). His birth name, Aye, naturally becomes his nomen, but he also includes his title "god's father" within his cartouche, an unusual choice. Just as the titularies of the person or persons immediately succeeding Akhenaten reveal an evolution from the name of Nefertiti and demonstrate a desire to link the holders of those titularies to the rulers at Amarna, so the name of Aye incorporating the title "god's father"—his chief title at Akhet-aten—within the nomen cartouche may reveal Aye's desire to link his nomen to the court of Akhenaten. Aye's continued use of the title "god's father" also may indicate his earlier status as "caretaker" of Tutankhamun. Even if his devotion were not entirely sycophantic, Aye's decision to maintain his connection with the family of Akhenaten appears to have been enough to ensure his inclusion in Horemhab's damnatio memoriae of all rulers from Akhenaten through Aye.

The unusual promotion of the god's father Aye to the rank of pharaoh appears to have created a certain amount of conflict within the ranks of the civil and military administration. Aye's coronation might have overridden the general Horemhab's stronger claim to the throne. In his coronation text, Horemhab claims to have been appointed heir to the throne by Tutankhamun. If this represents historical fact and not later propaganda, how did Aye become king? The answer lies not in Egyptian documents, but rather in Hittite sources. A Hittite historical retrospective suggests that the Egyptian and Hittite armies clashed in the region of Amki at the time of a pharaoh's death; the unnamed pharaoh is almost certainly Tutankhamun. As chief general, Horemhab would have been on campaign at the time of Tutankhamun's death and unable to return to assume the throne.[204] Horemhab might even have assented to Aye's kingship, knowing that the old courtier would rule for only a short time, during which Horemhab could consolidate Egyptian control in Syria-Palestine.

Although Aye's own accession to the throne might have gone uncontested, once king, Aye appears to have further distanced Horemhab from the royal succession. The name of the general Horemhab appears nowhere in the tomb of Tutankhamun,[205] but a general named Nakhtmin donated five *ushebtis* (funerary statuettes) to the royal funerary equipment.[206] Aye may have promoted this Nakhtmin—perhaps a member of at least the extended family of Aye if not the son of Aye—to chief military commander and heir apparent. Aye would then have retired Horemhab from his martial duties, and possibly attempted to remove Horemhab from the line of succession. Either during the reign of Aye or following his death, Horemhab—or the gods of Egypt—removed Aye's intended heir, Nakhtmin, and guaranteed Horemhab's own succession to the throne.[207]

Horemhab: The General

Horemhab began his military career during the reign of Akhenaten, and by the time of Tutankhamun's death was the chief army general and a seasoned veteran.[208] Horemhab was not related to the royal family; although some have identified his wife, Mutnodjmet, as a sister of Nefertiti, no certain evidence of this connection exists.[209] Horemhab compensated for his apparently modest family background through an outstanding energy in military and civil service. Upon his coronation as pharaoh, Horemhab brought a similar dedication to the office of king, a position that Horemhab claimed he owed to the divine intervention of the falcon god Horus.

While still a general, Horemhab began construction on a large tomb at Saqqara,[210] much of the decoration of which concerns itself with martial themes—military scribes take dictation, chariot officers lounge alongside their horses, and a group of soldiers carrying a rolled-up tent help prepare a camp. Detailed reliefs lining the second courtyard of the tomb depict row after row of Nubian, Asiatic, and Libyan prisoners led before Horemhab.[211] An associated text describes Horemhab's military victories on behalf of the pharaoh Tutankhamun: "He was sent as royal envoy as far as the limit of the rising of the sun disk, returning after he triumphed, his [attack] having succeeded. No land stood firm against him, and he overawed it in a single moment."[212] The phraseology of the inscription grants

Horemhab qualities normally reserved for the pharaoh himself; after Horemhab indeed became pharaoh, he altered the reliefs in his Memphite tomb to reflect his new status, adding a royal uraeus to his brow.

Although Horemhab's assumption of the throne may appear to be the final act of a military coup, no evidence survives to support such a view, and Horemhab's career, like that of many other Egyptian officials, had included both civilian and military training and roles.[213] He was not a member of the royal family, but neither apparently had Thutmose I been of royal blood. Only Horemhab's own apparent hostility to the memory of his predecessors' reigns indicates any irregularities in the pharaonic succession, but that animosity does not appear to have been driven by Horemhab's military connections. Indeed, Horemhab's coronation text,[214] which justifies the general's claim to the throne, emphasizes not his military achievements but royal and divine recognition of his administrative abilities: "Now this god (Horus) elected his son (Horemhab) in front of the entire population . . . the heart of the king (Tutankhamun) was pleased with his (Horemhab's) deeds and rejoiced at his choice. He appointed him to be chief of the land, in order to execute the laws of the two banks as heir apparent of this entire land."[215]

Another passage describes Horemhab's role as adviser under Tutankhamun and his effectiveness in aiding the king during the difficult restoration: "When the palace fell into a frenzy, he was summoned before the sovereign. As soon as he (Horemhab) opened his mouth to respond to the king, he appeased him with the words which came from his mouth."[216] The text further describes Horemhab's successful leadership of the Two Lands; after many years, Horemhab is rewarded with the pharaonic throne: "Now this noble god Horus of Hutnesu, he wished to establish his son on his eternal throne."[217] Horus and Horemhab sail south to Thebes, and the official coronation takes place under the auspices of the god Amun at Karnak Temple. Once Horemhab was led to the palace, all the gods rejoiced to heaven at the selection of their new vicar.

When the great celebration at Thebes was complete, the newly crowned pharaoh sailed north through areas still ravaged by the Amarna upheaval, and promptly began the serious work of his office. The concluding section of the coronation text of Horemhab mimics the restoration stela of Tutankhamun:

> He renewed the temples and domains of the gods, from the Delta marshes to Nubia. He fashioned all their cult images, more distinguished than the originals and more beautiful because of what he did on their behalf, so that Re rejoiced when he saw them, since they were ruined previously. . . .

He sought out the precincts of the gods that were like mounds in this land and reestablished them as they had existed at the beginning of time.[218]

Like Tutankhamun, Horemhab endowed the newly restored temples with material wealth, servants, and priestly staff. In recompense for his lofty deeds, Horemhab receives millions of jubilee festivals and victories against all the foreign lands.

The coronation text extols the legitimacy of Horemhab's rule and the continued restoration of temples throughout the country. Although Tutankhamun, and perhaps Aye, had already helped many of the religious institutions regain their pre-Akhenaten state, it was left to Horemhab and the first rulers of the Nineteenth Dynasty to complete the task of repairing the damages Akhenaten's reign had wrought on the civil administration. The internal situation Horemhab inherited may have been a picture of almost unbelievable corruption and abuse of power, as his decree—preserved on an enormous stela at Karnak Temple—suggests.[219] Using force and strongly worded new laws, Horemhab sought to restore order and strengthen the kingship again (see further in chapter 6).

Horemhab further compensated himself for his effort in restoring Egypt by subsuming the reigns of all the pharaohs who had ruled since the death of Amunhotep III, Akhenaten through Aye. Although Horemhab's actual reign probably lasted about twenty-seven years,[220] a tomb inscription from the Nineteenth Dynasty describes an event dated to "year fifty-nine" of the pharaoh Horemhab.[221] By backdating his reign to the end of the reign of Amunhotep III, whom he represented as the last legitimate ruler prior to his own accession, Horemhab could add about thirty-five years to his own rule. During his reign, Horemhab extinguished any vestige of the legitimacy of the rule of Akhenaten, and sought to obliterate the memory of the entire Amarna interlude with a thoroughness far surpassing that of Tutankhamun and Aye. Horemhab instituted a program of complete destruction of Akhenaten's monuments not already dismantled, and usurped monuments of Aye and Tutankhamun.[222] Horemhab also erased the name of Aye from the latter's tomb in the Valley of the Kings, although he did not behave in the same way toward Tutankhamun.[223]

Horemhab erased the memories of all the rulers of the Amarna Period and of those who demonstrated a strong desire in their titulary to associate themselves with the Amarna Period. The fact that Aye incorporated his old title "god's father" within his cartouche might very well express some reticence, at least in the political sphere, to abandoning the Amarna prototype, which in turn would give Horemhab an added incentive to erase any memory of Aye's reign. All of Akhenaten's successors, through

Aye, sought some legitimacy from at least furtive, if not overt, appeal to Akhenaten himself. Horemhab wanted none of it.

The case of Tutankhamun is perhaps somewhat different; although one must remember that Tutankhamun was most likely a son of Akhenaten and a member of the Amarna court. Horemhab's status as general of the army and perhaps heir apparent under Tutankhamun may have allowed the general become pharaoh to feel legitimately that most of the deeds for which Tutankhamun took credit on his monuments were carried out under the auspices of Horemhab himself. Although few of Horemhab's monuments remain,[224] no certain evidence exists for any campaigns fought by Horemhab as pharaoh, and blocks from his mortuary temple at Thebes and a small rock-cut temple at Gebel Silsila demonstrate his desire to take credit for his military activities as general by recasting them as victories he achieved while king (see further on pages 122–124 and 182).

The reign of Horemhab marks the end of the Eighteenth Dynasty and the conclusion of one of the most tumultuous times in Egyptian history, as well as the beginning of a new dynasty.[225] Horemhab wanted to be certain that history did not repeat itself, so he carefully chose his successor—a military colleague, Ramesses I.[226] Ramesses I, an old man, already had a son, Seti (the future Seti I), who himself already had a young son, Ramesses (the future Ramesses II). Horemhab could end his rule knowing that a strong dynasty would follow him.

The seventeen-year reign of Akhenaten, as well as the reigns of his four immediate successors (Merytaten/Ankh(et)kheperure, Smenkhkare, Tutankhamun, and Aye) were nearly obliterated from history. Horemhab, and the pharaohs of the Nineteenth Dynasty whom he chose to succeed him, made every attempt to expunge the heretic pharaoh's reign from the annals of kingship. In one case, when making reference to this eventful period in Egyptian history, a later inscription employed the euphemism "that rebel of Akhet-aten" rather than perpetuating Akhenaten's name.[227]

3

·:·+·:·+·:·+·:·◉·:·+·:·+·:·+·:·

TRAMPLING THE NINE BOWS: MILITARY FORCES AND WEAPONRY

All lands, all foreign countries, and all the Asiatic chiefs are joined as one beneath your two soles, like Re forever.

—Hieroglyphic inscription on the footstool of Tutankhamun

The physical manifestations and visual representations of pharaonic kingship were replete with metaphor and symbolism, but the ideal of Egypt's superiority over its neighbors was no idle boast. A professional and sophisticated military made the might of Tutankhamun and the other pharaohs of the Amarna Period a reality. During the late Eighteenth Dynasty, the Egyptian army fought enemies from all corners of Egypt's empire: Nubians in the south, Libyans in the west, and various Asiatic groups in the northeast, enemies to whom the ancient Egyptians referred collectively as the "Nine Bows" (see figure 7). The Egyptians placed considerable emphasis on the use of archers, and their predilection for archery derives no doubt ultimately from the early use of the bow and arrow in the remote prehistory of northern Africa.[1] "Bowtroop" early became virtually synonymous with "military force," both Egyptian and foreign, and led to the common description of hostile forces as "bows" or "bowtroops." Three strokes in the ancient Egyptian scripts represent plurality; a tripling of that plural indicator, the number nine, may then indicate the ultimate all-inclusive number, a "plural of plurals." The "Nine Bows" are thus all the

58

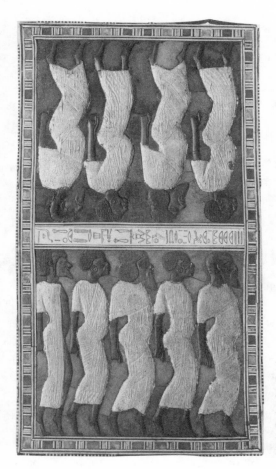

Figure 7. Footstool of Tutankhamun (JdE 62045). Inlays of nine bound enemies—the "Nine Bows"—of Asiatic, Nubian, and Libyan origin decorate this royal footrest. Courtesy of the Griffith Institute, Oxford University.

possible enemies of Egypt—both internal and external—who might exist at one time, whether fewer or greater than nine separate entities.[2]

The purpose of the Egyptian army, led by the pharaoh, was to smite these foes and bring the spoils of conquest back to Egypt. For the Egyptians, military success was not simply the result of proper strategy and overwhelming force, but more importantly, war was a divinely sanctioned activity. Particularly during the expansionist and imperialistic New Kingdom, armed conflict possessed the character of a holy war—every battle, no matter how trivial, could be construed as part of the Egyptian struggle against the forces of chaos outside the Nile Valley.[3] All enemies of Egypt appear literally as "rebels" in Egyptian inscriptions; they have either thrown off the proper suzerainty of pharaoh or have refused to acknowledge Egypt as their overlord.

Branches of the Egyptian Military

The physical force that made up the military might of Tutankhamun and the other pharaohs of the Amarna Period incorporated both native Egyptians and foreign auxiliaries and was divided into three major branches: infantry, chariotry, and navy.[4] Professional military units existed in Egypt during the Old Kingdom (ca. 2500 B.C.E.)[5] and possibly even earlier,[6] and a military hierarchy, with its accompanying titles and ranks, appears during the Middle Kingdom.[7] The necessity for military innovation during the Second Intermediate Period was the mother of New Kingdom invention. The Seventeenth Dynasty ruling in Thebes was beset by enemies to the north and the south; during the ensuing hostilities, which eventually led to final expulsion of the Hyksos by the pharaoh Ahmose, two new weapons that would considerably affect Egypt's military capabilities—the composite bow and the chariot—appear for the first time in widespread use by the Egyptian army.

The addition of the composite bow and the chariot to the Egyptian arsenal is probably due to the influence of the Hyksos, the foreign power that directly ruled the eastern delta and controlled to some degree the rest of Lower Egypt and northern Middle Egypt during much of the Second Intermediate Period. The Hyksos and the Thebans did engage in trade with one another, but the Thebans were not confined to dealing with the northern invaders.[8] Trade routes in the vast desert west of Thebes may have allowed the southern Egyptian kingdom to bypass the Hyksos and trade directly with other Mediterranean powers.[9] The Egyptians quickly adopted and adapted the technology, reorganizing their army to incorporate the new weapons. By the beginning of the Amarna Period, the infantry and newly created chariotry, both equipped with the powerful new bow, became the twin arms of the Egyptian land forces, with mercenaries and foreign auxiliaries incorporated into both branches.

Infantry

In the "Satire of the Trades," an ancient Egyptian scribe extolled the virtues of his own profession and described in harsh terms the lives of others, including that of the infantry soldier:

> He labors until the sun sets in the darkness of night. He is hungry and his stomach hurts; he is dead while he is still alive. . . . His march is uphill through the mountains. . . . His body is ravaged by illness. The enemy

comes, surrounding him with arrows, and life is far from him! . . . If he comes out alive, he is weak from marching. . . . Be a scribe and be spared from soldiering![10]

Despite the pessimistic scribe's description—exaggeration as scribal class propaganda[11]—the very vehemence of the scribe's polemic against the military profession suggests that at least some young men voluntarily chose to become soldiers, some following their fathers and grandfathers into military service.[12] Not a few of these men would have risen through the ranks, and surviving autobiographical texts suggest that those soldiers may have found their far-ranging travels and exotic experiences at least as interesting as the rewards they received for their service.[13]

The Egyptian infantry had a hierarchical structure that resembled most other armies of developed societies.[14] During the Middle Kingdom, the highest rank in the Egyptian infantry was the "great overseer of the army," which corresponds well to the rank of general in Western armies.[15] The Egyptian word for "army" in this title, mesha, did not imply a specific number of troops and could encompass the infantry, and later the chariotry as well; one Ramesside period text suggests that a standard army unit was five thousand men, including archers and foreign auxiliaries.[16] During the transformation of the Egyptian military, from the Second Intermediate Period through the early New Kingdom, the title "general" appears only rarely. The reign of Amunhotep III marks another reorganization of the armed forces, including the reintroduction of the title "general," often with the addition of the epithet "of His Majesty" or other royal designations,[17] and a more thorough division of infantry and chariotry branches. The title of general conveyed a number of responsibilities upon its holder, both administrative duties within the military[18] as well as command of a military force on campaign. As the Eighteenth Dynasty progressed, men could spend their entire career in the military, but careers combining experience in both the civil and military administrations remained more common.[19]

Below the general was the "lieutenant general," and lower-level officers such as the "troop/regiment commander," and "standard-bearer."[20] The "troop/regiment commander," like the general himself, was not in charge of a specific number of men but rather commanded a subdivision of the army at a particular time. When not serving on the battlefield, the troop commanders could be assigned to fortresses in Egypt or in the northern and southern parts of the Egyptian empire,[21] the number of soldiers under the authority of the "troop/regiment commander" depending on the strength of the garrison at a particular fortress. The "standard-bearer," who commanded a company, shared some responsibility in recruitment and

Figure 8. Running infantry soldiers accompanying Tutankhamun and the divine barks during the Opet Procession; from a relief in the Colonnade Hall of Luxor Temple. The first four soldiers carry shields and are armed with spears and axes; the following three men carry staves and *khepesh* swords. Epigraphic Survey, *Luxor Temple* 1, pl. 98. Courtesy of the Oriental Institute of the University of Chicago.

conscriptions, and may have carried a standard into battle. The army secretariat fulfilled several important roles within the officer corps, and support personnel, such as commissariat positions and military doctors, appear in the ancient Egyptian record.[22]

The basic unit of the Egyptian infantry was the company, which consisted of several groups of fifty men, further divided into five platoons of ten men;[23] Akhenaten's military escort appears also to have comprised ten-man units.[24] Companies differed in their armaments, and most if not all were provided with names, often referring to the king and his prowess in battle. Some companies consisted of archers, while others were infantry armed with close-combat weapons, particularly spears and axes (see figure 8). Company names during the reign of Akhenaten were as affected by the religious revolution of Aten worship as other aspects of Egyptian culture, and alongside the "company of Neferkheperure-Waenre (Akhenaten)" served companies called "Pacifier of the Aten" and "the Aten shines."[25]

During the Middle Kingdom, a number of military titles refer to troops of a city, sometimes the city being specified by name.[26] Expedition inscriptions of the same date often describe the units making up a force as deriving from a number of local garrisons. While local military garrisons persisted into the New Kingdom, military titles did not typically retain a local identity.[27] The names of military units in the New Kingdom instead related to the place where those units were stationed or to the deity whose temples provisioned the force. The overall historical trend suggests that the increase in regional loyalties during the First Intermediate Period and the Middle Kingdom gave way to a more national military force by the time of the early New Kingdom.

The process of recruitment began at an early age, and boys from military families may at times have served in the same units as their fathers.[28] To maintain a numerically powerful army, the Egyptians also conscripted individuals into the infantry.[29] Young soldiers underwent a rigorous training process, learning marching techniques, weapons proficiency, and military discipline.[30] Akhenaten took a particular interest in bringing up young soldiers; in a tomb at Amarna, soldiers recited the following hymn: "He trains thousands of recruits, being the chief of eternity like the Aten."[31]

Chariotry

The warfare of New Kingdom Egypt, and her allies and foes of the Near East, rapidly and increasingly became warfare between elite units, especially the chariotry.[32] The creation of a chariot corps required great skill and expense, and the host of specialists needed to build and maintain the vehicles, and the breeders, grooms, and stall workers were a force much greater in numbers than the chariotry itself.[33] Because of the agricultural land necessary for provisioning the horses of the teams, and the people needed to support them, only wealthy states could field sizable chariot armies. The perhaps somewhat ritualized tactics of the great wheeling formations of chariot units and the skill needed to shoot a bow and hit a moving target from one's own vehicle required constant practice by professional troops. These features of chariot warfare probably in the end had positive effects on Bronze Age warfare, and even contributed to the development of more complex and effective diplomatic relations. Lesser powers would need to ally themselves, either in great coalitions of smaller groups or as satellites of the great powers.[34]

Kamose refers to Hyksos chariotry, and the chariot first appears as a part of the Egyptian arsenal during the reign of Ahmose, founder of the Eighteenth Dynasty.[35] Throughout the first half of the Eighteenth Dynasty, Egyptian chariots participated in campaigns in Syria-Palestine and began to develop a more sophisticated hierarchy of officers. The titles "overseer of horses"[36] and "chief of the stables (of His Majesty),"[37] in use from the beginning of the New Kingdom, further emphasize the importance of an administrative infrastructure for the chariotry, but from the late Eighteenth Dynasty onward, holders of these titles were not restricted to non-combat positions.[38] During the reign of Amunhotep III and the following Amarna Period, new titles enter into use, providing chariotry equivalents to infantry ranks, such as "lieutenant general of the chariotry"[39] and "first chariot officer."[40] Like the infantry, the chariotry was organized into groups of fifty.

Egyptian chariots were lightly constructed and carried a two-man crew—the chariot warrior and the shield-bearer/driver. Chariot warriors were most often drawn from the upper classes of Egyptian society, including the sons of the most powerful families in Egypt as well as royal princes; the shield-bearer, on the other hand, was of lower rank, possibly a cadet.[41] Besides holding the shield that protected both himself and the warrior, the shield-bearer was the primary driver of the chariot during combat, leaving the other man free to shoot the bow, throw javelins, or wield a sword. The construction of the chariot and the makeup of its crew created a fast-moving platform for projectile weapons, especially the powerful composite bow.

Although no ancient texts explain the mechanics of an ancient chariot battle, chariot forces most likely fought one another in a series of wheeling maneuvers and attempts by one chariot force to outflank its opposing counterpart; arrows shot from composite bows, along with well-thrown javelins, would have inflicted most of the casualties. Chariot tactics against infantry forces, particularly the tribal levees in Nubia and Libya, would have differed, since horses cannot effectively charge into massed infantry formations.[42] Against massed infantry and with no opposing chariot forces, at the start of a battle Egyptian chariot crews could drive across the front of the opposing infantry, raking it with arrows, softening the enemy's front just before the Egyptian infantry collided with it. At the conclusion of the battle, chariots could pursue a routed enemy. The chariotry also possessed infantry support, foot soldiers called *pehreru* (runners), whose duties included countering opposing skirmishers, capturing enemy chariots, and providing aid if a horse they were supporting became injured.[43] The armaments of the runners included a small round shield, spear, and sword for close combat.

Among the chariot warriors of the ancient world, the most flamboyant were probably the *maryannu*, elite equestrians who first fought for the Hurrian kingdom of Mitanni in northern Mesopotamia. The term maryannu probably derives from a Sanskrit term for "young man, hero" and appears to have designated in the Hurrian world an important class of "knight," paid for his services and given authority over particular territory, after the feudal fashion.[44] Egyptian military texts often highlight the capture of small numbers of maryannu, which was equivalent to the capture of a high-level military official, whose loss would be greatly felt by the opposing force.[45] The reputation of these warriors led charioteers throughout the ancient Mediterranean world to adopt the mode of dress and even hairstyle of the maryannu. Egyptian charioteers sometimes wore their hair in three pigtails or grew beards, perhaps in imitation of the foreign charioteers they hoped to mimic on the battlefield.[46]

Navy

By the early New Kingdom, Egypt had a long tradition of seagoing vessels and long-distance trade. Navigation in the ancient eastern Mediterranean world seems to have placed a greater emphasis on coastal routes as opposed to open sea lanes, and Egypt was no exception. Amphibious troop landings in foreign territory are known as early as the late Old Kingdom (ca. 2300 B.C.E.), and a naval force existed at that time.[47] Much of the ancient Egyptian organization of manpower, from workmen to priests, appears to have employed terminology similar to the watches and crews of naval vessels.[48]

Egypt may have relied primarily on the navy and naval personnel in most of its military activities prior to the New Kingdom.[49] Even desert operations and the administration of desert activities and outposts through the First Intermediate Period appear to have owed some debt to the navy, and some early desert administrators were in fact naval officers.[50] Perhaps the peculiar combination of navigational abilities and commissariat foresight necessary for a good naval officer were ideally suited to operations in the deserts, in which forces moved like ships between the oasis islands. Egyptian troops were not entirely focused on the Nile, however, even in the internecine wars of the First Intermediate Period desert operations were as much of an Egyptian specialty as nautical encounters.[51] During the reconquest of Middle Egypt and the Delta by Kamose, desert and naval troops worked in tandem; as the Egyptian fleet carried infantry to the Hyksos strongholds in Middle Egypt, Nubian auxiliaries patrolled the desert cliffs, making forays farther west, into the oases.[52]

Egyptian naval forces could engage in sophisticated maneuvers, even on the Nile. Kamose's progress culminated in a naval assault on the harbor of the Hyksos stronghold of Avaris. When he reached Avaris, defended by the Hyksos fleet, Kamose literally spearheaded the Egyptian attack, sailing in his flagship "like a falcon."[53] The remainder of his war-ships formed into three lines ahead—the central line breaking the enemy line, the two flanking lines preventing enemy escape.[54] Kamose could thereby defeat the line of the Hyksos battle squadron and sail into the harbor of Avaris. While the Hyksos women stared helplessly down from the battlements, Kamose captured the Hyksos merchant fleet and its rich cargo.

In addition to launching amphibious attacks, one of the main functions of the Egyptian navy was to transport and supply the infantry and the chariotry; one of the ships built at the naval base of Perunefer was even called "the Stable," an appropriate name for a horse transport.[55] The ability to move large numbers of men and matériel far north into Syria-Palestine without relying exclusively on overland routes was critical to the expansion of the Egyptian empire at the beginning of the Eighteenth Dynasty (see pages 139–141).[56] The Egyptians appear to have been so adept at amphibious operations that Thutmose III, determined to employ such maneuvers in his year thirty-three campaign against Mittani, had vessels constructed on the Levantine coast and transported overland, to be floated on the Euphrates.

A ship's crew of rowers was under the supervision of a commander of rowers and a standard-bearer, who in turn served under the ship's captain.[57] At the top of the hierarchy was the "commander of all the king's ships," chief admiral of the Egyptian fleet. The few men known to hold this title were administrators as well as warriors, and several held titles related to the Egyptian treasury (for the economic aspects of the Egyptian navy, see chapter 6). Egyptian naval forces also included amphibious troops, "marines," who often carry their ship-topped standards in religious processions. By the end of the New Kingdom, the Egyptian navy possessed a complex structure, including at least three different classes of vessels.[58] The close ties between the infantry and the navy led to overlap among the personnel of both branches, and the careers of several prominent individuals and even entire units indicate that naval officers and soldiers could be transferred to the infantry and vice versa. The hierarchy of the navy during the New Kingdom thus resembled that of the infantry and chariotry,[59] and Egypt favored a combined arms approach in its military campaigns.

The Egyptian navy may have had bases throughout Egypt, but the most well known are those in the northern part of the country. New Kingdom Memphis was not only a center of weapons production and a place for training and marshaling the chariotry, but an important naval base as well. Another port and military base was Perunefer, on the Pelusiac branch of the Nile adjacent to the former Hyksos stronghold of Avaris, founded in the early Eighteenth Dynasty, and providing a direct link between Egypt and the Mediterranean world.[60] Perunefer was an active base during the Amarna Period, and Horemhab added additional fortifications to the site during his reign.

Auxiliaries

A number of foreign troops served in each branch of the Egyptian army, and particular foreign groups favored specific weapons and tasks (see figure 9). These auxiliaries could be integrated into a particular unit, such as the royal bodyguard, or form separate units of non-Egyptian troops.[61] Foreign troops in the Egyptian military appear to have served for long periods of time and to have become members of Egyptian society, unlike the temporary service mercenaries of more recent eras.[62] A text from the reign of Ramesses II suggests that foreign troops could be intentionally assigned to posts far from their homeland;[63] such isolation would have been particularly important for foreign auxiliaries acquired as prisoners of war.[64] To help guarantee loyalty, the Egyptians used acculturation, including—at least during the Old and Middle kingdoms—circumcision,[65] instruction in the Egyptian language,[66] and rewards—upon retirement, foreign soldiers could be provided with fertile plots of land along the Nile Valley.[67]

The earliest attested auxiliaries in the Egyptian army were troops from Nubia,[68] and during the First Intermediate Period, Nubia became an important recruiting ground for soldiers who could aid the rulers of Upper Egypt in their conflicts with the northern Heracleopolitan dynasty.[69] Soldiers from a Nubian group known as the Medjoy[70] became particularly renowned as archers, scouts, and policeman in the Egyptian army (for their role in military intelligence, see below).[71] These tribesmen are probably to be associated with the "Pan Grave Culture," known for its distinct ceramic tradition and shallow, oval-shaped graves, many of which are known from Upper Egypt.[72] Medjoy continued to be employed throughout the Middle Kingdom and served as an important desert column supporting Kamose's reconquest of northern Egypt. By the later Eighteenth Dynasty, the employment of Medjoy Nubians had become so widespread that the term was divorced from its original "tribal" designation and became the general designation for police forces and patrolmen.[73] The fame of Nubian soldiers spread beyond Egypt, and several of Egypt's vassals in Syria-Palestine during the Amarna Period requested that Kushite troops be sent to help defend their cities.[74]

Soldiers in Egyptian service from the Libyan Desert or from Syria-Palestine are much less common than those from Nubia during the earlier periods of Egyptian history. Asiatics served in the Old Kingdom Egyptian navy, and from the time of the Middle Kingdom, Asiatic military units could be settled within the confines of Egypt itself;[75] certain groups of Asiatics may have helped defend the Middle Kingdom border in Nubia and patrol the desert hinterlands of Egypt.[76] Apart from the Asiatic members of Akhenaten's bodyguard,[77] few Syro-Palestinians appear in the service of the New Kingdom Egyptian military prior to the Ramesside Period.[78] The reign of Akhenaten might also mark the appearance of Mycenaeans in the Egyptian army (see pages 198–199) presaging the use of Sea People troops by Ramesses II and Ramesses III.[79] Libyan auxiliaries appear most often in New Kingdom texts as prisoners of war who have been transformed into Egyptian soldiers.[80]

Images of prisoners from Tutankhamun's northern and southern wars, depicted in the Memphite tomb of Horemhab, are early versions of a cycle of scenes recording the transformation of Egypt's defeated enemies from the rabble of chaos into orderly members of Egyptian society. The clearest example of this pictorial cycle is the depiction of the aftermath of the Sea Peoples campaign of Ramesses III at Medinet Habu.[81] There, Egyptian guards first push roughly along the contorted and bound Philistines; the bonds of the Philistines are then removed, and the Egyptian guards raise their hands not to strike their charges, but rather to give homage to the king. The Egyptians then mark (apparently brand) the prisoners with the name of the king, register them, and seat them all on the ground in ordered ranks. As the Egyptian scribes write their names, the prisoners become part of the ordered world—the magical power of writing is such that the ordering of names can effect the ordering of those very people.

So in the Memphite tomb of Horemhab, bound Nubians are pushed and driven under the blows of their guards, but eventually they sit with docility. The latter scene does not emphasize, however, so much that they are cowed, but rather reveals that the seated prisoners are now enrolled in Egyptian society. Similarly the northern prisoners are a colorful but disorganized throng, awkwardly posed with their manacles, but they, too, eventually appear as ordered inductees into the pharaonic world. Probably as a result of lessons learned after earlier conflicts, the Egyptians did not continue to employ captured soldiers exclusively in a military capacity, but rather sought to assimilate them into Egyptian society in more pacific and agricultural undertakings. According to the Restoration Stela, one result of

Tutankhamun's military campaigns was an influx of servants—*hemou(t)*—into the temples, something lacking under Akhenaten. During the New Kingdom, prisoners of war appear on the whole to have been inducted into Egyptian society as *hemou(t)*, closely associated with the agricultural activities on temple lands, and this induction entailed education, primarily in the Egyptian language. Interestingly, in his Memphite tomb Horemhab does not then stress the tactics or strategic vision of his military prowess; by depicting the transformation of northern and southern prisoners, he emphasizes the economic and social results of his campaigning.

Military Intelligence

Egyptian military accounts emphasize the importance of accurate information about the location of enemy forces, their strength, and their intentions. In the Nubian battle texts of Seti I, the pharaoh delayed his own decisions concerning the campaign so that he might "learn their plans thoroughly."[82] Seti's son Ramesses II, on the other hand, demonstrated the dangers of reacting on the basis of unsubstantiated intelligence. During its march toward the city of Kadesh, the Egyptian army captured two apparent bedouin, who reported to Ramesses II that the Hittites were far north of Kadesh. To Ramesses' dismay, only after the Hittite chariotry had ambushed an element of the Egyptian army as it crossed the Orontes did the pharaoh learn that the bedouin were spies in Hittite employ, sent to provide false information.[83]

The Egyptian military seems to have employed different types of scouts for various regions of the Egyptian empire. Border patrols within Egypt and Nubia could be the responsibility of scouts called "overseers of hunters."[84] Often accompanied by dogs, these hunters used their knowledge of local geography to collect military intelligence. Modern parallels for the military function of hunters are provided by the German *Jägern* and the Belgian *chasseurs ardennais* who fought in World War II. Egyptian scouts employed in Syria-Palestine, called *meher*, were expected to memorize extensive information about the region, including any geographical features that might be important when planning a military expedition—the location of cities, towns, roads connecting them, as well as the topography of each area (see further on page 143).[85] Nubian auxiliaries served as desert scouts and patrolmen; similar corps of Libyan scouts, called Tjukten, assisted Egyptian expeditions west of the Nile Valley.[86] During campaigns in Syria-Palestine and elsewhere, mounted scouts were essential to provide intelligence and monitor rapidly changing situations.[87] The Nubians were renowned for their abilities in horse breeding and riding, which they combined with their skills as desert scouts to become highly effective mounted units.[88]

Weapons and Armor

In the modern imagination, the Great Sphinx and the pyramids of Giza have little to do with military affairs, yet the pharaohs of the New Kingdom used the Giza Plateau as a place to practice their equestrian skills. A monument near the Sphinx records the activities of the pharaoh Amunhotep II: "He raised horses without equal who did not tire when he took the reins and who did not sweat when galloping. He would yoke them with the bit in Memphis, and he would stop at the abode of Horemakhet (the Sphinx). He would spend time circling around it, while he saw the magnificence of this abode of Khufu and Khafre, justified (the two largest pyramids at Giza)."[89] During the New Kingdom, the serene eyes of the Sphinx overlooked royal displays of horsemanship in preparation for war.[90]

Not far from Giza lay the ancient capital at Memphis, which served as an important arsenal during the New Kingdom.[91] Many of the soldiers and craftsmen who manned the arsenal were buried at Saqqara, just west of Memphis, and scenes from their tombs provide us with a wealth of detail about the production of weapons and armor.[92] Carpenters, metallurgists, and leather workers gathered in workshops to produce the bows, arrows, swords, chariots, armor, and myriad of other equipment necessary for the Egyptian army at war. Such scenes, royal military depictions and texts, and actual surviving weapons, particularly the panoply from the tomb of Tutankhamun, provide considerable information on the development and capabilities of Egyptian weaponry.

Archery Equipment

The bow was one of the first weapons depicted in the hands of the early Egyptians,[93] and throughout pharaonic history, archers remained central to the Egyptian military.[94] From the earliest periods of Egyptian history until the beginning of the New Kingdom, Egyptian and Nubian archers fought on foot. From the reign of Ahmose onward, the chariot-mounted archer appears. The introduction of the chariot in the Egyptian army occurred shortly after the appearance in Egypt of another key technological innovation: the composite bow. Until around 1700 B.C.E., the Egyptian army relied solely on "self-bows," single staves of wood to which a bowstring was attached. The composite bow was more sophisticated than the simple bow and had much greater penetrating power. Composite bows were, however, also more time-consuming and expensive to manufacture than the self-bow, and the self-bow continued in use long after the introduction of the new technology.

The Egyptians and the Nubians employed two types of simple self-bows: the "segment" self-bow, in which the profile of the wood is a single curve; and a slightly more complicated and powerful bow, in which the tips curve away from the bowstring. The manufacture of either type of self-bow was a fairly straightforward process.[95] After an appropriate piece of wood had been cut to the desired size of the bow, the shaft was shaped with an adze.[96] For the self-bow with recurved tips, grooves were cut perpendicular to the shaft on one side near the ends; made pliable with steam, the wood was bent in the areas of the scoring to provide the curves at the two ends of the bow. After the bow had dried and the wood had properly cured—probably within some sort of frame to provide the final shape—the bowyer cut the string notches and achieved the final smoothing of the shaft with small sandstone smoothing blocks, the equivalent of modern sandpaper. Once the bow was ready to use, it would be strung with twisted strands of animal gut.[97]

Composite bows were constructed, as the name suggests, by gluing together different woods, horn, and sinew to provide many more pounds of pull.[98] Each material had to be carefully shaped to ensure a proper fit in the overall construction of the bow, and after each step in construction the bowyer was obliged to wait until the glue was dry before continuing to the next stage.[99] After the composite materials were properly fused, the bow would be finished much like a self-bow. Two different shapes of composite bow appear in the Egyptian arsenal: recurved and triangular. The triangular bow appears in the hands of Asiatic tribute bringers within tombs from the reign of Thutmose III and in the hands of several pharaohs.[100]

The tomb of Tutankhamun contained fourteen self-bows, all of the more complex recurved shape. Three of the self-bows from the tomb of Tutankhamun are almost 2 meters in length, and all but one of the others measure 1.2 to 1.8 meters long. The remaining bow is just over 65 centimeters in length, leading to speculation that this may have been a weapon of the "boy king" when he truly was a boy. Some of Tutankhamun's bows consist of simple wooden staves, while some of the composite bows are elaborately gilded and decorated. The tips of one composite bow are even carved and painted to resemble bound enemies, whose necks serve as the indentation where the bowstring was tied[101]—each time the king drew this bow, he symbolically strangled his foes.

Figure 9. Egyptian and foreign infantry soldiers with different armaments. From left to right: an Egyptian soldier (mostly destroyed), a Nubian wielding a long self-bow, an Egyptian carrying a *khepesh* sword, a Libyan armed with an ax and short bow, another Nubian with long bow and a sporran, another Egyptian, and finally a Libyan whose cloak billows out at the end of the scene. Epigraphic Survey, *Luxor Temple* I, pl. 93. Courtesy of the Oriental Institute of the University of Chicago.

A scene of foreign members of Tutankhamun's bodyguard from Luxor Temple suggests that the longest and shortest of Tutankhamun's self-bows may relate not to the size of the user as much as to his cultural identity (see figure 9). In the scene, one Nubian soldier carries a long bow, approximately 1.5 meters long based on the size of the soldier, which would correspond to the longer bows of Tutankhamun's panoply. A nearby Libyan soldier carries a bow only half as long as that of his Nubian compatriot. Other depictions of Libyan troops suggest that they favored these shorter bows,[102] and the smallest bow from the tomb of Tutankhamun may be of the same type as those carried by his Libyan bodyguards.

The different bow lengths used by the Egyptian army and its foreign auxiliaries were also suited to different purposes. The long self-bows (1.5 meters and above) would not lend themselves well to firing while moving, either on foot or mounted, but would be ideal for use by a stationary unit firing at various trajectories to lay down a barrage of arrows, foreshadowing the tactic best known from English archers of the Hundred Years War.[103] The short bows (less than 70 centimeters), like those carried by the Libyans, could be used in rapid maneuvers and are more suited for shorter ranges. The expensive and powerful composite bows, which could range from 1.4 meters to 70 centimeters long, were ideal for chariot archers and smaller units of foot archers.[104]

Egyptian arrows could be pointed, at times barbed, causing deep wounds, and broad, even flat-tipped, causing broad, stunning injuries. Shafts were made of wooden dowels or reed[105] and fletched with bird feathers; tips could be of flint, horn, wood, bone, or copper.[106] By the time of the New Kingdom, bronze arrowheads were relatively common, although flint-tipped arrows continued in use. Although the Egyptians were well acquainted with poisonous serpents, their venoms, and the antidotes thereto, only slight evidence for poisoned arrows exists.[107]

Quivers were in use already by the Old Kingdom, and in the Middle Kingdom bows and arrows also could be carried in large leather sleeves open at both ends.[108] By the New Kingdom, quivers had achieved a more widespread use by archers on foot and in chariots, probably due to increased Egyptian activities in humid climates and the coeval rise in importance of the composite bow. Most New Kingdom quivers were slightly tapered leather containers with a cap, like the elaborately decorated quivers from the tomb of Tutankhamun.[109] Bow cases for the composite bow conformed to the triangular shape of the weapon, and officers' attendants are sometimes shown carrying bows in such cases made of leather;[110] similarly shaped cases were attached to the sides of chariots.

A final, but essential, piece of equipment for the Egyptian archer was the wristguard, which protects the skin along the inside of the arm holding the bow from the snap of the bowstring. Although some sort of wrist protection is probably as old as archery itself, the first Egyptian depictions of formal wristguards appear during the Old Kingdom (ca. 2250 B.C.E.).[111] The Egyptian pharaoh can wear a wristguard as he fires his bow, and in heraldic smiting scenes as well. This use of the wristguard alone to evoke the king's prowess in archery finds further expression in an elaborate gold and jeweled wristguard of the pharaoh Ahmose.[112] Leather wristguards were found in the tomb of Tutankhamun, and several objects in his tomb show the pharaoh wearing elaborately decorated wristguards.

Other Projectile Weapons

Although slings do not appear often in Egyptian military scenes and inscriptions, battle scenes from the Middle Kingdom depict slingers helping to besiege a fortified city,[113] and New Kingdom slingers fight from the crows' nests of Egyptian warships in the sea battle scenes of Ramesses III at Medinet Habu.[114] Nubian slingers have some prominence in the campaigns of the Twenty-fifth Dynasty pharaoh Piye. Nevertheless, slings from the tomb of Tutankhamun could be for hunting rather than military use.[115]

Another possible borrowing of a hunting weapon for warfare is the throwstick, perhaps best known from fishing and fowling scenes in Egyptian tombs. Scenes of Egyptian troops in religious processions occasionally depict officers holding throwstick-shaped objects.[116] The size of certain throwstick/club hybrids from the tomb of Tutankhamun would certainly allow for a military use of the weapon.[117] Throwsticks were principally weapons intended for fowling, and their use in warfare would certainly have a symbolic value for the Egyptians, who in numerous inscriptions liken their enemies to a flock of small birds among whom the pharaoh dove like a falcon.[118] The use against Egypt's enemies of a weapon for bird hunting would magically impart to those enemies the properties of the small birds to whom the Egyptians likened them.

Close-Combat Weapons

In spite of their predilection for projectile weapons, the ancient Egyptians recognized the inevitability of close combat in virtually every military encounter. As with most ancient cultures, the arsenal of close-combat weapons consisted of bladed weapons for cutting and thrusting, and non-bladed weapons intended to create blunt trauma injuries.

Maces and Clubs   Discoidal and pear-shaped stone maceheads are well attested in the Predynastic Period, and by the dawn of pharaonic history, the mace with pear-shaped head had already become an important symbol of royal power in Egypt.[119] The heraldic pose of the mace-wielding Egyptian ruler about to smite an enemy appears already during the Predynastic Period and survives well into the Roman Period. Some use of the mace on the battlefield appears to have persisted at least into the Middle Kingdom,[120] although by the time of the New Kingdom neither textual nor pictorial evidence attests to the use of the mace in actual combat. The primary function of the mace in pharaonic Egypt was to deliver the final killing blow to an already hopelessly wounded enemy.[121]

Although Tutankhamun may never have wielded a mace in battle, two gilded wooden maces lay in his burial chamber.[122] Even this traditional weapon underwent some modifications during the New Kingdom, with smiting scenes often adding a blade to the mace. This strange composite weapon may have been a new application for a primitive device, the stone macehead transmitting extra force to a bronze blade.[123] The added force would enable a bronze blade to penetrate the increasingly common body armor of the late second millennium B.C.E., in a time prior to the common use of tempered iron as a metal for bladed weapons.

The Egyptian army employed a variety of staves and clubs.[124] A First Intermediate Period warrior refers to a staff of copper, perhaps a metal-sheathed staff.[125] The successor of such a weapon is perhaps the fighting rod, which appears relatively frequently in Ramesside battle scenes.[126] These weapons could deliver crushing blows, and became more prevalent during the later New Kingdom as a means of combating armored foes.[127] Wooden clubs and staffs were also weapons popular with Nubian auxiliaries;[128] statues of the pharaoh Amunhotep II, as depicted in the tomb of one of his chief officials, show the pharaoh wearing a Nubian-style kilt while wielding a battle-ax in one hand and a wooden staff in the other.[129] In the same tomb, tribute from Nubia includes elaborate ebony staffs with gold wrappings to the top, and ferrules of silver. In the scenes of Horemhab's Nubian campaign, Nubian soldiers in the Egyptian army also carry long clubs,[130] Nubian members of Akhenaten's bodyguard carry similar clubs, and Nubian soldiers can perform a sort of war dance with such weapons.[131] A large club from the tomb of Tutankhamun has a shape similar to those wielded by Nubians in Egyptian reliefs and may have been a souvenir of Tutankhamun's Nubian War.[132]

Axes One of the most common weapons of the New Kingdom soldier was the ax. Although the use of the ax as a weapon is as old as the Predynastic Period, the shape of ax blades changed throughout Egyptian history.[133] Broad but short, curved blades attached to a long pole were common through the late Middle Kingdom. During the Middle Kingdom, the duck-billed ax, named for the overall shape and two cutouts resembling nostrils, was introduced from Syria-Palestine.[134] A narrow but long, chisel-bladed ax was a preferred weapon of the Hyksos forces but did not become popular in the Egyptian arsenal. During the New Kingdom, the standard shape for Egyptian axes is a long, roughly rectangular blade, convex on the cutting edge, with slightly concave sides.[135] Amarna Period reliefs portray Libyan auxiliaries using duck-billed ax types that would probably have appeared archaic to Egyptians of the late Eighteenth Dynasty (see figure 9).[136]

Although an effective weapon, the ax requires a soldier to use a hacking or swinging motion, and the soldier poised to bring down his ax would at that moment be vulnerable to a thrusting attack below the raised arm. Infantry armed with axes often carry both a spear and a shield in the other hand, and the New Kingdom Egyptian infantry would consequently have resembled in armament the Saxon forces at the Battle of Hastings.[137] In the absence of a sword with handle cast as one piece with the blade, a penetrating ax blade attached to a resilient wooden handle would have been the most effective slashing weapon in the Egyptian arsenal. Axes could also function as ceremonial weapons and insignia, and the ax of the warrior queen Ahhotep is made of precious materials; some axes, perhaps ceremonial as well, can have elaborate cutout designs in the blade.[138]

Swords and Daggers The primary long-bladed weapon of New Kingdom Egypt is the *khepesh,* a slashing implement with a curved bronze blade.[139] Often called a "sickle sword," the cutting edge of a khepesh is along the outside edge, as with a scimitar. The khepesh blade—wedgelike in cross section—widens considerably to the back, and the weapon functioned as a type of long and relatively thin ax. The Egyptians employed different sizes of khepesh swords, suited to a range of battlefield uses: the larger and heavier khepesh swords, like the "great khepesh" from the tomb of Tutankhamun, would have been useful for opening gaps in enemy armor and creating blunt-trauma injuries (see figure 10 top);[140] Tutankhamun's smaller and less curved scimitar possessed a much sharper blade that would be effective in thrusting and cutting at lightly armored enemies (see figure 10 bottom).[141] A leather loop attached to a ring at the end of the khepesh's handle could be worn around the wrist in case the weapon slipped during battle.[142]

Although Egyptian depictions do not attest to their use, archaeological evidence indicates that chariot crews could be armed with a long rapier with thin blade, only a small, narrow tang attaching the blade to the handle. This design made the rapier ideal for thrusting, particularly while the soldier wielding it was mounted on a chariot and stabbing down at an enemy on the ground, but the weakness of the blade's attachment to the handle rendered such rapiers unsuitable for slashing and parrying in hand-to-hand combat. Short swords, less than 70 centimeters in overall length, appear to have been wielded by charioteers and infantry soldiers.[143] Long swords with blade and handle formed of one piece (the Naue II type) do not appear until later in the New Kingdom, and coincide with the rise in armored infantry in the eastern Mediterranean, with a metallurgical and design pedigree leading back to southeastern Europe.[144]

Soldiers carried daggers of various lengths,[145] to use as weapons of last resort, and in the removal of a hand—or the phallus of an uncircumcised foe—from each slain enemy. This practice, well attested from the New Kingdom, allowed an accurate estimate of enemy casualties. In an unusual scene from battle reliefs of Tutankhamun, three Egyptian soldiers carry three hands each skewered on their spears.[146] Tutankhamun was buried

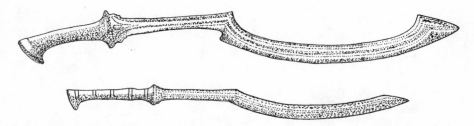

Figure 10. Two bronze *khepesh* swords from the tomb of Tutankhamun: (top) the "great" *khepesh* (Egyptian Museum, Cairo, JdE 61588), 59.7 cm long; (bottom) a smaller scimitar (Egyptian Museum, Cairo, JdE 61589), 41 cm long. Drawing by J. C. Darnell.

with two daggers;[147] his gold-bladed dagger was certainly a ceremonial weapon, but the other dagger was a more practical, iron-bladed weapon. Ironworking did not become widespread until after 1100 B.C.E., making Tutankhamun's iron blade an unusual object.[148] According to the Amarna Letters, the king of Mitanni gave Amunhotep III several iron objects, including a dagger and a mace, as bridal gifts.[149]

Spears and Javelins Spears and javelins were made of solid wooden shafts tipped by bronze blades of various lengths and shapes, although as with arrows, some use of stone tips may have persisted.[150] Both long, thrusting spears and short, stabbing spears appear early in the Egyptian arsenal.[151] Throwing spears, or javelins, are also in evidence by the New Kingdom.[152] In the immediate post–Amarna Period, two javelins appear in the chariot-mounted quiver of each Egyptian chariot soldiers, apparently for use should the chariot become disabled.

Horses and Chariots

The horse, like the composite bow and the chariot itself, entered Egypt between the collapse of the Middle Kingdom and the founding of the New Kingdom,[153] and physical evidence reveals that the domesticated horse had reached Nubia by the late Seventeenth Dynasty.[154] During the early Eighteenth Dynasty, Egyptian horses appear to have been a lightly built, long-backed breed. Depictions of horses change with the reign of Amunhotep II, suggesting more than a simple shift in artistic style and apparently reflecting the introduction of a new breed.[155] Probably first brought to Egypt as the result of wars in Syria-Palestine, this new stock is more heavily built with a shorter back, and typically appears with a roached mane. An Amarna Period relief carving of a horse's head has led some to suggest that the Egyptians slit the nostrils of their war horses, but numerous practical reasons argue against such an interpretation.[156]

The light, two-wheeled chariot drawn by a team of horses, in use throughout the Mediterranean world during the Bronze Age, reached its pinnacle of effectiveness in ancient Egypt (see figure 11).[157] Although the chariot was an import to the Nile Valley, the Egyptians quickly adapted and improved on its design; they also integrated the chariot into religious symbolism. From the Eighteenth Dynasty onward, Egyptian religious texts can describe the solar god traveling in a chariot;[158] chariots abound in representations of the daily royal journey at Akhet-aten, and Tutankhamun incorporated chariots into his commemoration of the Opet Festival celebrations at Luxor Temple.

The basic Egyptian chariot consisted of a cab with two rear-mounted wheels, a pole connecting the cab with the yoke and horses, and the tack and trappings of the chariot team itself.[159] The chariot cab had a roughly D-shaped floor plan formed by a wooden frame; chariot cabs were typically about 1 meter wide and 0.5 meter deep, and the axle projected a little over 0.5 meter to either side of the cab. The floor of the chariot was made of rope or leather mesh, a surface well suited to absorbing the shock of the chariot as it traveled over rough terrain. The chariot pole ran beneath the entire cab, providing further support for the vehicle. One or more vertical supports connected the floor frame to a curved wooden "banister" that ran at waist level along the front, curving back and down to the rear. The earliest Egyptian chariots had wheels with four spokes; during the middle of the Eighteenth Dynasty six spokes become standard, and some experimentation with eight-spoked wheels is evident.[160] The rim and spokes of the chariot wheel were constructed of carefully shaped wood pieces, and an outer wooden or leather tire could be added to decrease wear on the wooden rim.[161] The linchpins securing the wheels to the axle could be plain wooden dowels or elaborately decorated figures of bound foreigners.[162]

The wooden frame of the chariot body could be partially closed with wood or leather sidings,[163] and chariots with often elaborately decorated leather sides were particularly popular during the Amarna Period.[164] Egyptian chariotmakers utilized several types of wood, with elm, willow, and ash prominent in preserved examples.[165] The Egyptians appear to have understood the properties of different woods and combined them within relatively small elements of the chariot—the nave of the central portion of a wheel might have a composite construction of elm and tamarisk.[166] The composite wood construction and leather siding made

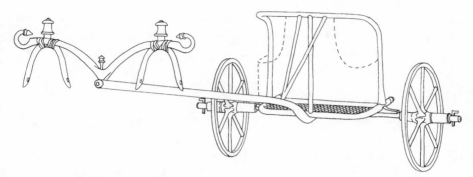

Figure 11. Light wood-frame Egyptian chariot (dashed lines represent the leather elements of the chariot body). After Herold, *Streitwagentechnologie*, abb. 1.

the chariot both durable and light; reconstructions estimate the weight at 30 kilograms, light enough for a single man to transport the vehicle when necessary.[167] A cutout in the chariot siding just below the railing could function as a handgrip for the charioteer or shield-bearer, and in some cases, looped thongs were attached as handles.[168] A bowcase and one or more quivers were fitted to the sides of the chariot; even chariots in religious processions at Amarna have these military accoutrements.[169]

The horses were harnessed to the chariot with yoke saddles attached to each side of the yoke, itself mounted at the forward end of the chariot pole. The yoke saddles were provided with a loose girth, which would tighten when the horse backed up, and a strap that passed around the horse's chest, producing an effective traction system.[170] Chariot horses often wore cloth bardings, which provided some protection for the horses against projectile weapons;[171] royal horses also wore gilded crests with ostrich feathers and had a golden disk attached to their yoke saddles. The remainder of the tack consisted of a bridle, with either a dropped noseband or bit,[172] and long reins, which ran through rings on the yoke saddle. Blinkers attached to the sides of the bridle limited the range of the horse's vision, preventing the horse from being distracted or frightened during battles and processions.[173] The tack and trappings of the chariot horses enabled the driver to maintain control and turn rapidly, even at a fast canter.[174]

Six separate chariots were part of the funerary treasure in the tomb of Tutankhamun, alongside elements of the harness and miscellaneous equipment,[175] such as fly whisks, whips,[176] and possible hoof picks.[177] Two chariots have gilded wooden bodies with inlays, adorned with images of Tutankhamun as rampant sphinx trampling his enemies, and rows of bound prisoners. The sumptuous decoration of these two chariots would have made them impractical for the battlefield but ideal for festival processions and other state occasions; two such decorated chariots await Tutankhamun and Ankhesenamun during the celebration of the Opet Procession, as depicted at Luxor Temple.[178] The four remaining chariots have wooden frames, which originally would have been covered with leather. These more lightly built chariots had wooden tires, at least one of which showed signs of replacement due to wear, and would have been suitable for hunting or warfare. One of the chariots in Tutankhamun's tomb lacks any decoration and is the most sturdily built, suggesting it was intended to be used during an actual campaign.

The New Kingdom Egyptian army could also travel with a type of transport chariot, a two-wheeled wagon that may be identical to the donkey-drawn "chariots" occasionally attested in Ramesside texts.[179] These may have been intended for general transportation of matériel, but this, as numerous later generals have learned and as the ancient Egyptians themselves would have known, could impede the progress of an infantry force by restricting its movement to areas across which a wagon could travel.[180] The lack of pulling ability of ancient harnesses in general shows that the two-wheeled carts depicted in the camp scenes of Ramesses II were not simply baggage carts, for they would have offered only a disadvantage with regard to weight-carrying ability, but were more probably fast-moving commissary wagons that could accompany the chariots.[181] Even under battle conditions, the transport chariots could supply armaments, ammunition, water, and food to men and beasts, allowing the Egyptian forces to maintain arrow fire and physical strength for a longer time than would be possible if the chariotry were supplied only by what each chariot crew could carry. Occasionally military forces might have employed much larger wheeled vehicles, as when Thutmose III used ox-drawn carts to transport prefabricated boats across Syria-Palestine to Mittani.[182]

War Dogs

As in hunting, so in warfare, dogs frequently accompany Egyptian soldiers, especially those engaged in desert operations and border patrol. Dogs appear in early predynastic art (ca. 4500 B.C.E.), most often in hunting scenes;[183] those most common in early hunting and police/military scenes are termed *tchesem* in ancient Egyptian, and are representatives of the breed now called basenji.[184] Some Old Kingdom scenes show such dogs in the company of desert huntsmen, while basenjis in a more explicitly military context appear on numerous monuments and depictions of the First Intermediate Period and early Middle Kingdom, particularly associated with the desert and Nubian troops.[185] On the "Hound Stela" of the Eleventh Dynasty ruler Antef II, one of the basenjis has the name Abaikur, meaning "hound" in Berber, suggesting a southwestern origin for that particular dog.[186]

Such depictions are rare by the time of the New Kingdom, and the dogs apparent in New Kingdom military contexts are more often of a grey-hound type, with floppy ears and long, gently curving tails.[187] At least one dog accompanies the Egyptian infantry attacking Asiatic troops on the painted box of Tutankhamun, particularly appropriate to that scene as the pharaoh was said to teach the Asiatics to obey Egypt and do "the dog walk."[188] In a scene of Ramesses II slaughtering a Libyan enemy, a small yet vicious female dog called "Anat Is Protection"—named for an Asiatic goddess who helps Egypt in war—bites the rump of the cowering foreigner.[189]

Clothing, Armor, and Defensive Weapons

Most Old Kingdom and First Intermediate Period depictions of soldiers show men wearing only kilts; in some Old Kingdom reliefs, recruits wear nothing more than a belt with three strips of cloth attached.[190] With Nubian auxiliaries of the First Intermediate Period, something like an actual military uniform appears. These Nubian troops usually wore a short fabric kilt in conjunction with a long, multicolored leather sporran hanging in front, attached by a belt knotted in the back.[191] The use of the sporran among Nubian troops may also have contributed to the development of formal Egyptian military aprons, which appear by the time of the New Kingdom.

Soldiers of the early Eighteenth Dynasty sometimes wore long, pointed, and relatively narrow aprons.[192] By the Amarna Period, two more voluminous and presumably padded sporrans were in use, one a long pleated apron widening to the bottom, the other an essentially heart-shaped sporran.[193] Soldiers, particularly in the naval branch, could wear a leather overkilt, which was cut into a net pattern, with a solid piece of leather covering the seat.[194] This item of clothing probably originated as a naval garment, intended to protect the linen kilt underneath from excessive wear during rowing.[195]

Climate and Egyptian emphasis on speed of movement apparently discouraged the development of body armor.[196] A metal breast protector appears in a Middle Kingdom scene,[197] but for the Old and Middle kingdoms, the only garments common on soldiers' torsos are crossed textile bands.[198] Quilted and leather protection for the torso appears during the New Kingdom, usually in the form of bands wrapped around the chest and over one shoulder. In some cases infantry soldiers could wear a jerkin with overlapping metal or leather scales, but such armor appears only rarely in Egyptian texts and depictions.[199] Tutankhamun was buried with a cuirass composed of numerous thick leather scales,[200] a more practical version of the elaborate corselet, made to look like overlapping wings of a protective falcon that pharaohs often wear in combat scenes.

No scene of Egyptian chariotry shows any member of an Egyptian chariot crew wearing armor, although Asiatic charioteers can appear with scale armor.[201] A depiction from the tomb of Qenamun, a contemporary of Amunhotep II,[202] suggests that the Egyptians also could use metal armor; among a number of items presented to the pharaoh during the New Year's festival is a type of scale body armor with solid metal gorget reminiscent of the "Dendra Panoply."[203] Both the scale armor from the tomb of Qenamun and the segmented suit from Dendra, Greece—combining a gorget and a helmet—provided considerable upper-body coverage with an almost complete neglect of the legs, a type of armor ideal for protecting a chariot warrior, whose lower body was protected by the chariot, and who required considerable protection for his upper body, but at the same time needed his arms free to wield weapons. The shield-bearer/driver, on the other hand, was normally lightly attired, since he could shelter himself behind the shield or crouch behind the body of the chariot; his lack of armor also contributed to the relative lightness of the Egyptian war chariot.

Footwear for Egyptian soldiers probably consisted primarily of sandals,[204] although soldiers in Egyptian battle scenes appear more often to have gone barefooted into the fray. Leather sandals and even elaborately laced bootlike sandals, harbingers of the Roman *caligae*, are attested already during the early Predynastic Period.[205] An expedition inscription of the Middle Kingdom refers to a large supply of spare sandals available for the troops on the march,[206] and another inscription suggests that an improperly shod soldier might have resorted to theft.[207] New Kingdom soldiers probably did wear sandals on the march,[208] but may have divested themselves of such during actual combat; constant marching and training without footwear can lead to remarkably thickened foot soles.[209] Curiously, even though a type of leg wrapping similar to military puttees common in the late nineteenth and early twentieth centuries c.e. is known from the New Kingdom, appearing at least once in an Amarna tomb scene, no such shin protectors appear in a clearly military context.[210]

At least some Middle Kingdom soldiers, as mummified remains from Deir el-Bahari reveal, could wear their hair thick and greased, forming a natural protection against blows to the head and neck, and such practice—perhaps Nubian in origin—probably persisted among Nubian auxiliaries during the New Kingdom.[211] Textile head coverings are well attested, and metal helmets appear during the New Kingdom,[212] Egyptian and foreign charioteers often wearing a bullet-shaped helmet with streamers attached to the top.[213] Egyptian infantry did not wear any sort of neck or face protection, although in scenes of ritual combat, Egyptian stick fighters/fencers could wear a type of chin and cheek protector.[214]

The shield was the predominant form of body protection at all periods of Egyptian history.[215] Predynastic shields, such as those depicted on the Hunters Palette, were small and irregular, perhaps made predominately of leather.[216] Shields during the earlier pharaonic period were often large, and tall, full-coverage shields are known from the Middle Kingdom.[217] Most New Kingdom shields were constructed of wood, either painted or covered by an animal skin; they were flat at the bottom, with a round top, some having sides tapering slightly to the bottom, and provided protection from the shoulders to the hip.[218] Shields could be flat or convex (like the Roman *scutum*) on the outer face, and some were provided with a metal boss near the center. The shape of the New Kingdom shield was a compromise between a defensive shield and one suitable for use as a pushing weapon in compressing a line of enemy infantry. New Kingdom soldiers in mêlées and on the march often appear with shields slung over their shoulders with a diagonal strap, the shields thereby protecting their backs and necks while freeing both hands. Shields also could be provided with a loop on the outer edge.[219] In their shape and configuration, Nubian shields differed from those carried by Egyptians, being oval or irregularly shaped pieces of leather or leather-covered wood, with a strap attached to the edge of the shield.[220]

Some of the few surviving ancient Egyptian shields come from the tomb of Tutankhamun. Instead of cowhide, two of Tutankhamun's shields are covered with cheetah skin, a much more expensive material (see figure 12). The outer edges are gilded, and the cartouches of the pharaoh adorn the center of the shield. Except for the unusual cheetah skin and gilded elements, these shields closely resemble those used by most infantry soldiers. Four further shields found in the tomb of Tutankhamun were purely ceremonial, their surfaces adorned with wooden cutout scenes of the king seated on a throne, smiting his animal or human foes, and trampling his enemies as a sphinx (see figure 13).[221]

Signaling Equipment

Once the fog of war descended on the ancient battlefield, effective communication between a commander and his troops was of paramount importance. As with most ancient armies, the Egyptians appear to have

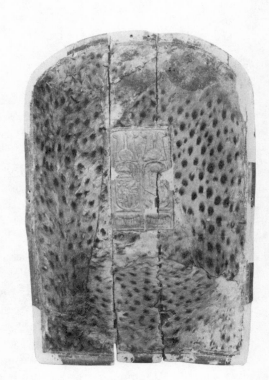

Figure 12. Shield of Tutankhamun
(Egyptian Museum, Cairo, JE 61581).
Wood-backed shield covered with
cheetah hide and decorated with
a gold plate bearing the cartouches
of Tutankhamun. Courtesy of the
Griffith Institute, Oxford University.

Figure 13. Openwork shield of
Tutankhamun (Egyptian Museum,
Cairo, JE 61577). The gilded and
painted wood of this shield shows the
pharaoh Tutankhamun as a human-
headed sphinx trampling two Nubian
enemies; the open fan behind the royal
sphinx emphasizes his divine nature.
The hieroglyphic text to the right reads
"The perfect god who tramples the
foreign lands, who smites the chiefs of
all of the foreign lands. Lord of strength
like the son of Nut (Seth), valiant like
Montu who dwells in Thebes," followed
by Tutankhamun's cartouches. Courtesy
of the Griffith Institute, Oxford
University.

employed both visual and aural signals in military maneuvers. Standards identified the branch of the army to which a unit belonged—infantry, chariotry, and navy.[222] Depictions of standards within the tombs of officials at Amarna include images of the king smiting a foreigner,[223] royal cartouches,[224] boats,[225] rectangles (probably bearing painted scenes) adorned with a feather, and fans (see figure 14);[226] the wooden top of an actual military standard, decorated with a Wepwawet jackal on a standard and two running soldiers, was discovered at the workman's village at Amarna.[227] In addition to large standards for identification purposes, ancient Egyptian commanders also could employ smaller flail ensigns, wooden sticks with attached streamers, to communicate commands visually.[228] Signaling across long distances could be accomplished through intervisible towers (see page 194).

Visual signaling would not always have been possible, and units in battle would not always be free to glance from the oncoming enemy horde to check for a waving standard. Music could, however, pierce the din of combat.[229] The drum may have provided both marching beats and initial maneuvering signals to the troops.[230] Trumpeters, who often appear at the front of the army, probably sounded the charge and more complex commands.[231] Two trumpets, each made of precious metals and decorated with scenes of the deities Amun-Re, Ptah, and Re-Horakhty, were discovered in the tomb of Tutankhamun;[232] wooden cores fitted into each trumpet and maintained the shape of the thin metal instruments.[233] A scene from a tomb at Amarna shows just how trumpets such as those from the tomb of Tutankhamun would have been used.[234] The entire scene consists of five registers, four of which are occupied by units of ten armed soldiers; the central register is empty but for a single figure on the far left facing to the right and holding a trumpet to his lips (see figure 25). The space stretching away from him to the right seems not to be empty, but reserved for the now silent notes of the signal blasts.

Fortifications, Camps, and Siege Technology

Defensive architecture is probably as old as cities themselves, and in the Nile Valley, fortifications existed by 3200 B.C.E. before the unification of Upper and Lower Egypt.[235] Textual and archaeological evidence for Old Kingdom fortresses is scant,[236] and the First Intermediate Period and early Middle Kingdom appear to have witnessed a number of developments in defensive military architecture. Desert outposts appear already to have functioned in far-flung corners of Egyptian hegemony during the late Old Kingdom.[237] To control Egypt's colony in Nubia, the pharaohs of the Twelfth

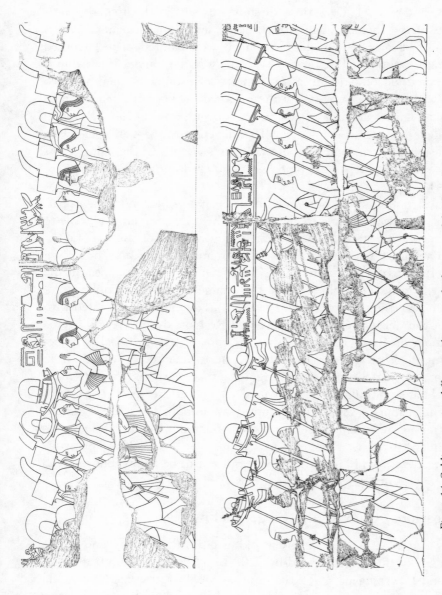

Figure 14. Soldiers carrying different military standards as part of the Opet Procession, from reliefs in the Colonnade Hall of Luxor Temple carved during the reign of Tutankhamun. (top) Epigraphic Survey, *Luxor Temple* 1, pl. 93. (bottom) Ibid., pl. 98. Courtesy of the Oriental Institute of the University of Chicago.

Dynasty erected a series of large mud-brick forts in strategic locations (see chapter 4). These monumental defensive structures were not isolated outposts, but were the centerpieces of a network of smaller forts and watchposts, all connected by patrol roads that traversed the desert hinterlands.

With advances in fortifications came advances in siege technology.[238] Wheeled siege ladders appear during the late Old Kingdom and the First Intermediate Period.[239] Several early Middle Kingdom tombs at Beni Hasan depict sapping on a large scale: three men within a protective testudo work a long, crowbarlike pole against the walls of a fortress.[240] Reed mats embedded between the courses of bricks in the Middle Kingdom Nubian fortresses decreased the effectiveness of such sapping methods. Similarly, the use of a sloping glacis at the base of fortress walls deterred the use of battering rams.[241] During the wars of the late Second Intermediate Period and early New Kingdom, the Egyptians appear to have been content to invest enemy cities rather than to mount any destructive siege or sapping attack. This should not be construed, however, as evidence that the Egyptians were incapable of attacking fixed fortifications; Ramesside Period battle reliefs demonstrate that when they chose, the Egyptians could destroy a fortification.[242]

Egyptian armies on the move, when no established fortification was available, appear to have constructed temporary laagers,[243] the best evidence for which appears in New Kingdom depictions. Particularly lively images of camp life from the time of Tutankhamun appear in the Memphite tomb of General Horemhab.[244] The tableau accompanying Ramesses II's commemoration of the Battle of Kadesh depicts the royal encampment; a large central tent belongs to the king, with the army encamped roundabout, the entire camp surrounded by a square palisade of shields. The command tents would have been quite large, with tall central pole and resulting conical roof. Such a tent appears in the Memphite tomb of Horemhab (see figure 15) and shows that the commander would have taken with him folding furniture of a sort well attested in actual examples from the tomb of Tutankhamun. Ancient texts provide evidence of tents made of both cloth and leather, the latter having the advantage of durability and the disadvantage of weight.[245] A scene in the tomb of Horemhab shows a large number of soldiers struggling with what must be a heavy and thick roll of tent material—probably leather, given the number of men carrying it and the difficulties they are evidently having.[246] Inside the camp, in keeping with the age-old Egyptian image of the basic layout of a city, two streets crossed at the central command area, dividing the enclosure into quadrants; the formal layout of the camp suggests that the Egyptians may well have followed a pattern later adopted by Roman and

Figure 15. Scene of a military camp from the Memphite tomb of Horemhab. In the upper register, a man sits in a chariot resting on a stand, while the spirited horses are held by a groom. Below is a peak-roofed tent with provisions and a folding stool. To the right, a donkey feeds from large vessels and a young boy carries a platter of fruit. A jumble of furniture, including a headrest, appears in the lower right corner. Courtesy of the Bildarchiv Preussischer Kulturbesitz/Art Resource, NY.

Byzantine armies whereby temporary camps possessed a consistent, even codified layout.[247]

How the common soldiers prepared their personal bivouacs remains unclear.[248] Egyptian soldiers rarely appear carrying anything like a backpack or a purpose-made carrying pole of the sort attested for the Roman army.[249] However, the Egyptian hieroglyphic representation of a herdsman, another person commonly living out of doors, shows a man carrying a bundle hanging from a stick that he could balance on his shoulder (𓀒); this hieroglyph and a similar representation of a soldier carrying objects in a camp scene from the tomb of Horemhab[250] suggest that Egyptian soldiers might have carried their camp gear in a manner not unlike that of Roman soldiers after the reforms of Marius. No particular nonroyal accommodations appear in the scenes of Ramesses II's camp near Kadesh, and Amarna talatat depict what are probably soldiers apparently sleeping under the stars, with their blankets pulled over their heads.[251] While on active campaign, the army may purposefully have traveled light.

Archaeological and textual evidence suggests that the Egyptians also constructed semipermanent outposts that were something between the large, well-established fortresses and the temporary camps set up on campaign. Such intermediate constructions could function as elements in a larger system of fortifications; Middle Kingdom rock inscriptions in Nubia refer to fortified enclosures for which no readily apparent remains have been discovered (see page 96). The conflicts of the Second Intermediate Period fueled the construction of a number of smaller fortifications for specific purposes; the defensive system west of Thebes was crucial to the military success of the Seventeenth Dynasty, creating a "back door" into Hyksos-controlled territory to the north, and enabling Theban patrols to capture enemy messengers attempting to bypass the area of direct Theban hegemony.[252] Two freestanding towers at the northern border of ancient Thebes served as defensible lookouts as well as checkpoints along the Wadi Alamat Road, a heavily traveled track in the Western Desert.[253]

Other semipermanent encampments in remote locations facilitated the control of strategic routes in places impractical for a large fort and garrison. One Second Intermediate Period/early New Kingdom encampment, halfway between the Nile Valley and Kharga Oasis, consisted of two drystone and partially subterranean tent bases; a third, smaller stone circle a short distance away functioned as a cooking area.[254] The twin towers of the Wadi Alamat Road and the deep desert tent emplacements on the road to Kharga also guarded cisterns along their respective tracks; the cistern on the high plateau between the Nile and Kharga, approximately 33 meters deep, is a testament to the hydrological engineering skills of the Egyptians. In Nubia, where desert tribes continued to threaten Egyptian colonial interests throughout the New Kingdom, Egypt continued to construct semipermanent outposts. During the reign of Tutankhamun, Nubian policemen were stationed in the oasis of Kurkur, manning a portion of what a stela of Tutankhamun from the region (see pages 113–117) calls the "Wall of Pharaoh." No easily identifiable fortification is visible in or near the oasis, so this "wall" might have been constructed from perishable materials, such as wood and thorn bushes, much like the temporary fortifications of British armies on campaign in Africa during the nineteenth century.[255]

The great civilization so well known for sprawling architectural complexes and cyclopean edifices also applied its magisterial talents for the organization of human labor to militaristic pursuits. Just as Egyptian building tools did not undergo much change over thousands of years, the Egyptians rarely made alterations to their arsenal of weapons. The chief innovations of Egyptian military thought were more in strategy and tactics. Although many Egyptian armaments remained relatively unchanged for millennia, the Egyptian emphasis on indirect engagement and speed of movement—more than cultural conservatism—accounts for this lack of innovation. In general, the Egyptians valued mobility and the use of projectile weapons above the development of armor and the heavy infantry so necessary for the set-piece battles of the later Graeco-Roman world. The Amarna Period is no less militarized than any other period of Egyptian history, and Akhenaten and his successors put their forces to good use defending Egypt's interests in its northern and southern empires.

4

LAND OF GOLD:
THE SOUTHERN EMPIRE

*A further matter to the viceroy of Nubia: "Do not be lenient! Be on guard
against their people and their sorcerers!"*

—Amunhotep II to Usersatet, viceroy of Nubia[1]

B y the reign of Tutankhamun, Nubia had been an Egyptian colony for
two centuries, yet Egypt's southern neighbor never lost its reputation
for potentially inimical magical potency so apparent in Amunhotep II's
advice to his viceroy.[2] Nubia contributed more than strong magic, however, to the world of Egypt. Before the rise of pharaonic civilization, and
during the formative phases of Egyptian history, cultures to the south and
west exerted considerable influence on developments in the Egyptian Nile
Valley.[3] After the emergence of the pharaonic state during the late third
millennium B.C.E., Egypt began to surpass Nubia in cultural complexity,
but the regions south of Aswan remained an integral part of Egypt's religious, cultural, and economic identity. Nubia was not only the source of
much of Egypt's gold; through her Nilotic and desert routes, she was also
Egypt's primary link with trade routes to the south. From these areas came
many valuable products, not the least important of which were those
essential to religious cults—leopard pelts for priestly costumes, ostrich
feathers for elaborate divine fans and official costumes, and the myrrh and
incense burned continuously in the sanctuaries.[4] A natural antagonism,
born of a cultural, economic, and military interdependence between Egypt
and Nubia, combined with their close cultural and religious ties to create
a unique and often fluid colonial relationship.[5]

91

During their long history, the two regions shared much in religious ideology and cosmic outlook; although Egypt's traditional southern border was at the city of Aswan, a cultural continuum existed between southern Egypt and northern Nubia.[6] The two areas were closely connected between ca. 5000 and ca. 3200 B.C.E., near the end of which period native regional powers in both Egypt and Nubia developed into more unified kingdoms. Conflict between the Egyptian and Nubian polities was inevitable, and successful forays by early Egyptian rulers into Lower (northern) Nubia proved a major setback for the developing Nubian kingdom.[7]

In addition to the often stifling effects of direct Egyptian influence and control, climatic change also affected the course of Nubian history. During the time of the Old Kingdom in Egypt, between 2600 and 2300 B.C.E., increased aridity in northeastern Africa forced a number of different but interconnected groups into ever closer contact as the seasonal lakes and desert oases in the eastern and western hinterlands of the Nile Valley diminished in number and moisture.[8] The influx of nomadic desert groups into the southern Nile Valley displaced Nilotic Nubians already living in the region, and appears ultimately to have led to the creation of a series of allied Nubian states that threatened Egyptian trade interests in Nubia in about 2300 B.C.E.[9]

At the same time, the decline of Old Kingdom power after the end of the Sixth Dynasty, and the onset of the First Intermediate Period in Egypt, with a weakened shadow of central government far to the north, and warring monarchs in the south, allowed the fledgling Nubian polities to flourish—the Nubians even provided auxiliary troops for the armies of Egypt, soldiers whose presence and martial talents appear ultimately to have fanned the flames of civil strife throughout the Nile Valley.[10] The Theban reestablishment of a strong central government and the founding of the Middle Kingdom in 2055 B.C.E. again led to Egyptian military domination of Nubia.

Although Egyptian outposts existed in Nubia during the Old Kingdom, those early manifestations of Egyptian control could not compare to the extensive and complexly conceived fortress system the rulers of Egypt's Twelfth Dynasty (ca. 1985–1773 B.C.E.) constructed between the First and Second cataracts. The Twelfth Dynasty's defensive network in Lower Nubia remained the physical basis for many of the later New Kingdom policies in northern Nubia. To understand the Nubian strategies of Egypt's Amarna Period rulers, one must first examine the Middle Kingdom fortification system in Nubia, and understand how the conflicts of the Second

Intermediate Period and the lessons the Egyptians learned during that politically dark period led the pharaohs of the early Eighteenth Dynasty to alter the architecture of Egyptian imperialism in Nubia.

Egyptian Fortifications in Nubia

Though their imposing and massive mud-brick walls were among the earliest and most impressive large-scale fortifications surviving from antiquity, many of the remains of the enormous Egyptian fortress system in Nubia are now lost beneath the lake formed by the successive Aswan dams. Rescue archaeology throughout the first quarter of the twentieth century and again during the 1960s resulted in the excavation and publication of a number of the fortresses.[11] However, recognition of ancient Egypt's brilliant strategy of fortification and the flexibility of that strategy in adapting to a changing threat appear to be as hidden to military history as are now the physical remains of most of the fortresses.[12]

During the First Intermediate Period (2160–2055 B.C.E.), Upper Egypt entered a period of war and civil unrest; local rulers and their partisans besieged the capitals of their rivals, and governors annexed neighboring districts, all the while often acknowledging but seldom heeding a shadowy line of rulers at Heracleopolis in the north. Even after the late Eleventh Dynasty, fighting and ruling from Thebes, had reestablished the control of a centralized administration over all the country, internal strife continued, even marring the reign of Amenemhat I (1985–1956 B.C.E.), first ruler of the Twelfth Dynasty. Amenemhat I campaigned at least once in Nubia, following upon the successes of the founder of the Middle Kingdom, Nebhepetre Montuhotep II.[13] The consolidation of Middle Kingdom hegemony over Lower Nubia came with the reign of Senusret I (1956–1911 B.C.E.), son and successor of Amenemhat I, who established a major chain of fortresses between Aswan and the point of the ultimate extent of Egyptian-controlled territory in early Middle Kingdom Nubia.[14] During the reign of Senusret I, this southern border of Egyptian control in Nubia coincided with the Second Cataract, an area of the Nile where the granite bedrock is elevated and impedes the progress of the river, creating a series of rapids and at times virtually unnavigable waters. The Nile forces its way across a total of six such granitic barriers between the confluence of the Blue Nile and the White Nile at Khartoum and the traditional southern border of Egypt proper at Aswan. As the cataracts were natural barriers to river traffic, they greatly influenced placement of the Egyptian southern frontier throughout the Middle and New kingdoms.

Senusret I appears to have constructed five fortresses north of the Second Cataract, each sited for a different strategic purpose.[15] The northernmost, twin forts of Ikkur and Kuban were constructed on opposite sides of the Nile at the terminus of the roads leading into the Wadi Allaqi gold-mining region.[16] The fortress at Aniba, approximately halfway between Buhen and Ikkur/Kuban, guarded a fertile agricultural region that possessed a number of native Nubian C-Group settlements. The fortresses of Buhen and Kor marked the southernmost extent of Egyptian control. Despite the different motivations for the locations of the fortifications, they all possessed a similar rectangular ground plan, with one side abutting the Nile and a single main gateway oriented toward the desert.

The most elaborate construction in Senusret I's fortress system was the fortress of Buhen.[17] In its earliest incarnation, Buhen contained a central fort measuring approximately 150 by 138 meters, enclosing all of the administrative, economic, and residential buildings. A daunting defensive system surrounded this central unit. The mud-brick walls, nearly 5 meters thick at the base and originally more than 9 meters high, were reinforced with wooden beams and reed matting; along the base of the main wall ran a lower, outer wall punctuated with round towers containing multiple loopholes, which overlooked a ditch, about 7 meters wide and 3 meters deep, with a counterscarp opposite the parapet. An outer defensive wall, reinforced by small round towers, enclosed a much greater area of about 420 by 150 meters. The location of the early Middle Kingdom fortresses on open ground would have made them vulnerable to a long-term siege by a technologically sophisticated opponent, but such did not exist in Nubia at the time of the early Twelfth Dynasty;[18] instead, the flat terrain invited a massed attack by infantry, an attack that must ultimately fail in the rain of arrows the defenders would have poured onto their hapless foes from the loopholes along the protected walls of the elaborate central fortification. The fortresses of the early Middle Kingdom were also effective campaign bases for conflicts fought farther south or deeper in the surrounding deserts in regions beyond direct Egyptian control.

The fortresses constructed during the reign of Senusret I served as stunning architectural expressions of Egypt's domination over Lower Nubia, and their main function was militarily pragmatic.[19] At the same time, however, the fortresses could serve economic functions, facilitating the storage and transportation of raw materials, particularly gold. An inscription from the Nubian amethyst quarry at Wadi el-Hudi suggests that Senusret I's fortress construction was paralleled by economic integration of the Nubian population, particularly as workmen on large mining expeditions.[20] Fortresses could possess their own granaries and treasuries, which could supply military expeditions and provide a basis for trade.[21]

Toward the end of the Twelfth Dynasty, the political situation in Upper (southern) Nubia appears to have changed dramatically, and Senusret III (1870–1831 B.C.E.) made extensive alterations to at least some of the earlier forts, and constructed a new series of fortresses to adapt to the evolving threat from the south. The fortress plans of the late Middle Kingdom did not rely on the rectilinear shapes of the plains fortresses, but rather conformed to the topography of the rocky hilltops the later fortresses occupied in the southern portion of the Second Cataract region, part of the area known in more recent times as the Batn el-Hagar (Belly of Stones). The imposing fortress of Buhen already guarded the northern portion of the Second Cataract; probably as part of Senusret III's modifications to the southern limes,[22] the outer wall of Buhen was rebuilt with defenses mirroring those of the inner fort: a wall with continuous parapet and rectangular towers overlooking a ditch and a counterscarp. Additional barracks and other buildings might have been built in the northern portion of the extensive area between the inner fortress and the improved outer line of fortifications.[23] The fortress of Kor, just south of Buhen, also appears to have been enlarged during the reign of Senusret III.[24]

As the late Middle Kingdom Egyptians altered the earlier fortifications, they also transformed the entire system of fortifications. Within the Batn el-Hagar, Senusret III commissioned a string of new hilltop fortresses: Mirgissa, Shalfak, Uronarti, and Askut.[25] Although each of these fortresses possessed a unique ground plan contoured to the rocky outcrops that formed its foundation, all of the fortresses within the Batn el-Hagar share similar defensive features. Buttressed walls with projecting towers were combined with spur walls, giving defenders access to high areas and outcrops near the fortresses without requiring those areas to be enclosed in larger walls, and allowing control of the approaches to the promontories upon which the forts were built. Projecting towers, a feature already incorporated into early Middle Kingdom Buhen, guarded the entrances to the fortresses, while enclosed stairways connected the fortresses with the river, providing a constant access to water in case of a prolonged siege. A unit of three additional fortresses guarded the southernmost point of Egyptian control at the southern end of the Batn el-Hagar: Semna, Kumma, and Semna South.[26] Semna, the largest of the complex, had a L-shape ground plan nearly 130 meters on each long side. Semna South, the first line of defense, was much smaller than either Semna or Kumma, but possessed the same basic defensive features: bastions projected from the main wall approximately 2 meters, beyond which was a 7.5-meter-wide ditch. Surrounding the ditch was a counterscarp with glacis. Semna South had a particularly secure access to water—a subterranean staircase that ran beneath the outerworks.

A mud-brick wall with parallel track ran from just beyond the fortress of Semna South to near the fortress of Uronarti, bypassing an area of the Nile particularly difficult for navigation.[27] Such a use of a wall to defend a road, and perhaps to function at least in part as an elevated path for armed patrols, parallels the Middle Kingdom wall connecting Aswan to the area opposite the island of Philae.[28] To some extent these fortified paths are similar to the later "long walls" connecting Athens to the port of Piraeus.[29] The Egyptians might also have constructed a dam near the Semna complex of forts.[30] Naval communications among the fortresses may also have used portage points, such as the portion of a slipway discovered near the fortress of Mirgissa.[31]

Rather than functioning as isolated units, the Egyptian fortresses in Nubia were administrative centers, defended by fortifications and outerworks, integrated into a larger defensive system, in which some forts fulfilled specific roles. The island fortress of Askut possessed enough granaries and storerooms to provision the garrisons of nearly all the other Second Cataract forts and appears to have functioned primarily as a fortified grain depot for military expeditions into hostile Nubian territory. Mirgissa, at the northern end of the Batn el-Hagar, was a focus of trade between Egypt and Nubia. Watchtowers, desert outposts, and an extensive series of patrol routes were other important components of Egyptian hegemony in Lower Nubia.[32] The intervisibility of the fortresses and smaller outposts suggests that visual signals were communicated between neighboring components of the fortress system.[33] For more complicated messages, couriers traveling along the maintained roads could relay urgent information.[34] A unique set of military dispatches from the fortress of Semna, surviving as copies forwarded to the Theban military command center, records the movements of even small groups of locals Nubians and demonstrates the effectiveness of Egyptian patrols in Nubia during the late Twelfth Dynasty.[35]

The Nubian border defense system of the late Middle Kingdom appears to have been constantly on "high alert," and the virtually impregnable fortresses built during the reign of Senusret III were intended to oppose a very different threat from that for which their earlier Middle Kingdom counterparts had been designed. Between the reigns of Senusret I and Senusret III, a Nubian state centered around the Third Cataract, which would soon develop into the Kingdom of Kerma,[36] had become increasingly centralized and had expanded into the territory just south of the Egyptian border at Semna. Sitting astride major African trade routes and profiting from continual interaction with the Egyptians to the north, already by the Middle Kingdom the rulers of Kerma had amassed considerable wealth, as reflected in their burial goods, and appear to have improved the military technology or at least the military planning of the Upper Nubians, as the defenses of their capital Kerma reveal. Although the floruit of the classic Kerma culture would not occur for another hundred years, the Kermans of the late Middle Kingdom, during a transitional period between the Middle Kerma and Classic Kerma cultures, exhibited nascent forms of the traits that would transform Upper Nubia into a formidable foe.[37]

Senusret III's border defense system succeeded in keeping the Kerman threat at bay until the collapse of the Middle Kingdom nearly a century later. The Thirteenth Dynasty continued the foreign policy of the late Twelfth Dynasty,[38] but by the time of the Seventeenth Dynasty, many of the Egyptian military officials in Nubia—who may have been considered colonists by the late Middle Kingdom government, and some of whom were descended from families that had lived in Nubia for generations—seem to have viewed themselves as Nubians rather than Egyptians and allied themselves with the Kerman rulers.[39] At the height of its power, Kerma controlled—at least indirectly—the area from the Fourth to the First cataracts.[40] Near the end of the Seventeenth Dynasty in Egypt, at least one Kerman ruler was able to recruit auxiliary troops from throughout Upper Nubia and its surrounding regions and attack Upper Egypt.[41] The large-scale and audacious raid against the area of Elkab suggests that the Kermans might have possessed formidable military capabilities already during the late Middle Kingdom, when the Egyptians expended so many resources to construct and garrison the Nubian fortresses and their outlying patrol routes.

The third phase of Egyptian fortresses in Nubia began with the reconquest of Lower Nubia, inaugurated by Kamose, the last pharaoh of the Seventeenth Dynasty, and completed by his immediate successors.[42] The Egyptian army first recaptured the former Lower Nubian possessions of the Middle Kingdom[43] and began to restore the fortress of Buhen,[44] probably damaged during the Egyptian takeover of the stronghold.[45] Although New Kingdom Buhen was imposing, and a functional fortification, it lacked the elaborate outerworks and loophole system of the Middle Kingdom fortress—the appearance of power had become more important than the well-designed architectural means of manifesting that power. Kamose's two immediate successors, Ahmose and Amunhotep I, concentrated on reestablishing the earlier Middle Kingdom border and reducing the remnants of Kerman power.[46] Construction activities by Ahmose and Amunhotep I at Sai,[47] about 100 kilometers south of Semna, represent a first attempt at expanding the southern border past its Middle Kingdom location, presaging the major change in New Kingdom Nubian policy that commenced with the reign of Pharaoh Thutmose I, when the farthest known extent of Egyptian campaigns reached the area of Kurgus, north of the Fifth Cataract (see pages 102–105).

Instead of entirely reconstituting and restoring the architectural strongpoints of the Middle Kingdom defensive system in Nubia, the New Kingdom rulers transformed the border defense system of the Middle Kingdom into an effective colonial administration.[48] At the island fortress of Askut, a substantial portion of the interior fortified area was abandoned, but a large residence, comparable to mansions at Amarna, and other buildings were constructed outside of the original fortifications.[49] At Buhen many of the elaborate defensive features of the late Middle Kingdom inner fortification were abandoned; rebuilt walls and towers often stood directly on earlier debris, and the dry moat was filled and the counterscarp removed to construct a sunken roadway. Judging by jar sealings and dockets on wine amphorae, the rebuilt administrative center at Buhen flourished during the reigns of Amunhotep III and Akhenaten.[50] New military installations, on the other hand, appear to have been built during the reign of Thutmose I to prevent revolts by hostile Kushite leaders and to consolidate the Egyptian territorial gains between the Fourth and Fifth cataracts; although these installations were probably constructed near centers such as Tombos, Napata, and even Kurgus, without further archaeological examination, the nature of these fortifications remains unknown.[51]

When viewed against the impressive developments in military architecture in Middle Kingdom Nubia, the New Kingdom fortresses in Nubia are eloquent architectural testimony that Nubia by then had become a series of client states, not an occupied territory. During the New Kingdom, Egypt also established a series of lightly fortified settlements throughout Nubia, further evidence of Egypt's confidence in its new colonial system (see "Amarna Cities in Nubia" below). Modestly fortified native settlements and auxiliary forts in use during the Eighteenth Dynasty, such as Areika,[52] suggest that the local Nubian population participated in the policing of the new colonial system and its defense against threats from groups who had not accepted Egyptian hegemony. The open plans of the restored and renovated fortresses around the Second Cataract and the concomitant construction of fortified cities further demonstrate an emphasis on the economic role of the physical infrastructure of the New Kingdom Egyptian presence in Nubia.

The strategic sophistication reflected in the development of Egypt's Nubian fortresses finds excellent parallels in the Roman Empire's more well-known border defenses (see figure 16). Just as the designs of Roman fortresses corresponded to changes in Roman approaches to border defense, to changes in the enemy forces threatening those borders, and to the very concept of border, so the ancient Egyptian fortifications in Nubia appear to reveal similar physical manifestations of similar policies. Understanding the evolving concepts behind Rome's border defenses ultimately contributes to a more complete appreciation of the concepts behind the Egyptian fortresses in Nubia. In combination with archaeological evidence from Nubia, this in turn allows informed speculation regarding the nature of Nubian political organization and the sophistication of Nubian military forces at a given time.

Roman border defenses, and those of Egyptian Nubia before, may be said to consist of three basic types: mobile defense, perimeter defense, and defense in depth.[53] In the case of Rome and its foreign possessions and dependencies, these three approaches to border security followed one after another in that order. During the early empire (30 B.C.E. to 68 C.E.), client states guarded Rome's borders, and the legions themselves, their bases well protected within Roman territory by the intervening client states, ideally fought battles beyond Rome's borders. Permanent fortifications might be within Roman territory, but the camps of the legions on campaign were permanent elaborations of the temporary camps the units built when on the march. The combination of simple fortifications and client states in New Kingdom Nubia parallels the defense strategy of the early Roman Empire. The fortress of Buhen during the New Kingdom, like a legionary outpost in the territory of a client state, was impressive, and served the function of holding any possible attacker at bay long enough for the troops inside to draw up their ranks on the field of battle (see figure 16 D, G). The elaborate fortifications developed later in the Roman Empire were unnecessary in the Age of Augustus, when a series of allied states, quickly becoming Romanized, separated the empire from its enemies. Whereas the successful acculturation of the client states led Rome to create a new defense against the enemies still beyond its expanded borders, the New Kingdom Nubian colony lacked any powerful neighboring opposition. The outer fortresses of the early Roman Empire, and the forts and fortified cities of New Kingdom Egypt, were the protective enclosures of armies intending to meet the enemy as often as possible in the field; such structures were ultimately fortified sleeping areas for mobile forces.

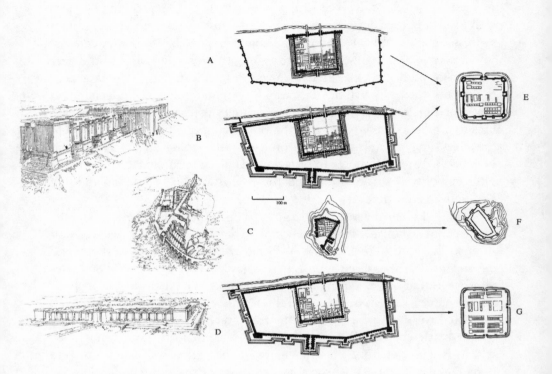

Figure 16. Development of Egyptian fortifications in Nubia. (A) Plan of the early Middle
Kingdom fortress at Buhen. (B) Plan and reconstruction drawing of the late Middle
Kingdom fortress at Buhen, showing Senwoseret III's modifications to the outerworks.
(C) Late Middle Kingdom fortress on the island of Askut. The fortress contained extensive
granaries and was made more defensible by the addition of spur walls. (D) New Kingdom
fortress at Buhen. The inner citadel lacks the sophisticated outer defensive elements of
the earlier fortress. (E) Roman fortress of the late third century, displaying towers and
wide ditch and berm. (F) Roman hilltop fortress of the late fourth century, with projecting
towers and complex gateway. G) Roman legionary fortress of the first and second centuries,
with thin walls and narrow ditch and berm. All Egyptian fortress plans are shown to scale.
Reconstruction drawings after Badawy, *Ancient Egyptian Architecture*, Vol. 2, 213, 221; Vol.
3, 460. Plans of Buhen after Emery, Smith, and Millard, *Fortress of Buhen*, pls. 2–4. Plan of
Askut after Smith, *Askut in Nubia*, fig. 2.8. Roman fortifications after Luttwak, *Grand
Strategy of the Roman Empire*, 164–165.

During the mid-first century C.E. and throughout the second, the Roman Empire incorporated most of its client states, leading to the formation of a static perimeter. The buffer of the earlier client states removed, the fortresses became more elaborate and more permanent, standing as they often did at the edge of barbarian territory, although the commanders of the legions had not yet abandoned the concept of mobility. The design of the Nubian forts of the early Middle Kingdom is the architectural manifestation of a strategy of border control closely paralleling the perimeter defense system employed by the Roman Empire from the second century C.E. to the middle of the third. The Roman perimeter defense consisted of legionary fortresses behind outer defenses, with patrol roads and watchtowers connecting the larger fortifications. Hadrian's Wall, which guarded the northern border of Roman Britain, is strategically equivalent to the Egyptian forts and the associated system of roads and smaller watchposts built during the reign of Senusret I. Functionally, the early Middle Kingdom fortresses and their outliers served the same purpose as their counterparts in Roman perimeter defense of the second and early third centuries, while architecturally, both early and late Middle Kingdom Buhen correspond to Roman fortifications constructed as the perimeter defense began to fail in the later third century (see figure 16 A, B, and E).

Both the Egyptian and the Roman defensive works visibly marked physical boundaries and served as staging points for military action beyond the fortifications. The forts constructed early in the reign of Senusret I, such as Buhen, functioned in year eighteen of his reign as bases for a Nubian campaign launched against enemies south of the Second Cataract.[54] The roads connecting the various defensive elements were the linchpins of both systems, providing rapid communication and the ability to coordinate a forward offense. Like the Nubian forts of the early Middle Kingdom, the Roman perimeter defense system was intended to protect against enemy groups who posed a continuous low-intensity threat and only occasionally mounted major attacks. The fortifications constructed during the reign of Senusret I appear to have been appropriate for the Nubian enemy of the time—the C-Group in Lower Nubia and the developing Kerman kingdom in Upper Nubia, neither of which appear to have possessed either sophisticated siege technology or the economic base for a prolonged conflict.

From the middle of the third century C.E. through the fifth century C.E. in the Roman Empire and during the late Egyptian Middle Kingdom in Nubia, a response to external threats transformed a perimeter defense into a system of defense-in-depth. In the case of Rome, increasingly numerous and ultimately more militarily sophisticated opponents required that fortresses be able to exist as islands of order in a sea of barbarian chaos, centers from which the legions and auxiliaries could counterattack the enemy hordes once the overwhelming flood of their initial onslaught had begun to ebb. In Nubia, the Kermans of the late Middle Kingdom, at the dawn of the classic Kerma culture and its military successes, provided a similar impetus for the creation of a new fortification strategy. The hilltop fortresses built on the rocks of the Batn el-Hagar during the reign of Senusret III find close parallels in the fortifications of the Roman defense-in-depth system developed during the third and fourth centuries c.e., in which fortifications were constructed with more elaborate defensive architecture and situated on more easily defendable high ground (see figure 16 C, F). In the face of stronger opposition, both the Egyptians and the Romans were unable to maintain a static perimeter, instead devoting a swath of border territory to the absorption of an enemy attack. While the declining Roman Empire was forced to sacrifice the integrity of its frontiers, the powerful and centralized government of Senusret III intentionally extended Egypt's Nubian fortresses into the southern region of the Second Cataract proper, incorporating the agriculturally unproductive region of the Batn el-Hagar as a defensive buffer.

The Egyptian fortifications in Nubia reflect Egypt's changing approach to its Nubian limes. Throughout the Middle Kingdom, the fortresses became more complex and defensible, and the border itself was extended in the late Twelfth Dynasty. After the expulsion of the Kermans from Lower Nubia and the conquest of Upper Nubia, the Eighteenth Dynasty pharaohs were able to create an effective colonial administration in Nubia, essentially reproducing the extensive bureaucracy of Egypt itself. By the time of the reign of Akhenaten, Nubia was in many ways a second Egypt, and less than six hundred years after the reign of Tutankhamun, a Nubian kingdom espousing thoroughly Egyptian ideology and pharaonic kingship would conquer Egypt itself.[55] The somewhat complex history of Egyptian fortifications in Nubia demonstrates the ingenuity of Egyptian strategy and the capability of the Egyptian military to adapt to a changing enemy—all of which contributed to the success of Egyptian colonization in New Kingdom Nubia.

The Southern Border of the New Kingdom

Although the toponym "Nubia" is omnipresent in modern descriptions of ancient Egypt's southern neighbor, the name does not actually appear in ancient Egyptian sources. For New Kingdom Egyptians, ancient Nubia consisted of two major Nilotic territories: Wawat, encompassing Lower (northern) Nubia from Aswan to the Second Cataract; and Kush, the area of Upper (southern) Nubia from the Second Cataract to Kurgus, between the Fourth and Fifth cataracts. The Egyptians also employed a number of other "tribal" names for the groups who inhabited the southern deserts. Geography primarily determined the border between Wawat and Kush, for the region of the Second Cataract, the Belly of Stones, was one of the longest impediments to riverine traffic along the Nubian stretch of the Nile River. The southern border of Kush at Kurgus might seem arbitrary, as there is neither a cultural break in that region nor a cataract. However, a combination of geographical factors, particularly the location of desert roads, dictated the extension of Egyptian control to the area of Kurgus and not beyond.

The reign of Thutmose I marked a transition in Egyptian policy in Nubia. Whereas the late Seventeenth Dynasty and the related first two rulers of the Eighteenth Dynasty appear to have followed to some extent an adaptation of Middle Kingdom policy, holding a main base in the area of the Second Cataract and launching punitive strikes, Thutmose I mounted a major campaign in which he expanded the southern border of Egypt far beyond that of any previous Egyptian pharaoh.[56]

The army of Thutmose I probably began their long trek toward Nubian domination in the city of Thebes and divided into a river and desert column as they progressed southward.[57] At Kerma, the army of Thutmose I annihilated a large enemy force,[58] killing a Kerman ruler and hanging his body upside down, as if the Nubian rebel were the chaos serpent Apep (see pages 18–19). Enjoying their military success, the Egyptian army probably camped in the fertile region around Kerma, an area of some comfort and relaxation, prior to beginning the arduous hauling of equipment along the Nile among the Third, Fourth, and Fifth cataracts, a stretch of the Nubian Nile called the "bad water." Between the Fourth Cataract, near the modern area of Kurgus, more than 500 kilometers south of Aswan, Thutmose I halted his forward advance and carved a triumphal boundary inscription on a large quartz boulder.[59] Thutmose I's far forward base in Nubia rendered obsolete the elaborate hilltop fortresses of the Second Cataract and contributed to the success of Egypt's Nubian policy for the remainder of the New Kingdom.

Two texts from the reign of Thutmose I explain why control over the region of Kurgus was essential to Egyptian domination of Nubia. The first text is the autobiography of the marine Ahmose, son of Ibana; the other document is the monumental stela of the pharaoh Thutmose I himself near Tombos at the Third Cataract. These two texts describe a particular portion of the Nile between the Fourth and Fifth cataracts where the Nile current flows from northeast to southwest. In general, a Nile journey from south to north involved use of the Nile current itself. When traveling from north to south, an ancient Egyptian was almost always sailing against the Nile current, but usually could rely on the north or northwesterly breezes that often prevail in Egypt.

In those portions of the Nile channel in which the river did not flow roughly from south to north, navigation against the current of the Nile could become extremely difficult. In bends where the Nile flowed in a more or less southerly direction, shipping was accomplished only with great difficulty and at times no little danger.[60] Upstream navigation of those portions of the river, such as the section of the Nile around the Fourth Cataract in Nubia, would entail a vessel moving against both current and prevailing wind. Ahmose, son of Ibana, simply and evocatively refers to the area of the Fourth Cataract as the "bad water": "Then I was brave before him (Thutmose I) at the bad water, during the hauling of the ships over the cataract."[61]

The Tombos Inscription of Thutmose I more fully, albeit in some ways more confusingly, refers to this same area as "that inverted water which flows downstream/northward while going upstream/southward." This somewhat confusing text could easily refer to the region of the Nile between the Third and Fourth cataracts, where the river flows downstream to the south and upstream to the north, the opposite of its accustomed direction. Thutmose I and his military forces witnessed the difficulties involved in transporting a major military force along the "inverted water."[62] The same problems, described quite clearly and in some detail by Winston Churchill, were encountered by the British forces in the late nineteenth century during Kitchener's advance for the reconquest of the Sudan:

On the 4th of August the gunboats *El Teb* and *Tamai* approached the Fourth Cataract to ascend to the Abu Hamed-Berber reach of the river [area south of the Fifth Cataract]. . . . About 300 local Shaiggia tribesmen had been collected, and their efforts were directed—or, as the result proved, misdirected. . . . The steamer, with her engines working at full speed, succeeded in mounting half the distance. But the rush of water was then so great that her bows were swept round, and after a narrow escape of capsizing, she was carried swiftly downstream. . . . Four hundred more Shaiggia were therefore collected from the neighboring villages, and in the afternoon the *Teb* attempted the passage. Her fortunes were far worse than those of the *Tamai*. Owing to the lack of co-operation and discipline among the local tribesmen, their utter ignorance of what was required of them, and the want of proper supervision, the hauling power was again too weak. . . . In ten seconds the *Teb* heeled over and turned bottom upwards.[63]

A prior recognition of the problems of navigating the Nile at these "upside-down waters" probably led Thutmose I to include the area of the Fourth Cataract in the territory under direct Egyptian control. The region around the Fourth Cataract is also the point of departure for desert routes crossing the desert filling the Bayuda Bend of the Nile toward the Sixth Cataract, just north of Khartoum, as well as points to the north, accessing the lower Nubian Nile in the area of Buhen.[64] Control of the Nile at a point sufficiently upstream of this juncture of inverted Nile course and desert routes would ensure direct Egyptian control of a difficult section of the Nile that would present a formidable challenge to an Egyptian force struggling against both wind and current when opposed by a hostile Nubian force. A permanent Egyptian presence at Kurgus also would ensure advance warning of any enemy force attempting to move directly against the Second Cataract via the desert routes of the Bayuda Desert.

A further consideration in favor of Kurgus as the location of the Egyptian southern border also may have been the site's connection with trade routes much farther to the southeast, particularly roads leading to an area the Egyptians called "Punt," most likely in eastern Sudan, northern Abyssinia, and possibly at times including the region across the Gulf of Aden into the southern Arabian Peninsula.[65] In Egyptian inscriptions, Punt often appears as "god's land," since it was an important source for myrrh, gold, ebony, ivory, and other products essential for religious cults. Two routes existed between the Egyptian Nile Valley and Punt—one overland from southern Nubia, and another through the Eastern Desert and then south through the Red Sea.[66]

The influence of Puntite trade on Egyptian policies in Nubia finds support in the activities of Hatshepsut (1473–1458 B.C.E.), who often mimics the policies of her father, Thutmose I. A woman ruling as a pharaoh, Hatshepsut had the particular desire to repeat the activities of Thutmose I, emphasizing her politically questionable role as legitimate successor to the throne.[67] An interest in the land routes from southern Nubia to Punt under Thutmose I may have led to Hatshepsut's great naval expedition to Punt. In the scenes and inscriptions of her Punt expedition she displayed so prominently in her mortuary temple at Deir el-Bahri, Hatshepsut refers to opening up new ways of access to Punt and eliminating middlemen in Puntite trade.

The Puntite expedition of Hatshepsut primarily traveled the Red Sea route to Punt, and her inscriptions imply that the maritime voyage was much more direct than previous expeditions, suggesting that her predecessors, Thutmose I and Thutmose II, relied on merchant middlemen and the land route to Punt. The importance of land routes and the Nile in Puntite trade with Egypt did not cease with Hatshepsut's great naval expedition, however, and a stela, possibly dating to the reign of Akhenaten, from Gebel Tingar in west Aswan[68] appears to refer to the products of divine Punt arriving via the Western Desert, probably along the route connecting Aniba with Aswan via the oasis of Kurkur.

Although no complete evidence about the Nubian strategy of Thutmose I exists, the actions of his successors suggest that the early Eighteenth Dynasty pharaohs established their border along the Fourth Cataract to secure the Nilotic and desert back door of the Second and Third cataracts, as well as to establish a forward Nilotic trading point for the religiously important exotica of Punt. If the Egyptians contracted their southern border, they might spend less resources maintaining control over southern Nubia, but then they would lose more direct control over trade. Based on the actions of early Eighteenth Dynasty kings, in addition to military reasons, we must consider the important influences of trade on Egyptian policy in Nubia during the Amarna Period.

The Viceroys of Nubia

The economic importance of Nubia, the almost constant interactions and even interdependence of the people and economies of Nubia and Upper Egypt, and the significance of Nubian trade routes fostered a New Kingdom administration of Nubia centered less around a military infrastructure and military command than was the case during the Middle Kingdom. New Kingdom Nubia instead represented a modified form of the Egyptian civil administration[69] influenced by military organization and earlier fortress administration.[70] The ultimate arbiter of justice and chief administrator in Nubia was the "King's Son of Kush," the viceroy of Nubia in Egyptological parlance.[71] Use of the term "viceroy" evokes the title of the chief administrative official of the British Raj in India. This evocation is illuminating, for New Kingdom Nubia functioned in many ways similar to British viceregal India, and the Egyptians' own aspirations and plans for Nubia during the New Kingdom presage to a great extent those of their British counterparts in India during the nineteenth and early twentieth centuries.

The Egyptian title "King's Son," which often appears as an abbreviation for the more complete designation "King's Son of Kush," was the continuation of a court title of the Second Intermediate Period, often involving military powers, and was not necessarily an indication of blood relationship to the king or to the royal family as a whole;[72] not until the very end of the New Kingdom was the holder of the title King's Son of Kush actually related to the pharaoh. The title "King's Son" possessed military connotations, and viceroys of Nubia often had military careers in addition to administrative and economic experience.[73] The pharaoh himself conferred the office of viceroy upon each new incumbent;[74] a unique scene in the tomb of Amunhotep, called Huy, viceroy during the reign of Tutankhamun, depicts this important investiture (see figure 17).[75] Huy appeared before the pharaoh Tutankhamun, while the chief of the treasury presented Huy with the seal of the latter's new office. As he handed over the seal, the chief of the treasury recited the following words: "I hereby delegate to you (authority) from Hierakonpolis to the region of Napata." Huy's responsibilities extended from the southernmost districts of Egypt to the Fourth Cataract—a stretch of the Nile as long as the entire course of the river in Egypt.

Huy had begun his official career under Akhenaten's viceroy Djehutymose, serving as the "scribe of correspondence" and "royal messenger in all foreign lands."[76] As royal messenger, Huy also would have participated in the network of letter carriers who transported these important missives throughout the Egyptian empire,[77] thereby acquiring the topographical knowledge necessary for a properly traveled military official.[78] Before becoming viceroy, Huy had achieved the rank of lieutenant general of the chariotry, and his investiture inaugurates a series of viceroys who began their careers as chariot officers. Upon his investiture, Huy took on another important function: "Overseer of all of the gold lands of Amun," a viceregal title since the reign of Amunhotep III. As the overseer of the gold lands, Huy not only monitored the economic aspects of gold production, but also was required to protect the mining regions from the incursions of hostile tribes, as had his predecessor Djehutymose (see pages 118–119).

After Huy's investiture in office, he probably administered his Nubian responsibilities from the fortified city of Faras. Although one of Huy's most important functions—of both an economic and a religious nature—was the presentation of southern tribute to the Egyptian ruler, when Huy first arrived in Nubia to assume his duties as viceroy, he was probably bringing gifts from Egypt to the local Nubian chiefs and administrators.[79] Some have cast doubt on Huy's vigilance in office, claiming that he performed most of his viceregal duties while living comfortably at Thebes, but no evidence exists to support such a claim.[80] Near the scene of investiture in Huy's tomb there is indeed a depiction of Huy's Theban house,[81] but the scene is associated with the return of the newly minted viceroy to his home, where family and friends acclaim him following his

Figure 17. Viceroy of Kush Huy receives his seal of office from the chief of the treasury. After Davies, *Tomb of Huy*, pl. 6.

appointment and prior to his inaugural voyage to Nubia. Although he may have maintained a household at Thebes, Huy probably spent much if not most of his time at Faras.

The viceroy of Nubia had charge over two deputy administrators, a deputy of Wawat in the north and a deputy of Kush in the south. The territory of Wawat extended from Aswan to the Second Cataract, while that of Kush stretched from the Second Cataract to Kurgus. This historically and geographically dictated division of the country was reproduced during another colonial era: the British governor-general of the Sudan was aided by two provincial governors of the provinces of Halfa and Dongola.[82] Like the viceroy himself, the deputies of Wawat and Kush often came from the ranks of the military. For example, Penniut, the deputy of Wawat for the viceroy Huy, was the deputy commander of the fortress of Faras at the time of Huy's investiture under Tutankhamun. In addition to the fortress commanders and mayors of the fortified cities in Nubia, the two deputies presided over ministers of agriculture (e.g., chief of cattle, overseer of the granaries), ministers of the Nubian treasury, and a large number of scribes who recorded all the details of day-to-day administration.

The exact relationship of the viceroy to the internal Egyptian administration is unclear. Although the chief of the treasury relays to Huy the pharaoh's statement of appointment, the viceroy appears by his very title to have reported directly to the ruler;[83] he was probably roughly on a par with the viziers of Egypt, perhaps not so important within Egypt as were they, but created more in the pharaoh's image and therefore of much more importance outside of Egypt than any other member of the Egyptian administration.[84]

In addition to an elaborate civil administration, Egypt's Nubian colony also possessed a large military force. Permanent garrisons were an essential component for the functioning of the fortresses as well as the fortress towns, construction of which continued through the Eighteenth Dynasty. The head of the military administration was the "chief of the troops/regiments (*pedjut*) of Kush." The term *pedjut* for battalion in the title also can have the more specific meaning of "bow troops, archers," and this particular nuance would be appropriate for native Nubian contingents, whose archery skills were prized. Several other types of troops—heavy infantry, naval forces, patrolmen, and some mounted patrols and messengers—would have supported the large forces of archers.

At the same time that Egyptian administration by Egyptian administrators was transplanted into Nubia, many local Nubian rulers found themselves suddenly elevated in status and groomed to be the mirrors of pharaonic society.[85] Following Thutmose I's establishment of the Nubian border at Kurgus, the area of Upper Nubia was divided into five districts, each under the control of a Nubian prince loyal to the Egyptian pharaoh; such a division may have been an attempt to mirror the nome administration of Egypt. A historical inscription from the reign of Thutmose II is the primary source for the administration of Upper Nubia, reorganized after a revolt by two Kushite leaders, probably sons of the former Kerman king.[86] The Egyptian army decisively crushed the rebellion and brought one of the Nubian leaders back to Thebes as a prisoner. His fate is unknown—he was possibly executed in a ceremonial fashion,[87] although the Kushite prince may have sworn an oath of loyalty to the pharaoh and returned to his native land.

In an attempt to minimize the likelihood of such a rebellion, Nubian princes often grew up in the Egyptian court, alongside the future pharaoh and similar young princes from other foreign lands. Many of the Egyptianized Nubian rulers boasted of their title "child of the nursery."[88] This policy of raising princes in the Egyptian court theoretically installed rulers sympathetic to Egyptian culture and religion in Nubia and Syria-Palestine without any military expenditure. In some cases the foreign children who did not return to rule in their native lands became close confidants to the pharaoh—for example, a Nubian man named Maiherper received the privilege of being buried in the Valley of the Kings (one of the few commoners ever to receive this favor) from a pharaoh of the mid-Eighteenth Dynasty.[89] As one would imagine, the indoctrination of foreign princes with Egyptian values was not always successful and could create backlash among the native population. During the reign of Ramesses III (1184–1153 B.C.E.), a Libyan prince sent from Egypt to rule over the previously rebellious tribes of the Sahara created dissatisfaction among the Libyans, precipitating an invasion of Egypt;[90] no similar failure is attested with Nubian princes.

In addition to the extensive role of native rulers in the Egyptian administration of Nubia, some foreign groups from regions north of Egypt were also sent to Nubia. In a letter written to Zalaya, the ruler of the city of Damascus, Akhenaten requests that Zalaya deport to Egypt a group of Apiru, seminomadic peoples who harassed the urban areas of the Levantine coast, to Egypt.[91] Akhenaten specifies that these Apiru will be sent to Egypt's colony Nubia, probably to garrison newly constructed fortified towns such as Gem(pa)aten (Kawa). The trade in auxiliary troops also affected the Nubian population directly—in another document from the reign of Akhenaten, the ruler of Ugarit requests palace servants from the "land of Kush."[92] The Nubians possibly sent to Ugarit might have been prisoners of war or groups who moved voluntarily; this potential deportation of Nubians may even be behind an interesting statement in an ancient Egyptian letter describing the ever-present arms of Akhenaten's deity the Aten; among the wishes for the health and well-being of the king, the letter states: "may he [the Aten] extend his arms and bring to you southerners."[93] Akhenaten appears to have continued the Egyptian practice of removing small, rebellious, or troublesome groups to a less familiar territory, far away from potential allies, resettling them in an area where they could function as effective auxiliary troops for the Egyptian state.[94]

Amarna Cities in Nubia

Although dense urban centers in Egypt often arose because of their strategic locations, in terms of both economic activity and military and administrative control,[95] the relatively narrow band of fertile land on either side of the Nile caused the population to be relatively evenly distributed.[96] During the late Old Kingdom, pharaohs created a series of officially founded "new" cities, which in turn fostered new power bases and burgeoning urban centers.[97] Sometimes these purpose-built cities filled a needed void in the country and increased the agricultural potential of the area. Other centers, such as Akhet-aten, appear to be viable population centers only as long as a state-sponsored program supported the city. The New Kingdom colony of Nubia benefited from the creation of a number of new urban areas, several of which were founded or expanded during the Amarna Period.

Although desert dwellers and populations south of the Fifth Cataract continued to harass Egyptian activity in Nubia, the extension of Egypt's border to Kurgus gave the Egyptians access to major desert routes, allowing them to deal swiftly with incursions, and the allied Nubian client states provided unmatched local expertise in defense. During the Eighteenth Dynasty, the Egyptians continued to alter the existing fortress system (see above), but New Kingdom Egyptian activity in Nubia focused on urban foundations[98] and religious constructions,[99] with military architecture in a subordinate position. Nubia shares fully in the religious upheaval during the reign of Akhenaten, as well as in the restoration of the cult of Amun following his death.

Akhenaten built extensively at two new cities in Nubia—Sesebi and Kawa—both of which contained temples dedicated to the Aten, and he sent his minions to Napata and other Nubian cult centers of Amun to hack out the name of the Theban deity. Kawa, whose ancient name Gem(pa)-aten means "the Aten is discovered," lay at the end of a desert route that led to Napata, a shortcut across a large portion of the bend of the Nile between the Third and Fourth cataracts; archaeological evidence suggests that the city was originally founded by Amunhotep III.[100] Akhenaten first erected a temple for Amun at his new city of Sesebi while he still ruled as Amunhotep IV and worshipped the traditional Egyptian pantheon; later, Akhenaten appears to have rededicated this temple to the Aten and built another temple for his solar cult;[101] Akhenaten's constructions at Sesebi might have been theologically as well as physically linked to his father's temple at Soleb.[102] Talatat from yet another Aten temple have been discovered at the site of Dokki Gel, a city founded earlier in the Eighteenth Dynasty just north of Kerma.[103]

The worship of the Aten at these remote Nubian sites lasted no longer than did the cult of the peculiarly Amarna era solar disk in Egypt. Tutankhamun replaced the Aten temple at Kawa with an edifice dedicated to Amun-Re; since Amun-Re was a syncretism between the god of Thebes, Amun, and the sun-god Re, the name of the city Gem(pa)aten was not altered, since the solar disk could easily be considered an aspect of Amun-Re. Tutankhamun or Horemhab might have built another temple to Amun-Re at Napata, which would become the center of Amun worship in Upper Nubia.[104] The mention of the area of Napata in the investiture of Huy as viceroy of Kush supports the existence of an Egyptian base of operations at Napata from at least the late Eighteenth Dynasty.[105]

Furthermore, nothing suggests that worship within these Nubian temples was limited to native Egyptians, and a number of texts and reliefs indicate that Nubians played an important role in Egyptian religion even within the Egyptian Nile Valley. Akhenaten's southern temple-building program strongly suggests that Nubia had assumed a fully integrated role in Egyptian religious ideology. The massive economic output required for Akhenaten's constructions probably surpassed the real or propagandistic needs of the Egyptian colonists, and the temples were most likely aimed at converting the local population to the new universal solar worship. The temple-building programs of Akhenaten and his successors provide important clues to the ultimate success, from an Egyptian point of view, of the transformation of Nubia into an extension of the perfect model of the world that was the land of Egypt. Implanting the developed pharaonic concept of the city and urbanism into Nubia also aided this transformation.

The city-building activities of Tutankhamun in Nubia were part of his program of economic development and increased governmental control, even altering the administrative bases of the chief Egyptian officials. A newly founded fortified city at Faras, incorporating the remains of an earlier Middle Kingdom fortress, appears to have represented the major base of pharaonic power during the reign of Tutankhamun, replacing Aniba as the seat of the viceroy of Nubia and the deputy of Wawat.[106] In addition to its administrative importance, Faras, whose ancient name was Neb-kheperu-re Sehetp-netcheru (Nebkheperure [Tutankhamun] is the pacifier of the Gods), housed a cult of the deified pharaoh Tutankhamun.[107] The cult of Tutankhamun at Faras recognized the pharaoh as a manifestation of the local form of Amun; one particularly eloquent stela of the Nubian viceroy Huy from Karnak Temple preserves a hymn to the deified Tutankhamun.[108]

A number of features made Faras a desirable site for the base of operations for Tutankhamun's Nubian administration, but its primary strategic importance was its connection to a number of far-reaching desert roads. Although Faras was north of the major waterway obstacle of the Second Cataract, an eastern desert track leading south from Faras connected the city with points as far away as Kurgus. Interestingly, Faras was near to Wadi Halfa, the starting point for the cross-desert railroad to Abu Hamed, next to Kurgus, constructed by the British forces during the Mahdist wars at the end of the nineteenth century;[109] the British railroad likely followed nearly the same track used by the Nubian administration of Tutankh-amun. From the west, two separate tracks led from Faras into the oases of Dunqul and Kurkur, the latter of which was the intersection of further roads leading to Aswan and Thebes; other routes led into small Nubian oases such as Selima. The existence of these routes and evidence of their use in pharaonic times indicate that Faras was a dynamic hub of land- and river-based traffic.

The Tutankhamun Stela from Kurkur Oasis

In March 1997, members of the modern Egyptian army stationed at an outpost near Kurkur Oasis discovered a stela with a unique text (see figure 18).[110] This monument sheds unexpected light on the border patrols of Lower Nubia, underscores the importance of Faras and its extensive net-work of desert roads during the reign of Tutankhamun, provides a glimpse of the somewhat surprising functions and importance of a modest Nubian patrolman, and highlights an otherwise little-known corner of Nubian administration—the frontier secret service. The text records a rebuke by the deputy of Wawat, Penniut, to an unnamed Medjoy patrolman who has failed to receive a seal on time; the text even gives the Medjoy's reply to this rebuke and his profession of loyalty to the pharaoh.

Below the offering scene, which depicts Tutankhamun presenting in-cense to the ram-headed god Khnum, two figures flank several columns of text. On the right side, in a flounced kilt typical of high Egyptian officials of the late Eighteenth Dynasty, is a man named Penniut, who possessed several important titles: overseer of the granary, chief in Duatneferet (pos-sibly the ancient Egyptian name for Kurkur Oasis), and deputy of Wawat. Penniut is one of the officials present at the promotion of Huy to viceroy, but when artists were decorating Huy's tomb, Penniut was only the deputy commander of the fortress of Faras, apparently a stage in his career prior to attaining the rank he possesses on the Kurkur stela. Penniut and Huy were both stationed at Faras, and they probably communicated fre-quently—Penniut even quotes Huy in his speech recorded on the stela.

Penniut has his right arm raised in a gesture of official address; the man to whom he speaks is a Nubian soldier, a Medjoy patrolman, in the lower left corner of the stela. The Nubian holds a bow in his right hand, and his left hand is raised to his mouth in a gesture of speech; his body is slightly bent, in a deferential bow. The bulk of the inscription on the stela records Penniut's address to the Medjoy and the latter's response. The text interestingly reflects spoken idiom rather than the more formal language

Figure 18. Kurkur Stela of Tutankhamun. Photo by C. Manassa.

typically found in hieroglyphic texts. Penniut reprimands the Medjoy patrolman for not coming in a timely fashion to receive an official seal and concludes with a not very subtle threat to the policeman:

> The fortress commander Penniut, as he speaks to the Medjoy who guides on the western wall: "What is the meaning of your not coming to show the way on the wall of Pharaoh, may he live, be prosperous, and healthy, since yesterday? You did not come to take the seal. Do you not know the advice of the King's Son (of Kush) Huy, by way of properly establishing the wall of pharaoh? 'Nay, put Pharaoh, may he live, be prosperous, and healthy, in your heart or you will die!'"

The Medjoy responds to his superior's criticism with an overview of his daily duties. The Medjoy says:

> "How great are they, the four *iteru* of travel which I make daily; five times going up (the mountain), five times going down (the mountain); so do not let me be replaced by another!"

The Medjoy describes his daily routine as a journey of four *iteru*, approximately 42 kilometers, a reasonable although slightly long distance for a small group of lightly armed men to cover in a day.[111] A larger group of people encumbered by draft animals would probably not achieve a rate of more than 25 kilometers per day, stopping in the evening. This suggests that the Medjoy patrol is not simply escorting caravans, but is part of a fast-moving series of patrols together perhaps covering all the borders of Egyptian Nubia, about which the Kurkur stela provides some of the only specific evidence.

If the Nubian soldier achieved an average speed of 2.5 miles per hour in the wadis and hills of Kurkur, the Medjoy would be on the move between 8.5 and 10 hours each day of his patrol. The fact that he refers to "ascending and descending" five times each day indicates that his patrol included Kurkur Oasis, which is in a depression surrounded by an escarpment. If the Medjoy were indeed covering on foot the approximately 26 miles each day, climbing steep hills, the Medjoy of Tutankhamun's Kurkur stela would certainly have reason for fatigue. Although on the stela he does not appear with a mount, the Medjoy may have belonged to a mounted patrol. Mounted Nubian patrolmen, at least some operating in desert areas, are attested for the New Kingdom, and the Medjoy of the Kurkur stela may have belonged to such a group for whom the 26 miles a day would be somewhat less taxing.

Although Kurkur lay along a track that led to Aswan, and was relatively close to that city, the Kurkur stela implies that the small oasis was one of the most distant outposts of the military administration centered at Faras. In the stela text, Penniut refers to the "wall of Pharaoh," most likely a system of outposts and patrol roads, which certainly incorporated Kurkur Oasis. Archaeological investigations of Kurkur, however, have as yet revealed no extensive remains or architecture, aside from a few dry stone huts and walls, and certainly no fortress. At no time need we expect that Kurkur, or any other of the smaller Nubian oases, possessed massive fortifications.[112] The Egyptian forces may have deemed small zeribas of brushwood and camel thorn to be sufficient protection, enabling the Egyptians to have fortified Kurkur sufficiently without leaving any obvious traces visible today. Perhaps military thinkers in ancient Egypt also had a philosophical opposition to large defensive works in many hinterland sites, concurring with some nineteenth-century strategists in the belief that such structures might contribute to the psychological advantage of the enemy.[113] During the Mahdist Wars of the late nineteenth century, the British employed local Ababde tribesmen to garrison Kurkur Oasis without constructing massive fortifications,[114] much like the ancient Medjoy during the time of Tutankhamun.

The Kurkur stela also reveals something of the chain of command of military patrols in New Kingdom Nubia. The viceroy of Nubia derives his authority directly from the pharaoh, and in turn transfers some of that authority to the deputies of Wawat and Kush. As deputy of Wawat, Penniut appears to be in charge of some sort of "changing of the guard" ceremony at Kurkur Oasis in which a Medjoy patrolman apparently receives a seal directly from a deputy of the viceroy of Nubia. One might initially find Penniut's direct concern with an apparently low-level patrolmen somewhat extraordinary. Penniut would more reasonably be annoyed, however, if his own journey to Kurkur Oasis for the transfer of the official seal was not promptly reciprocated by the officer he went to meet. Perhaps the Medjoy on the stela was—prior to his tardiness—a commander of the Medjoy auxiliaries at Kurkur Oasis and the surrounding region.

If one postulates that periodically the deputy of Wawat met particular patrol officers at border outposts, and delivered to them a seal in an official ceremony, a possible parallel appears from the Roman frontier intelligence system. The *beneficiarii consularis* were military veterans appointed to border stations, carrying out and overseeing surveillance and economic functions of frontier outposts as direct representatives of local governors.[115] At least on the northwestern marches of the empire, the beneficiarii were particularly associated with military roads. As emblems of their office, they carried a ceremonial lance, perhaps comparable to the seal our Medjoy was annoyingly late to receive. If this analogy is correct, then

Tutankhamun's Kurkur stela is one piece of evidence suggesting that New Kingdom Egypt and Nubia had a frontier surveillance system comparable to that of the Roman Empire. Along with the regular garrisons of border outposts and the patrols of the roads thereof, reporting to local commanders who report to district commanders who eventually report to the military governors, the viceroys of Nubia apparently had direct representatives in the frontier garrisons and patrols.

The administration of Nubia during the Amarna Period relied not only on the physical remains of the Middle Kingdom's system of fortifications but also on the extended borders that resulted from successful campaigns in the early Eighteenth Dynasty. Egyptian civil government was transplanted to a not wholly unfamiliar territory and actively recruited rulers from the native population. This vibrant interplay of Egypt and Nubia is reflected in the equally vibrant paintings in the tomb of Huy that portray Tutankhamun's peaceful and especially profitable rule over Nubia. The elaborate network of desert outposts that connected the cities founded by Akhenaten and Tutankhamun with the rest of Nubia and points beyond likewise functioned effectively, as demonstrated by the unique stela of Penniut and a Medjoy patrolman.

Nubian Wars of the Amarna Period

Although early Eighteenth Dynasty rulers suppressed the rebellion of still militant Kushite rulers and consolidated new administrative divisions in Nubia, all was not entirely peaceful in Nubia for the remainder of the Eighteenth Dynasty. As New Kingdom administration took hold in Nubia, much of the riverine population entered more fully into the cycle of pharaonic administrative life; groups on the fringes of the Nubian province, however, especially those inhabiting the desert regions beyond the Third Cataract, were particularly restive. The Nubian conflicts of the late Eighteenth Dynasty at first appear to have been little more than police actions or relatively safe demonstrations of pharaonic power. Some of these southern foes may, however, have been more dangerous than their relatively small numbers might indicate.

In fact, the enormous significance of the mineral wealth of Nubia and the great cultic importance of many of the products coming from and passing through Nubia meant that *any* group, no matter how small, that might disrupt commerce between Egypt and Nubia could very well present a potentially enormous threat far out of proportion to the actual size of the enemy force. Nineteenth-century "small wars" and many twentieth- and twenty-first-century conflicts similarly present opponents whose significance

lies not in their numbers or military prowess but rather in the simple economic and even psychological disaster they might inflict if their designs
proceed unhindered.

Nubian War of Akhenaten

An example of the colonial wars fought in Nubia during the Amarna
Period—and the often severe consequences for Egypt's enemies—occurred
during the reign of Akhenaten.[116] A stela set up by the viceroy of Kush
Djehutymose at Buhen and a nearly identical text at Amada, both quite
damaged, record a war sparked by the rebellion of the Akuyati tribe.[117]
The date of the conflict is also damaged, but the traces of the year date
suggest that the events occurred during year twelve of Akhenaten's reign.[118]
According to the fragmentary stelae, a messenger reported directly to
Akhenaten (probably in Akhet-aten) that troubles were brewing in Nubia.
Rather than donning his armor and seizing his bow and scimitar, like so
many of his illustrious ancestors, Akhenaten chose to delegate the con-
duct of a punitive expedition to his viceroy Djehutymose.

Charged with such an important expedition, Djehutymose would have
quickly called up the available Egyptian forces and the crucial Nubian
auxiliaries and equipped them for a desert expedition. As part of Djehutymose's planning for imminent military action, he would have received aid
from intelligence officers, such as the Medjoy patrolmen who traversed
such great distances over desert tracks. Careful preparation was essential,
since the Akuyati may have tried to use the harsh desert environment to
their advantage—a damaged portion of the text suggests that the Akuyati
retreated north of the wells of the mining region. Perhaps as the Sudanese
"Mahdi" would more successfully attempt in the late nineteenth century
with the Egyptian force commanded by the retired British general Hicks,
the Akuyati may have hoped to lure a larger and more unwieldy Egyptian
force into the desert in which the rebellious ones were at home. The strategy of the Akuyati failed in the face of Djehutymose's persistence and
organization.

The text gives no indication why the Nubians did not continue their
desert retreat or whether it was their choice to give battle at the wells.
Similarly, we can only guess at the precise tactics used by the opposing
forces, but the Egyptian documents leave no ambiguity as to the result of
the battle: Djehutymose carried off 145 live captives, including 12 children, with a total of 225 enemy casualties; additional booty, probably 361
head of cattle, also is recorded.[119] Considering the small population numbers supported by the Nubian desert, and in comparison with the casualty

numbers of more celebrated military conflicts, Akhenaten's combat against the Akuyati certainly qualifies as a colonial "small war."[120]

While the plunder list might appear to be the typical result of a battle against a nomadic population, the treatment of the prisoners by Akhenaten is anything but normal. Both texts record that some of the captured Akuyati tribesmen were "placed atop a stake," the Egyptian idiom for impalement. Unlike the Assyrians, the ancient Egyptians rarely employed the cruel practice of impalement. Merneptah (1213–1203 b.c.e.) is the only other pharaoh whom we know to have meted out this horrific punishment in a military context, following the invasion of Egypt by allied Libyan and Nubian armies.[121] Otherwise, impalement is reserved as a punishment for tomb robbery. The evidence is not sufficient to indicate whether the stakes were used to display already deceased enemies or whether the victims were still alive when impaled. Either way, the practice would serve to display the punishment and act as a deterrent for others who might share the sentiments of the impaled.

Interestingly, ancient Egyptian texts from later in the New Kingdom might explain why Akhenaten used such extreme measures against the Akuyati nomads. According to the Kuban stela from the reign of Ramesses II, the southern land of Akuta contained "much gold";[122] since Kuban is the Nile terminus of the main desert road leading to the gold-mining region in the Wadi Allaqi and considering the further content of the stela, Akuta appears to refer to the Wadi Allaqi itself, formerly one of the richest gold-mining areas in northeastern Africa.[123] The similarity of the two toponymns Akuyati and Akuta suggests that they may represent two attempts to write the same Nubian toponym in Egyptian script. If Akuyati and Akuta were indeed synonymous, then the troublesome tribe was near the precious gold mines, which would have provided Akhenaton with a motivation for supplying a particularly harsh and grisly warning to any who might attempt to tamper in any way with Egypt's gold supply. Impalement would have had a profound psychological effect even on those who did not join the Akuyati revolt, and the fragmentary stelae suggest that the gruesome display produced the desired result. The stelae preserve part of a speech of loyalty delivered by Nubian rulers who vow to strip their own lands for the pharaoh, presumably so he will not come and do it for them, and perhaps engage in impalement as a by-product.

Nubian War of Tutankhamun

The wealth of treasure buried in the tomb of Tutankhamun far overshadows the poorly attested historical events of the reign of Tutankhamun.

Ironically, the numerous objects in Tutankhamun's tomb adorned with images of defeated enemies may have contributed through their wealth of heraldic imagery to the view of Tutankhamun as a relatively pacific ruler. The plethora of scenes of royal domination of foreigners in such standardized settings contributed to the general impression of Tutankhamun as the politically ephemeral and militarily insignificant "boy-king." Nearly all items that might at some point find themselves under the pharaoh's feet, such as his sandals and footstools, are decorated with depictions of bound Libyans, Asiatics, and Nubians, so that he might symbolically crush his enemies and enact a phrase ubiquitous in Egyptian texts—"Your enemies are beneath your two soles." Even the curved tops of some of Tutankhamun's walking sticks are transformed into elaborately carved images of defeated enemies whose backs have been broken beneath the strong arm of the pharaoh.[124]

One object from the tomb of Tutankhamun—a small painted box—presents a juxtaposition of martial and hunting images.[125] The overall composition of the Nubian and Asiatic war scenes (see figure 1) on the long sides of the box is virtually identical to the two hunting scenes on the lid, and to the Egyptians, both hunting and warfare represented the triumph of order over the forces of chaos.[126] No text on the painted box mentions a date or a specific historical event; rather each tableau transforms this small item of furniture, which once contained Tutankhamun's clothing (possibly for battle), into a potent statement of pharaonic authority over the entire cosmos. Although the painted box and indeed all other objects depicting enemies from the tomb of Tutankhamun are devoid of specific historical information because their primary purpose was symbolic, one should not then assume that the Egyptian army fought no battles during Tutankhamun's reign.

Tutankhamun erected, decorated, and restored many monuments in ancient Thebes, but no fully preserved battle scenes survive from his reign. In the Colonnade Hall at Luxor Temple a series of scenes carved during the reign of Tutankhamun, and later usurped by Horemhab (and completed under Seti I), depict the elaborate celebration of the ancient Egyptian festival of Opet (see further in "Religious Functions of the Military" in chapter 6). In the depictions of that festival celebration, Nubians appear not as vanquished enemies but rather as celebrants. A very different representation of Nubians, however, appears in reliefs that once adorned a temple called "Nebkheperure [Tutankhamun] in Thebes." Although this temple was dismantled in antiquity and its blocks reused in other buildings, several fragments of a Nubian battle narrative from the Tutankhamun temple have emerged in diverse locations.[127]

The only block showing the battle in progress contains portions of two registers. In the upper register, a small-scale representation of a group of Egyptian infantry follows the enormous wheel of the king's much-larger-scale chariot, and completes the destruction of a Nubian enemy crushed beneath that wheel by removing a hand for the official tally of casualties.[128] In the lower register, another group of infantry marches in formation behind two men in a chariot; although the chariot itself is not preserved, the height and distinctive tasseled helmets of the vehicles' occupants mark them as charioteers.[129] Between the two groups of infantry is a hieroglyphic text recording the speech of the soldiers:

> [The Nubians collapsed] in the blink of an eye,
> their chiefs having succumbed to the slaughter whenever they violate our
> boundaries! His Majesty, may he live, be prosperous, and healthy [. . .].

In another small fragment, Asiatic and Nubian auxiliaries march along singing "Victory Be to the Ruler!" These foreign auxiliaries probably belong in the same scene as two further blocks, which show the triumphant return of the army, including two naval vessels that probably carried the majority of the plunder. A large-scale figure of Tutankhamun, of whom only his foot survives, holds the ropes of several groups of tortuously bound Nubian captives, whose contortions mimic those of sacrificial birds.[130] Behind the prisoners, a trumpeter turns back to blast a triumphant note as a series of standard-bearers and infantrymen—each bearing shield, khepesh-sword, and spear—recite a martial hymn recorded in the hieroglyphic text:

> Hymn of Victory which they sing:
> "You are like Montu, you are like Montu, O Ruler!
> You are like Montu! You are like Montu in the midst of your army,
>   the gods being the protection of your limbs,
>   your attack having succeeded against wretched Kush!"[131]

Although one can almost hear the piercing trumpet blasts and shouting voices of the Egyptian soldiers, the vivid scenes of Tutankhamun's Nubian war fail to provide specific geographic information. However, combined with the small snapshot of border activity in the Kurkur stela and another monument depicting the military exploits of the pharaoh Horemhab, the seemingly disparate pieces of evidence may actually reveal the location of Tutankhamun's activity in Nubia. Specifically, Tutankhamun's Nubian campaign may have involved an advance through the oasis of Kurkur, a proposition that finds support in scenes of a Nubian war in a small rock-cut temple at Gebel Silsila commissioned by Tutankhamun's general Horemhab, who later became pharaoh of Egypt. The Nubian war of

Horemhab was a conflict in which Horemhab was general and Tutankh-amun was pharaoh, this latter, unfortunate situation quietly overlooked in Horemhab's Nubian scenes in his monument at Gebel Silsila. Similarly, the scenes of Nubian war on the painted box from the tomb of Tutankha-mun and from the temple "Nebkheperure in Thebes" may simply repre-sent Tutankhamun symbolically taking personal, pharaonic credit for the conduct of a Nubian campaign actually led by Horemhab.

At Gebel Silsila, an enormous quarry approximately 65 kilometers north of Aswan, the Nile cuts through sandstone cliffs. There, at ancient Khenu, the Eastern and Western deserts reach the very edge of the Nile. Even at low ebb, the river touched the rocks of the desert margins, as it did else-where only during the height of the inundation. Appropriate to a Nilotic location in constant flood, Gebel Silsila was a site of important offerings to Hapi, the deified Nile inundation. Riverine festivals were popular cele-brations in Egypt, associated as they often were with the rising of the flooding Nile and the coming of the New Year. During such festivals, the ancient Egyptians would erect temporary booths and toast the occasion by drinking to the health of the gods and goddesses involved. Occasionally the Egyptians perpetuated the lives of their temporary festival structures, and at Gebel Silsila and elsewhere, such as Qasr Ibrim in Nubia, the river-ine shrines, where geology allowed, became rock-cut shrines.[132]

The largest of these chapels at Gebel Silsila, on the western bank of the Nile, is a *speos*, a T-shaped rock-cut temple with a wide transverse hall in front and an inner sanctuary leading back to an engaged statue group in the far wall. The chapel dates from the reign of Horemhab, who repre-sents himself in Nubian triumph scenes at the south end of the west wall of the transverse hall, covering unfortunately but a small portion of the wall decoration (see figure 19).[133] In the upper left portion of the scene, Horemhab travels in an elaborate sedan chair carried by soldiers. Before him are fettered Nubian prisoners, labeled as the "chiefs of Kush." Eight columns of hieroglyphic text summarize the scene:

> The good god (the pharaoh) has returned,
>> having triumphed over the chiefs of all the foreign lands.
> His bow is in his grasp like the Lord of Thebes (the war god Montu).
> Victorious king, powerful of might, who conquered the chiefs of wretched
> Kush. The King of Upper and Lower Egypt, Djeserkheperure-setepenre,
>> bodily son of Re, whom he loves, Horemhab,
>> beloved of Amun, may he be given life!
> Journey that the king made from the land of Kush,
>> bearing the plunder that his strong arm made, as his father, Amun, had
>> commanded to him.

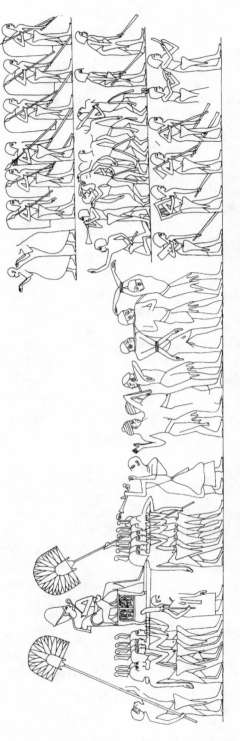

Figure 19. Horemhab's Nubian victory scenes from Gebel Silsila. On the left, Egyptian troops carry the triumphant Horemhab in his litter—adorned with the regal lion. Before him, the contorted positions of the bound arms of the Nubian prisoners is intended to mimic the pinioned wings of sacrificial birds. On the right, Egyptian and Nubian auxiliaries perform a leaping dance, while their comrades carry weapons and field equipment. After Wreszinski, *Atlas II*, pl. 162.

At the far right are three registers of Egyptian infantry; in the middle register, a trumpeter plays while Nubian auxiliaries perform a leaping war dance.[134] Beneath Horemhab's procession and the celebrating soldiers are further depictions of Nubian prisoners, some led by Egyptian soldiers; the hieroglyphic text above the Nubians records their lament and praise of the ruler:

> Greetings to you, king of Egypt,
>   solar god for the Nine Bows!
> Your great reputation is in the land of Kush,
>   your war cry in all of their places!
> It is your power, O good ruler,
>   which has made the foreign lands into heaps of corpses.
> The pharaoh is the light [of the world]!

As this dramatic speech indicates, Horemhab, pharaoh for Egypt, was the sun god for the rest of the benighted world.[135] Although this speech seems flowery and theologically oriented, Nubian prisoners may have made such a pronouncement as part of a formal surrender ceremony. A more informal speech appears in the lower left corner of the scene, where a Nubian runs while admonishing his compatriots for ever having roused the pharaoh's anger:

> O, children, overgrown in your minds—you have [surely] not yet forgotten that one already said to you: "Do not go out, for the lion has already entered into Kush."

Gebel Silsila is north of the traditional Egyptian border at Aswan, leading to suggestions that Horemhab's Nubian war scenes might simply be symbolic. However, earlier Egyptian military strikes into Nubia traveled desert routes originating in the area around Gebel Silsila.[136] These Western Desert tracks, passing through the small oases of Kurkur and Dunqul, provided a "back door" into points all along the Nubian Nile. Gebel Silsila was an appropriate place for Horemhab to commemorate his Nubian victory, since it might have been at the end of the road he used to return to Egypt.

If this is an accurate reconstruction, the Kurkur stela of Tutankhamun, in which Penniut chastises a Medjoy patrolmen for his late arrival to receive the official seal, is less of an oddity than it might seem. Trouble on the western fringes of Lower Nubia at some area accessed by routes through Kurkur Oasis would certainly have prompted a more than usual concern over the vigilance and diligence of the desert patrolmen in Nubia. The records of the Nubian campaign of Horemhab in the Gebel Silsila shrine suggest that Tutankhamun's campaign may have led across the desert just west of Aswan, being concerned with the western border of Lower Nubia. And despite the fact that both Tutankhamun and Horemhab attempted to take credit for each other's actions, careful examination of the surviving monuments enables us to set the record straight. A single Nubian war was fought during the short reign of the pharaoh Tutankhamun, during which the Egyptian army was almost certainly commanded by the general and future pharaoh Horemhab. Although the record for Tutankhamun's Nubian war is incomplete, the surviving evidence demonstrates that the "tragic boy king" was more energetic than most have supposed in securing the southern borders of Egypt—at least through policy, if not in person.

The Spoils of Battle: Durbars of Akhenaten and Tutankhamun

For the ancient Egyptians, every stage of a war possessed its own appropriate ritual activity. Temple reliefs portray a god—typically Amun—signaling divine justification for a campaign by handing a scimitar to the pharaoh;[137] the army marched beneath the banners and ribbons of divine standards as they set out for war,[138] and military texts record that before a battle a deity could appear to the pharaoh in a dream.[139] During the battle, the pharaoh manifested his divinely inspired strength by smiting the enemies with the divinely granted scimitar. After vanquishing Egypt's foes, the pharaoh rewarded his loyal army, and presented the enemy prisoners and plunder to the same gods who initially sanctioned the war. While most of this cycle of rituals could be enacted only during times of actual military conflict, the presentation of awards and commendations could occur whenever the pharaoh desired. An even greater, international event related to warfare, but not wholly dependent on actual military conflict, was the presentation of foreign tribute. Following the reign of Thutmose III and the eventual peace with Egypt's primary enemy, Mitanni, pharaohs such as Amunhotep II and Thutmose IV participated in fewer major campaigns, and turned to new venues in which to express their hegemony over the world.

Amunhotep II in particular became a "sporting king," devoting many of his monuments to the glorification of his skills in archery, equestrian pursuits, and other feats of physical prowess. His heroic actions at home were complemented by relatively few military campaigns abroad,[140] so Amunhotep II instead fostered an extended, ritualistic presentation of foreign tribute, often focused primarily on Nubia and the lands to the south. Private tombs in the Theban necropolis record many such presentations of tribute during the middle of the Eighteenth Dynasty.[141] During the reign of Akhenaten, the delivery of tribute attained its most intricate and sophisticated expression in a giant celebration that involved not only Nubia but also every corner of the known world; Tutankhamun continued his father's tradition, albeit on a slightly smaller scale.

For these festival presentations of tribute, Egyptologists have employed the Indian term durbar, and the modern use of a term from a land and a time far removed from Egypt is actually far more redolent of the true significance of the Egyptian ritual celebration than many might suppose. The durbar, as the modern West knows the term, derives from the Anglo-Indian Empire and refers to the ornate political ceremonies and presentations of tribute held before native princes and colonial officials.[142] The durbar in British India depicted in an actual ritual the desired political unity of the disparate districts and their semiautonomous rulers as elements of a single entity: India; the use of a formal ritualized presentation of tribute also assisted in the creation of the political fiction that India was a pendant element in the dual Anglo-Indian Empire.

Similarly, the Egyptian southern durbar reflected not only the internal unity of Nubia as an Egyptian dependency, but also the importance Nubia possessed as a mirror of Egypt. The ritual presentation of gold and other wealth of the south became incorporated within the festival cycle of the pharaonic realm and the occasion for the appointment of officials, both Egyptian and Nubian, who served in the Nubian administration. The durbar of Akhenaten, and most likely that of Tutankhamun, followed directly upon military success in Nubia, enabling real prisoners of war to be incorporated into the ceremony. These rituals, never before properly explained,[143] are crucial to understanding the Egyptian ideology of imperialism as it was applied to Nubia. Placed within their proper historical and religious contexts, the durbars also offer insights into the meaning of military history for the ancient Egyptians.

Akhenaten's great reception of foreign tribute in year twelve of his reign was recorded in two similar depictions in the tombs of the officials Meryre (II) and Huya in the necropolis of Akhet-aten (for an artist's reconstruction of the event, see the frontispiece).[144] In the center of the scene, Akhenaten and Nefertiti sit atop a raised throne-platform beneath an elaborate canopy topped with a frieze of cobras, representatives of the sun's rays.[145] Indeed, the rays from the Aten at the top of the scene pierce the ceiling of the canopy and touch the crowns of the pharaoh and his queen. Beneath the great royal throne are units of Egyptian infantry who guard the royal carrying chairs and chariots. Detailed representations of foreigners and their tribute fill the remaining space of the relief. Some of the foreigners bringing gifts to Akhenaten and Nefertiti include Aegean islanders bearing metal vessels, Puntites offering incense, Libyans with ostrich feathers and eggs, western Asiatics bringing horses and chariots, and Nubians presenting gold.

The great array of diplomats, tribute bearers, and prisoners presenting themselves before Akhenaten and Nefertiti bears a straightforward description in the accompanying hieroglyphic text:

> Appearance of the King of Upper and Lower Egypt and the wife of the king upon the great throne of electrum in order to receive the tribute of Syria and Kush, the West and the East, all foreign lands assembled on one occasion, even the islands in the midst of the sea, conducting presents to the king.[146]

Although Akhenaten's durbar included representatives of the entire Egyptian cosmos, his universalistic festival appears to have been more directly the expanded, official celebration of his year-twelve Nubian campaign, which took place a mere seventy-eight days prior to the durbar.[147] The relationship between the Nubian war and the durbar is suggested not only by their closeness in time, but also by the inclusion of a row of bound Nubian prisoners who are dragged before Akhenaten and Nefertiti in the tribute scenes. While one might suggest that the bound Nubians are slaves included in the tribute, they wear feathers—Nubian military insignia. The more detailed representations of similarly fettered Nubians in the tomb of Huy provide further evidence that the bound Nubians in the durbar scenes are indeed captured rebels and not slaves.

The durbar of Akhenaten was a ritual celebration of his successful Nubian campaign and expressed not only Egyptian domination and superiority over foreign lands but also reconfirmed the king's role as the divine ruler of Egypt. One of the most important religious roles of the Egyptian pharaoh was maintenance of the temples throughout Egypt and the performance of rituals that occurred each day within them. For the world to continue to exist, particularly the daily rising and setting of the sun, these rituals must be performed properly. The perpetuation of the world and the solar cycle depended on Egypt's domination of hostile, foreign groups. Furthermore, in the context of Egyptian theology, the foreigners at Akhenaten's durbar represent all the people illumined by the sun's rays, not only in Egypt but also throughout the world.[148] When foreigners from all corners of the Egyptian cosmos bow to Akhenaten and present him with their tribute, Akhenaten is transformed into the sun god himself.[149]

Like his father, Akhenaten, Tutankhamun presided over the presentation of royal tribute in the guise of the solar deity. Neither the date of

Tutankhamun's southern durbar nor the date of his Nubian war is known, and a connection between the two events is difficult to demonstrate. Fortunately, though, the vivid paintings from the tomb of the viceroy Huy record fascinating details that allow us to suggest that Tutankhamun celebrated his Nubian victory with a ritualized presentation of foreign tribute.

At least once in his career, the viceroy Huy returned to Thebes to present the treasures of Nubia to Tutankhamun. Scenes in Huy's tomb in Western Thebes show elaborate preparations and the gathering of goods from all over Nubia, as well as their careful loading onto cargo ships. After arriving safely in Thebes, Huy appears before his pharaoh Tutankhamun, who, seated on a throne with an elaborate canopy, wears a blue crown and holds the crook and flail in his left hand and the sign of life in his right. As the master of festivities, Huy presents the pharaoh with an ostrich feather fan, the special insignia of Huy's office, "fan-bearer on the right side of the king." All the treasures of Nubia are arrayed before the pharaoh—piles of gold, precious stones, ivory, ebony, leopard skins, elaborately wrought gold vessels showing entire Nubian landscapes,[150] furniture, a chariot of exquisite workmanship, weapons, and even a giraffe.

That the objects appearing in the scenes in the tomb of Huy are not all imaginary or simply generic, one should note the depictions of six shields. Three appear to be rather simply decorated, with cowhide coverings: two black and white, one red and white, all presumably with central metal bosses. The other three are more elaborate (see figure 20). One has a leopard skin covering with a central rectangular panel, containing two disk-topped cartouches, probably once bearing the names of Tutankhamun. The final two shields depicted in the tomb of Huy show Tutankhamun in human form spearing an enemy and as a divine ram-headed sphinx trampling two other foreigners.[151] Amazingly, three elaborate shields, nearly identical to those depicted in the tomb of Huy, were discovered in the tomb of Tutankhamun (see figures 12 and 13). Cheetah skin rather than leopard skin still adorns the shield with Tutankhamun's twin cartouches, and the elaborate wooden shields even now depict Tutankhamun triumphant over Egypt's enemies.

The tremendous natural wealth of Nubia displayed before Tutankhamun in the tomb of Huy is also accompanied by important human resources. Egyptian officials of the colonial administration are present, as well as the tribal rulers of Wawat and Kush, arrayed in elaborate costumes incorporating Egyptian and traditional Nubian elements. Some of the rulers also bring their sons, wearing almost entirely Egyptian clothing—they are presumably to be raised in the Egyptian court and eventually succeed their fathers as Nubian princes. A Nubian princess, bedecked in

Figure 20. Tomb of Huy, painted depiction of three shields included in the Nubian tribute presented to Tutankhamun. On the far left, a leopard hide shield bears twin cartouches. The center shield depicts Tutankhamun as a ram-headed sphinx trampling two Nubian enemies, while the final shield shows Tutankhamun—this time in his human manifestation—spearing another Nubian foe. After Davies, *Tomb of Huy*, pl. 24.

sumptuous jewelry and pleated gown, also arrives in style in a colorful chariot pulled by two cows; unfortunately, she is not labeled, but this princess may have become one of the young pharaoh's wives.

In fact, only one Nubian is labeled individually—in the upper register, one of the kneeling princes of Wawat is called "the ruler of Miam, Hekanefer." History has smiled on Hekanefer, for this is not our only evidence of his existence—during the Nubian salvage project prompted by the construction of the Aswan High Dam, Egyptologists discovered Hekanefer's tomb. This Nubian chief, who once stood in the presence of Tutankhamun, gives us a "southern" perspective on Egyptian colonialism. Another important aspect of the ancient Egyptian southern durbar required the presence of the Nubian chiefs and their Egyptian counterparts in the Nubian administration at the presentation of tribute: the confirmation of offices. This heretofore unrecognized aspect of the durbar is most apparent in a monument of Usersatet, the viceroy of Nubia during the reign of Amunhotep II (1427–1400 B.C.E.).

At Usersatet's shrine at Qasr Ibrim in Nubia, the viceroy records the durbar of Amunhotep I, which—like that of Tutankhamun—took place in Thebes.[152] In the scene, Amunhotep II sits beneath a canopy atop a dais, as does Tutankhamun in the tomb of Huy, and receives his Nubian

viceroy, who brings with him southern tribute. The inscriptions in Usersatet's shrine at Qasr Ibrim reveal that the true significance of the southern tribute is not just what products the viceroy has brought, or in what
quantities, but also the numbers of the Nubians who bring those items into
the royal presence. Another monument of Usersatet, which also depicts
the viceroy approaching the enthroned king, records advice the king dispensed to the viceroy—probably as part of the Nubian durbar of Amunhotep II—regarding the suitability of certain Nubians for holding administrative office.[153] Apparently the Nubian durbar was intimately related to
the organization and filling of the offices of the southern administration.

As the Nubian leaders presented Tutankhamun with gold, precious
stones, and other objects, some of which would ultimately be buried with
the pharaoh, those same leaders were reconfirmed in their offices or possibly promoted. The Nubians who wear Egyptian kilts along with their traditional wigs, gold earrings, and ostrich feathers are sharply distinguished
from a final yet significant part of Tutankhamun's durbar—five bound
Nubian men (see figure 21).[154] Based on their attire and fetters, these men
are not slaves presented as tribute, but rather captured Nubian rebel leaders. Each of the five men wears a kilt with a long forward sash typical of
Nubian military uniforms already by the time of the First Intermediate
Period, and has his hair adorned with an ostrich feather, a marker of high
tribal status as well as a military insignia. The first Nubian, presumably
the highest-ranking, wears an Egyptian-style linen kilt underneath his
sash, while the other four men wear short Nubian leather kilts.

If one compares these figures to those of the other unrestrained Nubians in the tomb of Huy, the major difference between these, aside from
their restraints, is that only one of the bound figures wears any sort of
Egyptian clothing. Based on the iconography of the images, we seem to
have a small band of Nubian rebel leaders, one perhaps partially Egyptianized. These rebels are clearly of some importance, since the same five men
appear elsewhere in the tomb of Huy, where they squat atop one of the
ships carrying tribute bound for Thebes. Their public display atop the boat
suggests that they might have been recognizable to Egyptians informed
about Nubian affairs. Careful attention to details of costume and compar-
isons with other scenes in the tomb of Huy thus provide evidence that the
southern durbar of Tutankhamun may have been part of the celebration of
his victories in Nubia.

The durbars of Akhenaten and Tutankhamun represent the ultimate
significance of military conflict for the ancient Egyptians—the triumph of
order over chaos. The ritual presentation of tribute from foreign groups
more specifically cast the Egyptian pharaoh in the role of the solar deity;

Figure 21. Tomb of Huy, five Nubian prisoners presented to the pharaoh Tutankhamun during the durbar. Two Nubian women carrying and leading their children follow the prisoners. After Davies, *Tomb of Huy*, pl. 30.

the subjugation of the foreign lands through which the sun traveled in turn maintains the solar cycle itself. On a more practical level, the durbar was a means of celebrating successful military campaigns and displaying captured prisoners. For Egypt's southern dependency, the Nubian durbar was a time for the confirmation of Egyptian and Nubian officials and a ritual, like the Anglo-Indian durbar, to symbolize the unity of the Nubian colony and its status as an extension of Egypt. When Akhenaten presided over the presentation of tribute from ambassadors of the known world and Tutankhamun received the homage of Hekanefer and the Nubian princes, all of these tributary groups affirmed their proper place in the newly extended and ordered cosmos.

The Nubian Experience of Colonization

From the time of the early Old Kingdom, Nubians entered into Egyptian service, primarily as soldiers, and during the civil wars of the First Intermediate Period, Nubian auxiliaries became an integral part of Egyptian political history. At colonies of Nubian soldiers, such as Gebelein, about 35 kilometers south of Luxor, the foreign troops set up modest personal monuments that attest to their adoption of many aspects of Egyptian culture, including their faith in an Egyptian-style afterlife.[155] Although most of the stelae show the Nubians in the appropriate Egyptian poses of receiving funerary offerings, many wear their traditional military costume, carry bows and arrows, and are represented with a darker skin tone. Other Nubian peculiarities, such as their preference for a breed of small, curly-tailed dog, are even adopted by members of the Egyptian population.

While most of the texts on the funerary monuments of the Nubian soldiers are stereotyped phrases, at least one early Middle Kingdom Nubian soldier, named Tjehemau, commissioned a fairly lengthy and literarily conceived autobiographical inscription that rivaled many contemporary Egyptian tomb inscriptions.[156] Tjehemau, whose name indicates his Nubian descent, is proud to refer to himself as "Nehesy"—the Nubian—in his description of his campaigns on behalf of the Egyptian pharaoh. Tjehemau presents himself as a champion of the Egyptian ruler who helps turn around a militarily unfortunate state of affairs for the benefit of Thebes:

> He (the king) traversed the entire land,
>   having decided to slaughter the Asiatics of Djaty.
> When it (the Asiatic force from Djaty) would approach,
>   Thebes was in flight.
> It was the Nubian (Tjehemau himself) who brought about the rally.

Tjehemau, like his compatriots at Gebelein and elsewhere in Egypt, seems perfectly comfortable with his dual Egyptian and Nubian identities and demonstrates that already by the beginning of the Middle Kingdom, Upper Egypt and Lower Nubia were home to a rather complex mixing of Egyptian and Nubian culture.[157]

At the same time that an Egyptianized Nubian commissioned a monument attesting to his loyalty and bravery as the pharaoh's soldier, generic Nubians also appear, as they had since the beginning of the pharaonic state, as members of the "Nine Bows."[158] These nine traditional enemies of Egypt typically appear in heraldic scenes emphasizing Egyptian dominion over foreign lands. Unlike the individualistic portrayal of Nubians on the Gebelein stelae and in Tjehemau's inscription, which one may classify as mimesis, scenes of royal power contain caricatured images of foreign enemies, an expression of topos. However, for the Egyptians this apparent stereotyping or topical representation is more accurately interpreted as a form of "hieroglyphic" representation, since the images of the bound enemies must visually contain clear signals to the viewer as to who he is seeing and what role that person plays within the Egyptian cosmos.

While particular Nubian groups remained enemies of Egypt and could represent a real threat to pharaonic interests, many of the traditional depictions of Nubians, especially those in which bound southern enemies appear alongside the other "Nine Bows," may be considered as a type of magical assurance of Egyptian domination over Nubia. Some of the earliest art in Egypt was intended to guarantee the triumph of the ordered world over chaos, be that chaos elements of the animal world or inimical humans.[159] By the time of the Middle Kingdom, the Egyptians employed an elaborate constellation of images and rituals to ensure the domination of Egypt and the ordered world over the forces of chaos, both internal and external.

The interplay of ritual activity and more mundane military activity in the Egyptian world led on at least one occasion to what might be considered human sacrifice—the so-called Mirgissa Deposit.[160] An intact assemblage from the Middle Kingdom fortress of Mirgissa contained the body of an executed man buried in a shallow pit along with a number of broken red clay vessels and several limestone and clay figurines of prisoners and associated images. The deposit appears to reveal the conjunction of three events: (1) a ritual called "breaking the red vessels," well attested in representations of Egyptian funerary practice; (2) an execration ritual in which certain individuals, both Egyptian and foreign, are ritually damned;[161] (3) finally, the actual execution of a human. By the time of the late Old Kingdom, the Egyptians had developed a magical rite in which the titles and names of enemies were written on clay (and perhaps even wax) images of bound human figures. These images were then broken or buried during the performance of some execratory ritual. At Mirgissa, ritual and reality appear to have coincided, and a human victim—decapitated and buried upside down—received the treatment meted out to ritual images. One cannot say whether the individual executed was simply chosen at random, the human sacrifice being the primary object of the ritual, or whether, as appears more likely, the deposit represents the religious significance of a ritualized execution that would have taken place on the basis of some military or legal precedent. Most likely the victim was a Nubian criminal or rebel leader whose execution took on greater cosmic meaning by the application of the execration rituals to his execution.

On the opposite side of the spectrum, Nubians could play important and positive roles in other Egyptian rituals. Nubians were key participants in the festivals celebrating the New Year, when the goddess Hathor returned to Egypt from her journeys southward in the winter (see "Religious Functions of the Military" in chapter 6). Without the dances and acclamations of the southerners, Hathor might not complete her journey back to Egypt, and disastrous results would ensue. No less important is the role the Nubians and their leaders fulfilled in the durbar festivals described above. The Nubian prince and ruler of Miam, Hekanefer, who participated in Tutankhamun's durbar, enables one better to understand how the Nubians themselves experienced such rituals.

Hekanefer, whose name means the "good ruler," was raised in the Egyptian palace, as his title, "child of the nursery," indicates, and might have formed close friendships with members of the royal family and other high officials in Egypt. His loyalist name expresses devotion to the Egyptian ruler and follows a pattern of Egyptian names adopted by foreigners entering Egyptian society. After his career as ruler of Miam, Hekanefer was buried in a decorated rock-cut tomb, decorated in Egyptian style, at Toshka.[162] Within his tomb, Hekanefer appears dressed solely in Egyptian clothing, and he was buried with tomb equipment resembling that of any high Egyptian official. One need not doubt that Hekanefer worshipped Egyptian deities and believed in an Egyptian afterlife.

Hekanefer's self-portrayal within his own tomb has been contrasted with his appearance in the tomb of the viceroy Huy, where he is attired as a Nubian chief;[163] claims have been made that he was forced to wear "barbaric" clothing for the presentation of tribute.[164] Hekanefer's mix of Egyptian and Nubian clothing, far from being "barbaric" in the eyes of the Egyptians, distinguishes him from other Egyptians and Nubians as an important Nubian ruler. There is no reason to believe that Hekanefer would not have been as comfortable moving between the two worlds as were earlier Nubians, such as the soldier Tjehemau. Within the context of standardized Egyptian tomb decoration Hekanefer is comfortable in Egyptian clothing; in the context of the durbar, since he is a Nubian ruler, he would be expected to appear as a Nubian and would be content if not proud to array himself in a combination of Egyptian and Nubian attire, to demonstrate both his local supremacy within the Nubian administration and his integral significance within the larger Egyptian world.

The pageantry of the Egyptian durbar appears to be similar in intent to the later British durbars and other ceremonies of the British Empire, during which local rulers were encouraged to wear their traditional attire. Indeed, while the creation of the Egyptian empire was driven by economic and political goals as well as ideology,[165] the expression and maintenance of Egyptian imperialism parallel the more symbolic approach of "ornamentalism,"[166] which for the British Empire bound "the British proconsular elite and the indigenous colonial elites into a unified, ranked, honorific body—'one vast interconnected world.'"[167] The elaborate dress of Egyptian and foreign participants at the universal durbar of Akhenaten and the Nubian durbar of Tutankhamun suggest that the Egyptians shared the "ornamentalist" approach to empire, which was particularly suited to the Egyp-

tians' own hieroglyphic worldview—the attire and attitude of the participants expressed their identity and thus their ritual role. Honors bestowed
during the Nubian durbar probably also linked Egyptian officials in Nubia
and Nubian rulers into a single unified hierarchy. As with later British
ceremonies, the Egyptians may have celebrated their durbars less for outward display to the general populace than to provide a venue in which
disparate titles could be interrelated, equated, and confirmed.

At the dawn of the Amarna Period, Akhenaten carried his religious iconoclasm deep into Nubia, destroying the images of Theban Amun and trans-
planting his own Atenist cult to his newly founded cities at Kawa and
Sesebi. Although he was much concerned with the affairs of western Asia,
described in the next chapter, he did deputize his viceroy Djehutymose to
launch at least one punitive expedition to protect the gold-mining region
of the Wadi Allaqi. This expedition resulted in the first of only two
attested examples of the ancient Egyptian use of impalement in a military
campaign. In addition to the so-called pacifist king's military mayhem
south of the First Cataract, Akhenaten enlarged upon earlier celebrations
involving the royal review of southern tribute and took on the role of the
sun god himself as he received homage from representatives of every foreign land.

Tutankhamun continued his father's grand festival displays, thereby
reinforcing the administrative and religious significance of Nubia; at the
same time he strengthened the southern borders, consolidated the Egyptian colonial administration, and further developed the religious role of
the Egyptian ruler as solar deity on earth in Nubia. At the newly constructed fortified city of Faras, the new home for the central administration
of Nubia, the viceroy Huy constructed a temple to the deified form of
Tutankhamun. A very few, but far-ranging, and even unique monuments
of his reign suggest that the adorations of the deified Tutankhamun was
well deserved, since he showed particular vigor in the deserts east and
west of the Nubian Nile Valley. Tutankhamun's Kurkur stela provides a
unique view of the border patrols in Egyptian Nubia and reveals what may
have been the complicated interrelationships of the upper and lower ech-
elons of Egyptian administration and military service in Nubia.

The reigns of Tutankhamun and Horemhab blur together to a certain
extent in Nubia, and the meager evidence for military activity under
Horemhab appears to be the result of a military campaign in Lower Nubia,
probably in the western fringes of the district, led by Horemhab as a general during the reign of Tutankhamun. The magnificence of the durbar

over which Huy presided also suggests that alongside his so-called return to religious orthodoxy, the reign of Tutankhamun should be recognized as a time of important consolidation of Egyptian power in Nubia and an increase in the efficiency and rigor of the Egyptian border administration. One of the shields from the tomb of Tutankhamun, perhaps a gift to the ruler at the time of Huy's durbar, may in many ways be an accurate representation of the reign of Tutankhamun in Nubia—the "boy-king" appeared in the south as a divine lion-bodied ruler trampling the enemies of Egypt and those who would violate the borders of Nubia and the desert hills of the far south.

5

✴∙✴∙✴∘✴∙◉∙✴∘✴∙✴∙✴

WRETCHED ASIATICS:
THE NORTHERN
EMPIRE

Why should messengers be made to stay constantly out in the sun and so die in the sun? If staying out in the sun means profit for the king, then let him (a messenger) stay out and let him die right there in the sun, (but) for the king himself there must be a profit. Or otherwise, why should they die in the sun?
— *The Amarna Letters*[1]

With these words, the Assyrian king Ashuruballit criticizes Akhenaten's treatment of his envoys. Ambassadors from throughout the ancient Near East may well have felt mistreated as they stood beneath the powerful rays of the Aten, while Akhenaten sat comfortably enthroned beneath the shade of a baldachin or leaned languidly over the cushioned balustrade of his ornately decorated Window of Glorious Appearances. For the Egyptian pharaoh, however, these outdoor ceremonies were important means of reinforcing his dominion over all foreign lands. Hieroglyphic texts on Akhenaten's throne and his footstool (compare figure 7) would probably have provided the Egyptian answer to any criticisms by Ashuruballit—"all foreign lands are united beneath the two soles of the king, like Re forever."

By the time of the Amarna Period, the patchwork of small city-states and great empires that made up the ancient Near East had long been connected to Egypt through trade routes. During the first fifteen hundred years of the pharaonic state, Egypt exerted only indirect influence on the politics of Syria-Palestine. After the end of the predynastic period, Egypt no longer showed serious interest in maintaining a permanent presence in southern Syria-Palestine,[2] but rather turned its attention to building close ties with the trading cities of the northern Levantine coast. As late as the Twelfth and Thirteenth dynasties, Egypt might engage in military razzias into Syria-Palestine, but did not appear to have concerned itself with direct, long-term control of local cities or groups.[3] The northern military expeditions of the Middle Kingdom were probably intended more to prevent the development of any locally unified political power in the area than to consolidate the area under Egyptian control.

Interactions between Egypt and its northern neighbors changed dramatically during the Second Intermediate Period, during which nearly half of the Egyptian Nile Valley was ruled by a foreign power. Toward the end of the Middle Kingdom, the increasingly weak Thirteenth Dynasty was unable to prevent a group of local military governors from seizing power in the northeastern Delta to form the Fourteenth Dynasty.[4] As a result of administrative weakness, pestilence, and population movements, the local Egyptian administrators and northern Levantine traders of the late Middle Kingdom Delta found themselves overseeing a population increasingly of a southern Palestinian origin. These factors combined to create the political power of the Hyksos, who filled the vacuum created by the collapse of the Thirteenth Dynasty and the weakening of the Fourteenth Dynasty.[5] This Hyksos Delta kingdom, the Fifteenth Dynasty, appears to have been a trade empire, aided by Egyptian officials and Egyptianized northern Levantine merchants,[6] augmented and supported by the large number of Syro-Palestinian "Bedouin" who had already infiltrated the depopulated eastern Delta. In the south, following the collapse of the Thirteenth Dynasty and the loss of the Memphite region, the independent Egyptian Seventeenth Dynasty ruled from Thebes and consolidated its power base in Upper Egypt.[7]

In 1552 B.C.E., the pharaoh Kamose led a successful naval attack against the Hyksos king Apepi, enabling Kamose to plunder and destroy the Hyksos merchant fleet at their capital city, Avaris.[8] Kamose's successor Ahmose attacked Avaris and drove the Hyksos forces entirely out of Egypt, finally besieging and ultimately vanquishing the last vestige of the Fifteenth Dynasty at Sharuhen. The expulsion of the Hyksos ultimately resulted in the powerful imperial state that was the Egyptian New Kingdom. The northern conquests of Thutmose I brought Egypt into contact with the far-flung states of the ancient Near East, many of which appear in Egyptian records for the first time during the Eighteenth Dynasty. While early Eighteenth Dynasty Egypt forged a broader and more directly controlled sphere of influence in Syria-Palestine, it engaged in a series of wars with its main rival, Mitanni. The eventual peaceful outcome of this century-long conflict occurred just in time for Egypt to meet the Hittites, who, beginning with the Amarna Period, would be Egypt's chief enemy for the century to come. To understand the machinations of Akhenaten and his successors, one must first examine the situation they inherited from their predecessors.

Prelude to Amarna: Early Eighteenth-Dynasty Wars with Mitanni

The military history of the Amarna Period involves a great many characters—expansive empires, proud kings, and a host of lesser rulers struggling to maintain power. The first of these characters is the kingdom of Mitanni, a complex state founded by the Hurrians, who spoke what was perhaps a distant relative of Northeast Caucasian languages.[9] Expanding out of the highlands of eastern Anatolia and playing their part in the cycle of outer "barbarians" preying on the settled populations of Mesopotamia, by 2200 B.C.E. the Hurrians had established a series of minor states in northwestern Mesopotamia. Early in the second millennium B.C.E., by virtue of their geographical location at the southern edge of the great steppes of central Asia, the Hurrians were the conduit for influence from Indo-European military societies passing into the ancient Near East. One of the most spectacular results of this influence was the arrival of the horse-drawn military chariot and an associated "knightly" social class, the *maryannu* (see pages 64–65).

By the beginning of the Eighteenth Dynasty the chief Hurrian state was Mitanni, located between the upper Tigris and Euphrates rivers, its capital at Washukanni, the exact location of which is still disputed.[10] By approximately 1500 B.C.E., Mitanni controlled not only its home territory along the upper Tigris and Euphrates rivers, but also a relatively large empire encompassing the southeastern corner of Asia Minor and all of northern Syria-Palestine south to the city of Kadesh. The Egyptian rulers of the late Seventeenth and early Eighteenth dynasties probably were aware of Mitanni, but seem to have shown little interest in any direct dealings with that Hurrian state, either warlike or pacific. The pharaoh Thutmose I changed that state of affairs. Although no evidence of any major Egyptian campaigning in Palestine north of Sharuhen for either Ahmose or Amunhotep I has survived,[11] and although no good evidence has thus far appeared for conflict in Syria-Palestine proper under Thutmose I, that true founder of the New Kingdom launched a preemptive strike against the heartland of Mitanni.

According to Ahmose, son of Ibana, Thutmose I reached the area of Naharin, a general designation for the riverine area of Mesopotamia and sometimes used synonymously with the term Mitanni; once there, Thutmose I learned of Mitanni preparations for a move into Syria-Palestine.[12] The Egyptian army appears to have struck preemptively, and according to another source, the ensuing battle occurred within the territory of Naharin. The pithy text of Ahmose, son of Ibana, suggests that the Mitanni forces were gathering near the border with Syria, intending an invasion into an area the Egyptians believed to be within their sphere of influence. A fragmentary inscription from the contemporary tomb of the horologist Amenemhat also refers to Thutmose I's campaign against Naharin, succinctly recording: "His Majesty traveled into this foreign land. It was retribution for [its] crime that he 'did' it (the country of Naharin)."[13] Following his military success against Mitanni, Thutmose I set up a victory stele on the Euphrates.[14]

How did Thutmose I manage this lightning strike against a mustering Mitanni force, and what did Mitanni plan? Thutmose I may well have slogged slowly north through Palestine, alternately accepting voluntary homage at one town, and slicing a path through forces that sought to bar his way at another. No evidence for such a scenario exists, however, and Ahmose, son of Ibana, to our everlasting thanks, was not shy in describing his bravery. Since we may suppose the warrior would have referred to at least some event in the campaign, a warlike progress by Thutmose I through Palestine is unlikely. Perhaps the local rulers, knowing of Mitanni preparations, welcomed Thutmose I and his force.[15] More likely, Thutmose was unconcerned with southern Syria-Palestine and simply mounted an amphibious operation, landing his force in a northern coastal town such as Byblos, a longtime ally of Egypt. Either way, Thutmose I, as in Nubia, set a wide mark for the Egyptian empire, and sought to identify future threats and neutralize them as far as possible from Egypt and its outer sphere of direct economic interest.

Just as in Egyptian art, where warfare and hunting are parallel means of expressing the extension of order over chaos,[16] so did Thutmose I mirror his warlike exploits in an equally novel and audacious feat of big-game hunting. In the land of Niye, on the Orontes River, Thutmose I hunted the now vanished herds of Syrian elephants.[17] Thutmose I was probably in northern Syria-Palestine when he learned that Mitanni was mustering its forces, so perhaps his hunting trip to the elephant grounds was a pretext for having an Egyptian force in place to pounce on Mitanni. Whether the elephant hunt occurred before or after the military campaign, Thutmose I was successful in hunting both bipeds and quadrupeds, and thanks to him, New Kingdom Egypt found itself in possession of a true Asiatic dominion.

Thutmose I was succeeded by Thutmose II, his son by the lesser queen Mutnofret. Perhaps quite young, Thutmose II married his probably older sister Hatshepsut, daughter of Thutmose I by his chief queen, Ahmose. These details of royal birth may have justified to Hatshepsut her final subsuming of the reign of Thutmose II into her own, after her husband died following three years of rule. Though she at first ruled as regent for the young king Thutmose III, son of Thutmose II by a lesser wife, Isis, the ambitious Hatshepsut soon transformed her titles and even her images into those of a male pharaoh. Hatshepsut launched a major expedition to the southeastern land of Punt, in her own way attempting both to copy and outdo her father in his Nubian expedition (see page 105). Hatshepsut also constructed extensively at Thebes and undertook minor military activity, but she does not appear to have engaged Mitanni in either warfare or any considerable dialogue, as far as one may judge from the surviving sources.

Though chastened by Thutmose I, Mitanni eventually gained influence over Assyria and the Hurrian state of Khanigalbat in the east, as well as the Hurrian centers Aleppo, Alalakh, and Tunip in northern Syria-Palestine. After the militarily rather uneventful reigns of Thutmose II and Hatshepsut,[18] the adult Thutmose III—freed from the restraints of his subordination to Hatshepsut—introduced western Asia to an Egyptian ruler who was not shy about employing force on a large scale and with some frequency. Thutmose III defeated a great alliance of rulers, led by the ruler of Kadesh, and possibly backed by the kingdom of Mitanni, at the Battle of Megiddo, on the plain of Armageddon, thereby eliminating any direct threat to Egyptian influence in western Syria-Palestine.[19] During his eighth campaign, having prepared transportable vessels on the Mediterranean coast, Thutmose III launched a land and river campaign against Mitanni, sailing on the Euphrates to the rear of what the Mitannian ruler must have believed to be his front lines. Thutmose III erected his own stele on the Euphrates, near that of his predecessor and spiritual father Thutmose I. Also imitating his predecessor, Thutmose III hunted Syrian elephants in Niye.

A campaign against Mitanni under Amunhotep II, son of Thutmose III, apparently accomplished little, but political developments soon propelled Mitanni literally into the lap of the pharaoh.[20] Already feeling southward pressure from the growing power of the Hittites in Anatolia, Mitanni sought an alliance with Egypt late in the reign of Amunhotep II. To cement relations, Thutmose IV (son of Amunhotep II) married a Mitanni princess. The peaceful relations and strong alliance between Egypt and Mitanni persisted during the reign of Amunhotep III, who continued the policy of his father, Thutmose IV, of taking a Mitanni princess as wife. After what must have seemed like the halcyon days of Amunhotep III, the reign of Akhenaten saw the ancient Near East become a more crowded and volatile, albeit more interesting, collection of political players.

The Egyptian Empire in Syria-Palestine

The population of Syria-Palestine during the Middle Bronze Age had experienced urbanization, the creation of literate bureaucracies, and the development of a myriad of separate city-states.[21] The complex and variegated political organization of Syria-Palestine made it impractical for the Egyptians to transplant their own administrative system to the northern part of their empire. Instead, Egypt developed an effective system for maintaining enough control over the region to satisfy its military and economic goals.[22] The overriding principle of Egyptian foreign policy in Asia from the reign of Amunhotep III to the death of Horemhab was to gain the greatest economic and political advantage from the smallest commitment of troops.[23] To achieve this goal, the Egyptians employed a number of non-military means. They placed Egyptian officials in key port cities to provide guidance, and Egyptian troops stationed nearby to enforce this "advice" if necessary. The sons of Syro-Palestinian rulers were sent to be raised in the Egyptian court, and thereafter installed upon the thrones of their fathers; the marriage of foreign princesses to the Egyptian pharaoh sealed further alliances. Diplomatic correspondence between the rulers of cities of Syria-Palestine and the Egyptian pharaoh and his high officials linked the Egyptian administration and the lesser indigenous bureaucracies of Syria-Palestine, and aided the functioning of Egypt's northern empire.

Foreign Service

The diverse geography of Syria-Palestine—coastal plains, mountains, deep valleys, and deserts—often hampers direct communication among its different regions. The natural environment was thus conducive to the existence of small city-states, none of whom could alone directly threaten Egypt's territories or interests on a broad front in a serious way.[24] At the same time, the geographical and political diversity of the region created certain challenges for Egyptian administration in the region. The Egyptians adapted their imperial framework to Syria-Palestine by dividing the northern empire into separate units;[25] three administrative areas in existence during the reign of Akhenaten included Amurru, the Syrian coastal region north of Byblos and inland to the Orontes River; Canaan, which stretched from Byblos south through most of Palestine; and Upe, the inland area just west of the Orontes and encompassing the region of Damascus. During the Amarna Period, Egyptian commissioners were associated—at least intermittently—with each of these regions and key cities within them:[26] Sumur in Amurru, Gaza in Canaan, and Kumidi in Upe. Sumur and Gaza were important ports, and all three cities sat astride major trade routes and strategic arteries.

Additional Egyptian officials were posted at equally important cities along the coast (e.g., Jaffa and Ullasa[27]) and at the intersection of major routes (e.g., Beth-Shean[28]). Thus organized, the Egyptian garrisons guarded the two land routes from Egypt into Syria-Palestine—the Via Maris, following a primarily coastal route, and another road through the highlands, passing through Jerusalem and Shechem to Megiddo. Egyptian commissioners and officials traveled among the various cities, and their jurisdiction was probably quite large. The Akkadian term $r\bar{a}bi\d{s}u$, denoting a "commissioner," corresponded to various military titles in Egyptian (such as "troop/regiment commander"); two classes of commissioners appear to have existed, a higher one bearing the Egyptian title "royal envoy in every foreign territory," and junior commissioners who held the title "overseer of all northern lands."[29] Details about the precise hierarchy of the Egyptian administration in western Asia are lacking, but the chief coordinator may have been one of the two Egyptian viziers.[30] By the reign of Amunhotep III Egypt had developed a true diplomatic service in the northeast, manned by a combination of civil and military administrators.

A Nineteenth Dynasty document, *Papyrus Anastasi I*, provides some clues about the knowledge expected of an official in the Egyptian foreign service. In this papyrus, which consists of a series of literary epistles, a teacher scolds his student for not knowing the precise locations and geographical context of various cities in Syria-Palestine.[31] Although few maps survive from ancient Egypt, the extant cartographic evidence and texts such as *Papyrus Anastasi I* attest to the Egyptians' mapmaking skills.[32] We can easily imagine an ancient Egyptian official who wanted to work in the northern empire submitting to a battery of tests, much like the British colonial administrators who served in India. The training of Egyptian officials seems to have reaped rewards for the pharaoh, whose vassals might invoke the local knowledge of his administrators.[33]

Egypt fielded two different types of troops to maintain control over its territory in Syria-Palestine. The first were garrison troops stationed in various cities, particularly ports, throughout the empire. Such garrisons need

not be large; fifty Egyptian soldiers were stationed in Jerusalem, and thirty
to fifty appear to have formed a standard contingent.[34] The second type of
Egyptian military force were mobile troops, called *piṭāti* in the Akkadian
documents, a rendition of the Egyptian term *pedjut* (bowtroops). These
mobile troops, who included archers and infantry, trekked across the different vassal states and could quickly deploy to a particular region if a
threat arose.[35] Egyptian vassals under pressure from other groups could
request aid from garrisons in other cities or ask that the mobile troops
assemble in their region.[36] The Egyptian administration in Syria-Palestine
appears to have been highly adaptable to the changing geopolitical reality
of the region,[37] with the small numbers of garrison troops representing
extreme economy of force. The ability to move commissioners and troops
easily from city to city enabled the Egyptians to curb overly aggressive vassals as well as to respond to threats by the other great powers.

Although the Egyptian empire in Syria-Palestine supplied Egypt with
goods of various types, and participated in the larger sphere of the Egyptian economy,[38] it was not as well integrated into that economy as was
Nubia. To some extent the reason for this difference may lie in the nature
of the goods; the enormous value and cultic significance of Nubia's gold
and ritual items led to a desire to integrate the southern domain more
directly into the pharaonic economy. Many of the taxes levied on the vassals in Syria-Palestine were not transported back to the Nile Valley, but
rather were used to support Egyptian military operations in the region.
Extensive tracts of land in the northern portion of the Egyptian empire
were the personal property of the pharaoh, and local rulers were required
to provide corvée labor for agricultural work.[39] Local products such as
wine, oils, timber, silver, Asiatic copper, metal vessels, and glass, as well as
military matériel such as horses and chariots, might be shipped back to
Egypt, but the fertile Nile Valley had no need to import grain. Instead, the
vassal rulers were responsible for storing and guarding grain for the use of
the Egyptian army during future campaigns in the region (for descriptions
of preparations for such a campaign, see pages 172–175).[40] Ironically, the
vassals most militarily troublesome to Egypt appear to have been among
the most consistent senders of tribute.[41] Egypt's chief interest in Syria-
Palestine was not its intrinsic economic value but rather the trade routes
that traversed the region,[42] combined with its strategic importance for
preventing invasions of Egypt itself.

Hostage Princes and Princess Brides
Syro-Palestinian vassals provided the Egyptian army with provisions, worked
alongside Egyptian commissioners, and sent tribute to the Egyptian court.

Included in this tribute were human resources—servants for Egyptian temples; princesses for the harem of the pharaoh; and most importantly for Egypt's political aims in the region, sons of local rulers to be raised in the Egyptian court. The pharaoh continually exercised his right to appoint successors to the rulers of the Egyptian vassal states, seeking to ensure loyalty while respecting dynastic traditions.[43] The princes sent to the Egyptian court would be raised from childhood in the Egyptian palace, exposed to Egyptian culture, religion, and loyalty to the pharaoh.[44] When a ruler died, one of these Egyptianized princes would often succeed his father as ruler. This practice of rearing future foreign rulers in Egypt was not confined to Syria-Palestine, but also was used with great success in Nubia and later in the New Kingdom, with less happy results in Libya (see pages 109–110).

Hostage princes and princess brides were effective nonmilitary means of maintaining Egyptian control over vassals in Syria-Palestine. At times this arrangement could be pleasing to both parties, and Egyptian vassals might even write to the pharaoh requesting that the son of their previous ruler be sent back to his home city. One poignant example is a letter from the "citizens of Tunip" to the king of Egypt: "And now, for twenty years, we have gone on writing to the king, our lord, but our messengers have stayed on with the king, our lord. And now, our lord, we ask for the son of Aki-Teshup from the king, our lord. May our lord give him."[45] Rulers of the cities in Syria-Palestine refer to their time in Egypt[46] and the debt they owed to the Egyptian pharaoh for their position; Abdi-Hiba of Jerusalem claims "neither my father nor my mother put me in this place, but the strong arm of the king brought me into my father's house."[47]

Once installed as rulers of the cities of Syria-Palestine, the Egyptian vassals considered themselves to be "kings," using the same Akkadian word (šarru) as the kings of Babylon or Assyria. The Egyptians, however, took a more practical view of those rulers' holdings and called them by the title "mayors" (haty-a), using the same word they applied to leaders of cities in the Nile Valley. During important festivals in Egypt, such as Akhenaten's jubilee festival and the year twelve durbar, the pharaoh could command the vassals to appear at the Egyptian court.

Egyptian vassals in Syria-Palestine could also be asked to provide a daughter to adorn the harem of the Egyptian king.[48] Diplomatic marriages were a particularly significant mode of interaction between the great kingdoms of the ancient Near East.[49] Foreign princesses sent to Egypt, often accompanied by hundreds of servants and rich dowries,[50] sealed peace negotiations,[51] and in return their countries would receive expensive bridal gifts.[52] Although the pharaoh might send his gold, he would never

reciprocate the trade in princesses and send one of Egypt's daughters—
royal or otherwise—to live as the wife of a "wretched Asiatic," as Egypt's
northeastern neighbors are most often called in military texts. According
to one letter, an apparently desperate Babylonian ruler, whose request for
an Egyptian princess had fallen on deaf ears, had made a request for any
Egyptian woman, whom he could pretend was a daughter of Amunhotep
III.[53] The Babylonian king laments that even that request was denied.
Although rulers of the ancient Near East might be concerned about
Egypt's haughty attitude toward foreign marriage and could take offense at
other slights,[54] Egypt's wealth in gold, which according to other rulers was
"more plentiful than dirt" in Egypt,[55] continued to grease the diplomatic
wheels.

Diplomatic Correspondence

Correspondence Egypt sent to its vassals enabled the pharaoh to convey
instructions directly to the leaders of cities throughout Syria-Palestine;
the commissioners and troops stationed in the region added an incentive for the leaders to obey the pharaoh's requests. Letters from the vassals
to Egypt, on the other, had helped apprise the pharaoh of the military
and diplomatic situation in the surrounding regions. In fact, intelligence-
gathering is a frequent topic of the correspondence between Egypt and its
vassals.[56] For example, Zimreddi, ruler of Sidon, quotes one of Akhenaten's
commands about collecting information: "Moreover, as to your ordering
with regard to the lands of Amurru, 'The word that you hear from there
you must report to me.'"[57] The diversity of Egypt's vassals allowed the
Egyptian pharaoh to receive reports from all angles; in another letter, Zimreddi's enemy Abimilki of Tyre also records: "The king, my lord, wrote to
me on a tablet, 'Write whatever you hear to the king.'" By comparing the
reports of his officials and messengers with those of frequently opposed
vassals, the pharaoh and his advisers could at best arrive at a relatively
accurate assessment of a situation and at worst realize where the available
intelligence required augmentation.

Such frequent correspondence between the kingdoms and vassal states
of the ancient Near East necessitated an organized courier service. In
Egypt, the title "messenger" or "royal messenger" appears as early as the
Old Kingdom, and by the time of the New Kingdom, a version of the
"pony express" existed at least in Upper Egypt.[58] Each ancient Near Eastern king possessed his own messengers, who not only transported the
actual missives but also aided in interpreting the text and conversing with
the foreign king.[59] Several Egyptian messengers, such as Mane and Hani,

figure prominently in the Amarna Letters. In some cases, messengers could be detained for years in the court of another ruler. The messengers might need to travel through unstable regions, and to prevent any interference and to aid their journey, messengers could be provided with "passports" that granted them free passage and released them from payment of any tribute along the way.[60]

The Amarna Letters

Due to a chance discovery in the late nineteenth century C.E., the reign of Amunhotep III marks a tremendous change in our understanding of Egyptian relations with western Asia. According to reports in 1887, a peasant woman from a village near Amarna was digging in the ancient ruins of Akhet-aten for *sebakh*, the remains of ancient mud-brick architecture and habitation debris used as fertilizer. Among the richly fertilizing remains she discovered a cache of clay tablets bearing correspondence between Egyptian pharaohs—Amunhotep III, Akhenaten, and his immediate successors through Tutankhamun—and rulers of the major kingdoms of the ancient Near East as well as the Egyptian vassal states in southern Syria-Palestine. These invaluable documents, commonly called the "Amarna Letters," paint a vivid picture of politics in the fourteenth century B.C.E. in which the "great powers" of the eastern Mediterranean threatened, cajoled, and deceived to acquire greater wealth and power.[61]

The Amarna Letters represent a portion of the archive once housed at the "Office of the Letters of Pharaoh," a building in the central city of Akhet-aten.[62] The tablets are covered in cuneiform, the wedge-shaped writing of ancient Mesopotamia (see figure 22). The language of the texts is almost entirely Akkadian; in rare cases, other languages, such as Hittite or Hurrian, appear within the archive.[63] A few of the tablets retained traces of ink notes in hieratic, the cursive Egyptian script, added for filing purposes.[64] The scribes who wrote the cuneiform documents dispatched from Egypt might have been Egyptian scribes who had trained in Akkadian, or foreign scribes employed in the Egyptian administration.[65] Monuments at Amarna attest to a number of Asiatics inhabiting Akhenaten's capital,[66] and in addition to their roles as members of the royal bodyguard, such foreigners also might have aided scribes with Akhenaten's international correspondence.

Despite the epistolary formulas used throughout the archive, the texts often portray annoyance, hope, hostility, and a range of other emotions. The letters between the great kings, who address each other as "brother,"

Figure 22. Cuneiform tablet from
the Amarna correspondence, a letter
of the Amorite ruler Aziru to an
Egyptian administrator, reporting
movements of the Hittite king
(EA 166, Vorderasiatisches Museum,
Berlin, VAT 250). Courtesy of the
Bildarchiv Preussischer Kulturbesitz/
Art Resource, N.Y.

differ greatly in their scope and tone from a vassal's letter to his overlord.
Vassals employ short opening statements emphasizing their subordinate
status, even when reporting disastrous events or blaming the pharaoh for
not sending aid in time; typical expressions include "I fall at the feet of
my lord seven times and seven times both on the stomach and on the
back, at the feet of the king, my lord."[67] Indeed, a scene in the Memphite
tomb of Horemhab[68] depicts a group of Asiatic chiefs assuming numerous
postures of abasement in the presence of the pharaoh—one man lies on
his stomach, another on his back, in just the positions described in the
letters.[69]

   Queens of the ancient Near Eastern kingdoms also participated in
diplomatic correspondence.[70] A series of letters from Tushratta, king of
Mitanni, to Akhenaten contain complaints about a gift of gold-plated
wooden statues from Egypt, despite Tushratta's insistence that he had been
promised solid gold statues. Exasperated with the new pharaoh, Tushratta
implores Akhenaten to speak with his mother, Tiye,[71] and sends at least
one letter directly to the Egyptian queen. In one letter Tushratta mentions
the messengers of his wife, Yuni, visiting Tiye.[72] The diplomatic role assumed by Tiye is fitting, considering she was the only Eighteenth Dynasty
queen granted the epithet "great of fear, mistress of all lands" (see page 24).

At least two other letters were written by the queen of Ugarit to the queen of Egypt (EA 48 and 50).

In total, 379 tablets or fragments thereof were found by illicit or official excavations at Amarna; of these documents, 355 are letters or texts related to international correspondence, while the remaining tablets contain other types of cuneiform texts, such as myths, scribal exercises, and vocabulary lists (for convenience, these documents are referred to by the designation EA, "El-Amarna," plus a number).[73] Fewer than 50 of the documents within the Amarna archive represent correspondence between Egypt and the major kingdoms and independent states of the ancient Near East—Mitanni, Babylonia, Hatti, Assyria, Arzawa, and Alashiya (Cyprus). The remaining letters, more than 300, are communications between Egypt's vassals and their overlord, the pharaoh.

Tushratta of Mitanni

The location of Hurrian Mitanni at the crossroads of Asia Minor, northern Mesopotamia, and the upper reaches of Syria-Palestine placed the kingdom in an ideal position to influence the growth of other powers in any of those regions. Mitanni was a check to any emerging power such as Assyria in northern Mesopotamia, and had already posed a serious military threat to the so-called Old Kingdom of the Hittites during the reign of Hattusili I (ca. 1650–1620 B.C.E.).[74] During the early Eighteenth Dynasty in Egypt, the influence of Mitanni was felt strongly in northern Syria-Palestine.[75] The autobiographical text of King Idrimi of Alalakh, a city on the northernmost stretch of the Orontes, recounted this new political reality.[76] Idrimi fled east from his ancestral home of Aleppo in the face of Hurrian incursions and later became a vassal of the Hurrian ruler.

During the early Eighteenth Dynasty, the kingdom of Mitanni was at its height. By the reign of Amunhotep III, Mitanni, the former archenemy of Egypt, had but recently been allied with Egypt. The alliance between Egypt and Mitanni, cemented by the marriage of Mitanni princesses to the Egyptian pharaoh, flourished at the same time that Mitanni began to decline. Amunhotep III married Gilukhepa, daughter of the Mitanni king Shuttarna II, and exchanged letters with the Mitanni ruler. After the death of Shuttarna II, Tushratta, the new king of Mitanni, continued the alliance with Egypt; behind the formalized nature of their correspondence, the letters between Amunhotep III and Tushratta suggest that the two rulers might even have developed a friendship. Upon the death of Amunhotep III, Tushratta attempted to forge a similar relationship with Akhenaten. Finding difficulty persuading the new pharaoh to keep the promises made by his father, Tushratta even wrote to the queen mother, Tiye (see pages 148–149).

Suppiluliuma I: King of the Hittites

The Hittite empire began with the reign of Hattusili I at Hattusas (modern Bogazköy, Turkey) in about 1650 B.C.E.[77] After turning his attention to securing trade routes to the Mediterranean and northern Syria, Hattusili I consolidated his hold on western Anatolia; his successor, Mursili I, greatly expanded the Hittite empire by capturing Aleppo and Babylon. After a period of checkered fortunes, the Hittites again became influential, in about 1380 B.C.E., with the accession of Suppiluliuma I, whose successful campaigns would destroy Mitanni and create a new rival to Egypt's empire in Syria-Palestine.

Ancient Egyptian texts refer to the "land of Hatti" from the early Eighteenth Dynasty, but when depicting a Hittite, the early New Kingdom Egyptians simply represented a person of Syro-Palestinian appearance. Northern Syrian states, mostly under the control of Mitanni, separated the Hittites from the Egyptians, and the Egyptians seem initially to have been acquainted with the politics and militarism of the Hittites through their Syrian surrogates. The standard Hittite of the Hatti homeland, as we know him in New Kingdom Egyptian depictions, with his clean-shaven face, prominent nose, sloping forehead, and long hair, first appears in an Egyptian representation in the Saqqara tomb chapel of Horemhab, carved during the reign of Tutankhamun or Aye.[78] Apparently the Egyptians first had any meaningful encounters with true Hittites during the Amarna Period.

Meaningful encounters the two empires would indeed have over the next century. The expansionist policies of Suppiluliuma I (c. 1350–1322 B.C.E.), although aimed against Mitanni, disrupted Egyptian interests in Syria-Palestine, particularly around the city of Kadesh and the region of Amki. The political events following Suppiluliuma's Great Syrian Campaign, which occurred in about year twelve of the reign of Akhenaten, are complicated and mostly reconstructed from later Hittite evidence, including historical retrospectives (e.g., "The Deeds of Suppiluliuma") and copies of treaties between the Hittites and the territories they conquered.

Burnaburiash II of Babylonia

Throughout the Amarna Period, the powerful and long-lived Kassite Dynasty ruled the kingdom of Babylonia.[79] At the southern end of Mesopotamia, Babylonia was too far from the sphere of Egyptian influence in western Asia to play much of a role in the political struggles of the great powers. Indeed, one of the Amarna Letters (EA 7) reveals that Babylonia's relative isolation from the great powers led to a certain ignorance of geography by the Babylonian king Burnaburiash II, a contemporary of Amunhotep III and Akhenaten. According to the letter, the king of Babylon had only recently recovered from an illness and was vexed at Akhenaten for not sending a messenger to visit during his illness. With a guilelessness to rival his geographic ignorance, Burnaburiash goes on to report to Akhenaten the following conversation with another Egyptian messenger present at the Babylonian court:

> (The Egyptian messenger) addressed me, s[aying], "It (Egypt) is not a place close by so your brother (the pharaoh) can hear (about you) and send you greetings. The country is far away. Who is going to tell your brother so he can immediately send you greetings? Would your brother hear that you are ill and still not send you his messenger?" I for my part addressed him as follows, "For my brother, a Great King, is there really a far-away country and a close-by one?"[80]

This letter also indicates the esteem in which even distant empires held the Egyptians—the Babylonian king seems to believe that Egypt cannot be far from any land. Egypt and Babylonia remained on friendly terms during the reign of Akhenaten (probably fortunate for any force Burnaburiash might have sent out), but their relationship has little significance for Egyptian foreign policy.

Ashuruballit I of Assyria

In about 1400 B.C.E., the kingdom of Assyria began to throw off the Mitanni yoke and to build a powerful empire in northern Mesopotamia.[81] Assyrian pressure on Mittani, already suffering from Hittite incursions, helped to usher in the downfall of the Hurrian state, but otherwise Assyria, like Babylonia, exerted little influence on Egyptian foreign policy. Indeed, not until the Neo-Assyrian Period during the seventh century B.C.E. did Assyria change the course of history in the Nile Valley, when successive invasions of Egypt by the Assyrian kings Esarhaddon and Ashurpanibal drove out the Nubian Twenty-fifth Dynasty and established an Egyptian puppet kingdom in the Delta, which would eventually lead to the Saite Renaissance.[82]

During the Amarna Period, Assyria was merely a small kingdom with dreams of empire. To improve his state's position among the great powers, Ashuruballit I sent a fact-finding mission to open contact with Egypt (EA

15).[83] Soon thereafter, the Assyrian king complained to Akhenaten about the inadequacy of his latest gift from Egypt (EA 16): "Is such a present that of a Great King? Gold in your country is dirt; one simply gathers it up. Why are you so sparing of it? I am engaged in building a new palace. Send me as much gold as needed for its adornment."[84] Burnaburiash of Babylon, who believed Assyrian territory to be under his control, expresses his annoyance at the efforts of Ashuruballit to establish independent contact with Egypt (EA 9): "Now, as for my Assyrian vassals, I was not the one who sent them to you. Why on their own authority have they come to your country? If you love me, they will conduct no business whatsoever. Send them off to me empty-handed."[85] Despite Akhenaten's diplomatic ties with Burnaburiash, the pharaoh appears to have continued to correspond with Assyria.

Arzawa and Alashiya

Two further independent kingdoms also attempted to interact on a more or less equal footing with the great powers: Arzawa and Alashiya. Arzawa controlled an area along the southern coast of Asia Minor west of the Hittite homeland and managed to remain independent of the growing Hittite empire during the entire reign of Suppiluliuma, but eventually fell to his son Mursili II (c. 1321–1295 B.C.E.).[86] Alashiya was the ancient name for the island of Cyprus, in the northeastern corner of the Mediterranean Sea.[87]

The main contact between Egypt and Arzawa occurred during the reign of Amunhotep III, when the Egyptian king requested a bride from Arzawa in exchange for gold.[88] This diplomatic marriage might have been an attempt to distract Hittite attention from northern Syria-Palestine and to impede any possible development of Hittite naval power by providing support to the still independent kingdom of Arzawa. Similarly, the island kingdom of Alashiya assumes a small role in the Amarna Letters, but its king sent messengers consistently to Egypt.[89] Along with his messengers, the king of Alashiya dispatched fairly large quantities of copper to Egypt, requesting silver in return.[90] Not surprisingly, some of the correspondence with Alashiya deals with maritime trade and piratical activities. In EA 38, the king of Alashiya responds to accusations by the Egyptian pharaoh:

> Why, my brother, do you say such a thing to me, "Does my brother not know this?" As far as I am concerned, I have done nothing of the sort. Indeed, men of Lukki, year by year, seize villages in my country.
>
> My brother, you say to me, "Men from your country were with them." My brother, I do not know that they were with them. If men from my country were (with them), send (them back) and I will act as I see fit.[91]

Apparently piratical Lukki and accusations from the Egyptian pharaoh are not all that cause the king of Alashiya concern (for Bronze Age pirates, see pages 197 and 203). In two further letters, the king of Alashiya informs the Egyptians and their governors that some ships from Cyprus belong to his merchants and "no one making a claim in your [the Egyptian king's] name is to approach my merchants or my ships."[92] Unfortunately, no further letters survive to indicate if the king's requests for "duty-free" status were honored.

Aziru of Amurru and the Apiru

Although the name originated as a more general term for the lands west of Mesopotamia, by the time of Akhenaten the toponym "Amurru" had come to designate a more limited geographical area: the land between the Mediterranean coast and the Orontes River, in the area of modern Lebanon and Syria.[93] Behind the lines of Thutmose I's thrust against Mitanni, and within the area of Egyptian influence during the reign of Thutmose III, the land of Amurru probably gave the early Eighteenth Dynasty rulers little hint of the importance it would attain during the reigns of Amunhotep III and Akhenaten. The rise of Amurru, a multifaceted event that looms large in the Amarna correspondence, was the result of two charismatic and cutthroat rulers: Abdiashirta and his son Aziru. Using all means at his disposal, Abdiashirta united the disparate population of Amurru, broadly termed the "Amorites," and created a state powerful enough to dispute terms with the two major superpowers, Egypt and the Hittites, between which the Amorites became a powerful buffer state. After consolidating the wilds lands of Amurru, Abdiashirta met his end under uncertain circumstances, but his sons, particularly Aziru, pursued the same goals as their father.

A key factor in the success of Abdiashirta and his sons was the alliance they forged with an infamous group of people known as the Apiru.[94] In the Amarna Letters, the Apiru appear as small, roving groups of brigands who attack caravans, destroy property, and wreak general havoc. The term appears initially to have referred to some specific element of the Amorite regional population, and to have undergone a change as that group was augmented and thereby changed through its associations with urban communities. By themselves, the Apiru could prove an annoyance to settled populations in Syria-Palestine, but properly manipulated by Abdiashirta and Aziru, the Apiru could move into an area and institute a reign of terror—the Apiru became a force of often violent social and political change. Much of the power of the Apiru lay not in their military strength but in their ability to inspire fear.

The realm of Amurru incorporated, even centered on, the great Biqa Valley of modern Lebanon. A northern extension of the Great Rift Valley, the Biqa is an excellent corridor for north–south trade, but a complex checkerboard of varying microecologies, increasingly arid toward the west and from south to north. The character of the Biqa Valley determined the nature of the Apiru and the flexible loyalties and policies of the Amorite state; for the past several millennia the inhabitants of the region have relied on a flexible approach to economy, switching between nomadism and farming as climate has dictated.[95] The Apiru exhibited traits of both sedentary and nomadic groups, as one would expect if at least some of the Apiru were people uprooted from settled groups and enticed or forced—by direct, social, or economic pressures—into a nomadic or a seminomadic lifestyle.

Some Apiru developed urban skills through association with former urbanites turned Apiru, and some of these latter carried the acculturative process in reverse. Apparently the term "Apiru" could apply to anyone who embraced or was swept up in the Apiru lifestyle, and the more recent term "gypsy," as it has specific linguistic and perhaps originally ethnic denotations, and a wide array of connotations, including itinerant but not destitute elements of the population of primarily sedentary populations, is an excellent and perhaps exact parallel.[96] The Apiru could function as auxiliary soldiers and workmen, a self-sufficient, self-propelled group of often skilled people who could augment the increasingly complex Near Eastern societies, taking advantage of the new internationalism, and turning the climatic peculiarities of the Biqa to the greatest economic advantage.

Ribaddi of Byblos

From the Egyptian Predynastic Period onward, vessels sailed between Byblos and Egypt, transporting skilled laborers, raw materials, and luxury goods.[97] The residents of Byblos adopted much of Egyptian theology and iconography. The patron goddess of Byblos, Baalat-Gebel, whose name means "Mistress of Byblos," was worshipped from an early period as a manifestation of the Egyptian goddess Hathor, who in turn could bear the Egyptian epithet Nebet-kepenet, "Mistress of Byblos."[98] Although the Egyptians did not consistently exert direct political control over Byblos, the city was a bastion of Egyptian culture on the coast of Syria-Palestine.

During the reigns of Amunhotep III and Akhenaten, the ruler of Byblos was a man named Ribaddi. Were it not for the Amarna Letters, we might not even know of his existence, and we certainly would not know so much about his personality. Ribaddi authored nearly seventy letters in the Amarna archive, a large proportion of all the correspondence from Egypt's northern vassals.[99] In his loquacious and often repetitive missives, Ribaddi reaches to the height of obsequiousness, including the poetic statement "I am a footstool for the feet of the king, my lord, and his loyal servant."[100]

Fortunately, Ribaddi's constant stream of letters provides a wealth of information about the political events in Syria-Palestine. While the Egyptian pharaoh might have appreciated the intelligence reports of Ribaddi, he seems also to have tired of the number and repetition of those reports.[101] In the end, Ribaddi's loyalty and undying devotion to the pharaoh were to no avail. As Ribaddi's letters tell us in often excruciating detail, the Amorite rulers Abdiashirta and Aziru were either directly or indirectly responsible for the murder of Ribaddi's family, the loss of his territories, and his eventual exile from his beloved city. He is a tragicomic figure, and Shakespeare would surely have made of him an Amarna Falstaff could he have written the tragedy *Akhenaten.*

Egyptian Vassals in Syria-Palestine

Besides Amurru and Byblos, who loom large in the Amarna correspondence, a number of other Egyptian vassals appear in the archive.[102] The majority of the correspondence is written by the vassals and addressed to Egyptian commissioners or the pharaoh; few copies of the pharaoh's letters to his vassals appear in the archive, but the sum of vassal correspondence suggests a yearly pattern of communication.[103] While the vassals' letters vary considerably in theme and content, missives from the pharaoh consistently stressed the need for obedience and vigilance by his vassals:

> The king herewith sends to you Hani, the son of Maireya, the stable overseer of the king in Canaan. And what he tells you heed very carefully lest the king find fault in you. Every word that he tells you heed very carefully and carry out very carefully. And be on your guard! Be on your guard! Do not be negligent! And may you prepare before the arrival of the archers of the king food in abundance, wine (and) everything else in abundance. Indeed, he is going to reach you very quickly and he will cut off the heads of the enemies of the king.[104]

The Syro-Palestinian vassals divide into a number of groups.[105] Those on the southern coastal plain, such as Gaza and Ashkelon, appear infrequently in the Amarna Letters, and posed few problems for Egypt, as one might expect from cities so close to the Nile Delta and within easy reach of the Egyptian navy. The southern vassals farther inland inhabited hilly territory that made direct control slightly more difficult. Labayu, the ruler of Shechem, one of the cities in this southern hill region, well represents the problems Egyptian vassals could create, even without the interference of another of the great powers. Labayu's expansionist policies brought him into conflict with a number of other Egyptian vassals. The Egyptians normally overlooked such internecine fighting, since it prevented any one group from gaining enough power to threaten Egypt's own interests in a particular region. Indeed, Labayu—like other unruly vassals—tried to exploit Egyptian tolerance of independent action by explaining in detail how his actions actually benefited Egypt (EA 254):

> To the king, my lord and my Sun: Thus Labayu, your servant and the dirt on which you tread. . . . I have obeyed the orders that the king wrote to me. Who am I that the king should lose his land on account of me? The fact is that I am a loyal servant of the king! I am not a rebel and I am not delinquent in duty. . . . How, if the king wrote to me, "Put a bronze dagger into your heart and die," how could I not execute the order of the king?[106]

Despite his protestations of innocence, however, Labayu's constant attacks on other vassals raised the ire of the pharaoh, and Amunhotep III eventually sent aid to a coalition of cities that had formed to defend themselves against the ruler of Shechem. Labayu's sons continued the aggressive policies of their father, much as the sons of the wickedly charismatic Abdiashirta carried on the work of their father in Amurru.

The northern vassals similarly divided into a coastal and an inland group. Along with the leaders of the port cities, such as Byblos, Beirut, Sidon, and Tyre, the main vassal in the coastal region was Amurru, discussed above. Farther inland was the area controlled by the ruler of Damascus, Biryawaza, who in the Amarna archive appears quite dedicated to the Egyptian pharaoh. When the Amorites allied themselves with the ruler of Kadesh, a Hittite confederate, Biryawaza clashed with Aziru.[107] At the northernmost extent of the Egyptian sphere of influence were the cities of Ugarit and Qatna, as well as the region of Nuhasse; during the Amarna Period, the rulers of all these northern areas entered either by force or voluntarily into the Hittite sphere of influence.

"The Vile Dog of Amurru"

From the time of the alliance between Mitanni and Egypt during the reign of Thutmose IV, a relatively peaceful balance of power prevailed in the ancient Near East. Although Egyptian and Mitanni vassal states in Syria-

Palestine continued to squabble with one another, the great powers were relatively pacific. The expansionist policies of Suppiluliuma I, king of the Hittites, would end this balance of power and force all the great powers to reevaluate their foreign policy. Mitanni would ultimately pay the greatest price in the Hittite rise to international prominence; while Egypt's home territory was never threatened, the Egyptian rulers of the next hundred years would have to trouble themselves with the problem of the "vile land of Hatti." The Amarna Letters reveal the events that surrounded the downfall of the empire of Mitanni as well as the surprising Egyptian response to the collapse of its ally. Although Akhenaten has often been accused of negligence in foreign policy, a new examination of the international correspondence instead suggests that he might have mastered a Machiavellian approach to diplomacy approximately three thousand years before it was codified.

The story of this complex series of events begins during the reign of Amunhotep III in the land of Amurru.[108] Amurru's location, between the southern Levantine ports, clearly under Egypt's hegemony, and Ugarit and the southern fringe of the Hittite realm to the north, predestined the region to enjoy the attentions of both Egypt and Hatti. Furthermore, the decline of Mitanni, which began during the reign of Amunhotep III and was nearly complete by the death of Akhenaten, left Egypt without an ally against the growing might of Hatti. But if a secondary power were to arise that might form a buffer to Hittite aggression and replace tottering Mitanni to the east, such a state might well center in the territory of Amurru. In spite of these geopolitical harbingers of political significance, Amurru, even early in the reign of Amunhotep III, probably seemed to lack the necessary social environment.

Nevertheless, the peculiarities of its human populations that may indeed have stunted her earlier political development suddenly became Amurru's greatest asset. Amurru proper was home to no major urban settlements, but was the center of the Apiru, who, due to the geography and climate of the Biqa Valley, alternated between nomadism and agriculture (see above). These ferocious bands of brigands, who existed around the fringes of settled society, alternately participating in and preying on their sedentary neighbors, were one of the most important weapons in the Amorite arsenal. At the time of Mitanni's collapse, Egypt and Hatti might well have found themselves without a buffer or even a distraction to avert the inevitable military confrontation. Fortunately for the two great powers, a crafty, duplicitous, and incredibly braggadocious politician arose in Amurru, a man who could communicate and maneuver in ways comprehensible to the large states to his south and north, and who could at the same time orchestrate a symbiotic relationship with the Apiru. The man was Abdiashirta, and the Apiru became his collective cat's-paw, the bringers of chaos and change whose onslaughts, at the behest of Abdiashirta, necessitated the arrival of Abdiashirta "to restore order."

Abdiashirta instituted this cycle of destabilization and incorporation to expand his territory and to create, for the first time, a unified power in Amurru. The details of one of Abdiashirta's strikes, against the Egyptian-controlled city of Sumur, indicate both the brilliance of his strategy and its inherent dangers. During the reign of Amunhotep III the commissioner of Sumur was a man called Pahhanate in the Amarna Letters, a cuneiform rendering of the Egyptian title Pa-hem-netcher, "the priest." Pahhanate found his area of responsibility under pressure from the Apiru; this constituted the first step of Abdiashirta's cycle of terror, in which he would unleash the Apiru to disrupt commerce in a particular region and threaten its urban inhabitants. When the commissioner Pahhanate left Sumur to visit Egypt, the Apiru moved in, with Abdiashirta on their heels. This was the second step in Abdiashirta's plan, in which the Amorite ruler would advance into the threatened area and "save" the city from the threat of the Apiru. While Abdiashirta's designs on the city of Sumur appear to have enjoyed military success, the Amorite king next had to extricate himself from the diplomatic consequences of invading one of Egypt's chief administrative centers in Syria-Palestine.

A letter from Abdiashirta to Amunhotep III tries to counter the denunciations made by the Egyptian commissioner Pahhanate[109] and Rib-addi, ruler of Byblos,[110] and seeks to justify his own actions against the city of Sumur (EA 60):

> To the king, the Sun, my lord: [Mess]age of Abdiashirta, your servant, the dirt under your feet. I fall at the feet of the king, my lord, seven times and seven times. As I am a servant of the king and a dog of his house, I guard all Amurru for the king, my lord. I have repeatedly said to Pahhanate, my commissioner, "Take auxiliary forces to guard the lands of the king." Indeed, all the kings under the king of the Hurri forces (king of Mitanni) seek to wrest the lands from my [. . . but I g]uard th[em]. [Look] there is Pahhanate, my commissioner. May the king, the Sun, ask him if I do not guard Sumur and Ullasa. When my commissioner is on a mission of the king, the Sun, then I am the one who guards the harvest of the grain of Sumur and all the lands for the king, my Sun, my lord. May the king, my lord, know me and entrust me to the charge of Pahhanate, my commissioner.[111]

Was Amunhotep III really convinced of Abdiashirta's protestations that he occupied Sumur for the Egyptians and was actually made a custodian of the area by the departed commissioner himself? If not, then why did Egypt allow Abdiashirta to remain in power in Amurru? A series of letters from Ribaddi, ruler of Byblos, to other Egyptian officials suggests that the Egyptian pharaoh might not have been receiving complete reports about the events surrounding the fall of Sumur.[112] Ribaddi felt certain Egypt's ruler would send troops to recover Sumur, if the pharaoh were only properly informed. Yet a failure of intelligence seems not to be the reason for Egypt's inaction. In yet another letter, Ribaddi accuses the pharaoh of knowingly abandoning his loyal servant to the depredations of Abdiashirta and the Apiru.[113]

Amunhotep III's disregard for the concerns of Ribaddi, and the pharaoh's apparent indulgence of Abdiashirta's aggression, may represent a calculated decision based on another troubling situation—the duplicity of Mitanni. At about the time that Abdiashirta gained control over Sumur, Ribaddi reported that Suppiluliuma "has seized all the countries that were vassals of the king of Mitanni."[114] Ribaddi's account is exaggerated, since Hittite dominance over *all* of Mitanni's vassals would not be achieved for two more decades; however, Hittite sources suggest that the king of Nuhasse did switch allegiance from Mitanni to the Hittites at this time.[115] Possibly to compensate for the loss of Nuhasse, Mitanni turned against Egyptian vassals in Syria-Palestine. Abdiashirta informed the pharaoh that local rulers loyal to the Hurrian king, subjects of Mitanni, were out to annex areas under Egyptian control; Hurrian aggression is one of the reasons Abdiashirta gives in EA 60 for his action against Sumur.

Did Abdiashirta exaggerate here, as he almost certainly lied about his commission from Pahhanate? Perhaps not. The appalled Ribaddi also had informed Egypt of a thrust by Tushratta as far as Sumur, a Mitanni incursion supposedly intended to reach Byblos itself (EA 85 and 95).[116] If these reports were accurate,[117] then Abdiashirta's claim might well have rung true, although his own visit to Mitanni, as reported by Ribaddi (EA 90),[118] could well leave one in doubt as for whom he was guarding Sumur. In either case, the combination of a Hittite menace and the duplicity Mitanni—even in its death throes—appears to have shown toward Egypt, would have increased Amurru's importance in the eyes of Egypt's rulers. Abdiashirta's success at creating an effective buffer on the Egyptian empire's northern border may well have made him worth the sacrifice of a few cities.

Unfortunately for Ribaddi, and to the ultimate annoyance of Amunhotep III, however, Abdiashirta did not cease his cutthroat tactics after the fall of Sumur. Under the guidance of Abdiashirta, the Apiru expanded the unsettled atmosphere of the region; as areas fragmented and collapsed before them, as settled populations became Apiru, Abdiashirta's nascent Amorite kingdom rushed in to fill the temporary political void. The more cities Abdiashirta consolidated under his rule, the more powerful he became and the quicker he could acquire important intelligence; as Ribaddi reports (EA 82): "All of the Apiru are on his side, and as soon as the mayors hear anything, they write to him. Accordingly, he is strong."[119]

While Egypt remained silent, all the more markedly so in contrast to the increasingly frantic and desperate appeals by Ribaddi, Amurru soon absorbed the hinterland of Byblos herself. Ribaddi sent his sister and her children south to Tyre and wrote again for help from Egypt. The pharaoh at last responded with an order to Beirut, Sidon, and Tyre to go to Byblos's assistance (EA 92), but by then those ports were in Abdiashirta's hands; even worse, the ruler of Tyre, along with Ribaddi's sister and her children, had been murdered by a Tyrian populace that did not want to oppose the Amorites (EA 89).[120] At about this time, Ribaddi even writes the Egyptian official Amanappa, threatening to abandon Byblos in the wake of an assassination attempt instigated by Abdiashirta (EA 82).[121]

Had Egypt miscalculated, or did it simply wait until it knew that only Byblos would be left on the Amorite littoral? Ribaddi was literally at his wits' end, alternately threatening to join the Amorites and begging the pharaoh to buy them off,[122] and Abdiashirta was poised to pounce on one of the few cities not yet under his control. Then, at the last minute, Egypt answered. In letter after letter, Ribaddi describes his situation with a particularly poetic turn of phrase: "Like a bird in a trap, so am I in Byblos."[123] At the twelfth hour the bird turned out to be not Ribaddi, but Abdiashirta; the unwitting Ribaddi had indeed been in a trap, but he was the bait in a trap of the pharaoh's setting.

Apparently Abdiashirta outlived his original purpose—to consolidate a backward area and provide a self-serving barrier to any possible Mitanni and Hittite interests. Abdiashirta might well declare his independent state loyal to Mitanni, but that self-serving ruler would be unlikely to hand over vast expanses to the Hurrians, and a potentially pro-Hurrian renegade was preferable to a potentially hostile and resurgent Mitanni in direct control of Sumur and Byblos. Egypt would have had every reason to want to remove Abdiashirta only at the very moment when his consolidation of Amurru had advanced so far that he could capture the last major Levantine port in Egypt's northern dependencies.

The task of removing Abdiashirta fell to Amanappa, an Egyptian official who had been monitoring the state of invested Byblos, and whose job
was probably to keep the pharaoh informed of just how long to wait, and
just when to strike. Amanappa arrived with an expeditionary force, apparently augmented shortly thereafter, and took Abdiashirta captive. Ribaddi
describes this episode in a "retrospective" portion of a letter he writes to
Akhenaten, already complaining about the negligence of the new pharaoh
toward the protection of Byblos and its loquacious ruler (EA 117): "I am
accordingly afraid and I have turned to my lord. Moreover, I sent a man
to your father. When Amanappa came with a small force, I wrote to the
palace that the king should send a large force. Did he not take Abdiashirta along with everything belonging to him, just as I said?"

Amanappa hauled Abdiashirta back to Egypt, where Amunhotep III
himself—dripping with the regalia of solar kingship—probably had an
amusing audience with a bewildered Amorite king—dripping with sweat
in his woolen robe. The fate of Abdiashirta is unclear, and the only possible reference to his death in the Amarna Letters leaves his murderer
unnamed (EA 101). Perhaps the pharaoh ordered the elimination of
Abdiashirta, or perhaps his own people murdered him in retribution for an
economic setback.[124] To judge from other letters by Ribaddi, even the subjects and henchman of Abdiashirta may not have been sorry to see their
leader depart (EA 73).[125]

Upon the death of their father, Abdiashirta's sons were left with a
challenge, and Egypt and Amurru were in the situation in which they
found themselves at the start of Abdiashirta's rise. Egypt, if it did nothing,
would see the sons perhaps struggle among themselves and then proceed
to repeat Abdiashirta's cycle of disruption of the cities and regions in the
vicinity of Amurru. Amurru would grow, and would consolidate within her
sphere the disparate smaller entities that might, without Amorite intervention, fall into the control of larger, more potentially menacing polities;
and Ribaddi would write increasingly desperate letters to the pharaoh.
Indeed, this did occur. Either Egypt did not learn its lesson, or what happened under Abdiashirta was what Egypt indeed wanted, and Egypt actually arranged to repeat the cycle. The Amorite realm served to protect the
populations of the area from themselves and from non-Egyptian intervention, and Egypt need literally do nothing to achieve this.

The Fall of Sumur and the Great Syrian Campaign

Probably not long after Abdiashirta's death, Amunhotep III died, and
Amunhotep IV ascended the throne, and a few years thereafter changed

his name to Akhenaten. For the first decade of Akhenaten's rule, events in Syria-Palestine followed the same pattern as in the latter part of the reign of Amunhotep III—vassals accused one another of aggressive behavior, Mitanni continued to lose territory to the Hittites, and Amurru consolidated its power. A few years after his accession, Akhenaten witnessed the rise of a powerful Amorite, whose ambition he could exploit just as Amunhotep III had exploited Abdiashirta. This leader of the sons of Abdiashirta was Aziru, who—like his father—was able to profess loyalty to Egypt in all he did, at least in the beginning.[126] Aziru appears to have expressed to several Egyptian officials his desire to become a formal vassal of Egypt, and those officials seem to have rebuffed Aziru each time (EA 157).[127]

Apparently the local Egyptian officials either did not understand or did not desire to play the Amorite's political game, while the pharaoh, it seems, understood—the pharaoh, after all, might have prepared the field for Aziru's game. Akhenaten saw a Mitanni truly tottering and soon to collapse, and pleased on the whole with the results of his father's Amorite experiment, Akhenaten was apparently prepared to allow the full and final establishment of the Amorite kingdom. Probably while Amunhotep IV prepared his new version of pharaonic power, and changed his name to Akhenaten, Egypt garrisoned Sumur again, installed another commissioner, and eventually Abdiashirta's sons threatened the area.

Akhenaten wrote to Ribaddi instructing the Byblian ruler to go to Sumur's assistance, but Ribaddi demurred, worried that if he went to Sumur the Amorites would take his own city (EA 104):

> Who are the sons of Abdiashirta, the servant and dog?[128] Are they the king of Kashu or the king of Mitanni that they take the land of the (Egyptian) king for themselves? Previously, they would take cities of your mayors, and you did nothing. Now they have driven out your commissioner and have taken his cities for themselves. . . . If in these circumstances you do nothing, then they are certainly going to take Sumur and kill the commissioner and the auxiliary force in Sumur. What am I to do? I cannot go personally to Sumur . . . they would attack me![129]

But would Akhenaten have been either surprised or entirely displeased if such did occur? Byblos was under attack by the land forces of Aziru and the Apiru, and by the fleet of the "people of Arwada."[130] Ribaddi's city also was filled with refugees, Egyptians among them, from other areas, and the Egyptian commissioner at Sumur does seem to have written to nearby cities for help that would never arrive. One of the unfortunate consequences of Akhenaten's inaction was one predicted by Ribaddi in EA 104:

the death of the Egyptian commissioner. With the fall of Sumur, the Amorite realm found itself possessed of all it had gained before Egypt removed Abdiashirta. Akhenaten turned a deaf ear to the pleas of his commissioner and the interests of the Egyptians living in Sumur. He apparently sacrificed a civilian and military population of his own people to a brutally efficient Realpolitik, but more would no doubt have died, and the outcome been perhaps more uncertain, if Egypt had consolidated and ultimately absorbed the Amorite region by direct application of its own military power.

An examination of trade routes and sea lanes, reveals that the loss of northern port cities such as Sumur to Amorite control during Akhenaten's reign might not have negatively affected Egyptian goals in the region. The current in the eastern Mediterranean flows counterclockwise, aiding vessels traveling north along the Syro-Palestinian coast from Egypt.[131] The low draft of warships discouraged voyages by galley forces in open water out of sight of land, and the Etesian winds blowing south toward the Delta out of the Aegean would in any event discourage a more direct journey from Egypt to the southern coast of Cyprus. In the spring, the *khamsin* winds blowing north out of the eastern Sahara might help propel vessels leaving the Nile Delta coast. Vessels sailing south along the Syro-Palestinian coast have the disadvantage of sailing against the current, although the daily regimen of coastal breezes might aid their passage.

A focus of Levantine sea lanes was the area of Tripoli and Beirut. Travel thence, north along the Syrian coast, was not overly difficult, but a continuation of the route west along the southern coast of Anatolia was complicated by the often narrow channel between the mainland and off-shore islands and by the dangerous katabatic winds, particularly in the much-to-be-avoided Gulf of Antalya. Similarly, vessels traveling to the eastern Mediterranean from the northwest would seek to avoid the southern Anatolian coast. A crossing between the area of Beirut and the coast of Cyprus would allow vessels traveling both to the east and to the west to avoid the hated winds and narrows of the southern coast of Anatolia.

An Egyptian fleet could attack north up the Levantine coast more easily than a northern fleet might attack to the south along the same coast. If a force based in Egypt controlled at least a few Levantine ports, it could water itself routinely, patrol the sea, and supply land armies that might thereby roam at will through even a hostile interior. A parallel situation is offered by medieval Egypt, when the Fatimid fleet from Egypt was able to assist Muslim land armies, and coordinate activities among the Muslim seaports during the early years of the Crusader states. Medieval Egypt did not lose its ability to influence the political events in Palestine until the loss of most of the ports, and the destruction of a fleet off Ashkelon and the loss of Tyre, its last northern base, during the 1120s C.E.[132] These latter events reveal that as long as certain key ports remained in Egyptian hands, Akhenaten could be rather complacent about events inland. Even with regard to the port areas of Amurru, Akhenaten did not necessarily have cause to worry. Allowing the Amorites some nautical trade could help strengthen the buffer state, and was a safe plan considering the relative ease with which Egyptian fleets could swoop down upon the ports when they so chose—witness the preparations for Akhenaten's Kadesh campaign (see pages 172–175). Beirut appears to have represented the northernmost port to which an Egyptian galley fleet might sail without stop from Egypt and be able to stay on station for a very few days before it would need to run for the Delta, or take on more water.

Ugarit might easily fall under Hittite control—at worst it would benefit the Hittite economy; at best, as a Hittite base on the Cypriot linked coast, Ugarit would bring new goods into the Egyptian-dominated eastern Mediterranean, and link the Hittite nautical economy—what there may have been of such—to the more robust Egyptian sea trade.[133] The port of Sumur was useful to Egypt, but may ultimately have benefited the pharaonic state more as an emporium to strengthen the economy and thereby the state of the Amorites—better to fund the economy of a buffer state than to drain one's own in the direct military confrontation that might well result from that very buffer state's demise.

Both Ugarit and Sumur lay north of the best route between the Levantine coast and Cyprus, the route Egyptian vessels traveling west and then south would take, and the route on which vessels of the north and west might sail on their way into the eastern Mediterranean.[134] Byblos was another matter, but Egypt could be somewhat cavalier, and use Byblos as a bait for the Amorites, even disregard its fate ultimately, as long as Beirut was in Egyptian hands. North of Beirut and Byblos, vessels would ideally sail south to the Byblos–Beirut route to Cyprus, or row south along the coast. As long as Egypt controlled the coastal cities, or at least a smattering thereof, north to Beirut, Nilotic power in the eastern Mediterranean need not be worried.

The coast of Lebanon from Ugarit in the north to Ullasa in the south is an area with no major rivers and few springs or seasonal streams. The coast south from Ullasa to Beirut has little cultivation in the hinterland of the port cities.[135] The scarcity of major water sources north of Ullasa combined with the relatively unfavorable sailing conditions along the southern coast of Anatolia to contribute yet further to the ease with which the Egyptians could disregard ports north of Byblos and Beirut. The limited direct supplies of food from the immediate hinterlands of the cities north of Beirut would also decrease the importance of those ports as major supply depots for Egyptian fleets or inland-bound military expeditions.

Aziru's capture of Sumur, which Akhenaten might have sacrificed for the sake of strengthening the Amorite buffer state, occurred in year twelve or thirteen of the reign of Akhenaten. In nearly all respects, the twelfth year of Akhenaten's reign marked a high point in the pharaoh's terrestrial power. Beneath the shining rays of the Aten, Akhenaten received tribute from all corners of the world, and he wanted his northern vassals to witness this display. Although the scenes do not label the figures, a group of elaborately attired Syro-Palestinians in the upper right-hand corner of the durbar scenes are almost certainly rulers of Egyptian-allied cities. Their subjects, also wearing colorful woolen robes, carry shields, spears, swords, helmets, and have chariots, and their compatriots lead in horses and captives. In just a few years, Akhenaten would employ these weapons against the Hittites, but for now Akhenaten's decisions with regard to Aziru and the rest of Egypt's vassals in Syria-Palestine would be shaped by events almost entirely out of the pharaoh's control.

While Akhenaten was playing sun god, Suppiluliuma was playing soldier. Probably slightly before the great durbar festivities at Akhet-aten, in approximately 1340 B.C.E., Suppiluliuma mounted a major offensive against Mitanni, the Great Syrian Campaign, and in one fell swoop conquered nearly all the Mitanni vassals in northern Syria-Palestine.[136] The Hittite juggernaut continued into the Mitanni homeland and overran the Mitanni capital, Washukanni, sending the king Tushratta fleeing from his own palace. The chronology of the events following the Great Syrian Campaign is uncertain, but at some point after the Hittite offensive, the cowardly behavior of the Mitanni king led to his murder[137] and the flight of his son Shattiwaza to the Hittite court.[138] The Hittites later established Shattiwaza as a client king over the Hurrian rump state of Khanigalbat,[139] which encompassed portions of Mitanni that the Hittites did not feel immediately disposed to incorporate directly into their territory, left perhaps as a buffer against encroachments by the Assyrians. Despite the overwhelming success of the Hittite blitzkrieg, Suppiluliuma and his son Mursili II would take several more decades to consolidate their rule over the remnants of the Hurrian empire.

Suppiluliuma's Great Syrian Campaign signaled a major change in the balance of power in the ancient Near East, but had relatively little effect on the territorial extent of Egypt's northern empire. Ugarit, previously an Egyptian ally at the northern extremity of Egypt's sphere of influence, was led into the Hittite fold by Niqmaddu II,[140] but the other Hittite territorial gains in the lands of Nuhasse and Niya were vassals of Mittani, not Egypt, and both of these regions would continue to revolt against Hittite rule. Hittite records indicate that Suppiluliuma's offensive was aimed directly at Mitanni and its vassals, and the Hittite king studiously avoided any direct conflict with Egypt. Suppiluliuma's intentions, however, were foiled by a fateful event. As the Hittite army traveled south to conquer one of the southerly vassals of Mitanni near the Egyptian-held territory of Upe, they were attacked by Shutatarra, the ruler of Kadesh, who claimed allegiance to the cause of Egypt and possibly to that of Mitanni as well.[141] Thus provoked, Suppiluliuma thrashed the small force of the ruler of Kadesh and took both Shutatarra and his son Aitakama hostage.

Although Mitanni would mount a counterattack against Suppiluliuma about ten years later during the reign of Tutankhamun (see pages 178–179), the Hurrian state's political influence was all but destroyed. At the same time, the vast majority of Egypt's sphere of influence remained intact. The Egyptians opted to wait and see what would result from the successful Hittite advance, and indeed no strong Hittite military presence developed in the southern portion of their new sphere of influence. Although the Hittites claim to have avoided confrontation with Egypt, the new Hittite vassals in Syria-Palestine did not maintain the same respect for Egyptian interests, a lack of respect probably fostered by the Hittites themselves. The Amarna Letters indicate that the chief thorn in Egypt's side was Aitakama, the ruler of Kadesh, installed as a Hittite vassal after the defeat of his father in the Great Syrian Campaign.

A few years after the Great Syrian Campaign, Aziru, once futilely seeking a place in Egypt's array of foreign vassals and agents, found himself personally summoned to visit Egypt. Akhenaten wanted to take the measure of the man he had probably already decided would be at the head of the state that would replace Mitanni as Egypt's chief northern buffer. Akhenaten appears also to have tired of Aziru's fraternization with loyal Hittite vassals such as Aitakama, ruler of Kadesh (EA 162):

Now the king has heard as follows, 'You are at peace with the ruler of Kadesh. The two of you take food and strong drink together.' And it is true. Why do you act so? Why are you at peace with a ruler with whom the king is fighting? . . . But if you perform the service of the king, your lord, what is there that the king will not do for you? If for any reason whatsoever you prefer to do evil, and if you plot evil, treacherous things, then you, together with your entire family, shall die by the ax of the king. . . .

And when you wrote, saying "May the king, my lord, give me leave this year, and then I will go next year to the king, my lord . . ."—the king, your lord, let you off this year, in accordance with what you said. Come yourself, or send your son, and you will see the king at whose sight all lands live. You are not to say, "May he give me this year, too."[142]

The invitation to visit Egypt was probably not fully explained to Aziru, and certainly not to his family, who feared that the Amorite king's visit to Egypt might be a permanent stay.[143] In their brother's absence, two other sons of Abdiashirta assumed the rulership of Amurru: Baaluya and Betili. Letters addressed to Aziru's brothers from nearby rulers even accuse them of betraying their brother to Egypt;[144] clearly these two Amorites would have their hands full maintaining their kingdom while their charismatic brother was away.[145] Without having to kill Aziru, Akhenaten had arranged for yet another phase of instability—though much more moderate this time—in the realm of Amurru, and left the sons of Aziru merely struggling to maintain order, rather than needing to build an ordered state again.

In Egypt, Aziru received a letter (EA 170) from Amurru reporting unverified accounts of the massing of Hittite forces in Nuhasse—probably in response to Nuhasse's friendly dealings with Egypt—and the Hittite capture of portions of Amki.[146] Whether Aziru voluntarily shared the letter with Akhenaten, one need not doubt that the vicar of the Aten probably learned of the letter's contents before the one to whom it was written. Akhenaten appears to have taken the reports of Hittite activity fairly seriously and allowed Aziru to return to Amurru; however, Akhenaten also dispatched the Egyptian commissioner Hani, who had become acquainted with the Amorite king during the latter's stay in Egypt, to watch over Aziru and report on what Akhenaten must already have realized would be the Amorite's inevitably unsavory behavior.

The letter EA 170 may have exaggerated the Hittite threat, but it almost certainly revealed Amurru's desire to show the pharaoh why a good buffer state, a strong Amorite kingdom, would be in Egypt's interest. The hint was taken, and Aziru soon returned to his wild homeland. Having learned of Egypt and probably having received the fright of his life thus far when ushered into the presence of the pharaoh, and having had his life spared, Aziru promptly set about doing what one would expect of a good son of Abdiashirta—he opened negotiations with the Hittites.[147] At the same time, Aziru probably tried to assert himself by avoiding an audience with the Egyptian commissioner Hani. Should we believe that Akhenaten really thought Aziru would be a loyal subject of Egypt, and picture him crying over his offerings to Aten when he later learned of Aziru's almost immediate overtures to the evil empire? Or did Aziru's visit assure Akhenaten of just such brazen duplicity and self-serving initiative? The latter is more likely. If Aziru had returned a true blue, cartouche-wearing pharaonic servant, he would have lost some of his value as leader of a self-sufficient buffer state.

Akhenaten's fears about Aziru's loyalty might have been further quelled by reports that the Amorite king was directing his military aspirations northward. At this time Aziru also wrote to Akhenaten, trying to respond to the king's accusations about avoiding Hani (EA 161): "The king, my lord, has spoken about Hani. My lord, I was residing in Tunip, and so I did not know that he had arrived. As soon as I heard, I went up after him, but I did not overtake him."[148] But what was Aziru doing in Tunip? Under Akhenaten, with Tunip's rightful new ruler held in Egypt (see page 145), and with the people of Tunip writing desperately in the face of Amorite aggression, Akhenaten did nothing, and Aziru occupied Tunip. Apparently Egypt indeed wanted Amurru to grow, and to appear to itself and to others to have done so by its own devices. If Egypt should seem weak and prevaricating to enemies, this was perhaps a small political price to pay for allowing Amurru to pay the real economic cost of consolidating the northern border of Egypt's realm. Tunip also would give Aziru a more direct access to territory in the Hittite sphere.[149] As the Amorite state began to turn its avaricious foreign policy from the south to the north, further expansion would remove other cities and small states allied or potentially allied with the Hittites. The preservation of the Amorite realm as the best hope for a buffer state between Egypt and Hatti would probably become as important to the Hittites as to the Egyptians.

Just so Aziru would stay on his toes, to keep him busy and ensure that he would not complacently assume that he had Egypt in his pocket, an Egyptian official in the north, Hatip, appears—according to Aziru, at least—to have urged some of the forces of Nuhasse to prick the sides of Amurru.[150] Akhenaten apparently asked why Aziru did not rebuild Sumur, the former Egyptian commissioner's seat, damaged by Aziru himself. Aziru reported that Nuhasse's attacks had delayed him, but he would deal with Sumur right away (EA 161).[151] Rather than the sly player of the political great game he believed himself to be, a view with which some more recent readers of his correspondence have concurred, Aziru looks a bit more like a third wheel not entirely sure what Akhenaten and Hatip are about. There is no reason to believe that Hatip did not tell Akhenaten he had arranged some "reconnaissance in depth" by Nuhasse into Amorite territory, and Akhenaten probably chose that time to write to Aziru with instructions to take care of Sumur, which was on the other side of the Amorite's realm.

Like his father before him, Aziru eventually turned his attentions on Byblos and its conscientiously corresponding ruler, Ribaddi. Akhenaten was apparently tired of Ribaddi's missives, even asking the ruler of Byblos, "Why does Ribaddi keep sending a tablet this way to the palace?,"[152] but Ribaddi persisted and asked for three hundred (presumably Egyptian) soldiers, a hundred Kushite soldiers, and thirty chariots to protect Byblos.[153] Was this seemingly modest force really all that Ribaddi thought necessary? Perhaps merely a show of Egyptian force was all that Ribaddi thought was needed to make Aziru desist his attacks. Similar requests for very small groups of soldiers appear in the letters of other vassals; one of the most extreme requests appears in a missive by Abimilki, ruler of Tyre (EA 150): "Should a single soldier guard the city of the king, my lord, then I would go in to behold the face of the king, my lord."[154]

The desperation of such statements reverberates to this day; indeed, a parallel situation occurred much more recently. From 1884 to 1885, besieged by the Mahdist army in Khartoum, British general Charles "Chinese" Gordon sent increasingly desperate appeals to the relief column slowly advancing south under general Sir Garnet Wolseley, at one point requesting a hundred men simply to show the colors.[155] Like Ribaddi, Gordon believed that such a small force might have been able to turn the tide against his enemies, since it would have had a powerful effect on both the besiegers and the besieged populace. If anything, the Amorites seem to have been more dangerous through their ability to turn the disaffected elements in their victims' populations into effective and often deadly fifth columns than in their own battlefield prowess.[156]

Although even Ribaddi's wife advised him to sue for peace with Aziru, Ribaddi fled Byblos and sought asylum in Beirut.[157] Upon Ribaddi's departure, his younger brother made himself ruler of Byblos and sought to ingratiate himself to Aziru by delivering up to the Amorite the sons of Ribaddi.[158] Ribaddi's own end is a bit unclear, but he reported to the Egyptian pharaoh that he was too ill to travel to Egypt, and we learn from other correspondence that Ribaddi's own brother barred him from reentering Byblos.[159] Most likely, Ribaddi died in exile from his beloved city that he had tried so long to protect from the Amorites. What is perhaps more important is that Egypt did not care to save Ribaddi from the second

Amorite advance. Apparently under Aziru, the puppet of Akhenaton's effi-
ciently "passive-aggressive" strategy, the pharaoh finally deemed the Amorite state ready to engulf Byblos.

The Realpolitik of Akhenaten

The reign of Akhenaten coincided with a series of major changes in
Egypt's relationship with western Asia. Mitanni began to crumple under
pressure from the Hittites in Anatolia and the growing menace of Assyria
to the east. The action and inaction of Akhenaten in the face of political
changes are often grossly misunderstood, contributing in a number of
works to the view of Akhenaten as a pacifist, when in fact as relatively
inactive as he may have been militarily, he certainly surpassed his predecessors in the cold-blooded Realpolitik of his reign. Akhenaten's apparent
inactivity continued on the diplomatic front the economy of force that
typified Egyptian military activity.

The Amarna Letters do not fully reveal the intentions or decision-
making processes of the great rulers of the ancient Near East and their
vassals. One cannot prove that Akhenaten had a particular strategy in
mind, and Akhenaten's foreign policy is most often characterized as a
failure due to negligence and religious obsession. However, the interpretation of events presented above, combined with modern theoretical
approaches, offer the most direct and unified explanation of the Atenist
ruler's actions. Realism, one of the prevailing theories in international
relations, postulates that human nature is aggressive and that each state
acts independently in a competitive environment; the realist theory also
assumes that rationality and self-interest are the bases of decisions by leaders of states.[160] Our reconstruction of Akhenaten's diplomatic and military strategy in Syria-Palestine, including his support of the untrustworthy
Aziru and abandonment of Egypt's ally Mitanni, conforms with realism—
Akhenaten's decisions are rational and in the best interest of the Egyptian state.[161]

Mitanni in its death throes appears to have sent mixed signals to the
Egyptians as to what it was or was not prepared to do. The Hittites were
rapidly surpassing Mitanni in the stability and military power of their
realm and would no doubt soon present an opponent more formidable
than the Egyptians had encountered since the Second Intermediate
Period. The genius of Akhenaten's Asiatic policy is that he allowed the
various groups involved to fight against one another, thereby eliminating
a weak and potentially duplicitous power (Mitanni) and creating an

equally duplicitous but militarily less powerful buffer state (Amurru), better placed geographically than Mitanni to separate Egyptian holdings from
the Hittite Kingdom. At the same time, Akhenaten refused to incorporate
Amurru more closely into the Egyptian sphere. Outer buffer states provided time for the "mother state" to react to outer threats, without the
need to maintain a static border. As Rome learned at the end of the first
century, when buffer states become loyal clients and virtually indistinguish-
able from the state they were originally intended to protect, a perimeter
defense becomes necessary.[162]

Akhenaten and his advisers might have foreseen a similar situation
occurring if they incorporated Amurru into the core of their northern
empire. Egypt needed Amurru as a client state, not as an Egyptian colony,
precisely so that Egypt would not need to commit the forces necessary if its
northern border were contiguous with the southern extent of the Hittite-
controlled territory. If Amurru were so interested in its own survival that
it were indeed willing to play a dangerous game with Egypt and Hatti,
then Egypt could be reasonably assured that Amurru probably would not
unconditionally open its gates to the Hittites either.[163] If the Hittites also
desired to avoid the expense and danger of maintaining a directly controlled forward border that abutted a forward Egyptian line, then a self-
serving buffer would be in place in Amurru. Akhenaten had cultivated a
strong Amurru probably with the idea that a self-important state headed
by self-important rulers like Aziru might bow and scrape to Egypt or Hatti,
but would never want to be truly occupied, and would thereby remain as
a buffer state, no matter to whom Amurru at the moment feigned open
alliance.

For Egypt's Asiatic foreign policy, the demise of Mitanni and the corresponding rise of Amurru allowed the replacement of one buffer state by
another farther to the west, situated more directly between the chief centers of Egyptian and Hittite control. The shift from Mitanni to Amurru
had one significant drawback to Egyptian foreign policy, however—the
limited eastward extent of the Biqa corridor led to a correspondingly limited expansion of Amurru to the east, resulting in a no-man's-land potentially open to the southern expansion of Hittite influence east of the
Orontes River. Near the center of this potential corridor east of Amurru
lay the city of Kadesh, and although Akhenaten's political machinations
served Egypt well at the time, the geopolitical situation he created in the
northern Levant would make Kadesh the flash point of conflict between
Egypt and the Hittites. The largest and most celebrated battle at Kadesh
would not occur until the reign of Ramesses II, but three earlier battles

were fought around the city, one each under Akhenaten, Tutankhamun, and Seti I.

Akhenaten's Attack on Kadesh

In contrast to Akhenaten's diplomatic policies, which allowed the Aten-worshipping pharaoh to maintain Egypt's northern empire with hardly any commitment of Egyptian forces, Akhenaten's one known Asiatic campaign—an attempt to assert direct pharaonic control over the city of Kadesh—appears to have failed. Kadesh, on the Orontes River, was essentially caught between the Hittite power to the north, Egypt's Palestinian dependencies to the south, Amurru to the west, and a sparsely settled and arid region to the east. Having initially belonged to Mitanni, Thutmose III added the city of Kadesh, initially a Mitanni dependency, to the Egyptian sphere of control during his string of Asiatic campaigns.[164] Kadesh remained in the Egyptian fold until Shutatarra's ill-fated attack on the Hittite army during the Great Syrian Campaign.[165] Since Suppiluliuma thus had a reasonable excuse for his attack on Kadesh, Akhenaten did not respond militarily at first, but waited to see how the Hittites would consolidate their new territories, and most importantly, whether they would seek to expand into the Egyptian portions of Syria-Palestine.

Akhenaten's patience was well rewarded, since the Hittites neither garrisoned the old Mitanni vassals with troops nor made any overt attempt to push farther southward. Even Shutatarra's son Aitakama, whom the Hittites installed as ruler of Kadesh, lost no time professing renewed loyalty to Egypt. However, Aitakama's letters about his allegiance to Akhenaten were entirely disingenuous, since at the same time, numerous Egyptian vassals reported Aitakama's attempts to persuade Egyptian vassals to switch their allegiance to the Hittites. Suppiluliuma himself maintained cordial relations with the Egyptian court and in later letters protested his friendly intentions. Yet the letters of Egypt's other vassals, such as Akizzi of Qatna, told a very different story (EA 53): "And now [Aitakam]a has written me and said, '[Come] with me to the king of Ha[tti].' I s]aid, 'How could [I go to the ki]ng of Hatti? I am [a ser]vant of the king, my lord, the king of Egypt.'"[166]

Aitakama was probably not making overtures to Egypt's vassals on his own initiative, without the blessing of Suppiluliuma. The Hittites were playing a double game, assuring Egypt of their peaceful intentions with their new empire in Syria-Palestine while encouraging the local rulers to foment discord among Egypt's vassals and positioning troops in key defensive positions.[167] For nearly five years, Akhenaten took no direct military action against the Hittites, probably trusting the self-interest of all the states in Syria-Palestine to maintain a balance of power. However, the continued treachery of Aitakama, and his dealings with Aziru in particular, might finally have stirred Akhenaten to action. Probably during or shortly after the time Aziru was a hostage in Egypt, Akhenaten began preparations for a campaign against Kadesh.[168] As Akhenaten's commanders marshaled the Egyptian forces, the pharaoh wrote to numerous Egyptian vassals, requesting that they prepare for the arrival of an Egyptian army.[169] Zimreddi of Sidon describes in particularly enthusiastic terms the announced arrival of Akhenaten's forces (EA 144),[170] and the Egyptian vassals even tried to outdo one another in providing assistance to the pharaoh; Abimilki of Tyre records (EA 155): "As the ruler of Beirut has done service with one ship, and the ruler of Sidon is doing service with two ships, I will do service with all your ships."[171]

The Egyptian army advanced to Kadesh in two contingents, one by sea and one by land.[172] The movement of a large force through Syria-Palestine would have greatly taxed the food and water resources of any given area, and even where supplies were sufficient, a massive army would have been hard pressed to replenish its stores and continue moving with some speed.[173] By dividing the army into land and sea contingents, the Egyptians made the most of the relatively sparse resources of the area. The fleet moving along the coast could access water and food supplies of the Syro-Palestinian coast and could bring supplies from Egypt to set up depots for its own use and that of the land forces. Considering the importance of rivers and streams for watering a large force, and given the fact that many of the water sources of the coastal cities, such as Ashkelon and Joppa, are rain-fed wells, Akhenaten's advance probably would have been timed to coincide with the greater supplies of water available during the winter months.

Although no Egyptian historical texts provide details about the campaign, one may reconstruct the route taken by each column, based on the names of the cities of the Syro-Palestinian rulers who report about their preparations to receive the Egyptian army. The land column almost certainly began its long trek northward at the gateway to Canaan—the Egyptian border fortress of Tjaru, on the eastern edge of the Delta.[174] Jar labels from throughout the Amarna Period attest to the richness of the vineyards surrounding Tjaru, and the soldiers probably tried to stock up on Tjaru's precious vintage before setting off on their march. Further supplies could have been garnished from the nearby fortress at Tell el-Borg, which might have contained a temple dedicated to the Aten; stamped jar handles with the names of Ankhkheperure and Tutankhamun reinforce the importance of this site as a staging point for operations during the late Amarna Period.[175]

Like the Egyptian armies sent northward during the Nineteenth Dynasty, Akhenaten's troops would have followed the "Ways of Horus," a military highway leading across the northern portion of the Sinai Peninsula and into the city of Gaza.[176] Three days' march from the Egyptian border at Tjaru and already halfway across the desert of the Sinai Peninsula, the army probably halted at the outpost of Bir el-'Abd, where a number of storage magazines and a large cistern would have allowed troops to restock their supplies.[177] Later armies crossing Sinai did not always have the advantage of water depots or cisterns, and even Akhenaten's land forces may have received assistance with water and supplies from the Egyptian fleet. Even with their water supplies augmented by shipments with the fleet and through access to the well at Bir el-'Abd, the force would almost certainly have wanted to cross with some rapidity, probably arriving at the border of southern Palestine within five to seven days after departing from the eastern Delta.[178]

Once into Syria-Palestine, the land contingent, swelled by contributions from several local rulers, moved north along inland routes between the coastal plain and the Jordan River. At the same time, the Egyptian naval contingent, which had probably assembled at Memphis or Perune-fer, sailed along the coast, stopping at major ports.[179] At these ports, including Tyre, Sidon, and Beirut, the navy could both resupply and deliver troops to reinforce the land column; Thutmose III placed similar emphasis on port cities in his own Asiatic campaigns.[180] The city of Byblos was mostly likely not included in the coastal stations employed during Akhenaten's campaign against Kadesh.[181] Byblos was both unnecessary considering the importance of Beirut and Tyre, and unlikely, considering the unsettled nature of the city at the time. Rather than landing and restoring Ribaddi, the Egyptians had allowed the former ruler of Byblos to drift on to Sidon (EA 162), vainly tried to get him to Joppa (EA 138), and during the time of the Egyptian preparations against Kadesh he was residing in Beirut. In fact, a letter from Ammunira of Beirut to Akhenaten (EA 142) relative to his preparations to receive the Egyptian forces provides news concerning Ribaddi, who is residing in Beirut, and Byblos, which is under the control of Ribaddi's brother, who has recently turned over Ribaddi's children to the Amorites. The Egyptians appear unconcerned about the actions of Aziru and the takeover of Byblos, and the correspondence with the coastal cities farther south suggests that Tyre, Sidon, and Beirut were sufficient for any Egyptian attack on Kadesh.

The dispositions of the armies at the resulting conflict at Kadesh remain unknown. In the end, the only information about the conflict was its result—a loss for the Egyptians and renewed pro-Hittite activity by Aitakama.[182] As Tutankhamun summarized in his restoration stela: "If an army was sent to Djahi (Syria-Palestine), to widen the boundaries of Egypt, they could not succeed."[183] Whether Akhenaten failed to achieve his military goals or not, his attack on Kadesh demonstrates two essential aspects of Egypt's approach to its northern empire: the importance of Kadesh as the focus of a great north–south corridor, and the crucial role port cities played in Egyptian strategy. The Syro-Palestinian campaigns of Seti I and Ramesses II reaffirm the significance of these two features, and reflections thereof appear even in the medieval Crusades.

A corridor to the east of Amurru and passing through Kadesh could indeed allow a northern enemy to threaten Egyptian control in Syria-Palestine, and might equally allow a northern military force to bypass Egypt's garrisons and dependencies on the Mediterranean coast. If a Hittite force slipped past Amurru on its way south, it might equally avoid Moab, the region of Transjordan east of the Dead Sea. The Kadesh corridor did not simply bypass Amurru, but provided access to the Wadi Sirhan, east of Moab, through which an army advancing south might bypass all major population and military concentrations to the west. During the early Islamic period the Wadi Sirhan provided the Umayyad rulers with a direct route between Damascus and the holy cites of Arabia, and they peppered the region of Moab and the Wadi Sirhan with a series of "hunting lodges" and postal stations.[184]

The history of the Crusader Kingdom of Jerusalem, both during its attacks on Egypt in the mid-twelfth century C.E., and in its attempts to support the fief of Transjordan later during the same century, make clear the threat a northern force might pose to Egypt by skirting the old region of Amurru. On five occasions during the 1160s C.E., King Amalric of Jerusalem invaded Fatimid Egypt. The second, third, and fourth of these invasions by Jerusalem via Ashkelon along the coast were countered by the army of Aleppo, advancing from Damascus—not far from old Kadesh— and traveling into the fiefdom of Transjordan—the old region of Moab— before crossing Sinai and reaching the eastern Nile Delta.[185] Even with the former Moab garrisoned, the Kingdom of Jerusalem could not easily block the southward movement of Syrian forces; if the Hittites had managed to hold Moab, they might also have been able to march directly to the border of the Nile Delta.

The result of Akhenaten's attack on Kadesh was a Hittite counterattack into Amki, a scenario repeated after Tutankhamun's later attack on Kadesh. The raids and counterraids between the regions of Amki and Upe reveal that both sides understood the problem of Amurru's eastern hinterland, where both sides would struggle but not press an advantage. Kadesh, however, fulcrum of the seesawing wrangle, became a prize too tempting to resist. If Akhenaten did not seek to capture Kadesh permanently, he probably at least sought to prevent the Hittites from doing the same, and later Seti I demonstrated that Egypt might indeed seize the Kadesh corridor. After the seeming quiet during the reign of Horemhab, who was probably tired from his military adventures under the late Amarna rulers, Seti I adopted an aggressive foreign policy.[186] Soon after his succession, Seti I secured the road to Gaza; advanced against rebels in Palestine; relieved beleaguered Beit Shean; and captured Yenoam, near the source of the Jordan River. Then, after his second regnal year, Seti advanced up the Levantine coast, and blew through Amurru like the blast of a flame, as the Egyptians were fond of saying. Seti then attacked Kadesh, still allied with the Hittites, and successfully captured the city. Either at the same time or shortly thereafter, Seti I defeated an actual Hittite military force.

Seti I's campaign did not directly alter the extent of Egyptian holdings in Syria-Palestine, and at the end of the campaign the Egyptians withdrew and Kadesh quickly returned to nominal Hittite suzerainty.[187] The inhabitants of Kadesh removed the stela Seti had erected at the city, but they carefully stored it away in case the stela needed to be reerected in the event of another Egyptian occupation. Seti I's lack of concern with the rapid reversion of Kadesh to the Hittite sphere implies that the goal of his Kadesh campaign and Hittite battle may have been to force a treaty with the Hittites; perhaps more likely, Seti's Kadesh campaign was an attempt to negotiate an already intended treaty from a position of greater strength, to wrest the greatest number of concessions from the Hittites.

Although Akhenaten's Kadesh campaign was perhaps not planned as wisely as Seti I's later military actions, Akhenaten may have hoped to achieve what Seti I later did achieve—not necessarily a long-term domination of Kadesh, but some sort of legal agreement with the Hittites that would serve the same purpose: the sealing off of the Kadesh corridor. The so-called Kurushtama treaty to which later Hittite historical documents refer was probably in place during Akhenaten's reign,[188] and the pharaoh might have desired a change in terms facilitated by military victory. Although Akhenaten's attack did not violate the treaty, the Hittite reaction to the Egyptian campaign—a retaliatory raid into the Egyptian territories in Amki—certainly did.[189]

The ultimate resolution to the Egyptian-Hittite conflict and the troublesome Kadesh corridor would not appear until the twenty-first regnal year of Ramesses II, sixteen years after his great battle against Muwatallis at Kadesh. Often credited as a Hittite victory, the Battle of Kadesh was actually a tactical victory for Ramesses II, even though he failed to take the city.[190] Hittite subterfuge enabled Muwatallis's chariotry to ambush a column of the Egyptian army, to put another to flight, and to descend upon Ramesses II's camp. Strategically Ramesses had blundered, racing ahead with but a portion of his force and leaving his other army groups strung out behind; but then, hemmed in by Hittites and facing capture or death, Ramesses revealed a tactical brilliance. Instead of merely retreating in headlong, self-preserving flight, Ramesses and his charioteer Menna, with one division of chariots, charged repeatedly into the attacking Hittites, engaging much of the Hittite chariotry; despite the Egyptian counterattack, Muwatallis did not send his infantry in support of the twenty-five hundred Hittite chariots. Confident attackers became the prey of the son of Re himself; Ramesses held on long enough for another Egyptian column, the army of Ptah, to arrive on the field, and the Hittites in response committed another one thousand chariots.

At this point a fifth Egyptian army, the Narin, probably sent along the coastal road and apparently unknown to the Hittites, arrived at Kadesh and threw itself into precisely those Hittites who were milling about confusedly in the face of Ramesses' counterattacks. Ramesses' precipitous move on Kadesh may have been necessitated by the desire to link up with the Narin, who apparently traveled by a western route. The Hittites panicked and retreated, some drowning in the Orontes. Although the Hittite losses were heavy, the Egyptians did not succeed in capturing the city of Kadesh. Ramesses made a grave strategic error, but the logistics of the Egyptian plans, particularly the arrival of the Narin, and the genius of Ramesses' retreat-as-counterattack tactics, combined with the poor tactics of the Hittite army, produced a tactical victory for the Egyptian army. Ramesses had reason to be disappointed with elements of his army, but at least most were living disappointments, and at least a fifth of his total force seems never to have been heavily involved in the major contest, whereas the Hittites had exhausted their chariot force and suffered heavy casualities, with major command losses as well.

After Ramesses withdrew from Kadesh, the Hittites appear finally to have attempted to outflank Egypt in a grand manner by gaining the allegiance of Moab. With Moab under the control of the king of Hatti, Hittite forces might have been able to march directly to the border of the Nile Delta. Hittites and their allies in Moab also might have been able to lure Egyptian and allied coastal forces across the Jordan. Again the history of Crusader Jerusalem provides support for such a scenario—Saladin, harassing Transjordan in response to a provocation by Renaud de Châtillon, was able to draw the forces of Baldwin IV of Jerusalem away from their bases west of the Jordan;[191] once those forces had left their familiar territories, Saladin's nephew—from his base at Damascus—was able to attack the undefended Galilee. To prevent such a scenario, probably during the summer bridging his seventh and eighth regnal years, Ramesses II attacked Moab, accusing its rulers of allying themselves with the Hittites.[192] By attacking Moab, Ramesses prevented any Hittite force from advancing south into allied territory via the Kadesh corridor, and prevented any turning of his own right flank while he advanced north again. By regnal year eight Ramesses II had returned to Galilee; by year nine he had taken Dapur, north of Amurru, and outflanked Kadesh. In year ten he was in coastal Syria-Palestine and attacked a pro-Hittite Dapur again. Ramesses eventually captured Qode in Naharin, revealing a collapse of Hittite military resistance in the south.

The events of the reign of Ramesses II demonstrate that the Hittites were indeed aware of the corridor leading south past Kadesh and were ultimately able to exploit that route. They also understood the importance of Moab as a base giving access ultimately to the Sinai and Egypt. Fortunately for Egypt, Ramesses II understood these factors as well. What lessons the armies on both sides of crusading warfare might have learned if they could have studied the Egyptian and Hittite struggle for Kadesh.

The Asiatic War of Tutankhamun

Akhenaten died soon after his attack on Kadesh, but the question of what to do about the area of Kadesh did not go away. The Hittite counterattack into the Egyptian territory of Amki breached the Egyptian-Hittite treaty of the time, but was probably no more than a retaliatory raid; as far as the sources indicate, Suppiluliuma did not follow with a major Hittite offensive. Major events in Syria-Palestine for most of the reign of Tutankhamun remain unknown, since Tutankhamun's abandonment of Akhet-aten brought the Amarna archive to an immediate halt; wherever Tutankhamun's diplomatic correspondence was stored—Thebes or more likely Memphis—the record lies as yet undiscovered. No Egyptian or Hittite historical texts unequivocally record any battles in Syria-Palestine prior to the final year of Tutankhamun's reign, but at about the time of the death of Tutankhamun, another Egyptian campaign was launched against Kadesh; details do not survive, but the timing of the Egyptian attack might have been intended to coincide with a Mittani counteroffensive.[193] The renewed attacks of the weakened but still existent state of Mittani precipitated the Second Syrian War, also known as the Six-Year Hurrian War, which culminated in the defeat of Carchemish and the complete destruction of the Mittanian state.[194] Tutankhamun's strike on Kadesh triggered a Hittite counterattack on Amki, the same reaction Akhenaten's attack on Kadesh had elicited. Both Akhenaten and Tutankhamun probably sought to force some conclusion to the Kadesh problem, for with the last vestige of the Hurrian state expunged, Hatti might decide to use Kadesh and the corridor east of Amurru.

The images of Tutankhamun's Asiatic campaign are fragmentary and provide few details about the location of the battle or the tactics involved.[195] Despite these problems, the lively carvings indicate that a chariot battle and an assault on fortifications were elements of the campaign. In one scene, an Asiatic warrior, with a typical bobbed hairstyle and kilt, is transfixed by the spear of an Egyptian charioteer (see figure 23 top). The ancient artist heightened the drama of the combat by showing the dead Asiatic draped across the legs of Egyptian chariot horses. Another block from this same tableau depicts an Asiatic tangled in the reins of his own chariot. In addition to the chariot battle, Tutankhamun's reliefs also depict an attack against fortifications. On one block, an Egyptian soldier armed with a spear, his shield slung across his back, ascends a ladder propped against a crenellated wall (see figure 23 bottom). The figure of a bearded Asiatic falling headlong from the fortress suggests the success of the Egyptian assault.

The Asiatic War scenes of Tutankhamun portray two different types of enemies, suggesting that the Egyptians fought a coalition of forces from throughout Syria-Palestine. The southern, Canaanite type have a short beard, a bobbed hairstyle tied with a fillet, and wear kilts. The northern Syrian or Mitannian type have short hair, a long beard, and wear long cloaks. The Tutankhamun battle scenes also provide a small but significant bit of information about the chariots of the "boy-king's" enemies. A poorly preserved block from the Tutankhamun Asiatic battle scene appears to depict a three-man crew in an Asiatic chariot.[196] The Asiatics

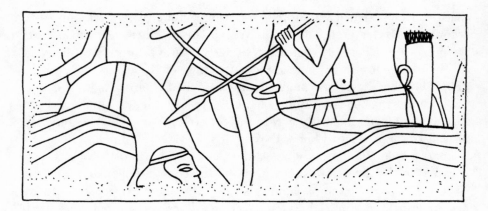

Figure 23. Two blocks from battle
scenes of Tutankhamun's Asiatic
campaign. (above) A charioteer,
with the horse's reins tied behind
his back, spears an Asiatic enemy,
whose body falls across the legs of
the horses. The shield-bearer wears
a heart-shaped sporran and stands in
front of a full quiver of arrows. After
Johnson, *Asiatic Battle Scene*, 156,
no. 10. (right) A soldier, armed with
a spear and a shield, climbs a ladder
resting against the battlements of an
Asiatic stronghold, while an enemy
defender falls to the ground. After
Johnson, *Asiatic Battle Scene*, 157,
no. 12.

against whom Tutankhamun fights are depicted as standard Canaanite
types, not as Hittites. The Syro-Palestinians, as they appear in scenes of
foreign tribute in the tomb of the vizier Rekhmire, in the heraldic image
of Asiatic combat on the chariot of Thutmose IV, and the Hittites in the
later war tableaux of Seti I, routinely appear with chariots virtually identical to those of the ancient Egyptians, and like the Egyptians, the Asiatics appear to have assigned two men to a chariot.[197]

The image of three Asiatic men in a chariot from the Tutankhamun
monument recalls the later three-man chariots of the Hittites in the
scenes of the Battle of Kadesh under Ramesses II. At Karnak, when Seti I
depicted his encounter with the Hittites, he shows the Hittites fighting
and dying with chariots manned by two men, similar to the Egyptian

chariots.[198] When Seti's successor Ramesses II depicts the chariotry swarms of his own Hittite enemies, those Hittite chariots have three-man crews.[199] Were it not for the Tutankhamun block, one might suggest that the Hittites simply adopted a new style of chariot, perhaps as a result of their loss to the forces of Seti I. The Tutankhamun scene reveals that some sort of experimentation with a different type of chariot crew, and almost certainly with a different sort of chariot, was already occurring during the reign of Tutankhamun.

Why would the Syro-Palestinian enemies of Tutankhamun or the Hittite opponents of Ramesses II add an extra man to the chariot crew? The added weight forced the Hittites to make their vehicles heavier, sacrificing both speed and maneuverability.[200] The Hittite chariotry that attacked Ramesses II also appear to have shifted away from the use of chariots to carry archers;[201] instead, the Hittite chariot crews consist of a driver, a shield-bearer, and a warrior armed with a spear or a lance, both weapons with ranges much shorter than that of the composite bow. While the Egyptian chariot was still suited for high-speed engagement as a platform for mounted archers, the makers of the Hittite chariots had sacrificed the potential for abrupt turns at speed, and seem uninterested in the vehicle's properties of maneuver. The Hittite chariot warriors of the Kadesh battle scenes appear to have become mounted infantry, the chariot transforming into a type of battle taxi; the apparent three-man chariot in the Tutankhamun battle scene suggests that experimentation with the chariot as battle taxi could well go back at least as far as the Amarna Period. The impetus for this apparent shift in chariot tactics, from mobile archery platform to battle taxi, remains to be explored.

The inscriptions accompanying the scenes of the Battle of Kadesh indicate that the Hittites secured soldiers from throughout their empire, including the western marches. From the western edge of the Hittite realm may have come the chief impetus for the three-man chariot. The groups who harassed the western borders of Hatti fought as massed infantry, appear as the Ahhiyawa in the Hittite record, and are one of the groups the Egyptians included among the Sea Peoples (see pages 203–204).[202] The chariot forces of the day, armed primarily with bows, had difficulty defeating the Ahhiyawa and other Sea People groups who wore armor and wielded close-combat weapons. The placement of Hittite infantry soldiers within the new three-man chariots was probably intended to make the chariotry more effective against the new Sea People foes. Considering the pressures on the Hittites in the west, and taking into account particular facets of the subsequent invasions of Egypt from the west and the north, the three-man chariot from the Tutankhamun battle scene is the swallow that heralds the dawn of the rise of massed infantry.

Fragments of relief from the mortuary temple of Horemhab contain further images of an Asiatic campaign.[203] Since Horemhab was responsible for the actual military command and Tutankhamun may have even died while the campaign was in progress, Horemhab probably felt no compunction about taking credit for the victory, as he had for the Nubian War he also led for Tutankhamun.[204] Without further evidence, the warfare in Syria-Palestine depicted on the monuments of Horemhab most probably took place entirely during the reign of Tutankhamun.

Images of the battle on blocks reused from Horemhab's mortuary temple include the royal chariot (only the names of the horses survive) and Egyptian charioteers shooting arrows and surrounded by slain Asiatic foes (see figure 24). At least two of the Asiatics have only a single hand—the stumps of their right arms indicate that their hands have already been severed to provide an accurate count of the enemy dead. Another block depicting part of the battlements of a city labeled "Fortress which his Majesty captured in the land of Kad[esh]"[205] provides the setting for this Asiatic battle.

Other reliefs from Tutankhamun's Theban memorial chapel show the triumphal return of the Egyptian military by sea. The royal flagship, with dozens of rowers and a large two-level cabin decorated with a frieze of uraeus serpents, also carries an important piece of cargo: an Asiatic captive.[206] This Asiatic appears in a cage hanging from the yardarm of the ship, a secure prison that allows Tutankhamun to display his military success. Unfortunately, no text accompanies this scene, and one can only speculate about the identity of the unfortunate captive. Earlier, Amunhotep III had Abdiashirta, the unruly Amorite leader, brought back to Egypt, and Tutankhamun may have copied this feat with the ruler of Kadesh, which would make the man in the cage Aitakama. In this case, while Akhenaten was not militarily successful, Tutankhamun's attack on Kadesh would have achieved at least one major objective.

Tutankhamun also commemorated the results of the Syro-Palestinian war on the eastern bank at the temple of Karnak. In a relief in the court between the Ninth and Tenth pylons, Tutankhamun presents the spoils of victory to the Theban triad.[207] Stacked before the king are elaborate metal vessels and other products from western Asia. Behind Tutankhamun are Asiatic prisoners, all bound by ropes that the king holds in his hand. The dress and coiffure of the captives indicate their diverse origins—some are from inland Syria-Palestine, while at least one is probably an Aegean islander or nautical type of the eastern Mediterranean (for more on such

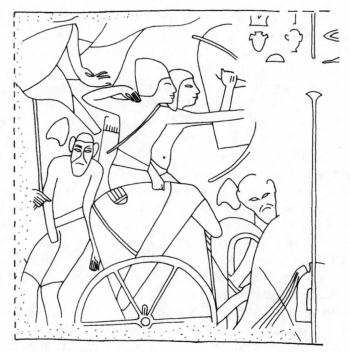

Figure 24. Block from the mortuary temple of Horemhab.
An Egyptian chariot team rides into battle against Asiatic foes.
While the helmeted charioteer shoots his bow, the shield-bearer
holds aloft a round-topped shield. The chariot is equipped with
a bow case (the limp flap indicates that it is now empty) and has
a six-spoked wheel and hand-hold on the body. Fallen Asiatics
and charioteers' helmets litter the scene. The right portion of
the block was recarved at a later date. After Johnson, *Asiatic
Battle Scene*, 170, no. 50.

pirates, see pages 202–203). In a parallel scene, Tutankhamun presents
tribute from Punt, accompanied by the high chiefs of the Puntites (for the
location of Punt, see page 105). However, the chiefs of Punt are not
bound, but stride freely, presenting the produce of their country. The differences between the representations of the Asiatics and the Puntites
demonstrate their contrasting relationships with Egypt. While the inhabitants of Syria-Palestine represent chaotic forces that must be subdued, the
Puntites, who inhabited a land far southeast of Egypt, peacefully traded
with the Nile Valley. Although some of the Asiatics led bound behind the
pharaoh lived closer to Egypt than the distant land of Punt, they were ideologically much farther from the ordered world that was Egypt.

The tomb that Horemhab commissioned while a general provides further depictions of the results of Tutankhamun's Asiatic War. Rows of bound Asiatic prisoners appear alongside Nubians and Libyans on the east wall of the second courtyard; the only accompanying text speaks of General Horemhab's victories in all foreign lands: "His reputation is in the [land] of the Hittites(?), after he traveled northward." The questionable mention of the Hittites in this text finds further support in two images from Horemhab's tomb that represent the first depictions of Hittites from their Anatolian homeland, otherwise known from the battle reliefs of Seti I.[208] The south wall of that same courtyard contains exquisitely carved reliefs of more Asiatic prisoners;[209] the manacles—some of them elaborately carved to resemble rampant lions—and ropes binding the men advertise their status as prisoners of war, and the emotion-filled expressions of the men indicate their reactions to their new status. Horemhab, who is called "one in attendance on his lord upon the battlefield on this day of smiting the Asiatics,"[210] leads these prisoners before the enthroned royal couple, Tutankhamun and Ankhesenamun.

In addition to the scenes of Asiatic prisoners, the tomb of Horemhab also contains images of other foreigners from all corners of the world—Libyans, Nubians, and Asiatics. In these scenes, the different ethnicities are juxtaposed, and none of the foreigners is bound. These two types of scenes reflect two separate historical events. The reliefs of the unbound foreigners allude to a durbarlike event, such as that depicted in two of the tombs at Amarna and in the tomb of Huy, and the incorporation of foreign captives into the Egyptian military (see pages 68–69). The gathering of foreigners appearing in vivid detail in the tomb of Horemhab may even represent the same northern and southern durbars as appear in the tomb of the viceroy Huy. On the other hand, the scenes of bound Asiatics correspond to a specific military event. Unfortunately, the general lack of toponyms in the tomb prevents a precise determination of the origin of the Asiatic prisoners, but one may reasonably suggest that they were captured during Tutankhamun's attack on Kadesh.

The Affair of the Egyptian Queen

Shortly after or even during the Egyptian campaign against Kadesh, and after only a decade on the throne, the young pharaoh Tutankhamun died. As the grieving widow Ankhesenamun placed a delicate wreath of flowers around the vulture and uraeus on the brow of Tutankhamun's golden coffin,[211] she might have wondered what role she would play at a court with no male heir. As Ankhesenamun is reported to have said, she had no desire to marry any of the officials who had played prominent roles during her husband's rule, such as the aging Aye or the general Horemhab. But Ankhesenamun's subsequent decisions led to one of the most surprising and bizarre events of ancient Near Eastern history. While the Hittite king Suppiluliuma was busy besieging one of the last Mitanni holdouts at the city of Carchemish, and immediately after he sent his two top generals to attack Egyptian holdings in Amki, in response to Tutankhamun's raid on Kadesh, he received a letter from Ankhesenamun. Within this letter, the Egyptian widow made a request the Hittite king could not believe—she asked for a Hittite prince, that she might marry him and thereby make him a pharaoh of Egypt. The Hittite king was probably not the only one aware of the queen's bizarre gambit.

The original letter Suppiluliuma received does not survive, nor do any Egyptian records of the event, but Hittite historical texts composed during the reign of Suppiluliuma's successor Mursili II record the event:

> My husband died. A son I have not. But for you, they say, the sons are many. If you would give me one son of yours, he would become my husband. Never shall I pick out a servant of mine and make him my husband! . . . I am afraid!"
>
> When my father heard this, he called forth the Great Ones for council (saying): "Such a thing has never happened to me in my whole life!" So it happened that my father sent forth to Egypt Khattusa-zita, the chamberlain, (with this order): "Go and bring the truth back to me! Maybe they deceive me! Maybe they do have a son of their lord! Bring the truth back to me!"[212]

The name of the recently deceased Egyptian pharaoh as it appears in Mursili's retrospective is Nibkhururiya, which best corresponds to the praenomen of the pharaoh Tutankhamun: Nebkheperure.[213] Although Akhenaten and Smenkhkare have been considered as possible identifications of the king Nibkhururiya, whose widow writes to Suppiluliuma, neither of their praenomens, Neferkheperure and Ankhkheperure, fits the Hittite writing of the Egyptian royal name; furthermore, for both Akhenaten and Smenkhkare, Tutankhamun was duly waiting in the wings. The name of the queen given in the Hittite document, Dakhamunzu, is not a name at all, but a rendering of the Egyptian title ta-hemet-nesut (Great Royal Wife). The identification of the king in the letter as Tutankhamun, the only logical alternative, implies that the widow is Ankhesenamun, and all other available evidence supports such a conclusion.

In the spring, when Khattusa-zita returned to Hatti, he was accompanied by the Egyptian messenger Hani.[214] They carried an indignant letter, part of which might actually appear in a tablet found in the Hittite capital,[215] from the Egyptian queen, who is perturbed that Suppiluliuma doubted the sincerity of her request:[216] "Never shall I take a servant of mine and make him my husband! I have written to no other country, only to you have I written! They say your sons are many: so give me one son of yours! To me he will be husband, but in Egypt he will be king." This new communication did not entirely assuage the fears of the Hittite king, who complained to Hani, the Egyptian messenger: "He will in some way become a hostage, but [king] you will not make him!"[217] Prophetic words, indeed—at least the final portion. Hani responded to this accusation by repeating the words of the queen—the king is dead, the queen seeks a Hittite prince to become pharaoh of Egypt, and only the Hittites have been honored with this incredible request; Hani even admits to the shameful nature of the queen's offer.[218] After consulting older treaties between Hatti and Egypt, Suppiluliuma finally decided to send his son Zannanza, possibly a rendering of the Egyptian title *sa-nesut* (Prince), to Egypt.

The subsequent tablets do not provide any further information about the Hittite prince and his preparations for a trip, which he must have hoped would end in his coronation as the pharaoh of Egypt. To the dismay of Suppiluliuma, the Hittite messengers bring the worst possible news: his son Zannanza is dead, and the Egyptian military, probably under the command of Horemhab, is on the offensive.[219] Following the death of his son, Suppiluliuma literally goes on the warpath and raids Egyptian territories in Amki. Despite his outrage at Zannanza's murder, Suppiluliuma also appears to have felt that his attack on Amki was still in violation of a preexisting treaty between Egypt and the Hittites. In the "Plague Prayers of Mursili II," Suppiluliuma's successor blames the plagues, which were brought back to Hatti after the Amki attack, on his father's rash action.[220] Mursili consults his own tablet archive about Egypt and asks the gods of Hatti the reason for the plague. Since Egypt and Hatti had agreed by treaty—sworn with an oath by the gods of Egypt and Hatti—not to attack one another, Suppiluliuma's offensive broke the treaty and thus angered the Hittite gods, who in recompense released the plague that ravaged Hatti.

Back in Egypt, the ultimate fate of the desperate Egyptian queen remains unknown. Was she forced to marry one of the courtiers she so despised? Signet rings with juxtaposed cartouches of Aye and Ankhesenamun suggest that such might have happened.[221] At any rate, Ankhesenamun's daring ploy failed, as did the royal bloodline that had begun over two centuries earlier with the reign of Thutmose I.

6

⊹·⊹·⊹·◉·⊹·⊹·⊹

UNITING THE TWO LANDS: DOMESTIC SECURITY AND THE ARMY IN PEACETIME

The two corps of the army, living in the agricultural areas, one in the south and one in the north, were wont to steal hides throughout the entire land, without stopping for a single year. . . . Now if it is reported about any soldier of the army that he still goes and steals hides up until today, then the law shall be executed against him consisting of beating him with one hundred blows and five open wounds and confiscating from him the hide, which he stole.

—Decree of Horemhab from Karnak Temple[1]

With these words the pharaoh Horemhab reversed one of the many abuses that plagued Egypt during the reigns of Akhenaten and his successors. The soldiers of the two corps of the Egyptian army—one stationed in Upper Egypt and the other stationed in Lower Egypt—inhabited "agricultural areas" that may have been the plots of lands awarded to them as part of their pay.[2] However, some of the soldiers appear to have desired further income, which they acquired by stealing hides. Horemhab's decree implies that the thieving was frequent and that it went unpunished, a state of affairs dramatically altered by the new king. Horemhab did not stop at correcting abuses by the army, but also issued new and harsh punishments concerning the requisitioning of boats or slaves owned by private individuals, fraudulent tax collection, and bias in the courts.[3]

187

During the reign of Akhenaten, local officials appear to have received less oversight than Horemhab later deemed appropriate. While the decree of Horemhab may also refer to situations that obtained prior to the reign of Akhenaten, the disk worshipper's closure of numerous temples and his concentration of activity at Amarna were probably the main causes for the local power vacuum, into which the more unscrupulous local officials and military leaders appear to have stepped.[4] A greater percentage of people in positions of power during the Amarna Period held their offices through direct royal patronage, which may have further contributed to corruption within the administration.[5] And whereas the concentration of power in the person of Akhenaten might have eliminated certain sources of corruption and patronage in middle levels of the bureaucracy, the resulting thinning of offices, especially in Upper Egypt, probably removed a number of checks and balances on the authority of local officials. As Horemhab's decree indicates, this corruption also spread to the military, and other evidence from Amarna suggests that Akhenaten particularly favored his armed forces. The descriptions of corruption during the reign of Akhenaten also read like specific descriptions of general social and political disruption bemoaned in some Middle Kingdom texts, such as the Admonitions of Ipuwer[6]—even in correcting actual abuses, Horemhab was able through allusion to a literary theme to depict Akhenaten's reign as an "intermediate period."[7]

During the Amarna Period, the Egyptian military fought relatively few major campaigns, but that did not lessen its importance in maintaining Egypt's empire. Even when not combating foes to the north or the south, the Egyptian military remained a significant element of Egyptian society. Outposts were needed to defend against the restive Libyan tribes to the west, to safeguard the Nile Valley as well as Egyptian settlements in the oases of the Western Desert. Along Egypt's northern border, fortresses and patrols were necessary to defend the Delta ports, essential to Mediterranean trade, from the pirate forces that plagued the maritime interests of the eastern Mediterranean world. The army could also function as a corps of engineers, aiding in building projects, particularly the procurement of stone and precious minerals from the Eastern Desert. Finally, with the restoration of the traditional Egyptian cults during the reign of Tutankhamun, elements of the Egyptian military were again able to participate in the great festival celebrations, wherein soldiers hauled divine barks while they sang hymns to the might of the pharaoh.

Akhenaten's Domestic Policy

In foreign policy, Akhenaten could be as aggressive as any previous or future pharaoh; this military prowess and a desire to confront potential threats were characteristics expected of the Egyptian ruler. Although the pharaoh might rage as a fierce lion abroad, he was expected to act as a beneficent shepherd at home.[8] This dual role of the king reflects the same roles of the Aten as they appear in the Great Hymn to the Aten:

> You (the Aten) are beautiful, great, scintillating, high over every land;
> your rays embrace the lands as far as all which you have made.
> As Re, you reach as far as them (the lands),
> and you curb them for your beloved son. . . .
> As for the lands of Syria and Kush and the land of Egypt,
> you set every man in his place;
> you make their necessities, every one of them according to his diet;
> his lifetime having already been reckoned.
> Tongues are separate in speech, and their characters likewise;
> their skins are different, for you differentiate the foreigners.
> In the Underworld you make a Nile, bringing it forth as you wish
> to feed the populace (of Egypt). . . .
> All distant lands, you make them live, for you place a Nile in the sky
> that it may descend for them, making waves upon the mountains
> like the sea to irrigate the fields in their towns.[9]

The Aten both "curbs" the foreign lands and fashions "a Nile in the sky" to nourish those same countries; the different populations who dwell in distant lands are all creations of the one solar disk. But the overtly universalistic aspects of Atenism just as obviously did not deter Akhenaten from impaling Nubians or sending an army against the city of Kadesh. However, Akhenaten's changes to Egyptian religion combined with his universalistic beliefs to effect his domestic policy and the means by which he enforced it.[10]

Some textual evidence for Egyptian hostility toward Akhenaten's plans appears in the fragmentary and damaged conclusion to the first set of boundary stelae at Amarna:

> It was worse than the things which I heard in regnal year 4;
> it was worse than the things which I heard in regnal year 3;
> it was worse than the things which I heard in regnal year 2;
> it was worse [than the things which I heard in regnal year 1].

It was worse than the things which [Nebmaat]re (Amunhotep III) heard. . . .
It was worse than the things which Men[kheper]re (Thutmose III) heard.
[It was] worse [than the thing]s which any of the kings who had ever
assumed the White Crown (of Upper Egypt) heard.[11]

The unique nature of this section of the boundary stelae text renders
interpretation difficult.[12] However, a following fragmentary passage mentions "offensive" things that Egyptians and Nubians have spoken against
the Aten, suggesting that the things that Akhenaten and previous pharaohs heard were blasphemies against the solar disk. The truly damned, as
the Netherworld Books of the New Kingdom reveal, were those who
sinned against Re, upsetting the balance of *maat*, of whom the solar disk
was the ultimate arbiter.[13] The supreme representative of Re on earth, and
his chief solar priest, was the king.[14] One may therefore read these sections of the boundary stelae as descriptions of civil unrest during the reign
of Akhenaten and evidence for opposition to his new religious program.[15]

Perhaps Akhenaten wanted to make the still obscure evil in his reign
seem all the worse so that his righting of those wrongs would seem all the
more significant. Other pharaohs employed similar rhetoric for the same
purpose. In a building inscription on the facade of the rock-cut Speos
Artemidos temple near Beni Hasan, Hatshepsut describes her own constructions as part of Egypt's recovery from the depredations of the Hyksos
period—for the Egyptians of the time of Hatshepsut a distant time of disorder and one from which Egypt had already recovered.[16] A number of
building inscriptions, from before and after the reign of Akhenaten, describe
a ruler encountering a temple in the final stages of collapse and then restoring and rebuilding the temple in a form far better than what he found.[17]

Nevertheless, Akhenaten is unusual in portraying the nadir of the situation as something occurring during his own reign, and worsening during
his reign at that, rather than depicting his rule as a golden time that by its
own inception ended the troubles of the "before time." The political ten-
sion evident in the passage from the boundary stelae is complemented by
another text, which expresses the religious bankruptcy of the Amarna
Period. An ink graffito left by a man named Pawah in a Theban tomb
describes in poignant terms the spiritual desolation he feels in the absence
of the god Amun:

My wish is to see you . . . may you give satiety without eating and intox-
ication without drinking! My wish is to look at you, so that my heart
rejoices. O Amun, protector of the lowly! You are the father of the moth-
erless and the husband of the widow. They are pleased at the mere utter-

ance of your name. . . . Come back to us, lord of eternity! You were here before anything had come into being, and you will be here at the end of time. As you have caused me to see the darkness that is yours to give, make light for me that I may see you![18]

While the members of the court at Amarna appear to have worshipped the Aten with as much fervor as Pawah felt for the god Amun, much of the country might well have commiserated with Pawah's emotional state at the abandonment of the traditional Egyptian gods. The graffito of Pawah dates to the reign of Akhenaten's successor Ankhk(et)heperure Neferneferuaten,[19] but similar views expressed during Akhenaten's own reign could have been one of the many "offenses" that are so disturbing to the pharaoh in the boundary stelae of Akhet-aten.

Evidence for unrest and dissatisfaction during the reign of Akhenaten finds overwhelming support in the thorough *damnatio memoriae* carried out by Tutankhamun, Horemhab, and even Seti I of the Nineteenth Dynasty. Even without further explicit references to rebellion against Akhenaten, the rapid abandonment of his capital and the cult of the Aten following his death are evidence that even during his reign, Akhenaten may have been considered "that enemy from Akhet-aten." Bits of pictorial and archaeological evidence from Akhet-aten provide the final tesserae to this mosaic of civil discontent. In nearly every scene of the royal family, Akhenaten is surrounded by soldiers, many of them foreign, and an examination of police and military installations at Akhet-aten reveals that Akhenaten might have been particularly concerned with his own physical safety.

Police and Military Installations at Akhet-aten

Reliefs in the tombs in the eastern cliffs of Akhet-aten portray significant political and religious events as well as mundane daily activities: sculptors sit within their workshops carving pieces of statuary, brewers and bakers transform grain into beer and bread, and shepherds lead their goats out to graze. All of these industries were essential to the existence of Akhet-aten, but in scenes of the royal family, one profession achieved particular prominence: the military. Wherever Akhenaten and his family went in the city of Amarna, groups of running soldiers accompanied them. Sometimes these soldiers are identifiable only by their military uniform—the heart-shaped sporrans worn over their kilts—but in most cases they carried an assortment of weapons and standards. A scene from the tomb of Ahmes at Amarna displays the multiethnic identity of Akhenaten's bodyguards and their range of armament (see figure 25).[20]

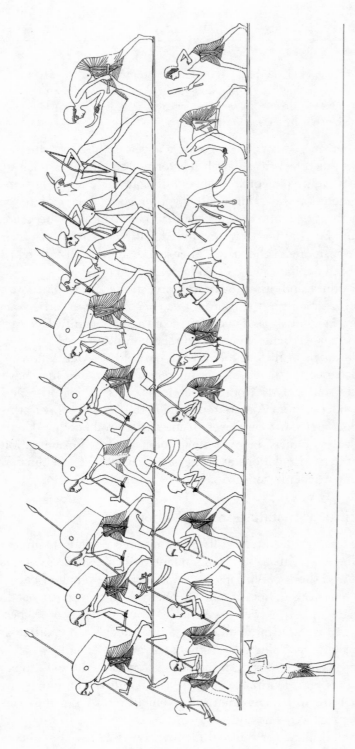

Figure 25. Two units of running soldiers from the tomb of Ahmes at Amarna, including a number of foreign auxiliaries armed with a range of weapons. Below, a trumpeter signals the troops, the notes of his instrument filling the blank space of the entire register. After Davies, *Rock Tombs III*, pl. 31.

Four platoons of soldiers appear between a depiction of the great Aten temple and an image of Akhenaten and Nefertiti riding in a chariot. A single trumpeter, the sole figure in the central register, accompanies the troops; the running soldiers, like all military escorts at Amarna, move in a semibowed posture. The Egyptian soldiers, dressed in kilts and heart-shaped sporrans, are armed with long spears, axes, and shields with central boss, while the officers carry a sickle sword, baton, or both. Other soldiers hoist aloft a series of standards. Alongside the Egyptian troops in the top two registers runs a group of foreign soldiers—two Asiatics, two Nubians, and a Libyan. The Asiatics are dressed in decorated kilts with a distinct point in the front, distinguished in form and fabric from the Egyptian kilt; they wear their hair in traditional Asiatic style, tied with a band around the forehead, and they sport a short, pointed beard. Each Asiatic soldier carries a spear and a *khepesh* sword but no shield. The weapons and accoutrements of the two Nubians differ. The Nubian in the upper register wears a linen kilt with a long sporran, an ostrich feather in his hair, and carries a long self-bow (see pages 72–73). The lower Nubian wears a dangling animal skin over his kilt, his head is shaved, and he wields a long club. The Libyan soldier carries a relatively short, triangular bow, and what may be a baton or an ax in his other hand; he wears a short kilt in place of the expected penis sheath, but wears the traditional long leather cloak tied over one shoulder, trailing far out behind him as he runs.

Scenes in other Amarna tombs reinforce the multiethnic nature of the military forces at Akhet-aten, and their constant presence in the entourage of the royal family.[21] The Egyptian and foreign soldiers are there when Akhenaten grants honors at the Window of Appearances, when the king visits the temples of Akhet-aten, and when he and his family ride their chariots into and out of the Central City. Since Akhenaten's chariot ride and many of his other daily activities replaced the traditional festival celebrations of Egypt, and seeing that the military played an important role in such celebrations during the reigns of other pharaohs (see "Religious Functions of the Military," pages 204–209), one might suggest that the soldiers merely emphasized the festive nature of daily life at Akhet-aten. Even if Akhenaten did employ the military at Akhet-aten to express the religious significance of his daily life, and the ritual into which he made the outward expressions of that daily life, the plentiful armaments of Akhenaten's soldiers also betray a practical function.

Military barracks occupied the eastern edge of the central city of Akhet-aten, separated by libraries and other scribal buildings from the central administrative district and palace.[22] Alongside the barracks was a horse stable, which housed the animals who probably served as patrol mounts and pulled chariots through the streets of the city. This sector of the city contained its own well and commissariat, as the large number of pottery sherds from bread molds and beer jars reveal. These barracks and their associated buildings probably housed and provisioned the local military garrison.

One of the well-preserved tombs in the eastern cliffs of Akhet-aten belongs to the chief of police of Amarna, Mahu. Scenes in the tomb depict events and activities with which Mahu would have been familiar, such as the training of policemen in running. From his tomb scenes we even learn otherwise unattested details of routine police life. For example, to cope with the chill winter nights, Mahu used bowls in which he lit small fires;[23] because of the relative prominence they receive, Mahu appears to have been quite fond of them.

As Akhenaten rides his chariot along the great royal road of Akhet-aten, Mahu is there to greet the ruler. Above and below the image of the king are the policemen in Mahu's employ, many of whom stand outside small, one-man stations that apparently were strung out along the main north-south road. Similar one-room buildings are placed on elevated platforms, which functioned as a line of intervisible signaling platforms. The nature of ancient Egyptian signaling remains unknown, but Roman watchmen could transmit complex messages by means of various techniques.[24] Another scene from the tomb of Mahu shows a series of altarlike platforms with ramps, atop which stand military standards and fans;[25] a man sits on a folding stool beside each of these platforms and receives a message from a running youth. This suggests that the platforms may have functioned, among other things, as communication outposts that could relay both verbal and visual signals. These Amarna posts would be smaller—in both scale and geographical scope—but functionally similar to those the Romans constructed in the Eastern Desert of Egypt and elsewhere.[26]

Akhet-aten as a whole does not appear to have possessed city walls, but the tomb of Mahu portrays a system of watchposts and watchtowers that formed a defensive system for the city.[27] Temporary supply depots were also part of the physical infrastructure of Akhet-aten's patrols. In one such depot, Mahu stands in front of a fire in a large bowl and before him is a chariot beneath a tree and a group of running policemen.[28] In another scene, donkeys and people with shoulder yokes bring supplies to an outpost.

The outpost appears as a much larger structure than the guard posts—a three-story tower with crenellations. Inside the tower are amphorae, various types of food, and a cache of weapons, including shields, axes, and

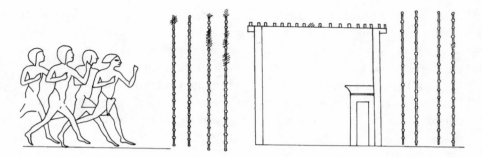

Figure 26. Running policemen patrol the city of Akhet-aten, as depicted in the tomb of the chief of police, Mahu. The crenellated outpost appears between sets of parallel lines, the latter probably representing swept tracks lined with stone piles. After Davies, *Rock Tombs* IV, pl. 21.

bows and arrows. This tower and others like it were primarily intended to guard the items stored within rather than to provide refuge from an attack. Yet another large rectangular building depicted in the tomb of Mahu is associated with parallel lines marked with small circles (see figure 26); these lines are perhaps the edges of patrol routes, and the circles are the rocks removed from the track that were used to line the paths. The patrol routes around this building as well as those that connected the other guard posts indicate that the defense of Akhet-aten rested primarily on roving patrols; considering the extent of the city and its layout, such a system was more effective than a static defense.[29]

The depiction of a motley bunch of criminals in the tomb of Mahu sheds light on life and security at Akhet-aten and suggests that Akhenaten might not have felt wholly safe in his private horizon. Mahu himself appears leading three handcuffed prisoners before a group of Amarna officials: the vizier, the chief officials of the pharaoh, and the commanders of the army "who stand before his Majesty."[30] Mahu greets the grandees, and the vizier responds, perhaps echoing Mahu's own words: "As Aten endures so does the ruler endure." Mahu summons the officials to interrogate the prisoners: "Investigate, O officials, people who climbed the gebel!"[31] Two of the handcuffed prisoners wear long, thin beards, and may be Libyans, while the other appears to be an Egyptian.

Why Mahu chose to depict this particular occurrence remains unfortunately unclear. The only recorded accusation against the men is that they were "climbing the gebel," but a concern about such men might be one reason for the location of the North Riverside Palace. Aside from the fact that the palace would be at the edge of the horizon, it also is near sheer cliffs virtually impossible to climb or descend easily.[32] The North Riverside Palace, which served as the main residence of Akhenaten and his family, also was surrounded by a double wall with engaged towers.[33] These fortifications, combined with the placement of the North Riverside Palace, would have made the residence easily defensible by roving police patrols, who could follow tracks on the plateau above the city.[34]

The Western Frontier

The narrow beards of Mahu's gebel-climbing prisoners suggest that they came from the Western Desert, the land of the potentially hostile Libyan tribes. While the ancient Egyptian civilization flourished along the Nile Valley and established settlements in the oases of the Western Desert, the area of modern Libya remained a region sparsely populated by nomadic tribes. By the time of the New Kingdom, certain of these Libyan groups had become more organized under powerful chiefs, had acquired more wealth, and had even constructed some settlements.[35] Egyptian terms for the eastern Sahara and its inhabitants reflected the changing nature of ancient Libya. During the New Kingdom specific tribal designations, such as Lebu and Meshwesh, augmented the earlier terms Tjehenu, describing Libyan tribes inhabiting the desert north of middle Egypt, and Tjemehu, encompassing all tribes living west of Egypt and Nubia.[36]

Conflicts between the Nile Valley dwellers and tribes of the western Sahara began as early as the Predynastic Period, and the pharaohs of the Old and Middle kingdoms fought periodic campaigns against the Libyans on the fringes of Egyptian territory.[37] Although from the Second Intermediate Period through the late Eighteenth Dynasty, relatively few detailed references to Libyan tribes appear in Egyptian texts,[38] the recruitment of Libyans for the Egyptian military during the reign of Akhenaten as well as possible conflict along the western border during the Amarna Period provide some background for the Libyan wars of the Ramesside Period.[39] From the reign of Seti I onward, conflicts with Libyans became a more visible part of the Egyptian historical record, culminating in the massive wars of Merneptah and Ramesses III against coalitions of Libyan tribes.[40]

Unlike Nubia and Asia, the lands west of Egypt had few local economic resources to attract Egypt's imperial interests. Some of Libya's products were light and seemingly ephemeral objects, such as ostrich eggs and feathers. The eggs might well be canteens,[41] and could be exported farther afield,[42] while the feathers were useful for elements of fans and military insignia. Libyan cattle may have been another trade product linking Egypt and the western Saharan tribes.[43] Other, more exotic products that became important in the classical era, such as the medicinal plant silphium, but that have not left any major archaeological or epigraphic trace in earlier sources, might also have benefited Libya's economic intercourse with Egypt and other lands.[44] Despite the barrenness of their native land, however, the Libyans lived along north-south trade routes that linked sub-Saharan Africa with the Mediterranean coast, giving them access to a wide range of trade goods and contact with foreign traders and soldiers of the Mediterranean world.[45]

The dual local and long-distance trade economies of Libya are reflected in the tribute presented to Akhenaten and Nefertiti during the year twelve durbar at Akhet-aten. In the lower left-hand corner of the durbar scene in the tomb of Meryre II, a Libyan delegation brings the expected ostrich feathers and eggs.[46] Despite the modest nature of such goods, the Libyans appear on a par with Puntites presenting incense and with Aegean islanders bringing elaborate metal vessels. The durbar scene in the tomb of Huya suggests that the Libyans were an additional conduit for metals, including perhaps gold.[47] Texts of the Ramesside Period also occasionally reveal an unexpected wealth and diversity of materials acquired as plunder from defeated Libyans. Plunder lists concluding the accounts of the Libyan campaigns of Merneptah and Ramesses III include not only cattle, livestock, and human captives, but also metal vessels and swords, products of eastern Mediterranean craftsmen and trade routes.[48] The swords captured from the Meshwesh tribe during the reign of Merneptah and wielded by the same tribe in battle scenes of Ramesses III suggest that the military technology of northern Mediterranean groups influenced that of the Libyans.[49]

The Libyan trading post on Bates Island, near modern Marsa Matruh, provides ceramic evidence for the presence of traders from the Aegean, Syria-Palestine, and Egypt from the mid-fourteenth to the end of the thirteenth century B.C.E.[50] Exploitation of such connections enabled the Libyans to become a threat to Egyptian hegemony during the Nineteenth and Twentieth dynasties. The Libyans who invaded Egypt during the reign of Merneptah brought with them not only the weapons of the Mediterranean world but human representatives of that world as well. Mediterranean pirates had become a problem for the northern coast of Egypt proper already by the reign of Amunhotep III, and most likely they also reached the Libyan coast as well. During the Ramesside Period Mediterranean groups known as the "Sea People" found employment in the military forces of Egypt and other Near Eastern kingdoms;[51] the military experience that the Sea People acquired in turn assisted their later attacks against Egypt and the eastern Mediterranean littoral. The otherwise unique appearance in the New Kingdom of Libyan troops in full native attire in Egyptian service during the Amarna Period suggests that the Libyans themselves, by the time of Akhenaten, may have been gaining military experience in Egyptian service.[52]

An enigmatic painted papyrus from Amarna may show the beginnings of conflicts between the Libyans and the New Kingdom Egyptians, and at the very least demonstrates the participation of yet another foreign group in the Egyptian army. The papyrus fragments, now housed in the British Museum, were discovered in a structure that was probably dedicated to the worship of a statue of Akhenaten.[53] The painted scenes on the papyrus depict three different military types—Egyptians, Libyans, and Mycenaeans—distinguished by their mode of dress (see figure 27). The Egyptians wear only linen kilts, and for the most part their armaments are not preserved, but one Egyptian soldier appears to wield a dagger. The Libyans sport long cloaks, open at the front and revealing elaborate tattoos and their exposed genitalia (an artistic misunderstanding of the penis sheath?); one Libyan holds a short bow and carries his arrows in a quiver.

The third type of warrior in the fragmentary composition, and the most surprising element of the papyrus decoration, is clad in an animal hide tunic and wears a conical helmet, decorated with vertical striations. The iconography of the helmets corresponds most closely to the boar's tusk helmets popular among Mycenaean warriors.[54] While the identification of the warriors on the papyrus is certain, their relationship to one another is much less straightforward. The first scene portrays three figures—two striding Libyans and a kneeling Egyptian; the position of the Libyan's arms suggests that he is about to kill the Egyptian. In the second scene, intermingled Egyptian and Mycenaean warriors run to the right. At the top of this scene, an Egyptian soldier appears to thrust a dagger into another man of uncertain identity, who wears a kilt and ox-hide tunic but no helmet. Are the Libyans fighting against a coalition of Egyptians and their Mycenaean auxiliaries? Or are all three groups part of Akhenaten's multiethnic bodyguard, who are quelling a revolt by Egyptians? The former appears more likely, because the Libyans on the papyrus do not wear Egyptian kilts, while the Libyan auxiliaries at Amarna normally add this bit of Egyptian clothing to their traditional dress. Mycenaean soldiers do not otherwise appear in the pictorial record at Amarna; yet the same house in which the painted papyrus was found also contained a complete Myce-

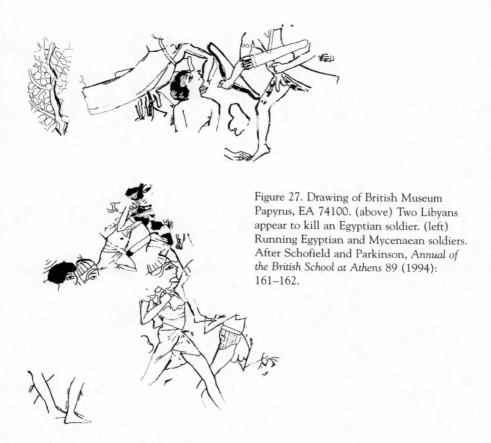

Figure 27. Drawing of British Museum Papyrus, EA 74100. (above) Two Libyans appear to kill an Egyptian soldier. (left) Running Egyptian and Mycenaean soldiers. After Schofield and Parkinson, *Annual of the British School at Athens* 89 (1994): 161–162.

naean vessel, and a large number of Mycenaean sherds have been recovered from Amarna.[55]

The Egyptian, Libyan, and Mycenaean soldiers on the painted Amarna papyrus may or may not refer to an actual historical event. However, the running warriors certainly hint at historical events to come. Reliefs from the reign of Horemhab also depict conflict with Libyan tribesmen, or at least the successful outcome thereof (see figure 28).[56] The pharaohs Seti I and Ramesses II also appear slaying Libyans and hauling prisoners before the gods, but like the fragmentary Horemhab scenes, no detailed historical texts accompany the early Nineteenth Dynasty Libyan battles. However, Ramesses II constructed a series of fortresses along the Western Delta and the Mediterranean coast, an indication that the scale of the Libyan threat at the cusp of the Eighteenth and Nineteenth dynasties was larger than the textual record suggests.[57] No archaeological evidence of a corresponding fortress system of the Eighteenth Dynasty has thus far been

Figure 28. Relief from the mortuary
temple of Horemhab. An Egyptian
soldier chastises a Libyan prisoner
with his ax. After Johnson, *Asiatic
Battle Scene*, 176, no. 58.

discovered,[58] but a series of small desert outposts could have served the
same function as the later Ramesside fortresses.

Such outposts would have served as an early warning system and provided physical support for retaliatory raids. The forward defense in the
Western Desert not only protected the Nile Valley, but also important
Egyptian settlements in the oases, which were renowned for their vineyards.[59] In fact, at least one vineyard in Kharga Oasis, called Perwesekh in
antiquity and now known as Qasr el-Ghueita, supplied large quantities of
wine for the jubilee festival of Amunhotep III.[60] The strategic location of
Kharga and the other oases made them important militarily, but their natural resources also made them vulnerable to Libyan incursions. In the fifth
year of Merneptah's reign, a large coalition of Libyans and Sea People
mercenaries launched an attack on the Nile Delta;[61] avoiding the coastal
forts, the invading forces captured the oasis Farafra and may have used the
interoasis routes of the Western Desert to foment a simultaneous rebellion
of Nubian tribes in the south. Although the Egyptians defeated the combined Libyan and Sea People forces at the fields of Perire, a city in the
western Delta, the invasion demonstrated the vulnerability of the oases
and the potential danger posed by the increasingly sophisticated and
wealthy Libyan tribesmen.

Corps of Engineers

The Egyptian military served multiple functions, only one of which was its
role in war. The relative geographic isolation of Egypt made an army on
constant alert unnecessary, and the state's economic investment in the
military made impractical the maintenance of a large and inactive force in

peacetime. Furthermore, as the Egyptians learned in the aftermath of the
First Intermediate Period, men accustomed to combat do not always transform into model citizens when the conflict ceases.[62] To make the military
more economically advantageous, troops worked on both military and
civil construction projects.[63] Prominent among these projects were quarrying expeditions in the Sinai and the Eastern Desert, where the military
served not only as protection against nomads but also provided added
manpower. The harsh desert environments in which the quarries were
located also may have provided important training for the troops, who
might have to travel to those same regions during campaigns. For example, the war against the Akuyati tribe during year twelve of the reign of
Akhenaten was fought in a gold-mining region of Nubia, and some of the
troops who fought in that campaign might have worked in the region on
earlier mining expeditions. Several inscriptions of Amunhotep IV appear
in the Wadi Abu Qwei, and one large inscription of the Aten in the
nearby Wadi Hammamat was later transformed into a scene of Amun-Re
during the reign of Seti I.[64]

An inscription dating to the beginning of the reign of Amunhotep
IV/Akhenaten from Gebel Silsila describes the role the military could ful-
fill in quarry expeditions. Next to a scene of Amunhotep IV offering to
the god Amun is the following text:

> The King of Upper and Lower Egypt, the high priest of Horakhty, who
> rejoices in the horizon in his name of Shu who is in the sun disk, Nefer-
> kheperure Waenre, the son of Re [Amunhotep], whose lifetime is great,
> living forever and ever, beloved of Amun-Re, lord of heaven, ruler of eter-
> nity. The first occasion of his Majesty commanding [. . .] in order to exe-
> cute all the work projects from Elephantine to Sambehdet (in the Delta).
> The commanders of the expeditionary force were set to carrying out a
> large compulsory labor project, consisting of quarrying sandstone in order
> to make the great *benben*-stone for Horakhty, in his name of Shu who is
> in the solar disk, in Karnak, while at the same time, the officials, compan-
> ions, and chief standard-bearers were tax assessors for the stone statue.[65]

Naval and Port Security

At some time during the reign of Akhenaten a large trading vessel, packed
with goods from Egypt, Syria-Palestine, and the northern Mediterranean
littoral, was plying a counterclockwise route through the eastern Mediterranean Sea. Raw materials formed the majority of the vessel's cargo,
including ten tons of copper and tin ingots, many of them in the "oxhide"
shape; some of this copper came from Cyprus, whose wealth in metal was

a topic of the Amarna correspondence (see page 152). Nearly 150 amphorae carried a range of foodstuffs and wine, and smaller ceramic vessels from all over the Mediterranean held various precious oils and perfumes. The ship also transported jewelry and luxury items, including a gold ring bearing the name of Queen Nefertiti. Off the coast of Turkey, this richly laden trading vessel—now known as the Uluburun shipwreck—sank and lay beneath the waters of the Mediterranean for the next $3^1/2$ millennia. While most of the timbers disintegrated, much of the vessel's cargo remained quite well preserved.[66]

Based on the places of origin of the objects, the Uluburun ship was on its way from Egypt or elsewhere in North Africa, and had already stopped in Syria-Palestine before heading farther north, where its journey would tragically end. The remains of the ship indicate that it was quite large and probably belonged to the class of vessel the Egyptians called *menesh,* a large, seagoing vessel, with tall, vertical prow and stern posts.[67] The deck was surrounded with a type of fencing, probably of wooden vertical elements and horizontal roping, some of which has actually survived in the Uluburun shipwreck.

The crew of the Uluburun ship followed the currents and winds of the eastern Mediterranean, visiting various ports in a primarily counterclockwise cycle.[68] The combination of goods discovered in the Uluburun shipwreck suggests that the crew may on occasion have taken on cargo that might have remained on the ship for some time; while the vessel may have been on an official mission, it could equally fit the profile of a private merchant ship. Private Egyptian trading ventures could lease ships from temples, bridging the private and state-controlled economies of the Nile Valley.[69]

The men who manned the Uluburun ship and the other ships that sailed the wine-dark waters of the Mediterranean were probably not all from the same region. In their eclectic mixture of clothing and accoutrements brought from home and acquired in their ports of call, these sailors might have resembled the perplexing hybrid figures that appear occasionally in Egyptian depictions. A man in the Eighteenth Dynasty tomb of Anen wears Hittite shoes, a Syrian robe, and a Libyan sidelock, yet he is labeled "Keftiu," the Egyptian name for an inhabitant of Crete. These depictions may not be the result of an overactive imagination, but could derive from accurate observations of the crews of the trading vessels that docked in Egyptian ports.[70] Like pirates and privateers of more modern times, the ancient traders may have intended their sartorial choices to represent the breadth of their travels.

The North African coast between the Delta and Cyrenaica was not endowed with natural harbors, with the exception of the Libyan trading emporium on Bates Island. Such a situation, along with the general lack of suitable ports and points of disembarkation along the northern coast of Sinai, concentrated southeastern Mediterranean nautical activities on the Egyptian Nile Delta.[71] Once traders reached the shores of Egypt, they would have to navigate the mouths of the Delta channels, a task made difficult by the silt mounds just beyond the shore. For much if not most of the year, larger vessels would not have been able to sail into and out of these channels, and a certain amount of transshipping from larger to smaller vessels was required.[72]

Ships docking for trade—foreign and Egyptian—could be accompanied by a military escort called the *meshkebu*. Based on their duties with the chariotry, the meshkebu were not strictly nautical but involved with a range of commissariat activities.[73] Armed guards would have been present not only at Delta ports, but also at harbors along the Nile. Police outposts at the riverbank appear in the tomb of Meryra at Amarna, where a fleet of ships are docked and where three armed men, holding shields, spears, axes, and an ensign, stand guard.[74] Further evidence of police activity along the river appears in the Theban tomb of Neferhotep, a man contemporary with the reigns of Aye and Tutankhamun. Next to a harbor where large vessels are docked appears a scene of judgment and punishment; as an official decrees the sentence for three men, a scribe records it, and guards armed with bastinados stand by to carry it out.[75]

The Egyptians were well equipped to control activity within their own harbors and ports, but Egyptian ships sailing elsewhere in the Mediterranean could be prey to piratical groups, who became increasingly dangerous during the Amarna Period. Already in the early Eighteenth Dynasty, pirates and heavily armed northern mercenaries appear in Egyptian documents.[76] The incursions of pirates had become so serious by the reign of Amunhotep III that the Egyptians constructed coastal forts and patrolled the mouths of the Nile.[77] Egypt was not the only great power threatened by these piratical groups. In one of the Amarna Letters, the ruler of the island kingdom of Alashiya, modern Cyprus, not only complains of pirates raiding his land, but also reassures the Egyptian pharaoh that his own men have not turned pirate and joined in attacks on other regions.[78] The term for pirate used in the letter is "men of the Lukki," the later Lycia, on the southern coast of Asia Minor.[79] The Lukki are one of the many groups the Egyptians classified as "Sea People," who attacked Egypt multiple times during the Ramesside Period. Some of these same Sea People groups fought as auxiliaries of the Egyptian army,[80] as we know from the Ramesside Period and as the fragmentary papyrus from Amarna may depict.

Religious Functions of the Military

In addition to participating in great engineering and mining projects, the military in peacetime also played a key role in religious activities, particularly large festival processions.[81] Egyptian military units appear to have taken part in such festivals from at least the time of the Old Kingdom, and probably even before. Already in the well-known Tomb 100 (the "Painted Tomb") at Hierakonpolis (ca. 3250 B.C.E.), ritual combat occurs in the context of a jubilee ceremony of royal renewal;[82] the combatants in that early festival, as in later depictions of ritual combat from the reigns of Ramesses II and Ramesses III, were probably warriors.[83] Another early depiction of the military in a religious context appears on a block from a temple of the Fifth Dynasty king Userkaf at Saqqara.[84] The scene shows units of running soldiers escorting a riverine procession in which, according to an accompanying inscription, someone, probably the king, is returning from a temple of Bastet. Similarly, during the New Kingdom, units of soldiers, marines, and foreign auxiliaries appear in numerous depictions of riverine celebrations associated with the Beautiful Festival of the Valley and the Opet Festival.[85] The presence of troops at religious celebrations probably always ensured proper security for the participants and crowd control in general, but beginning with the Eighteenth Dynasty, at least in Thebes, evidence indicates that the military presence is also an integral part of the ritual process.

One of the most elaborate portrayals of a Theban festival is the cycle of reliefs in the Colonnade Hall of Luxor Temple, which were carved during the reign of Tutankhamun and later usurped by Horemhab. The reliefs in the Colonnade Hall trace the course of the Opet Festival, in which the sacred barks of the triad of Karnak—accompanied from the reign of Tutankhamun by the bark of the king—sailed in great riverine barges from Karnak to Luxor and back again. The purpose of the Opet Festival was to celebrate the sacred marriage of the Egyptian pharaoh and his queen, which mirrored the union of Amun and his consort, Mut, thereby reaffirming the power and legitimacy of the current king as bearer of the royal *ka*, the immortal spirit of kingship.[86]

At the beginning of the festivities, which would last more than two weeks, the cult statues of the gods Amun, Mut, and Khonsu were placed within elaborately decorated shrines mounted on equally intricate barks, which were carried on the shoulders of groups of priests. Once the procession reached the Nile quay in front of Karnak Temple, the small barks that held the divine images were loaded onto larger riverine barks. While priests, dancers, and musicians sang praises to Amun, Mut, and Khonsu, sailors assisted with the navigation of the sacred barks, and other soldiers towed the great river barges against the current. In actual combat in Nubia, the Egyptian marines and soldiers of the early Eighteenth Dynasty had acquired considerable practice in hauling warships over the treacherous cataracts of the southland,[87] and no doubt on occasion similar activities occupied the troops of Akhenaten and his immediate successors. Naval officers could also be assigned to royal ships, not only that of the king, but also of the queen and royal heir.[88]

As the soldiers hauled the divine barks in the Opet procession, they proclaimed the power of their king, as the hieroglyphs above their heads record:

> [The vanguard] of the army proclaims before his majesty: "How flourishing is the perfect ruler! He has conveyed Amun so that he decrees for him valor against the south and victory against the n[orth]. Amun [is the god who decrees it]: 'Victory be to the ruler!'"

The soldiers' hymn of praise indicates that in return for fulfilling the rituals of the Opet festival, Amun will decree victory against Egypt's enemies. The great annual festivals, like nearly all religious activity in the temples that lined the Nile Valley, were ultimately intended to guarantee the proper functioning of the cosmos, which included the subjugation of any foreign groups who threatened Egypt. The participation of foreign groups, loyal to the Egyptian pharaoh, within these same festivals further enhanced the cosmographic significance of the religious processions.

Alongside the Egyptian soldiers who participate in the Opet festival are Nubian auxiliaries and Libyans—or Egyptians dressed as Libyans. The Nubians and the Libyans are representatives of regions south and west of Egypt, respectively, which was believed to be the winter home of the goddess of the eye of the sun.[90] This goddess, who could be called Hathor, Sakhmet, Bastet, and a host of other names, was the female counterpart of the solar deity and personified the solar eye, which is simultaneously the uraeus serpent who rests on his brow. According to Egyptian theology, Re offended this goddess by attempting to replace her, and she fled to the southwest, into the lands of Libya and Nubia. The goddess of the eye of the sun vented her rage on the populations in these regions until she was coaxed back to Egypt. The return of the goddess, heralded astronomically by the heliacal rising of the star Sirius in the middle of July, also corresponded to the inundation of the Nile River.

The presence of Nubian and Libyan celebrants in the Opet procession signals the glorious return of the goddess to Egypt from the southern deserts. Particularly lively depictions of Nubian dancers occur in Tutankhamun's Opet scenes (see figure 29).[91] The men wear traditional Nubian costumes, leather kilts with long, depending elements, at the bottom of which are gourds, probably serving as rattles.[92] They carry large wooden clubs, which other Nubians carry as weapons in some battle scenes. The dance of the Nubians as it appears on both walls of the Colonnade Hall finds a close parallel in a depiction of dancing Nubian warriors in the Gebel Silsila speos scenes of Horemhab's Nubian war (see figure 19).[93] The dance of the Nubians is a leaping and swaying performance, called the *gesges*, danced also by monkeys, a dance that—like the solar language of the baboons—the Egyptians believed to be an ancient form of solar worship, protected by nature, known to the king as supreme solar priest, and practiced by celebrants.[94] Some of the men hold their clubs vertically and leap into the air, while the rearmost man throws back his head and arches his body in a more ecstatic pose. A wooden club, virtually identical to those carried in the Opet scenes, was included in the furnishings of the tomb of Tutankhamun. These Nubian dances might not have been purely festive, but could have served as an integral part of their military training; similar uses of carefully choreographed dances to enhance coordination on the battlefield are attested for ancient Greek hoplites[95] and nineteenth-century Zulu warriors.[96]

In the scene of the celebration of the Opet procession in the Colonnade Hall at Luxor Temple, the lines of soldiers, musicians, and those hauling the towropes on the west wall is headed by a man in military costume who faces the approaching celebrants and chants a long hymn to Amun-Re.[97] This military officer singled out for particular prominence in the procession was probably never labeled by name, but may well represent General Horemhab. In fact, once crowned pharaoh, Horemhab used the Opet procession and its role in reaffirming the proper transmission of the royal ka to legitimize his own rule. Indeed, festivals and religious activity were so intimately related to pharaonic kingship that a king's political program could not be divorced from his theological agenda.

Such a combination of festivals and political expression is certainly true for Akhenaten—his peculiar form of solar worship is inseparable from his new capital, Akhet-aten, and his other political oddities, such as the emphasis on foreign bodyguards. Akhenaten's innovations ended the festi-

Figure 29. Carrying clubs and one irregularly shaped shield, Nubians perform a leaping dance as part of the Opet Procession festivities, as depicted in the Colonnade Hall of Luxor Temple. Epigraphic Survey, *Luxor Temple*, 1, pl. 94, courtesy of the Oriental Institute of the University of Chicago.

val processions of Thebes, and replaced them with a single daily procession at Akhet-aten—the appearance of Akhenaten riding into the center of his horizon city out of the North Riverside palace (see page 39). Perhaps great crowds thronged the processional way each day, and perhaps the soldiers involved in the procession are simply there because of the old involvement of the military in religious processions. At Amarna the ruler and his high officials carried out their daily lives as though they were enacting a religious drama for themselves, not for the populace as a whole. Akhenaten appears never to have ventured abroad without a military escort, perhaps to present every movement of Akhenaten as a ritual procession. No matter how many soldiers an Egyptian pharaoh might have brought with him to a festival celebration, no other pharaoh shows himself as constantly guarded by throngs of bowing and sycophantically scraping soldiers as does Akhenaten. The processions at Amarna did not differ from earlier and later processions in evincing a considerable military presence, but this military presence is all the more menacing and dominating in the relatively sterile environment of Akhet-aten's ritual life.

In addition to the chariot ride and the daily cycle of Akhenaten's activities, two further militaristic celebrations are commemorated in the Amarna tombs: the rewarding of loyal officials at the Window of Appearances, and ritual combat at the presentation of foreign tribute, both of

which relate to specific architectural features at Amarna. The royal audience in which the ruler appeared at the Window of Appearances was primarily associated with a ceremony during which officials receive rewards
and commendations.[98] The Window of Appearances was a large opening
in the wall of a palace, a short distance above the ground. A podium,
often adorned with a cushion placed at the front of the window, enabled
the king to reach over and cast rewards out to his officials and their families. The king alone might be present at this ceremony, or he might
appear with the queen; the queen herself also presided at least occasionally over a similar ceremony in recognition of the service of female members of the court and the administration.[99]

Officials, courtiers, and onlookers, often including foreign dignitaries,
gazed up at the pharaoh, surrounded by a host of images proclaiming his
domination of foreign lands.[100] Those foreign participants might themselves be present for a practical reason, perhaps receiving their own rewards
or an audience with the ruler, even though on occasion they may not fully
have understood the significance of the event and the venue (compare
the letter of Assuruballit I to Akhenaten quoted on page 137). Although
the foreigners might be there for a practical purpose, for the Egyptians,
they revealed the universal and cosmic significance of what was occurring
and reinforce the image of the ruler as the dominant figure in the political
world. Consequently, the Window of Appearances at Amarna—as elsewhere—was adorned with heraldic imagery. One of the principal motifs
consists of lotus and papyrus plants, representing Upper and Lower Egypt,
respectively, wrapped around a hieroglyph meaning "to unite." In the decorative scheme, the plants also serve to bind a series of kneeling Nubian
and Asiatic prisoners. A surviving Window of Appearances at the mortuary temple of Ramesses III displays a similar theme—just below where the
pharaoh would appear are carved the protruding, three-dimensional heads
of foreign enemies, so that the Egyptian king would appear to be standing
atop the prone bodies of his enemies as he made his glorious appearance.[101]

Military activity and display, particularly ritual combat, appear to have
been common occurrences at the Window of Appearances.[102] Beneath that
window in the first court of the mortuary temple of Ramesses III appear
elaborate and somewhat comical depictions of Egyptians soldiers wrestling
foreigners, possibly even foreign auxiliaries of the Egyptian military.[103]
The labels to these wrestling scenes even record the insults that the Egyptians hurled at their opponents: "Stand still, O Nubian opponent! I will
surely make you fall down, O weakling, in the presence of Pharaoh!"
Another wrestler details his next move: "Now see I have seized hold of

your legs and I shall throw you down upon your backside in the presence of Pharaoh, may he be living, prosperous, and healthy." Yet another Egyptian says: "Woe to you O Syrian enemy, boastful with his mouth. Pharaoh, may he be living, prosperous, and healthy, is against you." In addition to the pairs of wrestlers, the scenes show fencers,[104] one of whom says, "*En garde!* I will show you the hand of a warrior." This ritual combat also reinforced the image of the ruler as warlord; according to the texts at Medinet Habu, court officials and royal children (the latter perhaps including "children of the nursery"[105]) looked on and pronounced a short hymn to the ruler that sounded not unlike those sung by larger military units during festival events: "You are like Montu, O Pharaoh, may he be living, prosperous, healthy, our good lord. Amun has thrown down for you the foreigners, who have come in order to exalt themselves." Another combatant also evokes ritual hymns with his pronouncement, which begins, "Amun is the god who decreed it: 'Victory be to the ruler!'"

Ritual combat did not only occur at the Window of Appearances; at least in Akhet-aten such activities were part of the great durbar of year twelve. In the scenes of that exotic extravaganza in the tomb of Meryre II, the right central strip of attendants comprises wrestlers, fencers, and boxers, at least some wearing the heart-shaped sporrans of Egyptian soldiers, and apparently made up of Egyptians and Nubians, some of the latter apparently performing a military dance like that in which they participate in the Opet Procession scenes in Luxor Temple.[106] Ritual combat in the presence of representatives from the four corners of the Egyptian cosmos appears to have been an appropriate means of celebrating Akhenaten's rule over "all which the sun disk encircles," and helped transform the durbar—like so many events at Akhet-aten—into a ritual.[107]

EPILOGUE

W e may never know whether Tutankhamun actually rode his chariot into battle, just as we may never discover the real reason behind his untimely demise. If Tutankhamun had lived longer, what sort of impact might he have made on pharaonic history? Could he have lived up to the great reputation of his chief general, Horemhab, who had won victories for his young pharaoh in Nubia and Asia? Caught in the maelstrom of the religious changes of his father and forced to rule from an early age, Tutankhamun had little opportunity to prove himself a great warrior, like some of his illustrious predecessors of the Eighteenth Dynasty. Yet unknowingly, the "boy king" set the stage for what was to be one of Egypt's finest hours, the Ramesside Period. Having appointed a powerful general as his heir, Tutankhamun could travel to the Underworld knowing that Egypt would be protected. Although Horemhab would have to wait for the death of Aye before he assumed the throne, once pharaoh, he lost no time wiping away the memory of the Amarna Period. Monuments were smashed, names rewritten, and the hateful period became part of Horemhab's reign. The "rebel of Akhet-aten" was removed from history. To ensure the future glory of Egypt, Horemhab carefully chose his own successor—a man with proven military and administrative talents, who would become Ramesses I. Horemhab was not only appointing the next pharaoh, but also the next dynasty, since Ramesses I already had a son and a grandson, whose rule as Seti I and Ramesses II, respectively, would be a golden age in literature, art, and architecture. Although they would never admit it, the Nineteenth Dynasty pharaohs did owe a debt to the military achievements of the rulers of the Amarna Period.

NOTES

Abbreviations

Ä&L	Ägypten und Levante
ASAE	Annales du Service des Antiquités de l'Égypte
BACE	Bulletin of the Australian Centre for Egyptology
BASOR	Bulletin of the American Schools of Oriental Research
Bib. Or.	Bibliotheca Orientalis
BIFAO	Bulletin de l'Institut français d'archéologie orientale
BSEG	Bulletin de la Société d'Égyptologie de Genève
CAJ	Cambridge Archaeology Journal
CdE	Chronique d'Égypte
GM	Göttinger Miszellen
JARCE	Journal of the American Research Center in Egypt
JEA	Journal of Egyptian Archaeology
JNES	Journal of Near Eastern Studies
JSSEA	Journal of the Society for the Study of Egyptian Antiquities
KRI	K. A. Kitchen, Ramesside Inscriptions: Historical and Biographical
LÄ	W. Helck and W. Westendorf, eds., Lexikon der Ägyptologie
LEM	A. Gardiner, Late Egyptian Miscellanies
MDAIK	Mitteilungen des Deutschen Archäologischen Instituts Kairo
OLZ	Orientalistische Literaturzeitung
RdÉ	Revue d'Égyptologie
SAK	Studien zur altägyptischen Kultur
Urk. IV	Urkunden des ägyptischen Altertums IV: Urkunden der 18. Dynastie
ZÄS	Zeitschrift für ägyptische Sprache und Altertumskunde

1. Land of Desert and Nile

1. For the discovery of Tutankhamun's tomb, see Howard Carter, *The Tomb of Tut.Ankh.Amen*, 3 vols. (1923–1933; repr., London: Gerald Duckworth, 2000–2003); Zahi Hawass, *Tutankhamun and the Golden Age of the Pharaohs* (Washington, D.C.: National Geographic Society, 2005); T. G. H. James, *Tutankhamun: The Eternal Splendour of the Boy Pharaoh* (London: Tauris Parke, 2000); Nicholas Reeves, *The Complete Tutankhamun* (London: Thames & Hudson, 1990).

2. For overviews of Egyptian military history, see Andrea Gnirs, "Ancient Egypt," in *War and Society in the Ancient and Medieval Worlds*, ed. K. A. Raaflaub et al. (Cambridge, Mass.: Harvard University Press, 1999); Gnirs, "Military: An Overview," in *Oxford Encyclopedia of Ancient Egypt*, ed. D. Redford (Oxford, U.K.: Oxford University Press, 2001); Susanne Petschel and Martin von Falck, eds., *Pharao siegt immer: Krieg und Frieden im Alten Ägypten* (Bönen: Kettler, 2004); Alan Schulman, "Some Observations on the Military Background of the Amarna Period," *JARCE* 3 (1964): 51–69; Schulman, "Military Organization in

213

Pharaonic Egypt," in *Civilizations of the Ancient Near East*, ed. Jack Sasson (New York: Scribner, 1995); Ian Shaw, *Egyptian Warfare and Weapons* (Buckinghamshire, U.K.: Shire, 1991); Shaw, "Battle in Ancient Egypt: The Triumph of Horus or the Cutting Edge of the Temple Economy?" in *Battle in Antiquity*, ed. A. Lloyd (London: Gerald Duckworth, 1996); Anthony Spalinger, *War in Ancient Egypt* (Oxford: Blackwell, 2005); Spalinger, "Warfare in Ancient Egypt," in *A Companion to the Ancient Near East*, ed. Daniel C. Snell (Oxford: Blackwell, 2005). More popular and derivative overviews include William Hamblin, *Warfare in the Ancient Near East to 1600 B.C.* (London: Routledge, 2006), 308–463; Mark Healy, *Armies of the Pharaohs* (Oxford: Osprey Publishing, 1992); Roger Partridge, *Fighting Pharaohs: Weapons and Warfare in Ancient Egypt* (Manchester, U.K.: Peartree Publishing, 2002). For human remains and warfare, see Joyce M. Filer, "Ancient Egypt and Nubia as a Source of Information for Cranial Injuries," in *Material Harm: Archaeological Studies of War and Violence*, ed. John Carman (Glasgow: Cruithne Press, 1997).

3. Of the many possible references, compare Arthur Weigall, *The Life and Times of Akhnaton, Pharaoh of Egypt*, 3rd ed. (New York: G. P. Putnam's Sons, 1922); James Henry Breasted, *The Dawn of Consciousness* (New York: Scribner, 1933); see also Dominic Montserrat, *Akhenaten: History, Fantasy, and Ancient Egypt* (London: Routledge, 2000) and Erik Hornung, *Akhenaten and the Religion of Light* (Ithaca, N.Y.: Cornell University Press, 1999), 1–18, for an overview of the evolution of scholarly opinions about Akhenaten.

4. Philipp Hoelzmann, "Lacustrine Sediments as Key Indicators of Climate Change during the Late Quaternary in Western Nubia," in *Tides of the Desert: Gezeiten der Wüste* (Cologne: Heinrich-Barth Institut, 2002).

5. Fekri Hassan, ed., *Droughts, Food, and Culture: Ecological Change and Food Security in Africa's Later Prehistory* (New York: Kluwer Academic, 2002); Rudolph Kuper, "Routes and Roots in Egypt's Western Desert: The Early Holocene Resettlement of the Eastern Sahara," in *Gifts of the Desert*, ed. Renée Friedman (London: British Museum Press, 2002); Romuald Schild and Fred Wendorf, "Palaeo-ecologic and Palaeo-climatic Background to Socio-economic Changes in the South Western Desert of Egypt," ibid.

6. Detlev Franke, "Erste und Zweite Zwischenzeit: Ein Vergleich," ZÄS 117 (1990): 119–129; Renee Friedman, ed., *Egypt and Nubia: Gifts of the Desert* (London: British Museum Press, 2002).

7. Barry Kemp, *Ancient Egypt: Anatomy of a Civilization*, 2nd ed. (London: Routledge, 2006), 92–99; Dirk Huyge, "Cosmology, Ideology, and Personal Religious Practice in Ancient Egyptian Rock Art," in *Egypt and Nubia*, ed. Friedman; John Coleman Darnell, "Ancient Egyptian Rock Inscriptions and Graffiti," in *Oxford Handbook of Egyptian Archaeology*, ed. James Allen and Ian Shaw, forthcoming.

8. Kemp, *Ancient Egypt*, 2nd ed., 73–92.

9. Renée Friedman, Stan Hendrickx, and John Coleman Darnell in Darnell, *Theban Desert Road Survey in the Egyptian Western Desert*, vol. 1 (Chicago: University of Chicago Press, 2002), 10–19.

10. Toby Wilkinson, *Early Dynastic Egypt* (London: Routledge, 2001), 28–52.

11. Donald Redford, *Pharaonic King-Lists, Annals, and Day-books* (Mississauga, Ont.: Benben, 1986); Kemp, *Ancient Egypt*, 2nd ed., 61–69. For Egyptian historiography in general, see also John Tait, ed., *"Never Had the Like Occurred": Egypt's View of Its Past* (London: UCL Press, 2003).

12. For the Hyksos, see "Founding of the New Kingdom" in chap. 2, 13–16.

13. Donald Redford, "The Concept of Kingship during the Eighteenth Dynasty," in *Ancient Egyptian Kingship*, ed. David O'Connor and David Silverman (Leiden: Brill, 1995); Spalinger, *War in Ancient Egypt*, 101–109. See also "Eighteenth-Dynasty Kingship" in chap. 2.

14. Monumental inscriptions may compare the king's wisdom to that of the god Thoth; see Nicholas Grimal, *Les Termes de la Propagande Royal Égyptienne de la XIXe dynastie à la conquête d'Alexandre* (Paris: Imprimerie Nationale, 1986), 430–432.

15. For more on the history of Nubia, see chap. 4.

16. For imperialism, ancient and modern, from a cross-cultural perspective, see inter alia Susan Alcock et al., ed., *Empires: Perspectives from Archaeology and History* (Cambridge, U.K.: Cambridge University Press, 2001); Michael Doyle, *Empires* (Ithaca, N.Y.: Cornell University Press, 1986); Wendy Kasinec and Michael Polushin, ed., *Expanding Empires: Cultural Interaction and Exchange in World Societies from Ancient to Modern Times* (Wilmington, Del.: Scholarly Resources, 2002); Michael Cox, Tim Dunne, and Ken Booth, eds., *Empires, Systems, and States: Great Transformations in International Politics* (Cambridge, U.K.: Cambridge University Press, 2001). A useful treatment of medieval empires, particularly the religious and moral aspects of imperialism, is James Muldoon, *Empire and Order: The Concept of Empire, 800–1800* (New York: St. Martin's Press, Palgrave, 1999).

17. For overviews of Egyptian imperialism, see Paul Frandsen, "Egyptian Imperialism," *Power and Propaganda: A Symposium on Ancient Empires* (Copenhagen: Akademisk Forlag, 1979); Barry Kemp, "Imperialism and Empire in New Kingdom Egypt," in *Imperialism in the Ancient World*, ed. P. Garnsey and C. R. Whittaker (Cambridge, U.K.: Cambridge University Press, 1978); Stuart T. Smith, *Askut in Nubia: The Economics and Ideology of Egyptian Imperialism in the Second Millennium B.C.* (London: Kegan Paul, 1995); Smith, *Wretched Kush: Ethnic Identities and Boundaries in Egypt's Nubian Empire* (London: Routledge, 2003), 167–187. Further sources about specific aspects of the Egyptian empire are cited in notes in chaps. 4 and 5.

18. José M. Galán, *Victory and Border: Terminology Related to Egyptian Imperialism in the XVIIIth Dynasty* (Hildesheim: Gerstenberg, 1995); Grimal, *Les Termes de la Propagande*, 685–687.

19. Jan Assmann, *Ma'at, Gerechtigkeit, und Unsterblichkeit im Alten Ägypten* (Munich: Beck, 2001).

20. For military reliefs, see Susanna Heinz, *Die Feldzugsdarstellungen des Neuen Reiches: Eine Bildanalyse* (Vienna: Verlag der Österreichischen Akademie der Wissenschaften, 2001); Petschel and von Falck, eds., *Pharao siegt immer*, 54–71. Note also Anthony Spalinger, "The Battle of Kadesh: The Chariot Frieze at Abydos," *Ä&L* 13 (2003): 163–199 for the accuracy and detail contained within Egyptian military scenes. For temples as models of the cosmos, into which the military reliefs are integrated, see Byron Schafer, ed., *Temples of Ancient Egypt* (Ithaca, N.Y.: Cornell University Press, 1997). The association between temples and warfare also influenced temple architecture—compare the crenellations on a temple model (Kemp, *Ancient Egypt*, 2nd ed., 252–253) and the *migdol* at Medinet Habu (A. W. Lawrence, "Ancient Egyptian Fortifications," *JEA* 51 [1965]: 90–91).

21. Erik Hornung, *Geschichte als Fest* (Darmstadt: Wissenschaftliche Buchgesellschaft, 1966); Anthony Spalinger, *Aspects of the Military Documents of the Ancient Egyptians* (New Haven, Conn.: Yale University Press, 1982); Spalinger, *War in Ancient Egypt*, 76–78.

Chapter 2. The Amarna Interlude

1. H. S. Smith, *The Fortress of Buhen: The Inscriptions* (London: Egypt Exploration Society, 1976), pl. 29, bottom fragment, lines 1–2.

2. Historical overviews of the reign of Akhenaten and the Amarna Period abound; some recent investigations include Cyril Aldred, *Akhenaten: King of Egypt* (London: Thames & Hudson, 1991); Rita E. Freed, Yvonne J. Markowitz, and Sue H. D'Auria, eds.,

Pharaohs of the Sun (Boston: Museum of Fine Arts, 1999); Marc Gabolde, *D'Akhenaton à Toutânkhamon* (Lyons: Institut d'Archéologie et d'Histoire de l'Antiquité, 1998); Hornung, *Akhenaten*; Barry Kemp, *Ancient Egypt: Anatomy of a Civilization*, 1st ed. (London: Routledge, 1991), 261–317; R. Krauss, *Das Ende der Amarnazeit: Beiträge zur Geschichte und Chronologie des Neuen* Reiches (Hildesheim: Gerstenberg, 1978); William J. Murnane, *Texts from the Amarna Period in Egypt* (Atlanta: Scholars Press, 1995); Murnane, "The End of the Amarna Period Once Again," *OLZ* 96, no. 1 (2001): 9–22; Donald Redford, *Akhenaten: The Heretic King* (Princeton, N.J.: Princeton University Press, 1984); Nicholas Reeves, *Akhenaten: Egypt's False Prophet* (London: Thames & Hudson, 2001) (note also the comments in Marianne Eaton-Krauss, "Akhenaten Redux," *CdÉ* 77 [2002]: 95–98); Claude Vandersleyen, *L'Égypte et la vallée du Nil*, vol. 2: *De la fin de l'Ancien Empire à la fin du Nouvel Empire* (Paris: Presses Universitaires de France, 1995), 409–465; Jacobus Van Dijk, "Horemheb and the Struggle for the Throne of Tutankhamun," *BACE* 7 (1996): 29–42; Van Dijk, "The Amarna Period and the Later New Kingdom," in *Oxford History of Ancient Egypt*, ed. Ian Shaw (Oxford, U.K.: Oxford University Press, 2002), 272–313. Reviews and lists of works on the Amarna Period include Eaton-Krauss, "Akhenaten versus Akhenaten." *Bib. Or.* 47 (1990): 541–559; Eaton-Krauss, *CdÉ* 77 (2002): 93–107; Eaton-Krauss, *Bib. Or.* 58 (2001): 91–97; Geoffrey T. Martin, *A Bibliography of the Amarna Period and Its Aftermath: The Reigns of Akhenaten, Smenkhkare, Tutankhamun, and Ay* (London: Kegan Paul International, 1991).

3. K. S. B. Ryholt, *The Political Situation in Egypt during the Second Intermediate Period c. 1800–1550 B.C.* (Copenhagen: University of Copenhagen Press, 1997), 167–183; Wolfram Grajetzki, *Die höchsten Beamten der ägyptischen Zentralverwaltung zur zeit des Mittleren Reiches* (Berlin: Achet verlag, 2003), 262–263; David O'Connor, "The Hyksos Period in Egypt," in *The Hyksos, New Historical and Archaeological Perspectives*, ed. E. Oren (Philadelphia: University Museum, 1997), 45–67; Daniel Polz, "Theben und Avaris: Zur 'Vertreibung' der Hyksos," in *Stationen, Beiträge zur Kulturgeschichte Ägyptens*, ed. H. Guksch and D. Polz (Mainz: Philipp von Zabern, 1998). For an overview of Seventeenth-Dynasty chronology, see also Chris Bennett, "A Genealogical Chronology of the Seventeenth Dynasty," *JARCE* 39 (2002): 123–155.

4. Ceramic and epigraphic evidence—at least by the time of the late Seventeenth Dynasty—along the Western Desert roads linking the Thebaid with Kharga Oasis indicates that the Thebans were in control of these important tracks (J. C. Darnell, "Opening the Narrow Doors of the Desert: Discoveries of the Theban Desert Road Survey," in *Egypt and Nubia: Gifts of the Desert*, ed. Renée Friedman (London: British Museum Press, 2002); 139–140, 147–149; D. Darnell, "Gravel of the Desert and Broken Pots in the Road: Ceramic Evidence from the Routes between the Nile and Kharga Oasis," in *Egypt and Nubia*, 169–173; contra Janine Bourriau, "Some Archaeological Notes on the Kamose Texts," in *Studies on Ancient Egypt in Honour of H. S. Smith*, ed. A. Leahy and J. Tait (London: Egypt Exploration Society, 1999). For Theban control of the desert, note also Ryholt, *Second Intermediate Period*, 140–142, 327; M. Baud, "Balat/'Ayn-Asil, oasis de Dakhla: la ville de la Deuxième Période Intermédiaire," *BIFAO* 97 (1997): 27–28; Theban hegemony over the deserts might also have prevented the Hyksos from taking over any territory south of Thebes—for arguments against Hyksos rule in Upper Egypt, see Daniel Polz, "Die Hyksos-Blöcke aus Gebelen: zur Präsenz der Hyksos in Oberägypten," in *Timelines: Studies in Honor of Manfred Bietak*, ed. E. Czerny et al. (Leuven: Peeters, 2006), vol. 1, 239–247.

5. The mummy of Seqenenre Tao has a hole in the forehead corresponding to the shape of a Hyksos battle-ax—Vivian Davies and Renée Friedman, *Egypt* (London: British Museum Press, 1998), 111; Petschel and von Falk, *Pharao siegt immer*, 116. For the physical evidence, see Filer in *Material Harm: Archaeological Studies of War and Violence*, ed. John Carman, 65–66.

6. The exact relationship between Seqenenre and Kamose remains uncertain; Kamose may be a son of Seqenenre Tao II, or more likely they were brothers (Ryholt, *Second Intermediate Period*, 287; Thierry Stasser, "La famille d'Amosis," *CdÉ* 77 [2002]: 24).

7. For the account of Kamose's campaign, see Labib Habachi, *The Second Stela of Kamose, and His Struggle against the Hyksos Ruler and His Capital* (Glückstadt: Verlag J. J. Augustin, 1972); H. S. Smith and A. Smith, "A Reconsideration of the Kamose Texts," *ZÄS* 103 (1976): 48–76; Claude Vandersleyen, *Les guerres d'Amosis, fondateur de la XVIIIe Dynastie* (Brussels: Fondation Égyptologique Reine Élisabeth, 1971), 61–64; Spalinger, *War in Ancient Egypt*, 1–4, 19–24; Frédéric Colin, "Kamose et les Hyksos dans l'oasis de Djesdjes," *BIFAO* 105 (2005): 35–45. A useful summary of archaeological discoveries at Avaris is Manfred Bietak, *Avaris: The Capital of the Hyksos* (London: British Museum Press, 1996). For the Battle of Avaris and its naval tactics, see John Coleman Darnell, "Two Sieges in the Aethiopic Stelae," in *Ägypten im Afro-orientalischen Kontext (Gedenkschrift Peter Behrens)*, ed. D. Mendel and U. Claudi (Cologne: Institut für Afrikanistik, 1991), 86–93.

8. W. L. Rodgers, *Greek and Roman Naval Warfare* (Annapolis, Md.: Naval Institute Press, 1964), 190–192.

9. Such a principle is well expressed by the late Roman military strategist Vegetius; see N. P. Milner, *Vegetius: Epitome of Military Science* (Liverpool: Liverpool University Press, 1993), 101.

10. Vandersleyen, *L'Égypte*, 221–225. For the location of Sharuhen, see Ryholt, *Second Intermediate Period*, 132 and 464n; Eliezer Oren, "The 'Kingdom of Sharuhen' and the Hyksos Kingdom," in *Hyksos*, 253–255. For a summary of archaeological remains, see Ellen Fowles Morris, *The Architecture of Imperialism* (Leiden: Peeters, 2005), 60–66.

11. Franz-Jürgen Schmitz, *Amenophis I: Versuch einer Darstellung der Regierungszeit eines ägyptischen Herrschers der frühen 18. Dynastie* (Hildesheim: Gerstenberg Verlag, 1978), 45–46.

12. See "Prelude to Amarna: Early Eighteenth Dynasty Wars with Mitanni" in chap. 5.

13. Vandersleyen, *L'Égypte*, 247–255; Aidan Dodson and Dyan Hilton, *The Complete Royal Families of Ancient Egypt* (Cairo: AUC Press, 2004), 126–128.

14. Michel Gitton, *L'épouse du dieu Ahmes Néfertary* (Paris: Belles Lettres, 1975), 20–21, 83–84.

15. For Middle Kingdom activity in Syria-Palestine, see 133–134.

16. *Urk.* IV, 1–11; Vandersleyen, *L'Égypte*, 213–214; Vandersleyen, *Les guerres d'Amosis*; Regine Schultz, "Die Biographie des Ahmose—Sohn der Abana, Versuch einer Erzähltextanalyse," in *Gedenkschrift für Winfried Barta*, ed. Dieter Kessler and Regine Schulz (Frankfurt: Peter Lang, 1995); Lutz Popko, *Untersuchungen zur Geschichtsschreibung der Ahmosiden- und Thutmosidenzeit* (Würzburg: Ergon Verlag, 2006), 187–206.

17. A presentation of the reign of Thutmose I as founder of the New Kingdom appears in John Coleman Darnell, "Studies on the Reign of Thutmosis I," M.A. thesis, Johns Hopkins University, 1985.

18. For early Eighteenth Dynasty expansion into Nubia and a comparison with contemporary events in Asia, see Spalinger, *War in Ancient Egypt*, 46–69.

19. For overviews of pharaonic kingship, see O'Connor and Silverman, eds., *Ancient Egyptian Kingship*; Wilkinson, *Early Dynastic Egypt*, 183–199; Rolf Gundlach and Christine Raedler, eds., *Selbstverständnis und Realität* (Wiesbaden: Harrassowitz, 1997); Gundlach and Klug, eds., *Das ägyptische Königtum im Spannungsfeld zwischen Innen- und Außenpolitik im 2. Jahrtausend v. Chr.* (Wiesbaden: Harrassowitz Verlag, 2004); Gundlach, *Der Pharao und sein Staat* (Darmstadt: Wissenschaftliche Buchgesellschaft, 1998).

20. Wilkinson, *Early Dynastic Egypt*, 200–208.

21. On the religious significance of pharaonic titulary see Cathie Spieser, *Les noms du Pharaon comme êtres autonomes au Nouvel Empire* (Fribourg: Éditions Universitaires, 2000).

22. Jürgen von Beckerath, *Handbuch der ägyptischen Königsnamen*, 2nd ed. (Mainz: Philipp von Zabern, 1999), 1–33.

23. Andrea Maria Gnirs, "Die ägyptische Autobiographie," in *Ancient Egyptian Literature, History, and Forms*, ed. Antonio Loprieno (Leiden: Brill, 1996); Miriam Lichtheim, *Ancient Egyptian Autobiographies Chiefly of the Middle Kingdom* (Freiburg: Universitätsverlag, 1988), 21–38.

24. Redford, *Pharaonic King-Lists*, 128–129, 147–151; Lilian Postel, *Protocole des souverains égyptiens et dogme monarchique au début du Moyen Empire* (Brussels: Fondations Égyptologique Reine Élisabeth, 2004); John Coleman Darnell, *The Birth of Victorious Thebes*, forthcoming.

25. On the "King's Novel" form, see Antonio Loprieno, "The 'King's Novel,'" in *Ancient Egyptian Literature*; Colleen Manassa, *The Great Karnak Inscription of Merneptah* (New Haven, Conn.: Yale Egyptological Seminar, 2003), 107–113; B. Hofmann, *Die Königsnovelle: "Strukturanalyse am Einzelwerk"* (Wiesbaden: Harrassowitz, 2004).

26. Detlev Franke, "'Schöpfer, Schützer, Guter Hirte:' Zum Königsbild des Mittleren Reiches," in *Selbsverständnis und Realität*.

27. Stephen Quirke, "Royal Power in the 13th Dynasty," in *Middle Kingdom Studies*, ed. Stephen Quirke (New Malden, U.K.: Sia Publishing, 1991).

28. Loprieno, in *Ancient Egyptian Literature*, 284–285.

29. For the context of this festival, see Renée Friedman, "The Ceremonial Centre at Hierakonpolis Locality HK29A," in *Aspects of Early Egypt*, ed. A. J. Spencer (London: British Museum Press, 1996); Alejandro Serrano, *Royal Festivals in the Late Predynastic Period and the First Dynasty* (Oxford: Archaeopress, 2000).

30. For the militant pharaoh as the omnipresent diety of the eastern horizon, see the references in Darnell, *Theban Desert Road Survey* I, 188.

31. *Urk*. IV 8, l. 14-9, l. 5; a scarab of Thutmose I may depict the pharaoh shooting the Nubian ruler (for an image, see Davies and Friedman, *Egypt*, 110). Amunhotep II inflicted a similar punishment on seven Syro-Palestinian captives; see Peter Beylage, *Aufbau der königlichen Stelentexte vom Beginn der 18. Dynastie bis zur Amarnazeit* (Wiesbaden: Harrassowitz, 2002), vol. 1, 267–281, vol. 2, 696–700; A. Klug, *Königliche Stelen in der Zeit von Ahmose bis Amenophis III* (Brussels: Fondation Égyptologique Reine Élisabeth, 2002), 278–292; for the elements of execration ritual in Amunhotep II's actions, see Robert Ritner, *The Mechanics of Ancient Egyptian Magical Practice* (Chicago: Oriental Institute, 1993), 170–171.

32. G. E. Kadish "The Scatophagus Egyptian," *JSSEA* 9 (1979): 203–217; John Coleman Darnell, *The Enigmatic Netherworld Books of the Solar Osirian Unity* (Freiburg: Universitätsverlag, 2004), 426–448.

33. Erik Hornung, *The Ancient Egyptian Books of the Afterlife*, trans. David Lorton (Ithaca, N.Y.: Cornell University Press, 1999), 38–39; Darnell, *Enigmatic Netherworld Books*, 286–289. For the royal flagship compared to the solar bark, see also *Urk*. IV 1546, l. 6–7: "His Majesty followed them (the army) in order to fell the one who attacked him in Nubia, brave in his golden ship like Re, when he settles himself in the night bark." (On this passage see also Klug, *Königliche Stelen*, 351–352.)

34. Donald Redford, *The Wars in Syria and Palestine of Thutmose III* (Leiden: Brill, 2003); for the annals in the context of Thutmose III's reign as a whole, see the essays in Eric Cline and David O'Connor, eds., *Thutmose III: A New Biography* (Ann Arbor: University of Michigan Press, 2005).

35. Wolfgang Decker, *Die physische Leistung Pharaos, Untersuchungen zu Heldentum, Jagd und Leibesübungen der ägyptischen Könige* (Cologne: Historisches Institut der Deutschen Sporthochschule, 1971).

36. For overviews of the reign of Amunhotep III, see the collected essays in Arielle P. Kozloff and Betsy M. Bryan, ed., *Egypt's Dazzling Sun: Amenhotep III and His World* (Cleveland: Cleveland Museum of Art, 1992); David O'Connor and Eric Cline, eds., *Amenhotep III: Perspectives on His Reign* (Ann Arbor: University of Michigan Press, 1997); Mechthild Schade-Busch, *Zur Königsideologie Amenophis' III. Analyse der Phraseologie historischer Texte der Voramarnazeit* (Hildesheim: Gerstenberg, 1992). For the art history of Amunhotep III's reign, see also Lawrence Berman, ed., *The Art of Amenhotep III: Art Historical Analysis* (Cleveland: Cleveland Museum of Art, 1990).

37. For the two Nubian campaigns of Amunhotep III, see chap. 4, n. 116.

38. The wild bull and lion hunts described on a series of commemorative scarabs indicate Amunhotep III's continuation of the "sporting king" tradition (Kozloff and Bryan, *Egypt's Dazzling Sun*, 67–72).

39. Erik Hornung, "Sedfest und Geschichte," *MDAIK* 47 (1991): 169–171; Jocelyn Gohary, *Akhenaten's Sed-festival at Karnak* (London: Kegan Paul International, 1992), 1–25; Wilkinson, *Early Dynastic Egypt*, 212–215; Ute Rummel, "Weihrauch, Salböl und Leinen: Balsamierungsmaterialien als Medium der Erneuerung im Sedfest," *SAK* 34 (2006): 381–407.

40. Bruce Beyer Williams and Thomas J. Logan, "The Metropolitan Museum Knife Handle and Aspects of Pharaonic Imagery before Narmer," *JNES* 46 (1987): 245–285; Darnell, in *Oxford Handbook of Egyptian Archaeology*, forthcoming.

41. Kemp, *Ancient Egypt*, 2nd ed., 99–110; Gundlach, *Pharao und sein Staat*, 68–73.

42. Epigraphic Survey, *The Tomb of Kheruef: Theban Tomb 192* (Chicago: University of Chicago, Oriental Institute, 1980), 43 and pl. 28. A palette dating to ca. 3500 B.C.E. and carved with *hed-sed* images has the cartouche of Queen Tiye on the reverse and remnants of a scene that depicted Amunhotep III and his chief wife, an indication that he did consult sources as old as the Predynastic Period (B. V. Bothmer, "A New Fragment of an Old Palette," *JARCE* [1969–1970] 8: 5–8; Aldred, *Akhenaten*, 162).

43. The temples on the western bank at Thebes are often designated "mortuary," a term retained here to distinguish them from the constructions on the eastern bank (for further discussion of the limitations of this term, see Gerhard Haeny, "New Kingdom 'Mortuary Temples' and 'Mansions of Millions of Years,'" in *Temples of Ancient Egypt*). Ancient Egyptians referred to the royal temples on the western bank as "Temples of Millions of Years," a designation they applied to any bark shrine, including the great hypostyle hall at Karnak Temple (ibid., 110–111; Vincent Rondot, *La Grande Salle Hypostyle de Karnak: Les architraves* [Paris: Éditions Recherche sur les Civilisations, 1997], 143–144, 149–153), and to temples outside of Thebes (Martina Ullmann, *König für die Ewigkeit—Die Häuser der Millionen von Jahren* [Wiesbaden: Harrassowitz Verlag, 2002]). The primary significance of the mortuary temples was not the cult of the deceased king per se, but the cult of the form of Amun or another deity as manifest in the ruler himself. All mortuary temples were essentially bark shrines, in which Amun of Karnak could unite with each of his other forms represented by the deceased pharaohs. A consummate example of this interpretation is the model of Ramesses III's mortuary temple built as a bark shrine in the first court at Karnak Temple.

44. Siegfried Schott, "The Feasts of Thebes," *Work in Western Thebes, 1931–33*, ed. H. H. Nelson and U. Hölscher (Chicago: University of Chicago Press, 1934), 73–74; Schott, *Das schöne Fest vom Wüstentale, Festbräuche einer Totenstadt* (Wiesbaden: Verlag der Akademie der Wissenschaften und der Literatur in Mainz, 1953); Agnès Cabrol, *Les voies processionnelles de Thèbes* (Leuven: Peeters, 2001), 543–564.

45. Gerhard Haeny, ed., *Untersuchungen im Totentempel Amenophis' III* (Wiesbaden: Franz Steiner, 1981); Betsy Bryan, "The Statue Program for the Mortuary Temple of

Amenhotep III," in *The Temple in Ancient Egypt: New Discoveries and Recent Research*, ed. S. Quirke (London: British Museum, 1997); W. Raymond Johnson, "Monuments and Monumental Art under Amenhotep III: Evolution and Meaning," in *Amenhotep III*, 71–78.

46. David O'Connor, "Malqata," in *LÄ* 3, 1173–1177; O'Connor, "The City and the World: Worldview and Built Forms in the Reign of Amenhotep III," in *Amenhotep III*, 160–162; Barry Kemp and David O'Connor, "An Ancient Nile Harbour: University Museum Excavations at the 'Birket Habu,'" *International Journal of Nautical Archaeology and Underwater Exploration* 3, no. 1 (1974): 112–115; Kemp, *Ancient Egypt*, 2nd ed., 276–281; Peter Lacovara, *The New Kingdom Royal City* (London: Kegan Paul International, 1997), 25–28; Dieter Arnold, *The Encyclopedia of Ancient Egyptian Architecture* (Cairo: American University in Cairo Press, 2003), 136; Manfred Bietak, "Neue Paläste aus der 18. Dynastie," in *Structure and Significance: Thoughts on Ancient Egyptian Architecture*, ed. P. Janosi (Vienna: Österreichischen Akademie der Wissenshaften, 2005), 131–134.

47. S. Nishimoto, "The Ceiling Paintings of the Harem Rooms at the Palace of Malqata," *GM* 127 (1992): 69–80.

48. John Coleman Darnell, "Two Notes on Marginal Inscriptions at Medinet Habu," in *Essays in Egyptology in Honor of Hans Goedicke*, ed. B. Bryan and D. Lorton (San Antonio: Van Siclen Books, 1994), 39–42; Darnell, *Enigmatic Netherworld Books*, 404–406.

49. For texts with the epithet "Dazzling Sun Disk," see Murnane, *Amarna Period*, 20–22. A palace called "Nebmaatre is the Dazzling Sun Disk" was either at Malqata (Gabolde, *D'Akhenaton à Tutânkhamon*, 85, n. 755) or at Karnak (David O'Connor, "Beloved of Maat, the Horizon of Re: The Royal Palace in New Kingdom Egypt," in *Ancient Egyptian Kingship*, 276–277). Amunhotep IV/Akhenaten also used the epithet "dazzling like the sun disk" on at least one occasion; see A. M. Blackman, "A Preliminary Report on the Excavations at Sesebi, Northern Province, Anglo-Egyptian Sudan, 1936–37," *JEA* 23 (1937): 148 and pl. 17, 2.

50. Sayed Tawfik, "Aton Studies," *MDAIK* 29 (1973): 77–82.

51. John Baines, "The Dawn of the Amarna Age," in *Amenhotep III*, 288–301, 306–312.

52. Kemp and O'Connor, *International Journal of Nautical Archaeology and Underwater Exploration* 3, no. 1 (1974): 101–136.

53. Gilles Néret, *Description de l'Égypte* (Cologne: Benedikt Taschen. 1994), 154–155 (reproduction of vol. 2, pl. 1), the East Bank harbor is labeled "Hippodrome"; see also Georges Daressy, "Le camp de Thèbes," *ASAE* 19 (1920): 242–246, who misidentified the artificial lake as a Roman camp. The outlines of portions of the Eastern Birket are preserved as eminences atop which sit modern structures, notably the village of el-Habeel above the southern and southwestern portions of the embankment, as observed by the authors in 2005. The general outline of the Eastern Birket is discernible between the villages of Naj al-Khudarat and Naj az-Anaqtah on Sheet NG36F6a (Luxor) of the series 1:50,000 maps produced by the Egyptian General Survey Authority in 1991.

54. Epigraphic Survey, *Kheruef*, 43 and pl. 28.

55. Elizabeth Thomas, "Solar Barks Prow to Prow." *JEA* 42 (1956): 65–79.

56. Like the sun god, Amunhotep III is accompanied by the goddess Hathor—Edward Wente, "Hathor at the Jubilee," in *Studies in Honor of John A. Wilson* (Chicago: University of Chicago Press, 1969).

57. Erik Hornung, *Das Amduat, die Schrift des verborgenen Raumes, Teil II: Übersetzung und Kommentar* (Wiesbaden: Otto Harrassowitz, 1963), 104–108.

58. Epigraphic Survey, *Kheruef*, pl. 24–26; note a similar depiction of Amenhotep III in Torgny Säve-Söderbergh, *Four Eighteenth Dynasty Tombs* (Oxford, U.K.: Griffith Institute, 1957), pl. 31. For parallel representations from the reign of Tutankhamun, see Lanny Bell, "Aspects of the Cult of the Deified Tutankhamun," in *Mélanges Gamal Eddin Mokhtar* (Cairo: Institut Français d'Archéologie Orientale, 1985), 34–35. Compare also royal stat-

ues where the king's back becomes that of a falcon (Catherine Roehrig, ed., *Hatshepsut, from Queen to Pharaoh* [New York: The Metropolitan Museum of Art, 2005], 90; Hourig Sourouzian, "Thoutmosis III-Faucon," in *Egyptian Museum Collections around the World* [Cairo: Supreme Council of Antiquities, 2002]) and the winged pharaoh in the tomb of Djehutyemhab (Christiane Desroches-Noblecourt, "Une coutume égyptienne méconnue," *BIFAO* 45 [1947]: 201–209).

59. For the king transforming into a falcon, compare (among many possible texts) Pyramid Text Spells 626 and 668; in Spell 655, the king possesses the plumage of a duck and flies like a falcon. For transformation texts in general, see W. Federn, "The 'Transformations' in the Coffin Texts: A New Approach," *JNES* 19 (1960): 241–257; F. Servajean, *Les formules des transformations du Livre des Morts à la lumière d'une théorie de la performativité* (Cairo: Institut Français d'Archéologie Orientale, 2003).

60. W. Raymond Johnson, "Images of Amenhotep III in Thebes: Styles and Intentions," in *The Art of Amenhotep III*, 34–36; Johnson, in *Amenhotep III: Perspectives on His Reign*, 84–85. For a newly identified sculpture relating to the jubilees of Amunhotep III, see John Coleman Darnell and Colleen Manassa, "A Fragmentary Pair Statue of Ptah of Ramesses and Herishef," *Yale University Art Gallery Bulletin 2005*, 110–114.

61. Kozloff and Bryan, *Egypt's Dazzling Sun*, 159–161, 198–199.

62. For the deification of Amunhotep III, see also W. Raymond Johnson, "Amenhotep III and Amarna: Some New Considerations," *JEA* 82 (1996): 67–72; Susanne Bickel, "Aspects et fonctions de la déification d'Amenhotep III," *BIFAO* 102 (2002): 63–90.

63. Robert Mond and Oliver Myers, *The Cemeteries of Armant* (London: Egypt Exploration Society), pl. 1.

64. Charles Bachatly, *Le Monastère de Phoebammon dans la Thébaïde*; vol. 1, *L'Archéologie du site* (Cairo: Publications de la Société d'Archéologie Copte, 1981), pl. 90.

65. Also known by the modern toponym Kom el-Abd; for this site, see Barry Kemp, "A Building of Amenophis III at Kom el-'Abd," *JEA* 63 (1977): 71–82; Wolfgang Decker, "Altägyptische Sportstätten," in *Gegengabe, Festschrift für Emma Brunner-Traut*, ed. I. Gamer-Wallert and W. Helck (Tübingen: Attempto Verlag, 1992), 67–69.

66. Compare the cleared track for military patrols associated with a pair of Seventeenth Dynasty towers along the Alamat Tal road—J. C. Darnell, in *Egypt and Nubia*, 139–140.

67. Publication of these inscriptions by J. C. Darnell is forthcoming.

68. Vandersleyen, *L'Égypte*, 396–401, and references therein.

69. Theodore M. Davis, *The Tomb of Iouiya and Touiyou* (London: Gerald Duckworth, 2000); J. E. Quibell, *Tomb of Yuaa and Thuiu* (Cairo: Institut Français d'Archéologie Orientale, 1908); Hawass, *Tutankhamun*, 128–139.

70. Audran Labrousse, "Sedeinga, métropole régionale au coeur de l'Empire méroitique," *Les Dossiers d'Archeologie* 196 (1994): 35–36; Kozloff and Bryan, *Egypt's Dazzling Sun*, 110.

71. Compare the deification of Amunhotep III at the Nubian temple of Soleb— William Murnane, "Soleb Renaissance: Reconsidering the Temple of Nebmaatre in Nubia," *Amarna Letters* 4 (2000): 6–19; Robert Morkot, "*Nb-M3't-R'*–United with Ptah," *JNES* 49 (1990): 329–330.

72. Silke Roth, *Gebieterin aller Länder* (Freiburg: Universitätsverlag, 2002), 19–20.

73. Epigraphic Survey, *Kheruef*, pl. 49; Roth, *Gebieterin*, 26–27.

74. William Murnane, *Ancient Egyptian Coregencies* (Chicago: Oriental Institute, 1977); for Middle Kingdom coregencies, see K. Jansen-Winkeln, "Das Attentat auf Amenemhet I. und die erste ägyptische Koregentschaft," *SAK* 18 (1991): 241–264; Jansen-Winkeln, "Zu den Koregenzen der 12. Dynastie," *SAK* 24 (1998): 115–135.

75. For persuasive arguments against the coregency theory and extensive bibliography, see Gabolde, *D'Akhenaton à Toutânkhamon*, 62–98; Peter Dorman, "The Long Coregency

Revisited: Architectural and Iconographic Conundra in the Tomb of Kheruef," in *Causing His Name to Live*, http://history.memphis.edu/murnane/.

76. The bibliography on Akhenaten is extensive and constantly expanding. For treatments of Atenism, particularly in the greater context of Egyptian religion, see Jan Assmann, "Die 'Häresie' des Echnaton: Aspekte der Amarna-Religion," *Saeculum* 23 (1972): 109–126; Assmann, *Egyptian Solar Religion in the New Kingdom: Re, Amun, and the Crisis of Polytheism*, trans. A. Alcock (London: Kegan Paul International, 1995); Assmann, *The Search for God in Ancient Egypt*, trans. D. Lorton (Ithaca, N.Y.: Cornell University Press, 2001), 208–230; Assmann, "Akhanyati's Theology in Light and Time," *Proceedings of the Israel Academy of Sciences and Humanities* VII: 4 (1992): 143–176; Erik Hornung, *Conceptions of God in Ancient Egypt: The One and the Many*, trans. J. Baines (Ithaca, N.Y.: Cornell University Press, 1996); Hornung, *Akhenaten and the Religion of Light*; Redford, *Akhenaten*, 169–181; L. Žabkar, "The Theocracy of Amarna and the Doctrine of the Ba," *JNES* 13 (1954): 87–101; further references are cited in following notes.

77. Jan Assmann, *Monotheismus und Kosmotheismus* (Heidelberg: Heidelberger Akademie der Wissenschaften, 1993); Assmann, "Monotheismus im pharaonischen Ägypten," in *Monotheismus im alten Israel und seiner Umwelt*, ed. O. Keel (Freiburg: Universitätsverlag, 1980), 83–97; a relatively recent overview of the history of Egyptological study of Egyptian religion, including the monotheism debate, is K. Koch, *Das Wesen altägyptischer Religion im Spiegel ägyptologischer Forschung* (Göttingen: Vandenhoeck & Ruprecht, 1989).

78. Ray Winfield Smith and Donald B. Redford, *The Akhenaten Temple Project*, vol. 1, *Initial Discoveries* (Warminster: Aris & Phillips, 1976); Redford, *Akhenaten*, 57–136; Redford, ed., *The Akhenaten Temple Project*, vol. 2, *Rwd-Mnw and Inscriptions* (Toronto: University of Toronto Press, 1988); Redford, "The Beginning of the Heresy," in *Pharaohs of the Sun*; Robert Vergnieux and Michel Gondran, *Aménophis IV et les pierres du soleil* (Paris: Arnaud, 1997); Vergnieux, *Recherches sur les monuments Thébains d'Amenhotpe IV à l'aide d'outils informatiques* (Geneva: Société d'Égyptologie,1999); Di. Arnold, *Ancient Egyptian Architecture*, 23–24.

79. Ramadan Sa'ad, "Les travaux d'Amenophis IV au IIIe pylône du temple d'Amon Re à Karnak," *Cahiers de Karnak* 3 (1970): 187–193; for the depiction of the third pylon of Karnak in the scenes of the Opet procession at Luxor Temple, see Epigraphic Survey, *Reliefs and Inscriptions at Luxor Temple*, vol. 1, *The Festival Procession of Opet in the Colonnade Hall* (Chicago: University of Chicago, Oriental Institute, 1994), 38–39 and pls. 104–107.

80. Aldred, *Akhenaten*, pl. 27; Redford, *Akhenaten*, 64 (for a slightly later version of Horakhty, see 65); Cyril Aldred, "The Beginning of the El-Amarna Period," *JEA* 45 (1959): 19–22.

81. Donald Redford, "The Sun-Disc in Akhenaten's Program: Its Worship and Antecedents, part 1," *JARCE* 13 (1976): 47–61; Redford, *JARCE* 17 (1980): 21–34. Suggestions that a disk-headed human statue dates to either Amunhotep III or Akhenaten remain uncertain, and stylistically the figure might better date to the Twenty-fifth Dynasty, perhaps relating to the decorative program of the so-called Edifice of Taharqa; for an Eighteenth-Dynasty date, see Robert Bianchi, "New Light on the Aton," *GM* 114 (1990): 35–40; Eugene Cruz-Uribe, "Another Look at an Aton Statue," *GM* 126 (1992): 29–32.

82. The almost spherical appearance of the solar disk in some representations combined with later Greco-Roman evidence suggests that the Egyptians might have conceived of the sun as a sphere; see Laszlo Kákosy, "Solar Disk or Solar Globe," in *Studien zur Sprache und Religion Ägyptens* (Göttingen: Hubert, 1984), vol. 2, 1057–1064.

83. Claude Traunecker, "Données nouvelles sur le début au règne d'Aménophis IV et son oeuvre à Karnak," *JSSEA* 14 (1984): 60–69; for further Amarna smiting scenes, see W.

Raymond Johnson, "An Asiatic Battle Scene of Tutankhamun from Thebes: A Late Amarna Antecedent of the Ramesside Battle-Narrative Tradition," Ph.D. diss., University of Chicago, 1992, 104–106; Vergnieux, *Recherches sur les monuments Thébains d'Amenhotpe IV*, 129, 152, and pl. 19, 109.

84. Some, if not most, of Akhenaten's architectural and artistic innovations may have been due to the pharaoh himself, since several artisans claim that the pharaoh instructed them personally. Maj Sandman, *Texts from the Time of Akhenaton* (Brussels: Fondation Égyptoloqiue Reine Élisabeth, 1938), 2, l. 14–15 and 175, l. 6–7.

85. Jesus Lopez, "Inscriptions hiératiques sur les talatât provenant des temples d'Akhenaton à Karnak," *Cahiers de Karnak* 8 (1987): 248 and n. 13.

86. Gohary, *Akhenaten's Sed-festival*; Karl Martin, "Der Luxortempel und Amenophis' IV. Sedfest(e)," *SAK* 30 (2002): 269–275. A year two or three date for the jubilee is espoused by Redford, in *Ancient Egyptian Kingship*, 180. For a year four date, see Gabolde, *D'Akhenaton à Toutânkhamon*, 26–28 and n. 211.

87. Hatshepsut may subsume the reign of her husband, Thutmose II, and perhaps some portion of the reign of her father, Thutmose I, to celebrate her *heb-sed* jubilee in year fifteen of her reign (Darnell, "Reign of Thutmosis I"); compare also how Horemhab subsumes the reigns of all the Amarna rulers (see below).

88. Gabolde, *D'Akhenaton à Toutânkhamon*, 28, is close to the proper understanding when he writes: "Amenhotep IV clearly desired that his early jubilee have a definitive and permanent impact."

89. James P. Allen, "The Natural Philosophy of Akhenaten," in *Religion and Philosophy in Ancient Egypt*, ed. William Kelly Simpson (New Haven, Conn.: Yale Egyptological Seminar, 1989), 91–94; Alessandro Bongioanni, "Considerations sur les 'noms' d'Aten et la nature du rapport souverain-divinite à l'epoque amarnienne," *GM* 68 (1983): 43–51; Florence Friedman, "3ḫ in the Amarna Period," *JARCE* 23 (1986): 99–106. Cathie Spieser, "Amarna et la négation du cycle solaire," *CdE* 76 (2001): 20–29. For a post year twelve date for the change in the Aten's names, see Gabolde, *D'Akhenaton à Toutânkhamon*, 110–118. For the more general phenomenon of divine cartouches, see Spieser, "Les cartouches divins," *ZÄS* 129 (2002): 85–95.

90. Von Beckerath, *Königsnamen*, 27–29.

91. The shining sun disk used as the icon of the Aten is not the image of the sun in the Egyptian hieroglyphic script, but rather a representation of light; see Assmann, *Saeculum* 23 (1972): 118.

92. Translations and commentary on the short and long versions of the Hymn to the Aten abound; see inter alia Jan Assmann, *Ägyptische Hymnen und Gebete*, 2nd ed. (Freiburg: Universitätsverlag, 1999), 210–227; Murnane, *Amarna Period*, 112–116.

93. Jan Assmann, "Die 'loyalistiche Lehre' Echnatons," *SAK* 8 (1980): 20–26. The teachings of Akhenaten are the only way in which the otherwise "mute" Aten reveals his will (ibid., 28–29). On the later survivals of loyalistic texts of the Amarna period, see Boyo Ockinga, "Zum Fortleben des 'Amarna-Loyalismus' in der Ramessidenzeit," *Die Welt des Orients* 14 (1983): 207–215.

94. William Murnane and Charles Van Siclen, *The Boundary Stelae of Akhenaten* (London: Kegan Paul International, 1993).

95. Ibid., 20–21, translation altered from 37.

96. Ibid., 1993: 23–24, translation altered from 39–40.

97. Geoffrey Martin, *The Hidden Tombs of Memphis* (London: Thames & Hudson, 1992); Martin, "Memphis: The Status of a Residence City in the Eighteenth Dynasty," in *Abusir and Saqqara in the Year 2000*, ed. Miroslav Barta and Jaromir Krejci (Prague: Academy of Sciences of the Czech Republic, 2000); Beatrix Löhr, "Aḫanjati in Memphis," *SAK* 2 (1975): 139–187.

98. Barry Kemp and Salvatore Garfi, *A Survey of the Ancient City of El-'Amarna* (London: Egypt Exploration Society, 1993); Kemp, "The Window of Appearance at El-Amarna, and the Basic Structure of this City," *JEA* 62 (1976): 81–99; Kemp, "The Amarna Workmen's Village in Retrospect," *JEA* 73 (1987): 21–50; Kemp, *Ancient Egypt*, 1st ed., 266–317; Peter Lacovara, "The City of Amarna," in *Pharaohs of the Sun*; O'Connor, in *Ancient Egyptian Kingship*, 284–290; Jan Assmann, "Palast oder Tempel? Überlegungen zur Architektur und Topographie von Amarna," *JNES* 31 (1972): 143–155; Arnold, *Ancient Egyptian Architecture*, 9–12. For more recent archaeological work, see the series of reports by Barry Kemp in *JEA*.

99. The boundary stelae and royal tomb wadi appear to have provided the bases for the alignment of all the major features of Amarna, which in turn dictated the alignment of the royal road; for analysis of the symbolic layout of Akhet-aten, see Michael Mallinson, "The Sacred Landscape," in *Pharaohs of the Sun*. For astronomical orientations for the temples at Akhet-aten, see Ronald Wells, "The Amarna M, X, and K Boundary Stelae Date: Ḥwt-itn Ceremonial Altar. Initial Results of a New Survey," *SAK* 16 (1989): 289–327; a thorough critique of Well's theory was presented by Edward Castle, "The Foundation Ceremony at Akhetaten," at the Annual Meeting of the ARCE, April 2007. We would like to thank Mr. Castle for making a copy of his paper (publication forthcoming) available to us.

100. Kemp, *Ancient Egypt*, 305–317.

101. For funerary beliefs during the reign of Akhenaten, see Robert Hari, "La religion amarnienne et la tradition polytheiste," in *Studien zur Sprache und Religion Ägyptens*, vol. 2, 1046–1055; Thomas von der Way, "Überlegungen zur Jenseitsvorstellung in der Amarnazeit," *ZÄS* 123 (1996): 157–164.

102. Assmann, *JNES* 31 (1972): 143–148; Arnold, *Ancient Egyptian Architecture*, 24. Note also the emphasis on ramps and balustrades in the architecture of Aten temples; see Ian Shaw, "Balustrades, Stairs, and Altars in the Cult of the Aten at El-Amarna," *JEA* 80 (1994): 109–127.

103. Compare the ground plan of a Heliopolitan temple in Herbert Ricke, "Eine Inventartafel aus Heliopolis im Turiner Museum," *ZÄS* 71 (1935): 111–133. Further Heliopolitan elements in Akhenaten's solar religion include the high priest title "Greatest Seer" and the transplantation of the burial of the Mnevis bull to Akhet-aten (Murnane and van Siclen, *Boundary Stelae*, 41).

104. Hassan Bakry, "Akhenaten at Heliopolis," *CdE* 47 (1972): 55–67; Labib Habachi, "Akhenaten in Heliopolis," *Aufsätze zum 70. Geburtstag von Herbert Ricke* (Wiesbaden: Franz Steiner, 1971).

105. C. Karlshausen, "L'évolution de la barque processionnelle d'Amon à la 18e dynastie," *RdE* 46 (1995): 119–138.

106. The art and artistic styles of the Amarna age have received copious attention. Discussions and bibliography may be found in most of the general publications cited in this book. See in particular the exhibit catalogs Cyril Aldred, *Akhenaten and Nefertiti* (New York: Viking Press, 1973); Freed, Markowitz, and D'Auria, eds., *Pharaohs of the Sun*.

107. For the artistic developments of the reign of Amunhotep III, see inter alia Kozloff and Bryan, eds., *Egypt's Dazzling Sun*; Berman, ed., *The Art of Amenhotep III*; Johnson, in *Amenhotep III*; Johnson, "The Setting: History, Religion, and Art," in *Pharaohs of the Sun*.

108. In ancient Egyptian theology, the shadows created by fans and sun shades showed the divine presence through sunlight; similarly, when the sun travels through the Underworld, the disk is called "great of shadow" (Darnell, *Enigmatic Netherworld Books*, 137).

109. Aldred, *Akhenaten and Nefertiti*, 48–57.

110. Such depictions of bowing and scraping by Egyptians are rare, but not altogether unattested; note the late Middle Kingdom sculpture of officials literally kissing the earth— C. Ziegler, ed., *The Pharaohs* (New York: Rizzoli, 2002), 197 and 438.

111. Aldred, *Akhenaten and Nefertiti*, 58–66.

112. Dorothea Arnold, *The Royal Women of Amarna: Images of Beauty from Ancient Egypt* (New York: Metropolitan Museum of Art, 1996), 41–84.

113. Translation of Murnane, *Amarna Period*, 66. Compare also the fragmentary taxation decree, which required payment from temples and estates throughout Egypt for the new Aten cult; see Traunecker, *JSSEA* 14 (1984): 60–69; Murnane, *Amarna Period*, 30–31.

114. Hari, in *Studien zu Sprache und Religion Ägyptens*, vol. 2, 1039–1043; see Gabolde, *D'Akhenaton à Toutânkhamon*, 32–34, for a list of monuments where the name of Amun and other deities were damaged during the Amarna Period.

115. Peter Der Manuelian, "Semi-Literacy in Egypt: Some Erasures from the Amarna Period," in *Gold of Praise: Studies on Ancient Egypt in Honor of Edward F. Wente*, ed. Emily Teeter and John Larson (Chicago: University of Chicago, Oriental Institute, 1999).

116. David Warburton, *State and Economy in Ancient Egypt* (Freiburg: University Press, 1997), 300–313; B. J. J. Haring, *Divine Households: Administrative and Economic Aspects of the New Kingdom Royal Memorial Temples in Western Thebes* (Leiden: Nederlands Instituut voor het nabije oosten, 1997), 12–20, passim.

117. Hari, in *Studien zu Sprache und Religion Ägyptens*, vol. 2, 1043–1046; Helmut Brandl, "Die Schutzgottheiten Sched und Thoeris in Amarna," in *Begegnungen, Antike Kulturen im Niltal*, ed. Caris-Beatrice Arnst et al. (Leipzig: Verlag Helmar Wodtke, 2001), 91–106.

118. Arnold, *Royal Women of Amarna*, 65–70.

119. Redford, *Akhenaten*, 72–78.

120. Roth, *Gebieterin*, 28–29; Petschel and von Falck, eds., *Pharao siegt immer*, 58; Edward Werner, "Montu and the 'Falcon Ships' of the Eighteenth Dynasty," *JARCE* 23 (1986): 120–122. Compare the stern of the queen Ankhesenamun's barge on the western wall of the Colonnade Hall of Luxor Temple, where the queen stands behind the king smiting an enemy and brandishing her own *khepesh* scimitar—Epigraphic Survey, *Luxor Temple* 1, pls. 28 and 29.

121. For a Meroitic queen in martial pose, compare S. E. Chapman and D. Dunham, *Decorated Chapels of the Meroitic Pyramids at Meroë and Barkal* (Boston: Museum of Fine Arts, 1952), pl. 17.

122. Anna Stevens, "The Material Evidence for Domestic Religion at Amarna and Preliminary Remarks on Its Interpretation," *JEA* 89 (2003): 143–168; Salima Ikram, "Domestic Shrines and the Cult of the Royal Family at El-Amarna," *JEA* 75 (1989): 89–102; Assmann, *JNES* 31 (1972): 153 and n. 64–65. On the stelae, see R. Krauss, "Die amarnazeitliche Familienstele Berlin 14145, unter besonderer Berücksichtigung von Massordnung und Komposition," *Jahrbuch der Berliner Museen* 33 (1991): 7–36; Arnold, *Royal Women*, 96–105.

123. Three other royal daughters are attested: Baketaten, Merytaten the younger, and Ankhesenpaaten the younger. The mothers of the latter two were most likely the princesses for whom they were named (Merytaten and Ankhesenpaaten, respectively), and their father may have been their own maternal grandfather, Akhenaten. See James Allen, "The Amarna Succession," in *Causing His Name to Live*, 9–14, http://history.memphis.edu/murnane.

124. For the parentage of Tutankhamun, see 47 below.

125. For the few documents mentioning Kiye, see Murnane, *Amarna Period*, 90–92.

126. For the debate over Kiye's identity, see Gabolde, *D'Akhenaton à Toutânkhamon*, 166–170; Peter Haider, "Menschenhandel zwischen dem ägyptischen Hof und der minoisch-mykenischen Welt?," *Ägypten und Levante* 6 (1996): 150–151; Vandersleyen, *L'Égypte*, 443–446; Jacobus van Dijk, "The Noble Lady of Mitanni and Other Royal Favorites of the Eighteenth Dynasty," in *Essays on Ancient Egypt in Honour of Herman te Velde*, ed. van Dijk (Groningen: Styx Publications, 1997).

127. For the history of scholarship on Akhenaten, see Montserrat, *Akhenaten*, 12–54, passim.

128. See among the many possible references Reeves, *Akhenaten*, 110–111.

129. Gabolde, *D'Akhenaton à Toutânkhamon*, 98–102. As Gabolde notes, many members of the clergy of Amun were also related to the "heretic pharaoh" through his mother, Tiye. For the interdependence of the temple and the state in the ancient Egyptian economy, see Warburton, *State and Economy*, 300–313.

130. The most common disease attributed to Akhenaten is Fröhlich's syndrome; for the proposal of Marfan's syndrome, see Alywn L Burridge, "Akhenaten: A New Perspective," *JSSEA* 23 (1993): 63–74. For an overview of the debate about the various diseases that might be reflected in Akhenaten's art, see Aldred, *Akhenaten*, 231– 236; Gabolde, *D'Akhenaton à Toutânkhamon*, 9–11; James Harris, "The Mummy of Amenhotep III," in *Gold of Praise* for the skeletal remains of the rulers of the late Eighteenth Dynasty.

131. The following discussion is a summary of portions of John Coleman Darnell, *"For I See the Color of His Uraei"*: *Amarna Solar Theology*, forthcoming, in which more complete references and textual parallels will appear.

132. Murnane and Van Siclen, *Boundary Stelae*, 37–38.

133. Kurt Sethe, *Amun und die Acht Urgötter von Hermopolis, eine Untersuchung über Ursprung und Wesen des ägyptischen Götterkönigs* (Berlin: Verlag der Akademie der Wissenschaften, 1929); Mark Smith, *On the Primaeval Ocean* (Copenhagen: Carsten Niebuhr Institute of Near Eastern Studies, 2002); David Klotz, *Adoration of the Ram: Five Hymns to Amun from Hibis Temple* (New Haven, Conn.: Yale Egyptological Seminar, 2006), 67–71, 137–138.

134. John Coleman Darnell, *The Birth of Victorious Thebes*, forthcoming; the religious policies of Monthuhotep II may even be a continuation of the temple-building of Antef II. For the New Kingdom Theban festival cycle, see Cabrol, *Les voies processionnelles*; Kemp, *Ancient Egypt*, 2nd ed., 264–273; O'Connor, in *Amenhotep III*, 154–160.

135. Evidence for the worship of Ogdoad at Thebes prior to the Greco-Roman Period is scarce but present. Compare the late Ramesside payprus mentioning the Ogdoad at a Theban Amun temple, probably Karnak but possibly Medinet Habu (O. Goelet, "A New 'Robbery' Papyrus: Rochester MAG 51.346.1," *JEA* 82 [1996]: 111, l. 11 and 26; for the location of the inspection, see 119–120).

136. Uvo Hölscher, *The Excavation of Medinet Habu*, vol. 2, *The Temple of the Eighteenth Dynasty* (Chicago: University of Chicago Press, 1939), 4–7, 44–46; no evidence for the cult of the original temple has appeared, but it may have been a foundation of Antef II or one of his successors and probably related to the cult of Amun and the establishment of the Theban festival cycle, for which Montuhotep II takes credit in the Deir el-Ballas inscription; see Darnell, *Birth of Victorious Thebes*.

137. Cabrol, *Les voies processionnelles*, 561–564.

138. Christine Strauβ-Seeber, "Amenophis III. in Medinet Habu," in *4. Ägyptologische Tempeltagung*, eds. R. Gundlach and M. Rochholz (Wiesbaden: Harrassowitz, 1998). Amunhotep III also builds opposite Medinet Habu/Malqata at Luxor Temple and the eastern equivalent of the Birket Habu, suggesting that he tried to link Amun of Luxor with Medinet Habu, presaging the later Decade Festival, in which Amun of Luxor journeyed to the small temple of Medinet Habu every ten days to unite with the Ogdoad. For the Decade Festival, see Cabrol, *Les voies processionnelles*, 65–66, 282, et passim.

139. For Akhenaten as the cult image of Aten on earth, see Assmann, *JNES* 31 (1972): 152–155; Assmann, *The Search for God*, 219–221.

140. For the ritual significance of the chariot ride at Amarna, see also O'Connor, in *Ancient Egyptian Kingship*, 289–290, 293–296. In the boundary stelae, Akhenaten rides forth "on the great chariot of electrum—just like Aten, when he rises in his horizon" (Murnane and van Siclen, *Boundary Stelae*, 36).

141. For this concept in Egyptian religion, see chap. 2, n. 48.

142. O'Connor, in *Amenhotep III*, 154–171.

143. Gabolde, *D'Akhenaton à Toutânkhamon*, 38 n. 218 and 82–85.

144. Or at least the Amun domains of Thebes as a unity—the *Pr-Imn*—comprised the *Akhet-ni-itn*; see William Murnane, "Observations on Pre-Amarna Theology during the Earliest Reign of Amenhotep IV" in *Gold of Praise*, 304–307.

145. Wolfhart Westendorf, "Amenophis IV in Urgottgestalt," *Pantheon* 21 (1963): 269–277; Erik Hornung, "Gedanken zur Kunst der Amarnazeit," *ZÄS* 97 (1971): 74–78; Aldred, *Akhenaten*, 234–236. On androgyny in Egyptian theology, see Lana Troy, *Patterns of Queenship in Ancient Egyptian Myth and History* (Uppsala: University of Uppsala, 1986), 15–21; Darnell, *Enigmatic Netherworld Books*, 360–362.

146. Compare the passage in Sandman, *Texts*, 84, l. 6–7: "You are the mother who gave birth to everybody and who raised millions by your *ka*."

147. Marianne Eaton-Krauss, "Eine rundplastische Darstellung Achenatens als Kind," *ZÄS* 110 (1983): 127–132.

148. Kozloff and Bryan, eds., *Egypt's Dazzling Sun*, 146–149, 204–206.

149. Freed, Markowitz, and D'Auria, eds., *Pharaohs of the Sun*, 107, 234; J. R. Harris, "A fine piece of Egyptian faience," *The Burlington Magazine* 119 (1977): 340–343. The tomb of Apy (Norman Davies, *The Rock Tombs of El Amarna*, part 4—*Tombs of Penthu, Manhu, and others* [London: Egypt Exploration Fund], pl. 31) depicts Akhenaten and Nefertiti offering images of themselves as Shu and Tefnut adoring the twin cartouches of the Aten. Amunhotep III is also described as being born "at the same time as Shu and Tefnut" (*Urk.* IV 1675, l. 5).

150. James Allen, *Genesis in Egypt: The Philosophy of Ancient Egyptian Creation Accounts* (New Haven, Conn.: Yale Egyptological Seminar, 1988), 14–21.

151. Assmann, *SAK* 8 (1980): 9–19.

152. Norman Davies, *The Rock Tombs of El Amarna*, part 2: *The Tomb of Meryra* (London: Egypt Exploration Fund, 1905), pl. 7, lower register, l. 13–19; as in Sandman, *Texts*, 24, 5–7.

153. Assmann, *SAK* 8 (1980): 23–24. On the more traditional relationship between Maat and the pharaoh, see Assmann, *Ma'at*, 200–212.

154. Compare the omission of the divine determinative after the name Aten, suggesting that the Aten transcends the category of "god"; see Orly Goldwasser, "The Essence of Amarna Monotheism," in *jn.t dr.w Festschrift für Friedrich Junge*, ed. G. Moers (Göttingen: Seminar für Ägyptologie und Koptologie, 2006), vol. 1, 267–279.

155. Assmann, *Saeculum* 23 (1972): 119, without noting the connection with the Ogdoad, reaches a similar conclusion: "The king . . . seeks a place, which has not been touched by any other traditions, where the 'primodial time' is still present and creation has yet to come. And is not Akhenaten's step in a certain sense a return to the primordial time, as a divine unity with duality not yet in existence, a dissolution of the multiplicity and differentiation of the world?" For timelessness as a defining principle of Akhenaten's religion, compare Sandman, *Texts*, 73, l. 6: "The ruler of Maat is born like the Aten, enduring forever according to his form, making millions of jubilees"; ibid., 84, l. 14: "The Aten gives birth to you each time that he appears and shines in heaven." Aten represents the eternity of the time before creation, while Akhenaten is the son of eternity; see passages collected in Zabkar, *JNES* 13 (1954): 90.

156. For the oneness of the Aten as the moment of creation, compare statements in the Coffin Texts that describe the uncreated world as "when two things did not yet exist" (A. de Buck, *The Egyptian Coffin Texts* [Chicago: University of Chicago Press, 1935–1961], vol. 2, 396, and vol. 3, 382). For this concept, see also Hornung, *Conceptions of God*, 170–172.

157. For the related association of crown, uraeus, and eye goddess, see John Coleman Darnell, "The Apotropaic Goddess in the Eye," *SAK* 27 (1997): 35–48; W. Guglielmi, *Die*

Göttin Mr.t. Entstehung und Verehrung einer Personifikation (Leiden: Brill, 1991); Troy, *Patterns of Queenship*, 20–25. For the solar hands as feminine elements, see Darnell, *Enigmatic Netherworld Books*, 394–396.

158. For the theological role of women at Amarna, compare the "Hathoric mode" of Egyptian queenship in general—Troy, *Patterns of Queenship*, 53–79. For another example of Hathoric theology adopted for Atenist theology, see Christian Cannuyer, "Aton, nourrice dans le sein, succédané des maîtresses de la ménat," GM 157 (1997): 11–14.

159. Murnane, *OLZ* 96 (2001): 9.

160. Redford, *Akhenaten*, 187. Plagues from the ancient Near East affected Egypt both before and after the Amarna Period. In about 1700 B.C.E., a plague entered the Delta; see Manfred Bietak, *Tell el-Daba V* (Vienna: Verlag der Österreichischen Akademie der Wissenschaften, 1991), 35–38; Bietak, "Avaris, Capital of the Hyksos Kingdom: New Results of Excavations," in *Hyksos*, 105; Hans Goedicke, "The Canaanite Illness," *SAK* 11 (1984): 91–105; for the Hittite records of the plague in the immediate post-Amarna period, see William Murnane, *The Road to Kadesh: A Historical Interpretation of the Battle Reliefs of King Sety I at Karnak* (Chicago: University of Chicago, Oriental Institute, 1990), 27–29. See also Eva Panagiotakopulu, "Pharaonic Egypt and the Origins of Plague," *Journal of Biogeography* 31 (2004): 269–275.

161. Davies, *Rock Tombs* II, pl. 41.

162. For overviews of the immediate successors of Akhenaten, see Vandersleyen, *L'Égypte*, 451–457; Gabolde, *D'Akhenaton à Toutânkhamon*; James Allen, "The Amarna Succession," in *Causing His Name to Live*, http://history.memphis.edu/murnane.

163. Vergnieux, *Monuments Thébains d'Amenhotpe IV*, 179–184.

164. The two epithets use elements of the nomen and praenomen of Akhenaten "beloved of Waenre" and "beloved of Neferkheperure" (Julia Samson, *Amarna, City of Akhenaten and Nefertiti, Nefertiti as Pharaoh* [London: University College, 1978], 108–109; von Beckerath, *Königsnamen*, 144–145). In some occurrences this name is associated with a nomen Neferneferuaten "beloved of Akhenaten" or "Waenre," apparently forming a single titulary.

165. The praenomen Ankhkheperure with "beloved of Neferkheperure" or "beloved of Waenre" (Akhenaten) also appears in mixed masculine and feminine forms; Gabolde, *D'Akhenaton à Toutânkhamon*, 151–153.

166. Roehrig, ed., *Hatshepsut*, 88–89.

167. Gabolde, *D'Akhenaton à Toutânkhamon*, 178–180.

168. Samson, *Nefertiti as Pharaoh*, 103–106; Gabolde, *D'Akhenaton à Toutânkhamon*, 155–156, 162–166.

169. Gabolde, *D'Akhenaton à Toutânkhamon*, 224–226.

170. The elevation of Neferure to the priestly office of "god's wife" after Hatshepsut assumed the male royal titulary (Vandersleyen, *L'Égypte*, 279–280) provides a rough parallel to the proposition that Merytaten might have become queen as Nefertiti masquerading as male ruler.

171. Compare the changes in titulary of Monthuhotep II (Eleventh Dynasty) and Piye (Twenty-fifth Dynasty)—von Beckerath, *Königsnamen*, 78–79, 206–207.

172. Compare EA 155 (William Moran, *The Amarna Letters* [Baltimore: Johns Hopkins University Press, 1992], 241): "Should the king, my lord, give water to drink to the servant of Mayati (Merytaten), then I will devote myself to his service (and that of) Mayati, my mistress, night and day." Mayati is first mentioned in EA 10, which may date shortly after her birth. For Merytaten and the Amarna Letters, see also Gabolde, *D'Akhenaton à Toutânkhamon*, 147–178.

173. At this stage of the Eighteenth Dynasty Manetho mentions a queen Akenkheres, perhaps Ankhetkheperure, whom the Greco-Egyptian historian describes as the daughter of her predecessor (Murnane, *Amarna Period*, 242; Krauss, *Amarnazeit*, 26–30).

174. Gabolde, *D'Akhenaton à Toutânkhamon*, 221–224, attempts to identify Smenkh-kare with the Hittite prince Zannanza, but no evidence confirms this identification. Furthermore, the Egyptian queen who wrote to Suppiluliuma is Ankhesenamun and not Merytaten, as Gabolde assumes (see further in chap. 5).

175. Murnane, *Amarna Period*, 207–208; Alexander J. Peden, *The Graffiti of Pharaonic Egypt* (Leiden: Brill, 2001), 69–70; Gabolde, *D'Akhenaton à Toutânkhamon*, 161–162.

176. G. Roeder, *Amarna-Reliefs aus Hermopolis* (Hildesheim: Gerstenberg, 1969), pl. 106.

177. Vandersleyen, *L'Égypte*, 467–468.

178. James Harris and Edward Wente, *An X-ray Atlas of the Royal Mummies* (Chicago: University of Chicago Press, 1980), 258, 333; Donald Redford, "Once Again the Filiation of Tutankhamun," *JSSEA* 9 (1979): 111–115.

179. Geoffrey T. Martin, *Royal Tomb at el-'Amarna*, vol. 2, *The Reliefs, Inscriptions, and Architecture* (London: Egypt Exploration Society, 1989), 38–40, discussing the scene in room alpha; the scene in room alpha, like that of gamma, might also depict the death of Meketaten and be unrelated to Tutankhamun (see Murnane, *OLZ* 96 [2001]: 14–16). For a detailed overview of discussions of the royal tomb at Amarna, see Gabolde, *D'Akhenaton à Toutânkhamon*, 105–146.

180. For a possible representation of Tutankhamun at Amarna, see Julia Pinch Brock, "Tutankhamun in the 'King's House' at Amarna? Cairo SR 11575/20647," *BACE* 9 (1998): 7–17.

181. Tutankhamun appears to have worshipped the god Amun prior to the change of his name; see Marianne Eaton-Krauss, "Die Throne Tutanchamuns: Vorläufige Bemerkungen," *GM* 76 (1984): 7–10; Brandl, in *Begegnungen*, 100.

182. Marianne Eaton-Krauss, "The Titulary of Tutankhamun," in *Form und Mass, Festschrift für Gerhard Fecht*, ed. J. Osing and G. Dreyer (Wiesbaden: Otto Harrassowitz, 1987).

183. For post-Tutankhamun remains at Amarna, see Stevens, *JEA* 89 (2003): 144, n. 3.

184. The following discussion is a summary of Gabolde, *D'Akhenaton à Toutânkhamon*, 227–276; see also Wolfgang Helck, *Das Grab Nr. 55 im Königsgräbertal* (Mainz: Verlag Philipp von Zabern, 2001).

185. *Urk.* IV, 2027, l. 1–18.

186. *Urk.* IV, 2028, l. 8.

187. For the size of the bark of Amun during the Eighteenth Dynasty and the number of its carrying poles, see J.-F. Carlotti, "Essai de datation de l'aggrandissement à cinq barres de portage du pavois de la barque processionelle d'Amon-Re," *Cahiers de Karnak* 11 (2003): 235–254.

188. *Urk.* IV, 2029, l. 14–15.

189. *Urk.* IV, 2030, l. 13–17.

190. Vandersleyen, *L'Égypte*, 472–474; Marianne Eaton-Krauss, "Tutankhamun at Karnak," *MDAIK* 44 (1988): 1–11.

191. Otto Schaden, "The Granite Colossi of Amun and Amonet at Karnak," *GM* 38 (1980): 69–73.

192. Epigraphic Survey, *Luxor Temple 1*. Some decoration appears to have been laid out in paint prior to the reign of Akhenaten, but the first carving in the Colonnade appears to date to the reign of Tutankhamun. Tutankhamun's scenes of the Opet procession cycle in the Colonnade Hall of Luxor Temple also reveal what appear to be a number of his own Amarna-influenced changes to the ancient processions, including two chariots decorated with a plethora of uraei that accompany the land processions between Karnak and Luxor temples, recalling the chariot at Amarna as both the processional vehicle of the rulers and

the carrying platform of the divine images. The bark of the deified image of Tutankhamun for the first time accompanies the procession of the barks of the divine triad of Karnak, reflecting the increased significance of the ruler as the exclusive vessel of divine inhabitation on earth; see Lanny Bell, "Luxor Temple and the Cult of the Royal Ka," *JNES* 44 (1985): 260–262.

193. Luc Gabolde, "Les temples «mémoriaux» de Thoutmosis II et Toutânkhamon," *BIFAO* 89 (1989): 139–144; this temple is likely the origin of the Asiatic and Nubian war blocks from the reign of Tutankhamun, for which see Raymond Johnson, *Asiatic Battle Scene*.

194. The cause of Tutankhamun's death remains a topic of debate; for the results of recent CT scans, which argue against any theories of Tutankhamun's murder, see Hawass, *Tutankhamun*, 263–270.

195. For the reign of Aye, see Otto Schaden, "The God's Father Ay," Ph.D. diss., University of Minnesota, 1977; Vandersleyen, *L'Égypte*, 478–484. For Aye's royal statuary, see Epigraphic Survey, *Reliefs and Inscriptions at Luxor Temple 2* (Chicago: University of Chicago, Oriental Institute, 1998), 73–74.

196. Helmut Brunner, "Der 'Gottesvater' als Erzieher des Kronprinzen," ZÄS 86 (1961): 90–100; Labib Habachi, "Gottesvater," in *LÄ* II.

197. Compare the rock-cut temple Aye decorated for Horus, Min, Isis, and Aperetset of Akhmim—Klaus Kuhlmann, "Der Felstempel des Eje bei Achmim," *MDAIK* 35 (1979): 165–188.

198. See Schaden, *Ay*, 7–10, for a survey of the evidence.

199. Vandersleyen, *L'Égypte*, 479; on Tiye, see also van Dijk, in *Essays on Ancient Egypt in Honour of Herman te Velde*, 39–41.

200. Norman Davies, *The Rock Tombs of El Amarna*, part 6—*Tombs of Parennefer, Tutu, and Ay* (London: Egypt Exploration Fund, 1908), pl. 29; Freed, Markowitz, and D'Auria, ed., *Pharaohs of the Sun*, 270, no. 232.

201. Boyo Ockinga, *A Tomb from the Reign of Tutankhamun at Akhmim* (Warminster: Aris & Phillips, 1997), 60–61 and pl. 35–39.

202. Theodore Davis, *The Tombs of Harmhabi and Touatankhamanou* (London: Gerald Duckworth, 2001), 127–129.

203. Hornung, *Books of the Afterlife*; for Ay and the tomb of Tutankhamun, see also Murnane, *Road to Kadesh*, 134–136.

204. Van Dijk, *BACE* 7 (1996): 29–42.

205. Reeves, *Complete Tutankhamun*, 94, noting that a seal once thought to bear the name of Horemhab actually does not.

206. Horst Beinlich and Mohammed Saleh, *Corpus der hieroglyphischen Inschriften aus dem Grab des Tutanchamnun* (Oxford: Griffith Institute, 1989) nos. 318a, 318c, 330i, 330j, and 330k. The treasurer Maya is the only other private individual known to have donated objects to the burial of Tutankhamun.

207. For Nakhtmin, see Ockinga, *Akhmim*, 54–61, and the earlier discussions of Alan Schulman, "Excursus on the 'Military Officer' Nakhtmin," *JARCE* 3 (1964): 124–126; Schulman, "The Berlin 'Trauerrelief' (No. 12411) and Some Officials of Tutankhamun and Ay," *JARCE* 4 (1965): 55–68.

208. The most detailed survey of Horemhab's preroyal career and his reign remains Rober Hari, *Horemheb et la reine Moutnedjemet* (Geneva: Imprimerie La Sirène, 1964); see also Geoffrey Martin, *The Memphite Tomb of Horemheb Commander-in-Chief of Tutankhamun* I (London: Egypt Exploration Society, 1989), 161–165; Gnirs, *Militär*, 44–51.

209. Vandersleyen, *L'Égypte*, 485; van Dijk, *BACE* 7 (1996): 29–42.

210. Martin, *Memphite Tomb*; Martin, *Hidden Tombs*.

211. Martin, *Memphite Tomb*, 78–84; pls. 78–95.

212. Ibid., pl. 90.

213. Gnirs, *Militär*, 44–53, 99–103; Spalinger, *War in Ancient Egypt*, 169–184.

214. Hari, *Horemheb*, 208–217 and pls. 37–39; Alan Gardiner, "The Coronation of King Haremhab," *JEA* 39 (1953): 13–31.

215. Gardiner, *JEA* 39 (1953): pls. 2, l. 5–6.

216. Ibid., l. 7.

217. Ibid., l. 12.

218. Ibid., l. 22–24.

219. This stela was set up at the back (northern side) of the western tower of the Tenth Pylon, at the southern end of the north–south axis of Karnak Temple.

220. Vandersleyen, *L'Égypte*, 487–488.

221. Alan Gardiner, *The Inscription of Mes* (Hildesheim: Georg Olms Verlagsbuchhandlung, 1905), 52.

222. Marc Gabolde, "Ay, Toutankhamon et les martelages de la stèle de la restauration de Karnak (CG 34183)," *BSEG* 11 (1987): 37–61.

223. Vandersleyen, *L'Égypte*, 484.

224. Ibid., 489–490; Hari, *Horemheb*.

225. Allan Philips, "Horemheb, Founder of the XIXth Dynasty, O. Cairo 25646 Reconsidered," *Orientalia* 46 (1977): 116–121.

226. For an image from the tomb of Horemhab possibly depicting the general rewarding the future Ramesses I, see Martin, *Memphite Tomb*, 40–43, and pl. 32, 34.

227. Gardiner, *Mes*, 11; in a fragmentary papyrus, an event is referred to as happening in "Year Nine of the Rebel," probably another euphemism for Akhenaten—Alan Gardiner, "A Later Allusion to Akhenaten," *JEA* 24 (1938): 124.

Chapter 3. Trampling the Nine Bows: Military Forces and Weaponry

1. Compare the violent deaths of the men, women, and children buried in shallow graves at Gebel Sahaba, with arrowheads still embedded in many of the bones—see inter alia Fred Wendorf, "A Nubian Final Paleolithic Graveyard near Jebel Sahaba, Sudan," in *The Prehistory of Nubia* (Dallas: Southern Methodist University Press, 1968), 954–995. For early projectiles of the Aterian culture, see David Phillipson, *Archaeology of Africa* (Cambridge, U.K.: Cambridge University Press, 2005), 131–134.

2. F. Uphill, "The Nine Bows," *JEOL* 19 (1965–1966): 393–420; David O'Connor and Stephen Quirke, "Introduction: Mapping the Unknown in Ancient Egypt," in *Mysterious Lands*, ed. O'Connor and Quirke (London: UCL Press, 2003), 12–13.

3. Thomas von der Way, *Göttergericht und "Heiliger" Krieg im Alten Ägypten: Die Inschriften des Merenptah zum Libyerkrieg des Jahres 5* (Heidelberg: Heidelberger Orientverlag, 1992).

4. The following discussion focuses on the military organization and capabilities of the Egyptian army; for the social impact of the military changes of the New Kingdom, see Gnirs, *Militär*; Spalinger, *War in Ancient Egypt*, 70–82, 182–184; Kemp, *Ancient Egypt*, 2nd ed., 297–300.

5. Eckhard Eichler, *Untersuchungen zum Expeditionswesen des ägyptischen Alten Reiches* (Wiesbaden: Otto Harrassowitz, 1993), 198–220. Reliefs from the reigns of Userkaf and Sahure depict training, apparently instruction in marching or running in formation, of military recruits; see Dorothea Arnold et al., *Egyptian Art in the Age of the Pyramids* (New York: Metropolitan Museum of Art, 1999), 318–321, 342–343.

6. For the Egyptian military of the predynastic period, see Gregory Gilbert, *Weapons, Warriors, and Warfare in Early Egypt* (Oxford: Archaeopress, 2004).

7. For military titles of the Middle Kingdom, see Stephen Quirke, *Titles and Bureaux of Egypt 1850–1700 B.C.* (London: Golden House Publications, 2004), 97–110; Grajetzki, *Die höchsten Beamten*, 126–129.

8. The Hyksos were not a barrier to the Egyptians' acquisition of new technology, as claimed by Ian Shaw, "Egyptians, Hyksos, and Military Technology: Causes, Effects, or Catalysts?," in *The Social Context of Technological Change: Egypt and the Near East, 1650–1550 B.C.*, ed. A. J. Shortland (Oxford: Oxbow Books, 2001).

9. D. Darnell, in *Egypt and Nubia*, 171; see also chap. 2, n 4.

10. Alan Gardiner, *Late Egyptian Miscellanies* (Brussels: Édition de la Fondation Égyptologique Reine Élisabeth, 1937), 108, l. 5–6, 10, 12–13, and 109, l. 3–4 and 8–9.

11. Hans-Werner Fischer-Elfert, "Morphologie, Rhetorik, und Genese der Soldatencharakteristick," GM 66 (1983): 45–65; Spalinger, *War in Ancient Egypt*, 266–269.

12. Torgny Säve-Söderbergh, *The Navy of the Eighteenth Egyptian Dynasty* (Leipzig: Otto Harrassowitz, 1946), 74.

13. E.g., Ahmose son of Ibana and Ahmose-Penniut (Vandersleyen, *Les guerres d'Amosis*); for the Egyptian system of promotion, see also Spalinger, *War in Ancient Egypt*, 70–74.

14. Alan Schulman, *Military Rank, Title, and Organization in the Egyptian New Kingdom* (Berlin: Bruno Hessling, 1964), with the important review of Jean Yoyotte and Jesus Lopez, "L'organisation de l'armée et les titulatures de soldats au nouvel empire égyptien," *Bib. Or.* 26 (1969): 3–19; Pierre-Marie Chevereau, *Prosopographie des cadres militaires égyptiens du Nouvel Empire* (Paris: Antony, 1994) Gnirs, *Militär*.

15. Grajetzki, *Die höchsten Beamten*, 126–129; Louise Gestermann, *Kontinuität und Wandel in Politik und Verwaltung des frühen Mittleren Reiches in Ägypten* (Wiesbaden: Otto Harrassowitz, 1987), 191–220.

16. Schulman, *Military Rank*, 10–13; Hans-Werner Fischer-Elfert, *Die satirische Streitschrift des Papyrus Anastasi I: Übersetzung und Kommentar* (Wiesbaden: Otto Harrassowitz, 1986), 149; Spalinger, *War in Ancient Egypt*, 229. For the equivalence of the terms *mšꜥ* and *mnfy.t* in the New Kingdom, see Gnirs, *Militär*, 12–17; Yoyotte and Lopez, *Bib. Or.* 26 (1969): 9. The term *mesha* can also refer to an expeditionary force sent on nonmilitary missions, such as quarrying activities. For more on the peacetime duties of the army, see chap. 6.

17. Gnirs, *Militär*, 3–7.

18. Compare the titles "scribe of recruits" (*sš nfr.w*) and "troop organizer/commander" (*tz pḏ.t*) that can be held alongside the title "general"; see Gnirs, *Militär*, 10–11; Chevereau, *Nouvel Empire*, 98–101; see Fischer-Elfert, *Papyrus Anastasi I*, 148–157, for the commissariat duties of the *tz-pḏ.t*. For the meaning of the term *nfr.w* as recruits and not elite troops, as argued in Schulman, *Military Rank*, 20–21, see Yoyotte and Lopez, *Bib. Or.* 26 (1969): 5; Manassa, *Merneptah*, 52–53.

19. Gnirs, *Militär*, 3–12, 21, passim. Compare also the dual military and civil careers of the military officials during the reign of Thutmose III, for which see Betsy Bryan, "Administration in the Reign of Thutmose III," in *Thutmose III*, 103–107.

20. In Egyptian, these three titles are respectively *idnw ny mšꜥ*, *hry-pḏ.t*, and *t3y-sry.t*. See Chevereau, *Nouvel Empire*, 34–38, 64–89, and 101–130; Yoyotte and Lopez, *Bib. Or.* 26 (1969): 7–8; Gnirs, *Militär*, 18, 29–30, passim; Schulman, *Military Rank*, 69–71.

21. Compare the number of men who jointly hold the titles "overseer of fortresses" and "regiment commander" (Chevereau, *Nouvel Empire*, 58–62; Schulman, *Military Rank*, 54–55).

22. For military scribes, see Donald Redford, *Egypt, Canaan, and Israel in Ancient Times* (Princeton, N.J.: Princeton University Press, 1992), 217–218; Gnirs, *Militär*, 10, 66; Chevereau, *Nouvel Empire*, 201–224. The logistics of provisioning the Egyptian army on campaign is addressed in Spalinger, *War in Ancient Egypt*, 32–42, et passim; Redford, *Wars in*

Syria, 200–201; for military ration tokens from Nubia, see Petschel and von Falck, eds., *Pharaoh siegt immer*, 174–175. The Edwin Smith papyrus may be a triage manual for military surgeons; see John Nunn, *Ancient Egyptian Medicine* (Norman: University of Oklahoma Press, 2002), 25–30; James P. Allen, *The Art of Medicine in Ancient Egypt* (New York: Metropolitan Museum of Art, 2005), 70–115.

23. Schulman, *Military Rank*, 26–30; Chevereau, *Nouvel Empire*, 168–169. Units of ten men appear as early as the Old Kingdom; see Arnold et al., *Age of the Pyramids*, 320–321.

24. Norman Davies, *The Rock Tombs of El-Amarna*, part 1—*The Tomb of Meryra* (London: Egypt Exploration Fund, 1903), pls. 10, 15; Davies, *The Rock Tombs of El-Amarna*, part 3—*The Tombs of Huya and Ahmes* (London: Egypt Exploration Fund, 1905), pl. 31.

25. Schulman, *Military Rank*, 74, 164; see Schulman, *JARCE* 3 (1964): 59, n. 67, for a list of different titles and unit names during the reign of Akhenaten.

26. For military units based on city levies, see Chris Eyre, "Village Economy in Pharaonic Egypt," in *Agriculture in Egypt: From Pharaonic to Modern Times*, ed. A. K. Bowman and E. Rogan (Oxford: Oxford University Press, 1999), 38; Gestermann, *Kontinuität und Wandel*, 212–217; O. D. Berlev, "Les prétendus 'citadins' au Moyen Empire," *RdE* 23 (1971): 23–48; Gnirs, Militär, 4–5; Quirke, *Titles and Bureaux*, 99–100.

27. Compare *Urk.* IV 1659, l. 13–15: "Then the [army of] the pharaoh was drawn up . . . organized into units and assigned officers, each man being with his town."

28. Compare the letter of congratulation sent to a son who attained the military position of his father (Ricardo Caminos, *Late Egyptian Miscellanies* [London: Oxford University Press, 1954], 238–241). The Nubian soldier Tjehemau describes joining the army of Monthuhotep II, apparently as a volunteer, and possibly even bringing his son to serve alongside him; see J. C. Darnell, "The Rock Inscriptions of Tjehemau at Abisko," *ZÄS* 130 (2003): 33–34; note also Ahmose son of Ibana, who followed his father into the military (see n. 13 above).

29. Schulman, *Military Rank*, 76–77; Caminos, *Miscellanies*, 16–17.

30. For training scenes, see Annelies Brack, and Artur Brack, *Das Grab des Tjanuni, Theben Nr. 74* (Mainz am Rhein: Philipp von Zabern, 1977). pls. 32–33; a collection of registration and provisioning scenes appears in Melinda Hartwig, *Tomb Painting and Identity in Ancient Thebes, 1419–1372 B.C.E.* (Turnhout: Brepols, 2004), 76–81. A stela of Taharqa indicates that running was an important aspect of military training—Ahmed Moussa, "A Stela of Taharqa from the Desert Road at Dashur," *MDAIK* 37 (1981): 332, l. 4, 12–15. The only mention of military schooling appears in a literary text, "The Blinding of Truth by Falsehood" (Alan Gardiner, *Late Egyptian Stories* [Brussels: Édition de la Fondation Égyptologique Reine Élisabeth, 1937], 32, l. 10–11): "He was sent to school and learned writing very well, and he practiced all the arts of war." The "Cambyses Romance," a Coptic text, imparts to most Egyptians of the Persian Period some training in warlike activities, such as horsemanship, and women are said to be proficient with slings (Darnell, in *Ägypten im Afro-orientalischen Kontext*, 89 n. 72).

31. Davies, *Rock Tombs*, 4, pl. 19, compares the parallel on pl. 17.

32. Robert Drews, *The End of the Bronze Age: Changes in Warfare and the Catastrophe ca. 1200 B.C.* (Princeton, N.J.: Princeton University Press, 1993), 104ff. For a critique of Drews's theories, see M. A. Littauer and J. H. Crouwel, "Robert Drews and the Role of Chariotry in Bronze Age Greece," *Oxford Journal of Archaeology* 15, no. 3 (1996): 297–305.

33. For Egyptian texts describing the agricultural resources and personnel needed for chariot teams, see Caminos, *Miscellanies*, 11–12, 307–308, 326, and 431. For the economy and Egyptian warfare in general, see Spalinger, *War in Ancient Egypt*, 140–159.

34. Compare the coalition of groups defeated by Thutmose III at Megiddo (Redford, *Wars in Syria*, 14–17) and the behavior of vassal states in the Amarna Letters (see chap. 5).

35. Stephen Harvey, "The Cults of King Ahmose at Abydos," Ph.D. diss., University of Pennsylvania, 1998, 316–320. The first example of the Egyptian term for chariotry, literally "that which belongs to the span (of horses)," appears in a taunt Kamose makes against the Hyksos ruler Apepi: "I seized the chariotry" (Labib Habachi, *Second Stela of Kamose* [Glückstadt: J. J. Augustin, 1972], 36).

36. Translated by Gnirs, *Militär*, 21–23 as "marshal"; on the use of this title, see ibid., 29–31; Chevereau, *Nouvel Empire*, 45–55, who translates the title "chief of the cavalry," noting that the title designated an officer position within the chariotry as well as command over mounted messenger troops.

37. Chevereau, *Nouvel Empire*, 135–165; Darnell, *Theban Desert Road Survey* 1, 139.

38. Gnirs, *Militär*, 19–21.

39. The Egyptian title *idnw (ny ḥm=f) n ti-n.t-ḥtri* means literally "representative [of His Majesty] in the chariotry." See Gnirs, *Militär*, 19–21, 31–34, who translates the title as "field marshal."

40. In Egyptian, *kḏn/ktn tpi ni ḥm=f.* For these titles, see Gnirs, *Militär*, 21; Chevereau, *Nouvel Empire*, 38–42, 173–186.

41. Through the mid-Eighteenth Dynasty both members of the chariot team were termed *snny*, while during the Amarna Period two different terms appear: *kḏn/ktn*, denoting the chariot warrior of higher rank, and *qrꜥ*, "shield bearer," of lower rank; see Yoyotte and Lopez, *Bib. Or.* 26 (1969): 11. See also Spalinger, *War in Ancient Egypt*, 176–177; Chevereau, *Nouvel Empire*, 187–189. For upper-class Egyptians supplying their own chariot equipment, see Caminos, *Miscellanies*, 95–99.

42. For an example of chariot tactics, combined with massed archers, against an infantry force, see the description of the Battle of Perire (1208 B.C.E.) in Manassa, *Merneptah*, 103–107. In both the Nubian and Libyan campaigns of Ramesses III, chariots support the infantry; compare Epigraphic Survey, *Medinet Habu 1: Earlier Historical Records of Ramses III* (Chicago: University of Chicago Press, 1930), pls. 8, 18, and 19.

43. Alan Schulman, "The Egyptian Chariotry: A Reexamination," JARCE 2 (1963): 89–90; Schulman, *Military Rank*, 38–39; Drews, *End of the Bronze Age*, 141–147; Richard Beal, *Organization of the Hittite Military* (Heidelberg: Carl Winter, 1992), 202–203.

44. A. F. Rainey, "The Military Personnel at Ugarit," JNES 24 (1965): 19–21; Peter Raulwing, *Horses, Chariots, and Indo-Europeans* (Budapest: Archaeolingua, 2000), 35–36, 117–118; Beal, *Hittite Military*, 178–184.

45. Redford, *Wars in Syria*, 37 and n. 217.

46. John Coleman Darnell, "Supposed Depictions of Hittites in the Amarna Period," SAK 18 (1991): 133–134.

47. The autobiography of Weni describes an amphibious attack—Kurt Sethe, *Urkunden des Alten Reiches*, 2nd ed. (Leipzig: J. C. Hinrichs'sche Buchhandlung, 1933), 98–100. For Asiatics in the Old Kingdom navy, see Manfred Bietak, "Zur Marine des Alten Reiches," in *Pyramid Studies and Other Essays Presented to I. E. S. Edwards*, ed. J. Baines (London: Egypt Exploration Society, 1988).

48. Ann M. Roth, *Egyptian Phyles in the Old Kingdom: The Evolution of a System of Social Organization* (Chicago: Oriental Institute, 1991); Chris Eyre, "Work and the Organization of Work in the Old Kingdom," in *Labor in the Ancient Near East*, ed. M. Powell (New Haven, Conn.: American Oriental Society, 1987), 11–12.

49. Spalinger, *War in Ancient Egypt*, 15–24, passim.

50. Compare the titles of several administrators in Dakhla Oasis; see Michel Valloggia, "Note sur l'organisation administrative de l'Oasis de Dakhla à la fin de l'Ancien Empire," *Méditerranées* 6–7 (1996): 61–72.

51. Darnell, *Theban Desert Road Survey*, 30–46.

52. For Kamose's campaign, see the references in chap. 2, n. 7; Nubian troops in naval and desert activities appear already in the early Middle Kingdom—see John Coleman Darnell, "The Route of Eleventh Dynasty Expansion into Nubia," ZÄS 131 (2004): 23–37.

53. Habachi, *Kamose*, 33.

54. For a reconstruction of the naval tactics of Kamose, see Darnell in *Ägypten im Afro-orientalischen Kontext*, 86–93.

55. S. R. K. Glanville, "Records of the Royal Dockyard of the Time of Tuthmosis III: Papyrus British Museum 10056 (Part II)," ZÄS 68 (1932): 16. Note also the horses transported in ships in the tomb of Huy, Norman Davies, *The Tomb of Huy* (London: Egypt Exploration Society, 1926), pls. 11, 12, and 31.

56. Redford, *Wars in Syria*, 204–205, describing the use of the navy as transport during the later campaigns of Thutmose III; for an overview of the logistics of travel for the ancient Egyptian army, see Spalinger, *War in Ancient Egypt*, 32–45.

57. Säve-Söderbergh, *Navy*, 78–87. For a listing of naval titles, see Dilwyn Jones, *A Glossary of Ancient Egyptian Nautical Titles and Terms* (London: Kegan Paul, 1988), 49–110.

58. Compare Ramesses III's deployment of three different types of vessels in his year eight naval battle against the Sea People (Epigraphic Survey, *Medinet Habu* 1, pl. 46, 1. 20).

59. Säve-Söderbergh, *Navy*, 82; Gnirs, *Militär*, 17–18.

60. Manfred Bietak, "The Thutmoside Stronghold of Perunefer," *Egyptian Archaeology* 26 (2005): 17–20; Bietak, "Egypt and the Aegean," in Roehrig, ed., *Hatshepsut*, 75–81.

61. Units of foreign troops could have their native chiefs as officers, who were in turn overseen by Egyptian officers (Schulman, *Military Rank*, 22–24; Chevereau, *Nouvel Empire*, 90–92); for foreigners holding military titles in the Middle Kingdom and Second Intermediate Period, see Schneider, *Ausländer in Ägypten*, vol. 2, 245–256.

62. See also the arguments of Spalinger, *War in Ancient Egypt*, 7–8.

63. *KRI* II 206, 1. 14–16.

64. For the employment of prisoners of war in the military and on other building projects, see Chris Eyre, "Work in the New Kingdom," in *Labor in the Ancient Near East*, 188–190.

65. Emoke Bailey, "Circumcision in Ancient Egypt," *BACE* 7 (1996): 15–28; note particularly the statement in the stela of Weha from Naga ed-Deir: "I was circumcised with 120 men." (Dows Dunham, *Naga ed-Deir Stelae of the First Intermediate Period* [London: Oxford University Press, 1937], 103–104, pl. 32, 1. 4).

66. For Libyan prisoners of war becoming auxiliary troops and learning Egyptian, compare a stela of Ramesses III from Deir el-Medina (*KRI* V 91, 1. 5–7).

67. See Kemp, *Ancient Egypt*, 2nd ed., 254–255, 297, and S. Katary, "Land Tenure in the New Kingdom: The Role of Women Smallholders and the Military," in *Agriculture in Egypt*, 61–82, for overviews of landholding information from the Twentieth-Dynasty Wilbour Papyrus, which provides some of the clearest evidence for the land plots owned by foreign auxiliaries.

68. The Asiatic campaign of Pepi I as reported by Weni records Nubian auxiliaries from several Nubian tribes, and so-called pacified Nubians appear in Old Kingdom decrees (see Rolf Gunlach, *Die Zwangsumsiedlung auswärtiger Bevölkerung als Mittel ägyptischer Politik bis zum Ende des Mittleren Reiches* [Stuttgart: Franz Steiner Verlag, 1994], 103–124, 132).

69. Manfred Bietak, "Zu den Nubischen Bogenschützen aus Assiut, ein Beitrag zur Geschichte der Ersten Zwischenzeit," in *Mélanges Mokhtar*; Sabine Kubisch, "Die Stelen der 1. Zwischenzeit aus Gebelein," *MDAIK* 56 (2000): 243–248; Henry G. Fischer, "The Nubian Mercenaries of Gebelein during the First Intermediate Period," *Kush* 9 (1961): 44–80; Darnell, ZÄS 131 (2004): 23–37.

70. Karola Zibelius, *Afrikanische Orts- und Völkernamen in hieroglyphischen und hieratischen Texten* (Wiesbaden: Dr. Ludwig Reichert, 1972), 133–137; Georg Meurer, *Nubier in Ägypten bis zum Beginn des Neuen Reiches. Zur Bedeutung der Stele Berlin 14753* (Berlin: Achet Verlag, 1996), 70–72; Rafed el-Sayed, "*r' n Md3.iw*—lingua blemmyica—*tu-bedawie*. Ein Sprachenkontinuum im Areal der nubischen Ostwüste und seine (sprach-)historischen Implikationen," *SAK* 32 (2004): 351–362; Thomas Schneider, *Ausländer in Ägypten während des Mittleren Reiches und der Hyksoszeit*, vol. 2, *Die ausländische Bevölkerung* (Wiesbaden: Otto Harrassowitz, 2003), 92–93. Medjoy may also have inhabited the Eastern Desert of Egypt, but an exclusive location in this area is untenable, contra Danièle Michaux-Colombot, "The MD3Y.W, not Policeman but an Ethnic Group from the Eastern Desert," *Études Nubiennes*, ed. Charles Bonnet (Neuchâtel: Compotronic S.A., 1994).

71. The armaments and fighting techniques of the Nubians as they appear in New Kingdom documents had changed little by the time of Diodorus Siculus in the second century B.C.E., who describes Nubians thus: "Some of them are armed with shields of raw oxhide and . . . wooden bows four cubits [1.8 m] long . . . when all their arrows have been spent, they continue fighting with wooden clubs." (translation of Tormod Eide et al., eds., *Fontes Historiae Nubiorum*, vol. 2 [Bergen: University of Bergen, 1996], 653).

72. See among the many references: M. Bietak, "The C-Group and Pan-Grave Culture in Nubia," in *Nubian Culture Past and Present*, ed. T. Hägg (Stockholm: Almquist & Wiksell International, 1987); Janine Bourriau, "Relations between Egypt and Kerma in the Middle and New Kingdoms," in *Egypt and Africa: Nubia from Pre-History to Islam*, ed. W. Vivian Davies (London: British Museum Press, 1991); Ryholt, *Second Intermediate Period*, 178–183; Karim Sadr, "The Territorial Expanse of the Pan-Grave Culture," *Archéologie du Nil Moyen* 2 (1987): 265–291.

73. Jaroslav Černy, *Community of Workmen at Thebes in the Ramesside Period* (Cairo: Institut Français d'Archéologie Orientale, 1973), 261–284.

74. Compare EA 70 and 95 (Moran, *Amarna Letters*, 139, 169); Horst Klengel, "Das Land Kusch in den Keilschrifttexten von Amarna," in *Ägypten und Kusch*, ed. E. Endesfelder (Berlin: Akademie Verlag, 1977).

75. Bietak, in *Pyramid Studies*; John Coleman Darnell, F. W. Dobbs-Allsopp, et al., *Two Alphabetic Inscriptions from the Wadi el-Hol: New Evidence for the Origin of the Alphabet from the Western Desert of Egypt* (Boston: American Schools of Oriental Research, 2005), 87 and references therein.

76. A. I. Sadek, *Wadi el-Hudi. The Amethyst Mining Inscriptions* (Warminster: Aris & Phillips, 1980), vol. 1, 56–57, and n. 212; for a possible Asiatic police official of the late Middle Kingdom, see Darnell, *Theban Desert Road Survey* 1, 56–58.

77. Donald Redford, "Foreigners (Especially Asiatics) in the Talatat," in *Akhenaten Temple Project 2.*

78. Compare a stela of Thutmose IV, which describes the pharaoh settling captives from Gezer near his mortuary temple (*Urk.* IV 1556, l. 10–11). For the *teheru* as a contingent of foreign troops, possibly Syro-Palestinians, in the Ramesside military, see Gnirs, *Militär*, 57–60; Redford, *Wars in Syria*, 66–67.

79. Manassa, *Merneptah*, 78–79; Sherden and Qeheq Libyans are mentioned together as auxiliaries in the historical retrospective of P. Harris I, 78, l. 9–10; see P. Grandet, *Le Papyrus Harris I* (Cairo: Institut Français d'Archéologie Orientale du Caire, 1994), 266, n. 955.

80. David O'Connor, "The Nature of Tjemhu (Libyan) Society in the Later New Kingdom," in *Libya and Egypt c. 1300–725 B.C.*, ed. A. Leahy (London: Centre of Near and Middle Eastern Studies, 1990), 88–89. Ramesses II employed captured Tjehenu in his bodyguard (*KRI* II, 289, l. 15–16), and the Meshwesh tribe provides auxiliary troops in Papyrus Anastasi (Fischer-Elfert, *Papyrus Anastasi I*, 149–151).

81. Epigraphic Survey, *Medinet Habu* 1, pls. 37, 42; for the scenes from the mortuary temple of Ramesses III and a discussion of *hemou*, see Bernadette Menu, "Captifs de guerre et dépendance rurale dans l'Égypte du Nouvel Empire," in *La dépendance rurale dans l'Antiquité égyptienne et proche-orientale*, ed. B. Menu (Cairo: Institut Français d'Archéologie Orientale, 2004), 187–209 (she does not, however, discuss the Horemhab tomb scenes).

82. *KRI* VII, 9, l. 11–14.

83. For a convenient summary of the events of the battle of Kadesh, see Spalinger, *War in Ancient Egypt*, 209–227, and references therein.

84. On this title, see Chevereau, *Nouvel Empire*, 230–232.

85. Jeffrey Zorn, "LÚ.pa-ma-ḫa-a in EA 162:74 and the Role of the MHR in Egypt and Ugarit," *JNES* 50 (1991): 129–138. For the northeastern patrol system in action during the reign of Merneptah, compare Caminos, *Miscellanies*, 108–113.

86. Caminos, *Miscellanies*, 176–181 (as in *LEM*, 46–47); *KRI* IV, 18, l. 9–10; Manassa, *Merneptah*, 93; Lisa Giddy, *Egyptian Oases* (Warminster: Aris & Phillips, 1987), 91–92.

87. Compare the man riding a horse in the tomb of Horemhab (Martin, *Memphite Tomb*, pl. 32). Note also the mounted scouts in the Kadesh battle scenes of Ramesses II; see Catherine Rommelaere, *Les Chevaux du Nouvel Empire Égyptien* (Brussels: Connaissance de l'Égypte ancienne, 1991), 123–134.

88. A.-P. Zivie, "Cavaliers et cavalerie au Nouvel Empire: À propos d'un vieux probleme," in *Mélanges Mokhtar*; for later associations of Nubians and horses, see Lisa Heidorn, "The Horses of Kush," *JNES* 56 (1997): 105–114. For inscriptions of Medjoy scouts at a desert watchpost, see J. C. Darnell in *Egypt and Nubia*, 143–144.

89. *Urk.* IV 1282, l. 16, to 1283, l. 2.

90. A perhaps ritualized display of horsemanship as part of actual military training is not an unreasonable suggestion and finds an excellent parallel in the ceremonial displays of the Roman cavalry; see inter alia Ann Hyland, *Training the Roman Cavalry: From Arrian's Ars Tactica* (London: Grange Books, 1993); M. Junkelmann, *Die Reiter Roms Teil II: Der militärische Einsatz* (Mainz: Philipp von Zabern, 1991), 142–174; for early Greek practice, I. G. Spence, *The Cavalry of Classical Greece: A Social and Military History* (Oxford: Clarendon Press, 1995), 77–78, 90, 186–188. The Giza Plateau may have been used in New Kingdom Egypt like the *campus martius* in Rome (compare the military activities of Thutmosis IV around the Sphinx, *Urk.* IV 1541, l. 8–15). The area of Memphis continued to be used to train soldiers into at least the Twenty-fifth Dynasty—Moussa, *MDAIK* 37 (1981): 331–337.

91. Serge Sauneron, "La Manufacture d'Armes de Memphis," *BIFAO* 54 (1954): 7–12; Jaromir Malek, "Two Problems Connected with New Kingdom Tombs in the Memphite Area," *JEA* 67 (1981): 156–165; Colleen Manassa, "Two Unpublished Memphite Reliefs from the Yale Art Gallery," *SAK* 30 (2002): 258; Ana Isabel Navajas Jimenez, "Reliefs décorés de la tombe de Kyiri," in *Egyptian Museum Collections*. For a collection of chariot manufacturing scenes from the Memphite necropolis, see Rosemarie Drenkhahn, *Die Handwerker und ihre Tätigkeiten im alten Ägypten* (Wiesbaden: Harrassowitz, 1976), 128–129.

92. For overviews of Egyptian weaponry, see James Hoffmeier, "Military: Materiél," in *Oxford Encyclopedia of Egyptology*; Partridge, *Fighting Pharaohs*, 21–74; Petschel and von Falck, eds., *Pharao siegt immer*; Shaw, *Egyptian Warfare*; Walther Wolf, *Die Bewaffnung des altägyptischen Heeres* (Leipzig: J. C. Hinrichssche Buchhandlung, 1926).

93. Gilbert, *Warfare in Early Egypt*, 44–48.

94. Wolfgang Decker, "Bogen," in *LÄ*, vol. 1; Petschel and von Falck, eds., *Pharao siegt immer*, 108–115, and references therein.

95. W. McLeod, *Self-Bows and Other Archery Tackle from the Tomb of Tutankhamun* (Oxford: Griffith Institute, 1982).

96. A. C. Western and W. McLeod, "Woods Used in Egyptian Bows and Arrows," *JEA* 81 (1995): 77–94.

97. For the means of attaching the bowstring to the bowshaft, see Herbert Winlock, *The Slain Soldiers of Neb-hepet-re Mentu-hotpe* (New York: Metropolitan Museum of Art, 1945), 10.

98. W. McLeod, *Composite Bows from the Tomb of Tutankhamun* (Oxford: Griffith Institute, 1970).

99. Richard Newman and Margaret Serpico, "Adhesives and Binders," in *Ancient Egyptian Materials and Technology*, ed. Paul Nicholson and Ian Shaw (Cambridge, U.K.: Cambridge University Press, 2000).

100. Norman de Garis Davies, *The Tomb of Rekh-mi-Re at Thebes* (New York: Metropolitan Museum of Art, 1943), pl. 22; Wolf, *Bewaffnung*, 82. Pharaonic examples include Thutmose IV: Howard Carter and Percy Newberry, *Tomb of Thoutmosis IV* (Westminster: A. Constable, 1904), pls. 10–11 (as in Wreszinski, *Atlas*, vol. 2, pl. 1–2); Tutankhamun (gold bracelet): Heinz, *Feldzugdarstellungen*, 237; Seti I: Epigraphic Survey, *The Battle Reliefs of Sety I* (Chicago: Oriental Institute, University of Chicago, 1986), pl. 4, 6, 12, 14, and passim; Ramesses II: Heinz, *Feldzugdarstellungen*, 252 (Abu Simbel), 256 (Aksha), 259 (Beit el-Wali, Libyan, and Asiatic campaigns), 268 (Karnak), 270–271, 275 (Luxor); Ramesses III: Epigraphic Survey, *Medinet Habu* 1, pl. 14, 17 (archers accompanying royal chariot). Egyptian soldiers during Ramesses II's Kadesh campaign also wield the triangular composite bow (Heinz, *Feldzugdarstellungen*, 284–286, 290); triangular bows are handed out to soldiers before the Sea People war of year eight (Epigraphic Survey, *Medinet Habu* 1, pl. 29). The frequency of these depictions contradicts this statement in Spalinger, *War in Ancient Egypt*, 121–122: "By Dynasty XIX the triangular compound bow had disappeared, at least from the official artistic repertoire."

101. McLeod, *Composite Bows*, pl. 5.

102. Davies, *Rock Tombs* III, pl. 31; Epigraphic Survey, *Medinet Habu* 1, pl. 18; Epigraphic Survey, *Medinet Habu* 2: *Later Historical Records of Ramses III* (Chicago: University of Chicago Press, 1932), pls. 68 and 70.

103. Andrew Ayton and Philip Preston, *The Battle of Crécy, 1346* (Woodbridge: Boydell Press, 2005).

104. Two smaller composite bows of 64 and 34 cm were also found in the tomb of Tutankhamun (McLeod, *Composite Bows*, 30).

105. Smoothing stones with regular grooves across their surface probably attest to the working of arrow shafts; these occur as early as the Neolithic Period: A. J. Arkell, *Early Khartoum* (Oxford: Oxford University Press, 1949), 69–70, pl. 40–41.

106. Gilbert, *Warfare in Early Egypt*, 48–58; Peter Behrens, "Pfeil," in *LÄ* 4; André Vila, "L'armement de la forteresse de Mirgissa-Iken," *RdE* 22 (1970): 185–187; for the development of flint arrowheads from the late Paleolithic through the pharaonic period, see Thomas Hikade, "Silex-Pfeilspitzen in Ägypten," *MDAIK* 57 (2001): 109–125; for bone arrowheads, see also Uvo Hölscher, *The Excavation of Medinet Habu*, vol. 5, *Post-Ramessid Remains* (Chicago: University of Chicago Press, 1954), pl. 3.

107. A. Lucas, "Poisons in Ancient Egypt," *JEA* 24 (1938): 199. For Egyptian knowledge of venomous serpents, see Serge Sauneron, *Un traité égyptien d'ophiologie* (Cairo: Institut Français d'Archéologie Orientale, 1989). Silius Italicus describes the Nubians as using javelins with poisoned tips (*Punica* 3.265–274). Strabo claims that southeastern Nubian tribes called "elephant eaters" used arrows dipped in snake venom for hunting—Tormod Eide et al., eds., *Fontes Historiae Nubiorum*, vol. 3 (Bergen: University of Bergen, 1998), 821, 824. For poison arrows throughout the ancient world, see Adrienne Mayor, *Greek Fire, Poison Arrows, and Scorpion Bombs: Biological and Chemical Warfare in the Ancient World* (Woodstock: Overlook Press, 2004), 63–97.

108. Decker, "Köcher," in *LÄ*, vol. 3.

109. McLeod, *Self-Bows and Other Archery Tackle*.

110. Norman de Garis Davies, *The Tomb of Ken-Amon at Thebes* (New York: Metropolitan Museum of Art, 1930), pl. 36.

111. Olaf Kaper and Harco Willems, "Policing the Desert: Old Kingdom Activity around the Dakhleh Oasis," in *Egypt and Nubia*, 85–88.

112. Hans Wolfgang Müller, *Der "Armreif" des Königs Ahmose und der Handgelenkschutz des Bogenschützen im Alten Ägypten und Vorderasien* (Mainz am Rhein: Philipp von Zabern, 1989).

113. P. E. Newberry, *Beni Hasan*, part 1 (London: Egypt Exploration Fund, 1893) pl. 14–16; Newberry, *Beni Hasan*, part 2, pl. 5, 15; note also the fortifications in B. Jaroš-Deckert, *Das Grab des Jnj-jtj.f: Die Wandmalereien der XI. Dynastie* (Mainz am Rhein: Philipp von Zabern, 1981), pl. 1; Karola Vogel, *Ägyptische Festungen und Garnisonen bis zum Ende des Mittleren Reiches* (Hildesheim: Gerstenberg, 2004), 44–54. Compare the military effectiveness of slingers in the Greek army: W. Kendrick Pritchett, *The Greek State at War*, part 5 (Berkeley: University of California Press, 1991), 56–58 (including siege operations).

114. Epigraphic Survey, *Medinet Habu* 1, pl. 36; for Greek slingers in naval operations, see Pritchett, *Greek State at War*, part 5, 60–61.

115. Carter, *Tut.Ankh.Amen*, vol. 3, 123 (noting pebbles that might have been ammunition) and pl. 72a; Reeves, *Complete Tutankhamun*, 175–176.

116. Gilbert, *Warfare in Early Egypt*, 69–70; Wolf, *Bewaffnung*, 78.

117. Some evidence suggests that the Egyptians might have discovered the returning properties of some throwsticks, much like the Australian boomerang; see Jacques Thomas, *The Boomerangs of a Pharaoh* (Lyons: J. Thomas, 1991); Reeves, *Complete Tutankhamun*, 176.

118. Darnell, in *Ägypten im Afro-orientalischen Kontext*, 91, n. 80; for the symbolism of the throwstick, see also Petschel and von Falck, eds., *Pharao siegt immer*, 32–34.

119. Decker, "Köcher," in *LÄ*, vol. 3; Emma Hall, *Pharaoh Smites His Enemies* (Munich: Deutscher Kunstverlag, 1986); Gilbert, *Warfare in Early Egypt*, 35–41.

120. Winlock, *Slain Soldiers*, 16–18; for a new analysis of the soldiers' remains, including a possible dating in the early Twelfth Dynasty, see Carola Vogel, "Fallen heroes?—Winlock's 'slain soldiers' reconsidered," *JEA* 89 (2003): 239–245.

121. Similarly, the wooden mace in the Zulu arsenal was considered a "mercy" weapon; see Ian Knight, *The Anatomy of the Zulu Army from Shaka to Cetshwayo 1818–1879* (London: Greenhill Books, 1995), 113.

122. James, *Tutankhamun*, 278.

123. The blade appears to have been attached partly to the mace itself and partly to an extension of the handle protruding beyond the top of the macehead. Earlier Egyptian weapons provide examples of the use of a blade or even an axhead to augment a staff or a clublike weapon (Arnold et al., *Age of the Pyramids*, 342–343).

124. Ali Hassan, *Stöcke und Stäbe im pharaonischen Ägypten bis zum Ende des Neuen Reiches* (Munich: Deutscher Kunstverlag, 1976); H. G. Fischer, "Notes on Sticks and Staves in Ancient Egypt," *Metropolitan Museum Journal* 13 (1979): 5–32.

125. Henry G. Fischer, *Dendera in the Third Millennium B.C.* (Locust Valley, N.Y.: J. J. Augustin, 1968), 144–145.

126. Ramesses II wields one himself at Karnak (Wreszinski, *Atlas* II, pl. 54a); for infantry contingents with rods, compare ibid., pl. 78; Epigraphic Survey, *Medinet Habu* 2, pl. 62, lowest register.

127. Peter Piccione, "Sportive Fencing as a Ritual for Destroying the Enemies of Horus," in *Gold of Praise*, 336.

128. Wolf, *Bewaffnung*, 62 and pl. 40; Epigraphic Survey, *Luxor Temple 1*, pl. 32 and commentary on p. 16; John Coleman Darnell, "Hathor Returns to Medamud," *SAK* 22 (1995): 64, 74, n. 141. For Nubians armed with clubs appearing alongside Nubian archers, see Herbert Ricke, George Hughes, and Edward Wente, 1967. *The Beit el-Wali Temple of Ramesses II* (Chicago: Oriental Institute, 1967), pl. 7 (bow troops), 9 (upper left, Nubian wielding clubs).

129. The wooden staff held by the statue of Amenhotep II is the *tisw* staff; see Davies, *Ken-Amun*, pl. 16–18; see also Fischer, *Metropolitan Museum Journal* 13 (1979): 13–14.

130. A.-C. Thiem, *Speos von Gebel es-Silsileh* (Wiesbaden: Otto Harrassowitz, 2000), pl. 8–9; Wreszinski, *Atlas*, vol. 2, pl. 161–162.

131. Davies, *Rock Tombs* III, pl. 31, 39.

132. Carter, *Tut.Ankh.Amen*, pl. 76; Reeves, *Complete Tutankhamun*, 175.

133. Eve Kühnert-Eggebrecht, *Die Axt als Waffe und Werkzeug im alten Ägypten* (Berlin: B. Hessling, 1969); Kühnert-Eggebrecht, "Axt," in *LÄ*, vol. 1; Gilbert, *Warfare in Early Egypt*, 63–68; Petschel and von Falck, eds., *Pharao siegt immer*, 119–125; A. M. Maier and M. J. Ponting, "'The Cutting Edge': Symbolism, Technology, and Typology of a New Kingdom Egyptian Axe," *MDAIK* 56 (2000): 267–276.

134. Petschel and von Falck, eds., *Pharao siegt immer*, 123.

135. W. Vivian Davies, *Tools and Weapons* I: *Axes* (London: British Museum Press, 1987).

136. Epigraphic Survey, *Luxor Temple 1*, 36 and pl. 93; compare also Davies, *Rock Tombs* II, pl. 17, second register, where a Libyan appears to wield an ax with a hemispherical blade, which resembles earlier Middle Kingdom Egyptian axes.

137. David Wilson, *The Bayeux Tapestry* (New York: Thames & Hudson, 2004), pl. 61–62, 64–66, 70–72, and p. 225.

138. Roehrig, ed., *Hatshepsut*, 250–252.

139. Hans Müller, *Der Waffenfund von Balata-Sichem und Die Sichelschwerter* (Munich: Verlag der bayerischen Akademie der Wissenschaften, 1987); Müller, "Zwei weitere Sichelschwerter," in *Festschrift Jürgen von Beckerath* (Hildesheim: Gerstenberg, 1990). The *khepesh* sword of ancient Egypt is probably behind the name of the Greek *kopis*, which had a similar short blade with curved shape (A. M. Snodgrass, *Arms & Armor of the Greeks* [Baltimore: Johns Hopkins University Press, 1999], 97–98).

140. Müller, *Waffenfund*, 149–150.

141. Ibid., 160.

142. Holes for the attachment of loops are not known from actual examples of *khepesh* swords, but do appear in representations—Davies, *Rock Tombs* I, pl. 1; Davies, *Rock Tombs* III, pls. 30–31; for later New Kingdom examples, see Epigraphic Survey, *Luxor Temple* 1, 36.

143. Compare the short sword that appears alongside chariot equipment in the tomb of Kenamun (Davies, *Ken-Amun*, pl. 22); Javier Martinez, "Ein Schwert aus der ersten Hälfte der 18. Dynastie," *GM* 208 (2006): 51–56.

144. Drews, *End of the Bronze Age*, 192–208.

145. Petschel and von Falck, eds., *Pharao siegt immer*, 126–135; Roehrig, ed., *Hatshepsut*, 252–253.

146. Redford, *Akhenaten Temple Project 2*, pl. 14, no. 3; Johnson, *Asiatic Battle Scene*, 69–71; Heinz, *Feldzugdarstellungen*, 239; Jose Galán, "Mutilation of Pharaoh's Enemies," in *Egyptian Museum Collections*.

147. Reeves, *Complete Tutankhamun*, 177.

148. Some have proposed that the blade was made of meteoritic iron, but analysis suggests that the dagger is an early example of ironworking; see Jack Ogden, "Metals," in *Materials and Technology*, 166–168. For early ironworking, see also Ünsal Yalçin, "Early Iron Metallurgy in Anatolia," *Anatolian Studies* 49 (1999): 177–187.

149. EA 22 (Moran, *Amarna Letters*, 51–57).

150. Flint blades are also attested for Middle Kingdom spears and javelins; see Vila, *RdE* 22 (1970): 174–184.

151. Wolfgang Decker, "Speer," in *LÄ*, vol. 5; Gilbert, *Warfare in Early Egypt*, 58–63.

152. Decker, "Lanze," in *LÄ*, vol. 3.

153. For the origin of the chariot, see M. A. Littauer and J. H. Crouwel, *Wheeled Vehicles and Ridden Animals in the Ancient Near East* (Leiden: Brill, 1979); Peter Raulwing, "Pferd und Wagen im Alten Ägypten: Forschungsstand, Beziehungen zu Vorderasien, interdisziplinäre und methodenkritische Aspekte. Teil 1," GM 136 (1993): 71–83.

154. Angela von den Driesch and Joris Peters, "Frühe Pferde- und Maultierskelette aus Auaris (Tell El-Dab'a)," *Ägypten und Levante* 11 (2001): 301–311; Louis Chaix and Brigitte Gratien, "Un cheval du Nouvel-Empire à Saï (Soudan)," *Archéologie du Nil Moyen* 9 (2002): 53–64; Smith, *Askut*, 121–122.

155. Rommelaere, *Chevaux*, 34–40; Spalinger, *War in Ancient Egypt*, 8–13.

156. Nadine Höveler, "Zu der Darstellung eines Pferdes der Amarna-Zeit mit angeblich aufgeschnittenen Nüstern." GM 198 (2005): 19–20.

157. Wolfgang Decker, "Wagen," in *LÄ*, vol. 6; Petschel and von Falck, eds., *Pharao siegt immer*, 98–107; M. A. Littauer and J. H. Crouwel, *Chariots and Related Equipment from the Tomb of Tut'ankhamūn* (Oxford: Griffith Institute, 1985); Anja Herold, *Streitwagentechnologie in der Ramses-Stadt: Bronze an Pferd und Wagen* (Vienna: Verlag der Österreichischen Akademie der Wissenschaften, 1999); Herold, *Streitwagentechnologie in der Ramses-Stadt: Knäufe, Knöpfe, und Scheiben aus Stein* (Vienna: Verlag der Österreichischen Akademie der Wissenschaften, 2006), and references therein. For chariots and horse riding in the Amarna Period, see James Hoffmeier, "The Chariot Scenes," in *Akhenaten Temple Project 2*; Marie-Agnès Matelly, "Un ostracon de cavalier," *BIFAO* 97 (1997): 193–200; Wolfgang Decker, "Ein Amarna-Block mit Wagendarstellung," in *Hommages à Jean Leclant*, vol. 1: *Études pharaoniques* (Cairo: Institut Français d'Archéologie Orientale, 1994).

158. L. Kakosy, "Bark and Chariot," *Studia Aegyptiaca* 3 (1977): 57–65; Epigraphic Survey, *Luxor Temple 1*, 11 and n. 30. Note also the hymn composed in honor of the royal chariot—Alan Schulman, "The So-Called Poem on the King's Chariot Revisited," *JSSEA* 16 (1986): 28–35, 39–44.

159. For chariot terminology, see Rommelaere, *Chevaux*, 89–107; Littauer and Crouwel, *Chariots*, 4–7; Herold, *Streitwagentechnologie in der Ramses-Stadt: Bronze an Pferd und Wagen*, XXI.

160. Manassa, *SAK* 30 (2002): 260–261.

161. Wolfgang Decker, "Bemerkungen zur Konstruktion des ägyptischen Rades," *SAK* 11 (1984): 475–488; Littauer and Crouwel, *Chariots*, 77–78.

162. Littauer and Crouwel, *Chariots*, 75; Ritner, *Magical Practice*, 122–25. For another depiction, see Davies, *Rock Tombs* I, pl. 26.

163. Littauer and Crouwel, *Chariots*, 71–72.

164. Manassa, *SAK* 30 (2002): 262–264.

165. Rowena Gale et al., "Wood," in *Materials and Technology*, 346.

166. Compare the partially preserved wheel from the tomb of Amunhotep III (Littauer and Crouwel, *Chariots*, 92–93).

167. Details of a recent chariot reconstruction appear in Petschel and von Falck, eds., *Pharao siegt immer*, 100; Herold, *Streitwagentechnologie in der Ramses-Stadt: Knäufe, Knöpfe, und Scheiben aus Stein*, with references to earlier literature. For representations of men carrying chariots, compare the scenes from the tomb of Kairy at Saqqara (J. E. Quibell, *Excavations at Saqqara*, vol. 4, *The Monastery of Apa Jeremias* [Cairo: Institut Français d'Archéologie Orientale, 1912], pl. 75; Anja Herold, "Ein Puzzle mit zehn Teilen—Waffenkammer und Werkstatt aus dem Grab des Ky-jrj in Saqqara," in *Es werde niedergelegt als Schriftstück*.

Festschrift für Hartwig Altenmüller zum 65. Geburtstag, ed. N. Kloth, K. Martin, and E. Pardey [Hamburg: Helmut Buske Verlag, 2003]); two men carrying chariots in the tomb of Huya (Davies, *Rock Tombs* III, pl. 14); and the Libyan carrying a chariot in the presentation scene at Medinet Habu (Epigraphic Survey, *Medinet Habu* II, pl. 75).

168. Epigraphic Survey, *Luxor Temple* 1, 11, and n. 31; Manassa, SAK 30 (2002): 264.

169. Hoffmeier, in *Akhenaten Temple Project* 2, 39. The chariots of Tutankhamun and Ankhesenamun depicted in Luxor Temple have bowcases as well.

170. Littauer and Crouwel, *Chariots*, 102.

171. Among the many depictions of bardings, compare Davies, *Ken-Amun*, pl. 22; Carter and Newberry, *Tomb of Thoutmosis*, vol. 4, 24; Gardiner, *Painted Box*, pl. 2–3; the tassels that depend from the bellies of the chariot horses in the battle reliefs of Seti I probably belong to bardings present only in paint, and numerous chariot teams from the war scenes of Ramesses II and Ramesses III depict bardings. For bardings/armor on Hittite horses, see Beal, *Hittite Military*, 152–153.

172. The bit certainly existed as early as the reign of Thutmose IV if not before, since a stela dating to his reign describes training horses with the bit; see John Coleman Darnell, *Enchoria* 24 (1997/1998): 158–162. For horse bits, see also Herold, *Streitwagentechnologie: Bronze an Pferd und Wagen.*

173. For blinkers from the tomb of Tutankhamun, appropriately decorated with udjat eyes, see Reeves, *Complete Tutankhamun*, 173; blinkers are depicted on Egyptian chariot horses in most battle scenes (e.g., the Karnak reliefs of Seti I, Epigraphic Survey, *The Battle Reliefs of King Sety I*, pls. 2, 4, 5, and passim).

174. Kathy Hansen, "Collection in Ancient Egyptian Chariot Horses," *JARCE* 29 (1992): 173–179.

175. The following summarizes the results of Littauer and Crouwel, *Chariots.*

176. For a talatat showing a chariot whip in use, see Aldred, *Akhenaten and Nefertiti*, 128–129; Akhenaten and Nefertiti both carry whips in a scene from the tomb of Panehesy (Davies, *Rock Tombs* II, pl. 16).

177. A dagger-shaped object found with the chariot equipment in the tomb of Tutankhamun has been identified as a linchpin, but the shape and size do not fit the linchpin holes on the actual chariots; see M. A. Littauer and J. H. Crouwel, "'Unrecognized Linch Pins from the Tombs of Tut'ankhamun and Amenophis II': A Reply," GM 100 (1987): 57–61; contra Robert Ritner, "Unrecognized Decorated Linch Pins from the Tombs of Tutankhamon and Amenhotep II," GM 94 (1986): 53–56. This enigmatic wooden object was most likely a tool used like a modern hoofpick. Egyptians might have used leather hoof covers like the Greco-Roman "hippo sandals"; (see Hans-Werner Fischer Elfert, "The Sufferings of an Army Officer (Anast. III 6, 8–10 = LEM 27, 11–15)," GM 63 [1983]: 43–45).

178. Epigraphic Survey, *Luxor Temple* 1, pl. 22, 95; note also the inclusion of Ankhesenamun's name on one of the chariots from Tutankhamun's tomb; see Wofgang Decker in *Studien zu Sprache und Religion Ägyptens*, vol. 2, 873–877.

179. For transport chariots at the Battle of Kadesh, see Heinz, *Feldzugdarstellungen*, 287, 291; Beal, *Hittite Military*, 134; U. Hofmann, "Fuhrwesen und Pferdehaltung im Alten Ägypten," Ph.D. diss., University of Bonn, 1989, 290–292. For donkey chariots, see Gardiner, *LEM*, 116; Edward Wente, *Late Ramesside Letters* (Chicago: University of Chicago Press, 1967), 40.

180. Donald Engels, *Alexander the Great and the Logistics of the Macedonian Army* (Berkeley: University of California Press, 1978), 16 and n. 26, 128; Ann Hyland, *Equus: the Horse in the Roman World* (New Haven, Conn.: Yale University Press, 1990), 216, 232, and 256; Sarva Singh, *Ancient Indian Warfare* (Leiden: Brill, 1965), 28.

181. The term used for these vehicles in the Gebel Barkal stela is *wrry.t* (*Urk.* IV, 1232, l. 4), the same term as used for war chariots.

182. A camp scene from Khonsu Temple possibly dating to the reign of Horemhab may also depict such transport chariots (Johnson, *Asiatic Battle Scene*, 176, no. 72); the tomb of Nebamun (TT17) contains a fragmentary scene of ox-drawn chariots (Säve-Söderbergh, *Four Tombs*, 26–27 and pl. 23).

183. Henry G. Fischer, "Hunde," in LÄ III, 77–81; Brigitte Dominicus, *Gesten und Gebärden in Darstellungen des Alten und Mittleren Reiches* (Heidelberg: Heidelberger Orientverlag, 1994), 151–153; the hunter's pointing gesture for the dog suggests that the breed is a sight hound, like the modern basenji.

184. For Egyptian dogs of the Middle and New kingdoms, see Jac. and Rosalind Janssen, "A Dog on a Tile," in *Egyptian Art in the Nicholson Museum, Sydney*, ed. K. N. Sowada and B. G. Ockinga (Sydney: Mediterranean Archaeology, 2006), although their doubts about the identification of the breed as the modern basenji on p. 113 are unwarranted.

185. Petschel and von Falck, eds., *Pharao siegt immer*, 221. Henry G. Fischer, *Inscriptions from the Coptite Nome* (Rome: Pontificium Institutum Biblicum, 1964), pl. 24, 32–34; Kubisch, *MDAIK* 56 (2000): 245; for the title "commander of leaders of dog packs," see Quirke, *Titles and Bureaux*, 99.

186. Peter Behrens, "Language and Migrations of the Early Saharan Cattle Herders: The Formation of the Berber Branch," in *Libya Antiqua*, ed. A. Leahy (Paris: UNESCO, 1986), 30; Behrens, "Wanderungsbewegungen und Sprache der frühen saharanischen Viehzüchter," *Sprache und Geschichte in Afrika* 6 (1984–1985): 135–216.

187. Well-bred Egyptian dogs also served to strengthen the Egyptian empire abroad. In one illuminating Late Egyptian text, an Egyptian official in Syria-Palestine is grateful for the puppy that is sent to him to drive off the local pariahs (Caminos, *Miscellanies*, 188–196, as in Gardiner, *LEM*, 48–49).

188. J. M. Galán, "What Is He, the Dog?," *Ugarit-Forschungen* 25 (1993): 173–180.

189. Ricke, Hughes, and Wente, *The Beit el-Wali Temple of Ramesses II*, pl. 14.

190. Arnold et al., *Age of the Pyramids*, 318–321.

191. Fischer, *Coptite Nome*, 66–75.

192. Compare the troops depicted in the mortuary temple of Hatshepsut—Petschel and von Falck, eds., *Pharao siegt immer*, 79; Roehrig, ed., *Hatshepsut*, 154.

193. For a few of the many depictions of heart-shaped aprons, see Petschel and von Falck, eds., *Pharao siegt immer*, 80; Gardiner, *Painted Box* (Tutankhamun's military escort, both in hunting and in combat, wear heart-shaped sporrans); Wreszinski, *Atlas* II, p. 162 (Horemhab's Nubian campaign, as in fig. 19 of the present volumes); such attire is standard among Akhenaten's bodyguard (compare fig. 25 in the present volume).

194. Rosalind Hall, *Egyptian Textiles* (Princes Risborough: Shire, 1986), 34–35; Brack and Brack, *Tjanuni*, pl. 8; Roehrig, ed., *Hatshepsut*, 70–74. Egyptian soldiers fighting Asiatic and Nubian enemies in the battle scenes on Tutankhamun's Painted Box also wear leather overkilts.

195. Säve-Söderbergh, *Navy*, 75–78.

196. Decker, "Panzer," in LÄ, vol. 4.

197. Davies, *Axes*, pl. 38, fig. 3. Breastplates of other materials might have been used as early as the Predynastic Period—a man engaged in ritual combat in the Painted Tomb at Hierakonpolis (Tomb 100) appears to wear an animal skin as a breastplate; see J. E. Quibell and F. W. Green, *Hierakonpolis*, part 2 (London: Histories and Mysteries of Man, 1989), pl. 75; for an alternate interpretation of the scene, see Stan Hendrickx, "Peaux d'animaux comme symboles prédynastiques: À propos de quelques représentations sur les vases white cross-lines," *CdE* 74 (1998): 203–230.

198. Gerry D. Scott, *Ancient Egyptian Art at Yale* (New Haven, Conn.: Yale University Art Gallery, 1986), 60–61; Fischer, *Kush* 9 (1961): 68, 70–71.

199. Wolf, *Bewaffnung*, 96–99.

200. Reeves, *Complete Tutankhamun*, 176.

201. Carter and Newberry, *Thoutmosis IV*, pl. 9, 10; bronze suits of mail are captured during Thutmose III's Megiddo campaign—see Redford, *Wars in Syria*, 35. For Hittite charioteers wearing scale armor, see Beal, *Hittite Military*, 150–152.

202. Davies, *Ken-Amun*, pl. 16.

203. P. Astrom, *The Cuirass Tomb and Other Finds at Dendra* (Göteborg: Paul Aströms Förlag, 1977); John Warry, *Warfare in the Classical World* (New York: St. Martin's Press, 1980), 12–13.

204. See Carol Van Driel-Murray, "Leatherwork and Skin Products," in *Materials and Technology*, 312–316, for an overview of Egyptian footwear.

205. A pair of leather sandals from a cave near the Wadi el-Hol, south of Hou, once belonged to a man of the Predynastic Tasian culture, and may be one of the oldest pairs of footwear (publication forthcoming).

206. Jules Couyat and Pierre Montet, *Les inscriptions hiéroglyphiques et hiératiques du Ouadi Hammamat* (Cairo: Institut Français d'Archéologie Orientale, 1912), 83, l. 6 (no. 114, l. 13).

207. Sethe, *Urkunden des Alten Reiches*, 2nd ed., 102, l. 13–14 (autobiography of Weni).

208. Compare the statement from the "Satire of the Trades" (Gardiner, *LEM*, 108, l. 8–9): "There are no clothes and no sandals, while the weapons of battle are gathered at the fortress of Tjaru."

209. For the thickened soles of Zulu warriors and their ability to cross difficult ground barefoot, see Knight, *Zulu Army*, 179.

210. Davies, *Rock Tombs* II, pl. 10; for a collection of references to putees and shinguards in Egyptian depictions, see Darnell, *Theban Desert Road Survey* 1, 81.

211. Winlock, *Slain Soldiers*, 9; for First Intermediate Period soldiers with unusually large amounts of hair, compare the tomb of Intef (Jaroš-Deckert, *Jnj-jtj.f*, faltkarte 2). For more recent examples, compare the practices of the Bisharin and Ababda; see Brian Robson, *Fuzzy Wuzzy: The Campaigns in the Eastern Sudan 1884–85* (Tunbridge Wells, U.K.: Spellmount, 1993), 14.

212. Rolf Kraus, "Helm," in *LÄ*, vol. 2.

213. Schulman, "Hittites, Helmets, and Amarna: Akhenaten's First Hittite War," in *Akhenaten Temple Project* 2, 54–55; Timothy Kendall, "*Gurpisu ša awēli*: The Helmets of the Warriors at Nuzi," in *Studies on the Civilization and Culture of Nuzi and the Hurrians*, ed. M. A. Morrison and D. I. Owen (Winnowa Lake, Ind.: Eisenbrauns, 1981).

214. Epigraphic Survey, *Medinet Habu* 2, pl. 111–112.

215. Alessandra Nibbi, "Some Remarks on the Ancient Egyptian Shield," *ZÄS* 130 (2003): 170–181; Wolfgang Decker, "Schild," in *LÄ* V.

216. Gilbert, *Warfare in Early Egypt*, 43–44; both turtleshell and leather shields continued to be used by Eastern Desert dwellers through the nineteenth century—see E. S. Thomas, *Catalogue of the Ethnographical Museum of the Royal Geographical Society of Egypt* (Cairo: Imprimerie de l'Institut Français d'Archéologie Orientale, 1924), 65–66).

217. Darnell, *Theban Desert Road Survey* 1, 74–75.

218. The shape of the New Kingdom Egyptian shield appears in an engraving of a West African Kanembu spearman in the early 1900s; see Robert S. Smith, *Warfare & Diplomacy in Pre-Colonial West Africa*, 2nd ed. (London: James Currey, 1989), 49.

219. Freed, Markowitz, and D'Auria, eds., *Pharaohs of the Sun*, 237, no. 107.

220. For oval Nubian shields, see Alan Gardiner, *Tutankhamun's Painted Box: Reproduced from the Original in the Cairo Museum by Nina M. Davies* (Oxford: Griffith Institute, 1962), pl. 2; Aldred, *Akhenaten and Nefertiti*, 121; Freed, Markowitz, and D'Auria, eds.,

Pharaohs of the Sun, 237, n. 107; J. C. Darnell, in *Egypt and Nubia*, 144; Uvo Hölscher, *The Excavation of Medinet Habu*, vol. 4, *The Mortuary Temple of Ramses III*, part 2 (Chicago: University of Chicago Press, 1951), pl. 25, fig. D. Nubians carry round-topped Egyptian-style shields in the Nubian battle scenes of Ramesses III; Epigraphic Survey, *Medinet Habu* I, pl. 8.

221. For descriptions of these shields, see Alessandra Nibbi, "The Four Ceremonial Shields from the Tomb of Tutankhamun," *ZÄS* 133 (2006): 66–71; her statements concerning the Nine Bows and other geographical designations, however, are entirely unsupported by the ancient evidence.

222. Raymond Faulkner, "Egyptian Military Standards," *JEA* 27 (1941): 12–18; Silvio Curto, "Standarten," in *LÄ*, vol. 5.

223. Davies, *Rock Tombs* IV, pl. 17.

224. Ibid. I, pl. 26.

225. E.g., ibid. II, pl. 9, 13.

226. For some of the many possible depictions, see ibid. I, pl. 10, 15, 16; II, pl. 13, 17; III, pl. 31. Note the particularly interesting group of soldiers carrying axes and palm branches, and one with a standard with fan and lion, in the mortuary temple of Hatshepsut; see Zbigniew E. Szafranski, ed., *Królowa Hatszepsut I jej swiatynia 3500 lat później/Queen Hatshepsut and Her Temple 3500 Years Later* (Warsaw: Agencja Reklamowo-Wydawnicza A. Gregorczyk, 2001), 256. The association of fan and lion probably alludes to the pharaoh as the victorious lion.

227. Kemp, *JEA* 73 (1987): 46–48 and fig. 5.

228. Wolf, *Bewaffnung*, 78–79; Faulkner, *JEA* 27 (1941): 16–17. For the possible Egyptian term for such flail standards, *sry.t*, see Epigraphic Survey, *Luxor Temple* 1, 8, n. 23 and p. 15, for the use of a flail by military officers, citing depictions such as Edouard Naville, *The Temple of Deir el-Bahari*, part 4 (London: Egypt Exploration Fund, 1901), pl. 90 and 89 (for naval officers) and Davies, *Rock Tombs* III, 28–29, pl. 31.

229. Lisa Manniche, *Music and Musicians in Ancient Egypt* (London: British Museum Press, 1991), 74–83. Compare the use of horns as signaling instruments for the Greek and Roman armies; see P. Krentz, "The Salpinx in Greek Warfare," in *Hoplites: The Classical Greek Battle Experience*, ed. V. D. Hansen (London: Routledge, 1991); G. Webster, *The Roman Imperial Army of the First and Second Centuries A.D.* (New York: Black, 1969), 141–142; M. Junkelmann, *Die Legionen des Augustus: Der römische Soldat im archäologischen Experiment* (Mainz: Philipp von Zabern, 1994), 216–218. Vegetius describes voiced (verbal), semivoiced (trumpets), and mute (signals from standards, etc.); see Milner, *Vegetius* 55 and 69–71.

230. Emhab, a soldier of the late Seventeenth Dynasty, uses drumming imagery in his description of his military career; see Jaroslav Černy "The Stela of Emhab from Tell Edfu," *MDAIK* 24 (1969): 87–92; Popko, *Geschichtsschriebung*, 173–178. Note also the drummer and two trumpeters in the tomb of Tjanuni (Brack and Brack, *Tjanuni*, pl. 33, 36a).

231. Henry G. Fischer, "The Trumpet in Ancient Egypt," in *Pyramid Studies*; Hans Hickmann, *La Trompette dans l'Égypte ancienne* (Cairo: Institut Français d'Archéologie Orientale, 1946).

232. Reeves, *Complete Tutankhamun*, 164–165.

233. Davies, *Rock Tombs* III, pl. 12, shows a trumpeter with his trumpet and wooden interior form, not two trumpets as in *Rock Tombs* III, p. 28, n. 2.

234. Davies, *Rock Tombs* III, pl. 31; for a further description of this scene, see chap. 6.

235. Compare the predynastic ceramic model (from Abadiya) of two figures leaning on wall as possible watchmen (J. C. Payne, *Catalogue of the Predynastic Egyptian Collection in the Ashmolean Museum* [Oxford: Oxford University Press, 2000], 17 and fig. 6); the fortified

enclosures depicted on the Libyan palette and the Narmer palette (A. J. Spencer, *Early Egypt: The Rise of Civilisation in the Nile Valley* [London: British Museum Press, 1993], 52–53); and the ivory model of a crenellated tower from Abydos (A. M. Donadoni Roveri and F. Tiradritti, eds., *Kemet, alle sorgenti del tempo* [Milan: Electa, 1998]: 219). For predynastic fortifications, see also Bruce Williams, "Security and the Problem of the City in the Naqada Period," in *For His Ka*, ed. D. P. Silverman (Chicago: Oriental Institute, 1994). An overview of fortifications and fortified cities in Egypt appears in Barry Kemp et al., "Egypt's Invisible Walls," *Cambridge Archaeological Journal* 14, no. 2 (2004): 259–288.

236. For the Old Kingdom title "overseer of fortresses," see Fischer, *Dendera*, 10–11 and n. 47. An overview of evidence for Old Kingdom fortresses, including Elephantine and Ayn Asil, can be found in Vogel, *Festungen*, 29–40.

237. Kaper and Willems, in *Egypt and Nubia*; an Old Kingdom outpost between the northern wells of Kharga Oasis and the Nile Valley was recently discovered by the Theban Desert Road Survey, publication forthcoming.

238. For an overview of ancient siege warfare, see Paul Bentley Kern, *Ancient Siege Warfare* (Bloomington: Indiana University Press, 1999).

239. Regine Schulz, "Der Sturm auf die Festung: Gedanken zu einigen Aspekten des Kampfbildes im Alten Ägypten vor dem Neuen Reiches," in *Krieg und Sieg: Narrative Wanddarstellungen von Altägypten bis ins Mittelalter*, ed. M. Bietak and M. Schwarz (Vienna: Verlag der Österreichischen Akademie der Wissenschaften, 2002).

240. Vogel, *Festungen*, 45–50, citing Newberry, *Beni Hasan*, vol. 1, pl. 14–16, and vol. 2, pl. 5, 15; note also the fortifications in Jaroš-Deckert, *Grab des Jnj-jtj.f*, pl. 1.

241. Yigel Yadin, "Hyksos Fortifications and the Battering Ram," *BASOR* 137 (1955): 23–32.

242. Compare Heinz, *Feldzugdarstellungen*, 277; note also the destruction of the western High Gate at Medinet Habu, which occurred at the end of the New Kingdom (Uvo Hölscher, *Excavation of Medinet Habu*, vol. 4, 8; Hölscher, *Excavation of Medinet Habu*, vol. 5, 1–2, pl. 3).

243. Temporary camps, including those for religious structures, were called *iḥзy* in Egyptian; for this term, see L. Kakosy, "Fragmente eines unpublizierten magischen Textes in Budapest," *ZÄS* 117 (1990): 151, n. v; Alan Schulman, in *The Egyptian Mining Temple of Timna*, ed. B. Rothenberg et al. (London: Institute for Archaeo-Metallurgical Studies, 1988), 114–115.

244. Martin, *Memphite Tomb*, 36–38, 43–44, and pl. 28–29, 35.

245. For cloth tents, see Wolfgang Helck, *Die Lehre des Dw3-Ḥty* (Wiesbaden: Otto Harrassowitz, 1970), 97, XVIe, 98–99; for leather tents, see R. J. Forbes, *Studies in Ancient Technology*, vol. 5 (Leiden: Brill, 1957), 31; see also Kemp, *JEA* 63 (1977): 77–78.

246. Martin, *Memphite Tomb*, pl. 32.

247. Davies, *Service in the Roman Army*, 125–137; Duncan Campbell, *Roman Legionary Fortresses 27 B.C.–A.D. 378* (Oxford: Osprey Publishing, 2006).

248. Small, round tents in painted decoration in the tomb of Horemhab might be examples of common soldiers' tents, if they are not instead tents belonging to a nomadic enemy force (Martin, *Memphite Tomb*, 26–27).

249. Compare the backpack carried by an Old Kingdom statuette (Francesco Tiradritti, ed., *The Treasures of the Cairo Museum* [Cairo: American University in Cairo Press, 1999], 100), and possible depiction from an Old Kingdom outpost near Dakhla Oasis (Kaper and Willems, in *Egypt and Nubia*, 85).

250. Martin, *Memphite Tomb*, pl. 29.

251. Aldred, *Akhenaten and Nefertiti*, 141 (no. 65) and 145 (no. 70).

252. See the references in chap. 2, n. 4.

253. J. C. Darnell, in *Egypt and Nubia*, 139–141.

254. Ibid., 147–149.

255. Compare the range of earthworks and simple fortifications constructed by the British in Zululand (Ian Knight, *British Fortifications in Zululand 1879* [Oxford: Osprey, 2005]) and the use of zeribas in the Mahdist wars (see chap. 4).

Chapter 4. Land of Gold: The Southern Empire

1. *Urk.* IV 1344, l. 10–12.

2. Y. Koenig, "La Nubie dans les textes magiques, l'inquiétante étrangeté," *RdÉ* 38 (1987): 105–110; H.-J. Thissen, "Nubien in demotischen magischen Texten," in *Ägypten im afro-orientalischen Kontext.*

3. David O'Connor, *Ancient Nubia, Egypt's Rival in Africa* (Philadelphia: University Museum, 1993), 10–23; L. Krzyzaniak, K. Kroeper, and M. Kousiewicz, eds., *Interregional Contacts in the Later Prehistory of Northeastern Africa* (Poznan: Poznan Archaeological Museum, 1996); Krzyzaniak, Kroeper, and Kousiewicz, eds., *Recent Research into the Stone Age of Northeastern Africa* (Poznan: Poznan Archaeological Museum, 2000).

4. Karola Zibelius-Chen, *Die ägyptische Expansion nach Nubien, Eine Darlegung der Grundfaktoren* (Wiesbaden: Dr. Ludwig Reichert, 1988), 69–135; Thomas Hikade, *Das Expeditionswesen im ägyptischen Neuen Reich, Ein Beitrag zu Rohstoffversorgung und Aussenhandel* (Heidelberg: Heidelberger Orientverlag, 2001), 71–75.

5. For overviews of Nubian history, see inter alia William Y. Adams, *Nubia: Corridor to Africa* (London: Allen Lane Adams, 1977); W. Vivian Davies, ed., *Egypt and Africa: Nubia from Prehistory to Islam* (London: British Museum Press, 1991); Meurer, *Nubier in Ägypten*; O'Connor, *Ancient Nubia*; Donald Redford, *From Slave to Pharaoh: The Black Experience of Ancient Egypt* (Baltimore: Johns Hopkins University Press, 2004); Karim Sadr, *The Development of Nomadism in Ancient Northeast Africa* (Philadelphia: University of Pennsylvania Press, 1991), 79–108; Torgny Säve-Söderbergh, *Ägypten und Nubien, Ein Beitrag zur Geschichte altägyptischer Aussenpolitik* (Lund: Hakan Ohlssons Boktryckeri, 1941); Derek Welsby and Julie Anderson, eds., *Sudan: Ancient Treasures* (London: British Museum Press, 2004).

6. The southernmost *nome* of Egypt even bore one of the traditional names of Nubia, *T3-sti*, "Bow-land," the land of archers (Wolfgang Helck, *Die altägyptische Gaue* [Wiesbaden: Dr. Ludwig Reichert, 1974], 68–71; for the fortress at Elephantine, the northernmost Nubian outpost, see M. Ziermann, *Elephantine 16, Befestigungsanlagen und Stadtentwicklung in der Frühzeit und im frühen Alten Reich* (Mainz: Philipp von Zabern, 1993); Vogel, *Festung*, 16–17.

7. Wilkinson, *Early Dynastic Egypt*, 175–182.

8. D. Gilbertson and C. Hunt with P. Smithson, "Quarternary Geomorphology and Palaeoecology," in *Farming the Desert: The UNESCO Libyan Valleys Archeological Survey*, ed. G. Barker (Paris: UNESCO, 1996); L. Krzyzaniak, M. Kobusiewicz, and J. Alexander, eds., *Environmental Change and Human Culture in the Nile Basin and Northern Africa until the Second Millennium B.C.* (Poznan: Poznan Archaeological Museum, 1993); B. E. Barich and M. C. Gatto, eds., *Dynamics of Populations, Movements, and Responses to Climatic Change in Africa* (Rome: Bonsignori Editore, 1997).

9. O'Connor, *Ancient Nubia*, 24–57.

10. Darnell, ZÄS 130 (2003): 31–48; ZÄS 131 (2004): 23–37.

11. For the Nubian fortresses, see inter alia, Adams, *Nubia*, 175–188; Alexander Badawy, *History of Egyptian Architecture*, vol. 2 (Berkeley: University of California Press, 1966), 198–230; Kemp, *Ancient Egypt*, 2nd ed., 231–241; Meurer, *Nubier in Ägypten*, 31–51;

Lawrence, *JEA* 51 (1965): 69–94; Claude Obsomer, *Sesostris Ier, Étude chronologique et historique du règne* (Brussels: Connaissance de l'Égypte ancienne, 1995), 253–269, 336–359; Säve-Söderbergh, *Ägypten und Nubien*, 80–98; Smith, *Askut*; Bruce Trigger, "The Reasons for the Construction of the Second Cataract Forts," *JSSEA* 12 (1982): 1–6; Bruce Williams, "Serra East and the Mission of Middle Kingdom Fortresses in Nubia," in *Gold of Praise*; Vogel, *Ägyptische Festungen*, 61–99. A late Middle Kingdom list of the fortresses provides the ancient names of the constructions; see Alan Gardiner, "An Ancient List of the Fortresses of Nubia," *JEA* 3 (1916): 184–192; Smith, *Askut*, 25–27; Petschel and von Falck, eds., *Pharao siegt immer*, 175.

12. One of the few exceptions is the appearance of the Second Cataract forts in John Keegan, *A History of Warfare* (New York: Vintage Books, 1994), 142–144.

13. Wolfram Grajetzki, *The Middle Kingdom of Ancient Egypt* (London: Duckworth, 2006), 27–28, 3; Darnell, *ZÄS* 131 (2004): 23–37.

14. O'Connor in *Social History*, 124–126; Adams, *Nubia*, 170–175. On the Nubian campaigns of Senusret I, see Obsomer, *Sesostris Ier*, 241–253, 311–335.

15. For arguments against any activity of Senusret I at Semna or Semna South, see Obsomer, *Sesostris Ier*, 337–340.

16. W. B. Emery and L. P. Kirwan, *The Excavations and Survey between Wadi es-Sebua and Adindan, 1929–1931: Mission archéologie de Nubie, 1929–1934* (Cairo: Service de antiquités, 1935).

17. W. B. Emery, H. S. Smith, and A. Millard, *The Fortress of Buhen: The Archaeological Report* (London: Egypt Exploration Society, 1979); Vogel, *Festungen*, 230–233.

18. The location on flat terrain was certainly intentional; as Säve-Söderbergh, *Ägypten und Nubien*, 84, notes, across the river from Aniba is the imposing rock outcrop of Qasr Ibrim, which later served as a fortified outpost in the Kushite Period.

19. For military titles at the fortresses, see Ronald Leprohon, "Les forces du maintien de l'ordre dans la Nubie au Moyen Empire," in *Hommages à Jean Leclant*, vol. 2.

20. Oleg Berlev, "A Social Experiment in Nubia during the Years 9–17 of Sesostris I," in *Labor in the Ancient Near East*, 143–158.

21. Brigitte Gratien, "Départements et institutions dans les fortresses nubiennes au Moyen Empire," in *Hommages à Jean Leclant*, vol. 2.

22. Senusret III also constructed at least one new fortress north of Buhen at Serra East; see Williams, in *Gold of Praise*, 443–449; Vogel, *Festungen*, 223–225.

23. Emery, Smith, and Millard, *The Fortress of Buhen*, pl. 82; Kemp, *Ancient Egypt*, 2nd ed., 235.

24. H. S. Smith, "Kor: Report on the Excavations of the Egyptian Exploration Society at Kor," *Kush* 14 (1966): 228–229.

25. J. Vercoutter, *Mirgissa 1* (Paris: Centre national de la recherche scientifique, 1970); Dows Dunham, *Second Cataract Forts 2: Uronarti, Shalfak, Mirgissa* (Boston: Museum of Fine Arts, 1967); Smith, *Askut*.

26. Dows Dunham and J. M. A. Janssen, *Second Cataract Forts 1: Semna-Kumma* (Boston: Museum of Fine Arts, 1960); Jean Vercoutter, "Semna South Fort and the Records of Nile Levels at Kumma," *Kush* 14 (1966): 125–131; L. Žabkar, "Semna South: A Preliminary Report on the 1966–1968 Excavations of the University of Chicago Oriental Institute Expedition to Sudanese Nubia," *JARCE* 19 (1982): 7–50; Karola Vogel, *Festungen*, 257–267.

27. Anthony Mills, "The Archaeological Survey from Gemai to Dal—Report on the 1965–1966 Season," *Kush* 15 (1967): 206 and pl. 38b; a summary of this material appears in Vogel, *Festungen*, 268–271.

28. Horst Jaritz, "The Investigation of the Ancient Wall Extending from Aswan to Philae: First Preliminary Report," *MDAIK* 43 (1986): 67–74; Jaritz, *MDAIK* 49 (1993): 108–119.

29. Darnell, *SAK* 31 (2003): 86 and n. 42.

30. Jean Vercoutter, "Les barrages pharaoniques. Leur raison d'être," in *Les problèmes institutionnels de l'eau en Égypte ancienne et dans l'antiquité méditerranéenne*, ed. B. Menu (Cairo: Institut Français d'Archéologie Orientale, 1994); Vercoutter, *Kush* 14 (1966) 132–164.

31. Vercoutter, *Mirgissa*, 204–214.

32. H. S. Smith, "The Rock Inscriptions of Buhen," *JEA* 58 (1972) 55–58; for the roads near the cataract fortresses, see also Ludwig Borchardt, *Altägyptische Festungen an der Zweiten Nilschwelle* (Leipzig: Otto Harrassowitz, 1923), 24. Some of these outposts or temporary places of refuge could be termed *ḫnr.t* in Egyptian; see Stephen Quirke, "The Regular Titles of the Late Middle Kingdom," *RdE* 37 (1986): 111 and n. 24; Z. Žaba, *Rock Inscriptions of Lower Nubia* (Prague: Universita Karlova, 1974), 99, 103–104.

33. For more on ancient Egyptian signaling, see chap. 6, 194.

34. Mills, *Kush* 15 (1967): 206, pl. 39a; Rex Keating, *Nubian Rescue* (London: Robert Hale, 1975), 127–128 and plate facing p. 159 publish a group of large, probably Middle Kingdom cairns with "windows" that might have been used for messages. A similar cairn appears along the road between Toshka and the Gebel el-Asr gneiss quarries; see R. Engelbach, "The Riddle of Chephren's Diorite Quarries Answered," *Illustrated London News*, March 26, 1938, 525.

35. Paul C. Smither, "The Semnah Despatches," *JEA* 31 (1945): 3–10.

36. For overviews of the Kingdom of Kerma and its capital city, see Charles Bonnet, *Edifices et rites funéraires à Kerma* (Paris: Éditions Errance, 2000); Bonnet, "The Kerma Culture" and "Kerma," in *Sudan Ancient Treasures*; Bonnet, *Le temple principal de la ville de Kerma et son quartier religieux* (Paris: Éditions Errance, 2004) and bibliography therein; David Edwards, *The Nubian Past: An Archaeology of the Sudan* (New York: Routledge, 2004), 75–111; Brigitte Gratien, *Les cultures Kerma* (Lille: Université de Lille III, 1978); Peter Lacovara, "Egypt and Nubia during the Second Intermediate Period," in *Hyksos*.

37. Gratien, *Les cultures Kerma*, 162–181, 279–280; Bonnet, *Le temple principal*, 19–28. Middle Kingdom execration figures contain the names of Nubian rulers, including the ruler of Kush, suggesting that the Egyptians monitored the developing situation in Nubia; Georges Posener, *Cinq figurines d'envoûtement* (Cairo: Institut Français d'Archéologie Orientale, 1987), 17–34.

38. Smith, *Askut*, 69–79. Ryholt, *Second Intermediate Period*, 90–92, argues that the Thirteenth Dynasty sees a pattern of abandonment of the Nubian fortresses that does not show a south-to-north progression, but rather reveals an attempt to consolidate the defense of the border by manning fewer key fortresses.

39. Smith, *Askut*, 90–106, 109–110; Torgny Säve-Söderbergh, "A Buhen Stela (Khartum no. 18)," *Journal of Egyptian Archaeology* 35 (1949): 50–58; Smith, *Fortress of Buhen, the Inscripitons*, 77–81; Welsby and Anderson, eds., *Sudan, Ancient Treasures*, 100 (stela of Ka).

40. Gratien, *Les cultures Kerma*, 280–281; Derek Welsby, "The Northern Dongola Reach," in *Sudan: Ancient Treasures*; Welsby, "The Amri to Kirbekan Survey: The 2002–2003 Season," *Sudan and Nubia* 7 (2003): 26–32; Elzbieta Kolosowska, Mahmoud el-Tayeb, and Henryk Paner, "Old Kush in the Fourth Cataract Region," *Sudan and Nubia* 7 (2003): 21–25.

41. W. Vivian Davies, "Kush in Egypt: A New Historical Inscription," *Sudan and Nubia* 7 (2003): 52–54; Davies, "Sobeknakht of Elkab and the Coming of Kush," *Egyptian*

Archaeology 23 (2003): 3–6. For Kerman naval capabilities, note the paintings of a flotilla from the funerary temple K XI (Bonnet, *Edifices et rites funéraires à Kerma*, 89–96).

42. W. Vivian Davies, "Egypt and Nubia: Conflict with the Kingdom of Kush," in *Hatshepsut*, ed. Roehrig, 49–51; Robert Morkot, "Studies in New Kingdom Nubia, 1: Politics, Economics, and Ideology: Egyptian Imperialism in Nubia," *Wepwawet* 3 (1987): 30–32; Zibelius-Chen, *Die ägyptische Expansion*, 192–197.

43. The mention of the land of Miu in the stela of Emhab (Wolfgang Helck, *Historisch-biographische Texte der 2. Zwischenzeit und neue Texte der 18. Dynastie*, 3rd ed. [Wiesbaden: Harrassowitz, 2002], 98) makes it possible that a small force under Kamose pushed as far as the Fifth Cataract, but the uncertainty surrounding the location of Miu indicates that this evidence should be used with caution; for the location of Miu, see David O'Connor, "The Location of Irem," *JEA* 73 (1987): 123–124; Lothar Störk, *Die Nashörner* (Hamburg: Verlag Born, 1977), 257–284; David Klotz, "Emhab and the *tmrhtn*: Monomachy and the Expulsion of the Hyksos," forthcoming.

44. Smith, *Fortress of Buhen, Inscriptions*, 8–9, and pl. 2 and 58; similarly, the fortress of Kor was resettled, but without reconstruction of its walls; the date of reoccupation is uncertain, but may belong to the early Eighteenth Dynasty—see Smith, *Kush* 14 (1966): 229–230.

45. Smith, *Askut*, 107–122.

46. Zibelius-Chen, *Die ägyptische Expansion*, 192–193; Schmitz, *Amenophis I*, 193–204.

47. Francis Geus, "Sai," in *Sudan: Ancient Treasures* and references therein.

48. For a summary of textual and archaeological evidence on Nubian fortresses from the late Eighteenth Dynasty, see Morris, *Imperialism*, 310–342.

49. Smith, *Askut*, 137–147, 154–156.

50. Smith, *Buhen, Inscriptions*, 188.

51. The Aswan-Philae stela of Thutmose II states that Thutmose I constructed fortresses to "to repel the rebellious lands of the bowmen of Khenethennefer" (*Urk.* IV 138.16–139.1); see further in Morris, *Imperialism*, 89–92, 108–112; Säve-Söderbergh, 149–150.

52. Josef Wegner, "Regional Control in Middle Kingdom Lower Nubia: The History and Function of the Settlement at Areika," *JARCE* 32 (1995): 127–160.

53. The following discussion of Roman fortifications relies on Edward Luttwak, *The Grand Strategy of the Roman Empire: From the First Century A.D. to the Third* (Baltimore: Johns Hopkins University Press, 1976); note also the contrasting interpretations of Benjamin Isaac, *The Limits of Empire: The Roman Army in the East* (Oxford: Clarendon Press, 1992) and J. C. Mann, "Power, Force, and the Frontiers of the Empire," *Journal of Roman Studies* 69 (1979): 175–183. Additional information about the first stage of Roman fortification—the legionary fortress—and its later development appears in Campbell, *Roman Legionary Fortresses*. For the fortresses in the late Western Empire, see H. Elton, *Warfare in Roman Europe A.D. 350–425* (Oxford: Clarendon Press, 1997), 155–174.

54. Obsomer, *Sesostris Ier*, 311–334, 336–337 (fortress of Kor as campaign base).

55. For archaeological evidence of the acculturation of Nubians in the early New Kingdom, see Brigitte Gratien, "La fin du royaume de Kerma—la situation dans l'arrière-pays," in *Tides of the Desert*; Smith, *Wretched Kush*, 188–206; Torgny Säve-Söderbergh, "Tekhet: The Cultural and Sociopolitical Structure of a Nubian Princedom in Tuthmoside Times," in *Egypt and Africa*, ed. Davies.

56. For Thutmose I's Nubian campaign and references to his monumental texts, see Davies in *Hatshepsut*, ed. Roehrig, 51–52.

57. A dual river and desert column is attested in Egyptian military strategy, particularly since the desert troops would control the high ground; compare Kamose's attack on the Hyksos in Habachi, *Kamose*, 41 (see also the references in chapter 2 note 7).

58. *Urk.* IV 82–88; see Beylage, *Aufbau der königlichen Stelentexte*, vol. 1, 209–219, vol. 2, 679–683; Klug, *Königliche Stelen*, 71–78.

59. For Thutmose I's boundary inscription at Kurgus (and the copy thereof by Thutmose III), see W. Vivian Davies, "Kurgus 2000: The Egyptian Inscriptions," *Sudan and Nubia* 5 (2001): 46–58; Davies, "The Rock Inscriptions at Kurgus in the Sudan," in *Séhel entre Égypte et Nubie—inscriptions rupestres et graffiti de l'époque pharaonique*, ed. A. Gasse and V. Rondot (Montpellier: Université Paul-Valéry, 2004).

60. Darnell, *Theban Desert Road Survey 1*, 1–3; J. Degas, "Navigation sur le Nil au Nouvel Empire," in *Les problèmes institutionnels de l'eau.*

61. *Urk.* IV, 8, l. 8–9.

62. Louise Bradbury, "The Tombos Inscription: A New Interpretation," *Serapis* 8 (1984–1985): 1–20.

63. Winston Churchill, *The River War* (New York: Award Books, 1964), 184; compare also H. E. Colville, *History of the Sudan Campaign* (Nashville: Battery Press, 1996), 117–118.

64. For pharaonic use of the northern tracks, see Alfredo and Angelo Castiglioni, "Pharaonic Inscriptions along the Eastern Desert Routes in Sudan," *Sudan & Nubia* 7 (2003): 47–51.

65. Kenneth Kitchen, "The Land of Punt," in *The Archaeology of Africa*, ed. T. Shaw et al. (London: Routledge, 1993); Kitchen, "Further Thoughts on Punt and Its Neighbors," in *Studies on Ancient Egypt in Honour of H. S. Smith*; Schneider, *Ausländer in Ägypten*, vol. 2, 100–104. For evidence relating Punt to the Arabian Peninsula, see Dimitri Meeks, "Locating Punt," in *Mysterious Lands*, ed. D. O'Connor and S. Quirke (London: UCL Press, 2003), although his argument that Punt is exclusively Arabia is indefensible; see Kenneth Kitchen, "The Elusive Land of Punt Revisited," in *Trade and Travel in the Red Sea Region*, ed. P. Lunde and A. Porter (Oxford: Archaeopress, 2004). For speculation about the effect of Egyptian trade on Puntite military capabilities, see D. M. Dixon, "Pharaonic Egypt and the Red Sea Arms Trade," in the same volume.

66. Louise Bradbury, "*Kpn*-boats, Punt Trade, and a Lost Emporium," *JARCE* 33 (1996): 37–60.

67. For the political agenda of Hatshepsut, see the essays in Roehrig, ed., *Hatshepsut*, particularly Davies for Nubian activity; for Hatshepsut in Nubia, see also Spalinger, in *Thutmose III*, 354; Morkot, *Wepwawet* 3 (1987): 32–33.

68. J. De Morgan et al., *Catalogue des monuments et inscriptions de l'Égypte antique* I, *Haute Égypte* I, *de la frontière de Nubie à Kom Ombos* (Vienna: Adolphe Holzhausen, 1894), 126; for the attribution of the stela to the reign of Akhenaten, see H. Jaritz, "Zum Heiligtum am Gebel Tingar," *MDAIK* 37 (1981): 241–246.

69. For overviews of New Kingdom Egyptian administration in Nubia, see among the many possible references, Morkot, *Wepwawet* 3 (1987): 39–48; Morkot, "Egypt and Nubia," in *Empires*, ed. Alcock, 232–244; O'Connor, in *Social History*, 252–270; Smith, *Askut*, 178–183.

70. Gnirs, *Militär*, 35–36, 134–135.

71. Following the reign of Amunhotep II, the Egyptian title of Nubian viceroy changed from "King's Son" to the more specific "King's Son of Kush." For more on these officials, see Tamas Bács, "A New Viceroy of Nubia," in *A Tribute to Excellence*, ed. T. Bács (Budapest: La Chaire d'Egyptologie, 2002); A. Gasse and V. Rondot, "The Egyptian Conquest and Administration of Nubia during the New Kingdom: The Testimony of the Sehel rock-inscriptions," *Sudan and Nubia* 7 (2003): 40–46; Labib Habachi, "Königssohn von Kusch," in *LÄ*, vol. 2; Silvia Rabehl, Silvia, "Der Königssohn von Kusch, *Mrj-msw*, in München," in *Jerusalem Studies in Egyptology*, ed. I. Shirun-Grumach (Wiesbaden: Harrassowitz, 1998); Christine Raedler, "Zur Repräsentation und Verwirklichung pharaonischer Macht in Nubien:

Der Vizekönig Setau," in *Das Königtum der Ramessidenzeit*, ed. R. Gundlach and U. Rößler-Köhler (Wiesbaden: Harrassowitz, 2003); Redford, *Slave to Pharaoh*, 40–43; George Reisner, "The Viceroys of Kush," *JEA* 6 (1920): 28–55, 73–88; Spalinger, in *Thutmose III*, 346–353.

72. Bettina Schmitz, *Untersuchungen zum Titel S3–NJSWT "Königssohn"* (Bonn: R. Habelt, 1976).

73. For the military background of the viceroys of Kush, see Gnirs, *Militär*, 35–36, 134–141.

74. Compare the investitute of Seni by Thutmose I (*Urk.* IV, 40, 1. 13–14) and Nehi by Thutmose III (*Urk.* IV, 988, 1. 9–12); on these individuals, see also Peter Pamminger, "Nochmals zum Problem der Vizekönige von Kusch unter Hatschepsut," GM 131 (1992): 97–100.

75. Davies, *Huy*, pl. 6.

76. See the overview of Huy's career in Christiane Desroches-Noblecourt, *Tutankhamen* (New York: New York Graphic Society, 1963), 192–201.

77. Michel Valloggia, *Recherche sur les "messagers" (WPWTYW) dans les sources égyptiennes profanes* (Geneva: Libraire Droz, 1976), 239–251.

78. Fischer-Elfert, Papyrus Anastasi I, 244–246.

79. Compare the inscription of the royal envoy Neferhor from the time of Siptah at the temple of Buhen; see Ricardo Caminos, *The New Kingdom Temples of Buhen* (London: Egypt Exploration Society, 1974), 25–27, and pl. 29–30.

80. Contra Smith, *Askut*, 180, who suggests that he administered from Thebes.

81. Davies, *Huy*, pl. 23, 29, and 39.

82. A parallel noted by Reisner, *JEA* 6 (1920): 84.

83. Smith, *Askut*, 183; Gnirs, *Militär*, 134, and n. 794.

84. The ability of Huy's family to retain the position for two more generations further confirms the power of the viceroy. Huy's son Paser serves under Aye and Horemhab, while Paser's son Amenemipet is viceroy during the reign of Seti I; see Georg Steindorf, *Aniba* II (Glückstadt: J. J. Augustin, 1937), 24, and pl. 12, no. 43; Michel Dewachter, "Nubie—Notes diverses (II)," *BIFAO* 79 (1979): 317–320; Gnirs, *Militär*, 73–74.

85. Säve-Söderbergh, in *Egypt and Africa*; William Kelly Simpson, *Heka-nefer and the Dynastic Material from Toshka and Arminna* (New Haven, Conn.: Peabody Museum of Natural History, Yale University, 1963); Robert Morkot, "Nubia in the New Kingdom: The Limits of Egyptian Control," in *Egypt and Africa*.

86. David Lorton, "The Aswan/Philae Inscription of Thutmosis II," in *Studies in Egyptology Presented to Miriam Lichtheim*, ed. S. Israelit-Groll (Jerusalem: Magnes Press, 1990), vol. 2, 668–679; Beylage, *Aufau der königlichen Stelentexte*, vol. 1, 21–27, vol. 2, 575–579; Klug, *Königliche Stelen*, 83–87.

87. Compare Alan Schulman, *Ceremonial Execution and Public Rewards* (Freiburg: Universitätsverlag, 1988).

88. For more on the raising of foreign princes in the Egyptian court, see 145.

89. On the tomb of Maiherperi and the date of various objects within his burial, see Roehrig, ed., *Hatshepsut*, 62–63, 70–74; however, none of Roehrig's arguments rules out a date in the beginning of the reign of Amunhotep II.

90. Manassa, *Merneptah*, 101–102.

91. Dietz Otto Edzard, "Die Keilschriftbriefer der Grabungskampagne 1969," in *Kamid el-Loz—Kumidi, Schriftdokumente aus Kamid el-Loz* (Bonn: Rudolf Habelt Verlag, 1970), 55–56.

92. Klengel, in *Ägypten und Kusch*, 227–232.

93. F. Ll. Griffith, *Hieratic Papyri from Kahun and Gurob* (London: B. Quaritch, 1898), pl. 38.

94. Gunlach, *Zwangsumsiedlung*, 192–194.

95. Karl Butzer, *Early Hydraulic Civilization in Egypt: A Study in Cultural Ecology* (Chicago: University of Chicago Press, 1976); J. A. Wilson, "Buto and Hierakonopolis in the Geography of Egypt," *JNES* 14 (1955): 209–236.

96. David O'Connor, "The Geography of Settlement in Ancient Egypt," in *Man, Settlement, and Urbanism*, ed. P. Ucko, R. Tringham, and G. W. Dimblleby (London: Duckworth, 1972); O'Connor, "Urbanism in Bronze Age Egypt and Northeast Africa," in *The Archaeology of Africa*, ed. T. Shaw et al. (London: Routledge, 1993). For example, the city of Thebes became one of the largest urban centers in Egypt because of the trade and military routes leading into and out of the Thebaid; see Darnell, *Theban Desert Road Survey* 1, 45–46; Darnell, *The Birth of Victorious Thebes*, forthcoming.

97. Kemp, in *Social History*, 85–92.

98. Barry Kemp, "Fortified Towns in Nubia," in *Man, Settlement, and Urbanism*; Frandsen, in *Power and Propaganda*, 170–174; Redford, *From Slave to Pharaoh*, 44–49.

99. Eleonora Kormyschewa, "Kulte der ägyptischen Götter des Neuen Reiches in Kusch," in *Wege öffnen, Festschrift für Rolf Gundlach*, ed. M. Schade-Busch (Wiesbaden: Harrassowitz, 1996). For economic connections between temple foundations in Nubia and their counterparts in Egypt, see Morkot, *JNES* 49 (1990): 329–330.

100. M. F. L. Macadam, *The Temples of Kawa* vol. 2, *History and Archaeology of the Site* (Oxford: Oxford University Press, 1955), 28–44.

101. Blackman, *JEA* 23 (1937): 145–151; H. W. Fairman, "Preliminary Report on the Excavations at Sesebi (Sudla) and Amarah West, Anglo-Egyptian Sudan, 1937–8," *JEA* 24 (1938): 151–154; for objects from Sesebi, see Bengt Peterson, "Archäologische Funde aus Sesebi (Sudla) in Nord-Sudan," *Orientalia Suecana* 16 (1967): 3–15. For the erased scene of Akhenaten and Nefertiti offering to the Aten, see Murnane, *Amarna Period*, 41.

102. M. Schiff Giorgini, "Soleb-Sedeinga," *Kush* 15 (1968): 267.

103. H. Bonnet and D. Valbelle, "Kerma, Dokki Gel," in *Sudan: Ancient Treasures*, 109–113.

104. Timothy Kendall, "A New Map of the Gebel Barkal Temples," in *Études Nubiennes*, vol. 2, 141.

105. Mechthild Schade-Busch, "Bermerkungen zum Königsbild Thutmosis' III. in Nubien," in *Selbstverständnis und Realität*; Irmgard Hein, *Die ramessidische Bautätigkeit in Nubien* (Wiesbaden: Otto Harrassowitz, 1991).

106. Janusz Karkowski, *Faras*, vol. 5, *The Pharaonic Inscriptions from Faras* (Warsaw: Editions Scientifiques de Pologne, 1981), 115–139.

107. Bell, in *Mélanges Mokhtar*.

108. Alan Rowe, "Newly Identified Monuments in the Egyptian Museum Showing the Deification of the Dead," *ASAE* 40 (1940): 47–50, pl. 9; Bell, in *Mélanges Mokhtar*, 37–38.

109. Adams, *Nubia*, 632–624.

110. John Coleman Darnell, "A Stela of the Reign of Tutankhamun from the Region of Kurkur Oasis," *SAK* 31 (2003): 73–91.

111. Darnell, *SAK* 31 (2003): 83, n. 24.

112. The Nubian War texts of Seti I refer to a hill fort, possibly somewhere along the Sinn el-Kiddab plateau (*KRI* VII, 10, l. 5–6); a new stela of Seti I from Kurkur will appear in a forthcoming article by J. C. Darnell.

113. C. E. Callwell, *Small Wars: A Tactical Textbook for Imperial Soldiers* (London: Greenhill Books, 1990), 277–285.

114. Karl Butzer and Carl Hansen, *Desert and River in Nubia: Geomorphology and Prehistoric Environments at the Aswan Reservoir* (Madison: University of Wisconsin Press, 1968), 334–335.

115. J. E. Austin and N. B. Rankov, *Exploratio: Military and Political Intelligence in the Roman World from the Second Punic War to the Battle of Adrianople* (London: Routledge,

1995), 195–204, 271; Roy W. Davies, *Service in the Roman Army* (New York: Columbia University Press, 1989), 60–61.

116. For the two Nubian campaigns during the reign of Amunhotep III, see Vandersleyen, *L'Égypte*, 371–375, David O'Connor, "Amenhotep III and Nubia," in *Amenhotep III*, 264–270; Klug, *Königliche Stelen*, 422–430; Zakeya Topozada, "Les deux campagnes d'Amenhotep III en Nubie," *BIFAO* 88 (1988): 153–164.

117. H. S. Smith, *The Fortress of Buhen: The Inscriptions* (London: Egypt Exploration Society, 1976), 124–129 (no. 1595), and pl. 29 and 75; Wolfgang Helck, "Ein 'Feldzug' unter Amenophis IV gegen Nubien," *SAK* 8 (1980): 117–126; Murnane, *Amarna Period*, 101–103; Alan Schulman, "The Nubian War of Akhenaton," in *L'Égyptologie en 1979* (Paris: Éditions du CNRS, 1982).

118. Schulman, in *L'Égyptologie en 1979*, 301 and n. 16.

119. Contra Helck, *SAK* 8 (1980): 121.

120. Schulman, in *L'Égyptologie en 1979*, 305–306.

121. Manassa, *Merneptah*, 100.

122. Kuban Stela of Ramesses II, *KRI* II, 355, l. 3.

123. Dietrich Klemm, Rosemarie Klemm, and Andreas Murr, "Ancient Gold Mining in the Eastern Desert of Egypt and the Nubian Desert of the Sudan," in *Egypt and Nubia*, ed. Friedman; Karola Zibelius-Chen, "Die Kubanstele Ramses' II und die nubischen Goldregionen," in *Hommages à Jean Leclant*, vol. 2; Hikade, *Expeditionswesen*, 69–71; Jean Vercoutter, "The Gold of Kush," *Kush* 7 (1959): 120–153; Redford, *From Slave to Pharaoh*, 49–53.

124. Reeves, *Complete Tutankhamun*, 155, 157, 178. Contra Smith, *Wretched Kush*, 184, who describes the enemy figures as the base of the walking stick.

125. Gardiner, *Painted Box*.

126. Compare the decoration on the backs (west faces) of the two towers of the first pylon of the mortuary temple of Ramesses III (Epigraphic Survey, *Medinet Habu* I, pl. 67–68, 116–117). For the association of hunting and warfare in the Egyptian artistic canon, see also Winfried Barta, *Das Selbstzeugnis eines altägyptischen Künstlers (Stele Louvre C 14)* (Berlin: Bruno Hessling, 1970), 104–120.

127. Johnson, *Asiatic Battle Scene*, catalog nos. 44–48.

128. Georges Legrain, *Les Temples de Karnak: Fragment du dernier ouvrage de Georges Legrain* (Brussels: Chez Vromant, 1929), 134, 136, fig. 87; Johnson, *Asiatic Battle Scene*, catalog no. 44.

129. For these helmets, see chap. 3, n. 213.

130. Hermann Junker, "Die Feinde auf dem Sockel der Chasechem-Statuen und die Darstellung von geopferten Tieren," in *Ägyptologische Studien*, ed. O. Firchow (Berlin: Akademie, 1955).

131. For parallels and discussion, see Epigraphic Survey, *Luxor Temple* 1, pl. 7 n. b. Egyptian martial hymns parallel the Greek use of "marching paians," for which see W. Kendrick Pritchett, *The Greek State at War*, part 1 (Berkeley: University of California Press, 1971), 105–108.

132. Martin Bommas, "Schrein unter Gebel es-Silsilah im Neuen Reich," in *Grab und Totenkult im alten Ägypten* (Munich: Verlag C. H. Beck, 2003).

133. Wreszinski, *Atlas 2*, pl. 161; Thiem, *Speos*, 141–153, 318–322, pl. 55–61.

134. A nearly identical depiction of dancing Nubians appears in the Colonnade Hall of Luxor Temple; see "Religious Functions of the Egyptian Military" in chap. 5.

135. The word for solar god used in the speech of the Nubians is Shu, who is luminous space, the combination of air and light.

136. Montuhotep II (2055–2004 B.C.E.) commissioned a stela just 10 kilometers south of Gebel Silsila at the Shatt er-Rigal, which relates to a campaign via desert routes, bypass-

ing the First Cataract and passing through Kurkur Oasis to descend into the Nile Valley in the region of the Second Cataract; see Darnell, ZÄS 130 (2003): 31–48; Darnell, ZÄS 131 (2004): 23–37. Horemhab's commemoration of his Nubian war may be an allusion to Montuhotep II's earlier activities and a likening of Horemhab's reign to a re-creation of the government and a new dynastic beginning; see Philips, *Orientalia* 46 (1977): 116–121. Gebel Silsila might also be the last of the Nubian fortresses in the Ramesseum onomasticon; see Gardiner, JEA 3 (1916): 185, 192.

137. Alan Schulman, "Take for Yourself the Sword," in *Essays in Egyptology in Honor of Hans Goedicke*, ed. B. Bryan and D. Lorton (San Antonio: Van Siclen Books, 1994).

138. Epigraphic Survey, *Medinet Habu* I, pl. 17; compare also the statement in the Great Karnak Inscription of Merneptah (l. 27): "The hand of god being with them did they proceed, Amun with them as shields!" (Manassa, *Merneptah*, 38–39).

139. Manassa, *Merneptah*, 117–119.

140. Vandersleyen, *L'Égypte*, 323–333.

141. Hartwig, *Tomb Painting*, 73–76; Petschel and von Falck, eds., *Pharao siegt immer*, 186–193; Diamantis Panagiotopoulos, "Foreigners in Egypt in the Time of Hatshepsut and Thutmose III," in *Thutmose III*, 377–389, 400–401.

142. David Cannadine, *Ornamentalism: How the British Saw Their Empire* (Oxford: Oxford University Press, 2001), 51–54, 109.

143. Compare Murnane's remark ("Imperial Egypt and the Limits of Power," in *Amarna Diplomacy*, ed. R. Cohen and R. Westbrook [Baltimore: Johns Hopkins University Press, 2000], 103): "It seems logical that a public demonstration of this magnitude [the durbar of Akhenaten] would mark an equally significant occasion, but our continuing inability to determine its precise significance (even with Egyptian and cuneiform sources combined at our disposal) only drives home how slender and anecdotal our information really is."

144. Davies, *Rock Tombs* II, pl. 37, 40; Davies, *Rock Tombs* III, pl. 13.

145. For the presence of Nefertiti at the durbar, see Roth, *Gebieterin*, 39–42.

146. Davies, *Rock Tombs* III, pl. 13.147.

147. The restored date of the Nubian war on the Buhen Stela is year 12, 3 Akhet, day 20, while the durbar scenes of Akhenaten bear the date year 12, 2 Peret, day 8 (Davies, *Rock Tombs* II, pl. 38; Davies, *Rock Tombs* III, pl. 13); the seventy-eight days intervening give a suitable amount of time for celebrating the victory, even if the date of the Buhen Stela refers to the royal declaration of war and not the date of the battle itself.

148. The composition "King as Solar Priest" (Jan Assmann, *Der König als Sonnenpriester* [Glückstadt: J. J. Augustin, 1970]) and the cryptographic portion of the Book of the Day and the Night (A. Piankoff, *Le livre du jour et de la nuit* [Cairo: Institut Français d'Archéologie Orientale, 1942], 83–97) both correlate terrestrial places with otherworldly toponyms of the solar cycle; natural and supernatural beings are defined by their local associations, and terrestrial geography and ethnography are extended beyond the boundaries of the created world. The description of the solar journey in toponyms both real and supernatural finds an appropriate visual expression in the durbar scenes of Akhenaten at el-Amarna, with the king in the role of the sun god surrounded by representatives of all the foreigners he visits during a day (Darnell, SAK 18 [1991]: 137 n. 82).

149. Akhenaten's self-deification is thus an extension of the New Kingdom expression of pharaonic divinity in the form of the pharaoh as the divine chief of foreign lands (Labib Habachi, *Features of the Deification of Ramesses II* [Glückstadt: J. J. Augustin, 1969]); the concept behind the epithet "Re of the Nine Bows (the traditional enemies of Egypt)" used by the Nubians in the Gebel Silsila reliefs of Horemhab (see pages 121–122). The deifications of Akhenaten and Horemhab have precedent in the reign of Amunhotep III, whose divinity, like that of other rulers, could be expressed in the form of divine statuary. The southern statue of the famous colossi of Amunhotep III at Thebes is an image of Amunhotep III

as "Ruler of the Rulers (of the foreign lands)" (see Labib Habachi, "The Qantir Stela of the Vizier Rahotep and the Statue Ruler-of-Rulers," in *Festgabe für Dr. Walter Will* [Cologne: Carl Heymanns Verlag, 1966]). When Akhenaten emphasizes the significance of the durbar and his position as living sun god, he is simply taking the deification of the pharaoh an extra step—rather than a deified statue being the sun god for foreign rulers, Akhenaten presents his own body as that deified form.

150. The elaborate golden "centerpieces" in scenes of Nubian tribute probably represent the Nubian landscape as the home of Hathor-Tefnut, whom the metal itself evokes; their reception by the king would be appropriate to the king as Shu. Compare S. Donnat, "Les jardins d'orfèvrerie des tombes du Nouvel Empire," in *Encyclopédie religieuse de l'univers végétal: Croyances phytoreligieuses de l'Égypte ancienne* 1, ed. S. Aufrère (Montpellier: Université Paul-Valéry, 1999).

151. The trampling ram-headed sphinx is a heraldic representation of the deified ruler as Amun ram, a depiction particularly suited to the Egyptian ruler as manifest in Nubia (Bell, in *Mélanges Mokhtar*).

152. Ricardo Caminos, *The Shrines and Rock-Inscriptions of Ibrim* (London: Egypt Exploration Society, 1968), pl. 28, 32.

153. The stela of Usersatet (Peter Manuelian, *Studies in the Reign of Amenophis II* [Hildesheim: Gerstenberg, 1987], 157), which has been interpreted as a letter written by Amunhotep II to his viceroy, more likely records a conversation between Usersatet and the pharaoh at the occasion of the Nubian durbar over which Usersatet presided (a new publication by J. C. Darnell in preparation).

154. Davies, *Huy*, pl. 30.

155. Fischer, *Kush* 9 (1961): 44–80; Kubisch, *MDAIK* 56 (2000): 243–248.

156. Darnell, *ZÄS* 130 (2003): 31–48; Darnell, *ZÄS* 131 (2004): 23–37.

157. The ability of some Nubians to adopt an Egypto-Nubian persona may be behind the two Nubian rulers of the First Intermediate Period who adopted pharaonic titulary (Säve-Söderbergh, *Ägypten und Nubien*, 42–50).

158. For an examination of these two different representations of foreigners, see Antonio Loprieno, *Topos und Mimesis* (Wiesbaden: Otto Harrasowitz, 1988); Smith, *Askut*, 184–188; Smith, *Wretched Kush*, 24–29.

159. Krzysztof Cialowicz, *La naissance d'un royaume* (Crakow: Ksiegarnia Akademicka, 2001), 151–207.

160. Ritner, *Magical Practice*, 153–180.

161. Posener, *Cinq figurines d'envoûtement*; Ritner, *Magical Practice*, 136–142; Petschel and von Falck, eds., *Pharao siegt immer*, 63–64.

162. Simpson, *Heka-nefer*; Bruce Trigger, "Toshka and Arminna in the New Kingdom," in *Studies in Honor of William Kelly Simpson*, ed. Peter der Manuelian (Boston: Museum of Fine Arts, 1996).

163. Compare Smith, *Askut*, 184–188; however, his "transitional" category between topos and mimesis, which includes the depictions of Hekanefer and other Nubians in the tomb of Huy, are actually mimetic. Hekanefer's adoption of full Egyptian attire and funerary practices in his tomb is as much a topos of "Egyptianness" as the bound Nubians from Tutankhamun's chariot are a topos of foreign enemies, while the mixed Egypto-Nubian clothing in the tomb of Huy might well reflect the reality of the appearance of high-ranking Nubians in the late Eighteenth Dynasty.

164. Smith, *Wretched Kush*, 173: "Thus the Nubian prince Hekanefer, whose family had been acculturated for well over a hundred years, had to don his 'barbaric' ethnic Nubian costume and bow down before Pharaoh as a *topical* Nubian."

165. Compare the review of Smith, *Askut* in *CAJ* 7:1 (1997): 123–137, particularly the response by Kemp; note also the works on Egyptian imperialism cited in chap. 1, n. 16.

166. The following description of ornamentalism in the British Empire is based on Cannadine, *Ornamentalism*.

167. Cannadine, *Ornamentalism*, 88.

Chapter 5. Wretched Asiatics: The Northern Empire

1. Moran, *Amarna Letters*, 39.

2. B. Andelkovic, *The Relations between Early Bronze Age I Canaanites and Upper Egyptians* (Belgrade: Faculty of Philosophy, Center for Archaeological Research, 1995).

3. Susan Cohen, *Canaanites, Chronologies, and Connections: The Relationship of Middle Bronze IIA Canaan to Middle Kingdom Egypt* (Winona Lake, Ind.: Eisenbrauns, 2002), 33–50; Miroslav Bárta, *Sinuhe, the Bible, and the Patriarchs* (Prague: Set Out, 2003).

4. For the contemporanity of the Thirteenth and Fourteenth dynasties, see Ryholt, *Second Intermediate Period*, 69–117.

5. The history of the Fifteenth Dynasty may be found in a number of sources, particularly Ryholt, *Second Intermediate Period*, 118–150, passim; Vandersleyen, *L'Égypte*, 163–178; Oren, ed., *Hyksos*.

6. Archaeological evidence and the emphasis on the Hyksos merchant fleet in the stela of Kamose suggest the existence of a naval-based trade empire; see Ryholt, *Second Intermediate Period*, 139–140; Oren, "The 'Kingdom of Sharuhen' and the Hyksos Kingdom," in *Hyksos*; Aharon Kempinski, "The Hyksos: A View from Northern Canaan and Syria," in *Hyksos*; Ezra Marcus, "Venice on the Nile? On the Maritime Character of Tel Dab'a/varis," in *Timelines*, ed. Czerny et al. During the Fifteenth Dynasty, vessels from the northern Levant made up three-quarters of imported vessels at Tell el-Daba; see Anat Cohen-Weinberger and Yuval Goren, "Levantine-Egyptian Interactions during the 12th to the 15th Dynasties Based on the Petrography of the Canaanite Pottery from Tell el-Daba," *Ä&L* 14 (2004): 81–84. Ryholt, *Second Intermediate Period*, 111–113, also argues that Tell el-Yehudiya ware and seals of Fourteenth Dynasty date suggest a similar trade empire in place earlier, but much of his evidence should be redated to the Fifteenth Dynasty, as noted in Daphna Ben-Tor, Susan Allen, and James Allen, "Seals and Kings," *BASOR* 315 (1999): 47–74. The conclusions of Patrick E. McGovern, *The Foreign Relations of the "Hyksos"* (Oxford: Archaeopress, 2000) should be considered alongside the review of D. A. Aston, *JEA* 90 (2004): 233–237.

7. The queen Ahhotep, wife of Seqenenre Tao II, received the title "mistress of the people of the Mediterranean littoral" (Roth, *Gebieterin*, 17–18; Bietak, *Avaris*, 80), indicating her at least theoretical control over the area that was so essential to the Hyksos economy and suggests Theban attempts to coordinate with eastern Mediterranean groups, possibly even Minoan Crete.

8. On the tactics of the naval battle, see chap. 3, 65–67.

9. For overviews of the Hurrians and their kingdom of Mittani, see Gernot Wilhelm, *The Hurrians*, trans. J. Barnes (Warminster: Aris & Phillips, 1989); Wilhelm, "The Kingdom of Mitanni in Second-Millennium Upper Mesopotamia," in *Civilizations of the Ancient Near East*, ed. J. Sasson (New York: Scribner, 1995); Amélie Kuhrt, *The Ancient Near East c. 3000–330 B.C.*, vol. 1 (London: Routledge, 1995): 283–300; Jacques Freu, *Histoire du Mitanni* (Paris: L'Harmattan, 2003).

10. Lauren Ristvet and Harvey Weiss, "The Habur Region in the Late Third and Early Second Millennium B.C.," in *The History and Archaeology of Syria*, ed. W. Orthmann (Saarbrucken: Saarbrucken, 2005), 9; Klengel, *Geschichte des hethitischen Reiches*, 86.

11. The blocks from Karnak Temple that represented the primary evidence for Amunhotep I's northern campaign (Donald Redford, "A Gate Inscription from Karnak and Egyptian Involvement in Western Asia during the Early 18th Dynasty," *JAOS* 99 [1979]:

270–287) are either of Middle Kingdom date or represent an archaistic production of the reign of Thutmose I (Redford, *Wars in Syria*, 185–186). For a complete publication and discussion of the reliefs, see Françoise Le Saout, "Un magasin à onguents de Karnak et le problème du nom de Tyr: mise au point," in *Cahiers de Karnak* VIII (1987): 325–338; the amphorae carried by the personifications of the Syro-Palestinian cities are most similar in their shape and handle placement to Middle Bronze Age IIA storage jars, which support a Middle Kingdom date for the Karnak reliefs (compare Ruth Amiran, *Ancient Pottery of the Holy Land from its Beginnings in the Neolithic Period to the End of the Iron Age* [New Brunswick, N.J.: Rutgers University Press, 1970], 102–105).

12. "After this (the Nubian campaign of Thutmose I), proceeding to Retchenu in order to slake his (the king's) ardor throughout the foreign lands. His majesty reached Naharin and he discovered that the enemy was marshaling troops" (*Urk.* IV, 9, l. 8–12). The soldier Ahmose-Pennekhbet also records fighting in Naharin (Mitanni) and the capture of horses and chariots (*Urk.* IV, 36, l. 9–11).

13. Helck, *Historisch-biographische Texte*, 3rd ed., 110; Popko, *Geschichtsschriebung*, 179–185; for the religious implications of the word "crimes" in the inscription of Amenemhat, see Ritner, *Magical Practice*, 170, n. 787.

14. Anthony Spalinger, "A New Reference to an Egyptian Campaign of Thutmose III in Asia," *JNES* 37 (1978): 35–41.

15. For Thutmose I's Asiatic campaign, compare Spalinger, *War in Ancient Egypt*, 49–52.

16. See note 126 in chap. 4.

17. The only records of Thutmose I's hunting exploits are an extremely fragmentary text from Deir el-Bahari (*Urk.* IV, 103–105; it is only Sethe's conjectural restoration that mentions hunting *after* military conflict) and a possible reference by Thutmose III about his forefather when he also hunts elephants in Niye (Gebel Barkal). The tradition of hunting while on campaign in the north may begin as early as the reign of Ahmose—compare a short inscription mentioning "[going to] Qedem for recreation [. . .]" (Howard Carter, "Report on the Tomb of Zeser-Ka-Ra Amen-hetep I, Discovered by the Earl of Carnarvon in 1914," *JEA* 3 [1916]: pl. 21, no. 4).

18. Redford, *Wars in Syria*, 189–194.

19. Redford, *Wars in Syria*; Redford, "The Northern Wars of Thutmose III," in *Thutmose III*; Spalinger, *War in Ancient Egypt*, 83–100.

20. For overviews of Egyptian-Mitanni relations, see Betsy Bryan, "The Egyptian Perspective on Mitanni," in *Amarna Diplomacy*; Freu, *Histoire du Mitanni*, 55–90.

21. Horst Klengel, *Syria 3000 to 300 B.C.* (Berlin: Akademie, 1992), 84–180.

22. For overviews of the Egyptian administration in Syria-Palestine during the late Eighteenth Dynasty, see Rolf Hachmann, "Die ägyptische Verwaltung in Syrien während der Amarnazeit," *Zeitschrift des deutschen Palästina-Vereins* 98 (1982): 17–49; Thomas Hikade, *Das Expeditionswesen im ägyptischen Neuen Reiches* (Heidelberg: Heidelberger Orientverlag, 2001), 109–122; James Hoffmeier, "Aspects of Egyptian Foreign Policy in the 18th Dynasty in Western Asia and Nubia," in *Egypt, Israel, and the Ancient Mediterranean World: Studies in Honor of Donald B. Redford*, ed. G. N. Knoppers and A. Hirsch (Leiden: Brill, 2004); Kuhrt, *Ancient Near East 1*, 317–333; Murnane, in *Amarna Diplomacy*; Redford, *Egypt, Canaan, and Israel*, 192–213; Redford, *Wars in Syria*, 255–257; Michael Several, "Reconsidering the Egyptian Empire in Palestine during the Amarna Period," *Palestine Exploration Quarterly* 104 (1972): 123–133; James Weinstein, "The Egyptian Empire in Palestine: A Reassessment," *BASOR* 241 (1981): 1–28; Weinstein, "Egypt and the Levant in the Reign of Amenhotep III," in *Amenhotep III*, ed. O'Connor and Cline.

23. Compare, among others, A. Bernard Knapp, "Response: Independence, Imperialism, and the Egyptian Factor," *BASOR* 275 (1989): 65–67.

24. Leon Marfoe, "Between Qadesh and Kumidi: A History of Frontier Settlement and Land Use in the Biqa, Lebanon," Ph.D. diss., University of Chicago, 1978, 492–530; Alan James, "Egypt and Her Vassals: The Geopolitical Dimension," in *Amarna Diplomacy*, 112.

25. Some maintain that the Egyptians created only two distinct regions in the north (Nadav Na'aman, "Economic Aspects of the Egyptian Occupation of Canaan," *Israel Exploration Journal* 31 [1981]: 183–185); for an overview of the debate, see Morris, *Imperialism*, 293, n. 87.

26. Marfoe, *Between Qadesh and Kumidi*, 494–498, suggests that Kumidi was not a "capital" city but an important frontier outpost critical for communications and staging military activities.

27. On Egyptian activity at these sites, see Morris, *Imperialism*, 252–253.

28. For Beth-Shean in the Eighteenth Dynasty, see Morris, *Imperialism*, 249–252.

29. William Murnane, "'Overseer of the Northern Foreign Countries': Reflections on the Upper Administration of Egypt's Empire in Western Asia," in *Essays on Ancient Egypt in Honour of Herman te Velde*.

30. Murnane, in *Amarna Diplomacy*, 108–109.

31. Fischer-Elfert, *Papyrus Anastasi I*.

32. James Harrell and Max Brown, "The Oldest Surviving Topographical Map from Ancient Egypt (Turin Papyri 1879, 1899, and 1969)," *JARCE* 29 (1992): 81–105.

33. Compare EA 148 (Moran, *Amarna Letters*, 235): "May the king ask his commissioner, who is familiar with Canaan."

34. Nadav Na'aman, "The Contribution of the Amarna Letters to the Debate on Jerusalem's Political Position in the Tenth Century B.C.E.," *BASOR* 304 (1996): 20 and n. 2, citing EA 139, 238, and 295.

35. José Galán, "The Heritage of Thutmosis III's Campaigns in the Amarna Age," in *Essays in Egyptology in Honor of Hans Goedicke*. For possible yearly tours of the bow troops, compare EA 76 (Moran, *Amarna Letters*, 146–147).

36. For a few of the many possible examples, see EA 286 from Ribaddi, where he requests both types of troops; in EA 76 and 362 he asks only that the mobile "archers" be dispatched with all possible haste.

37. Morris, *Imperialism*, 254–256.

38. The tax and tribute systems of the Amarna Period are a direct development from the system in place during the reign of Thutmose III; see Panagiotopoulos, in *Thutmose III*, 371–377. For the differences between the economic integration of the southern and northern territories of Syria-Palestine, see Panagiotopoulos, "Tributabgaben und Huldigungsgeschenke aus der Levante, die ägyptische Nordexpansion in der 18 Dynastie aus strukturgeschichtlicher Sicht," *Ä&L* 10 (2002): 139–158.

39. Shemuel Ahituv, "Economic Factors in the Egyptian Conquest of Canaan," *Israel Exploration Journal* 28 (1978): 93–96; an amphora stamped with the cartouche of Thutmose I, discovered in the Western Desert at a site almost exactly between the Nile and Kharga Oasis, provides further archaeological evidence of the pharaoh's estates in the northern empire (publication forthcoming).

40. Panagiotopoulos, *Ä&L* 10 (2002): 143–144, 155–157. For the coastal grain storage depots, see Morris, *Imperialism*, 228–230; Spalinger, *War in Ancient Egypt*, 134–136. Compare the statement in the annals of Thutmose III (*Urk.* IV 719, l. 7–11): "Meanwhile, every harbor was supplied with all good supplies according to their yearly custom . . . including the labor of Lebanon and the harvest of Djahy."

41. Na'aman, in *Amarna Diplomacy*, 129–130.

42. Ahituv, *Israel Exploration Journal* 28 (1978): 93–105.

43. For a few examples among the many in the Amarna Letters, compare EA 147, 149, 185, and 286. See also Na'aman, *BASOR* 304 (1996): 20–21.

44. A particular part of the palace, known as the *per-kap*, could be used for the upbringing of foreign princes and other high officials; on this institution, see Ericka Feucht, "Kinder fremder Völker in Ägypten," *SAK* 17 (1990): 177–204; Feucht, *Das Kind im alten Ägypten* (Frankfurt: Campus, 1995), 266–303; Bernard Mathieu, "L'énigme du recrutement des 'enfants du *kap*': Une solution?," *GM* 177 (2000): 41–48. The *per-kap* might originally been termed the *per-djamu* "house of the recruits" (see Darnell, *Theban Desert Road Survey* 1, 123–24).

45. EA 59, Moran, *Amarna Letters*, 130.

46. For one of many examples, see EA 296 (Moran, *Amarna Letters*, 338).

47. EA 286, Moran, *Amarna Letters*, 326.

48. In EA 99, one of the few letters in the archive from the Egyptian pharaoh to one of his vassals, the king requests a daughter from the vassal ruler as well as a variety of luxury goods (Moran, *Amarna Letters*, 171).

49. Samuel Meier, "Diplomacy and International Marriages," in *Amarna Diplomacy*; Roth, *Gebieterin*, 85–93, 108–130.

50. For inventories of such dowries, compare EA 13, 22, and 25 (Moran, *Amarna Letters*, 24–27, 51–61, 72–84).

51. The role of the princesses might not have been entirely passive; one Babylonian princess appears to have written a letter to her future Egyptian husband (EA 12, Moran, *Amarna Letters*, 24).

52. E.g., EA 14, Moran, *Amarna Letters*, 27–37.

53. EA 4, Moran, *Amarna Letters*, 8–9.

54. Kevin Avruch, "Reciprocity, Equality, and Status-Anxiety in the Amarna Letters," in *Amarna Diplomacy*.

55. For one of many examples, see EA 20 (Moran, *Amarna Letters*, 48).

56. R. Cohen, "Intelligence in the Amarna Letters," in *Amarna Diplomacy*.

57. Moran, *Amarna Letters*, 231.

58. J. C. Darnell, in *Egypt and Nubia*, 132–139.

59. Samuel Meier, *The Messenger in the Ancient Semitic World* (Atlanta: Scholars Press, 1988); Mario Liverani, *International Relations in the Ancient Near East, 1600–1100 B.C.* (New York: Palgrave, 2001), 71–76; Trevor Bryce, *Letters of the Great Kings of the Ancient Near East: The Royal Correspondence of the Late Bronze Age* (London: Routledge, 2003), 63–74.

60. E.g., EA 30; for this and references to other "passports," see Moran, *Amarna Letters*, 100; Westbrook, "International Law in the Amarna Age," in *Amarna Diplomacy*, 33–34.

61. For overviews of the Amarna Letters and their historical context, see Bryce, *Letters of the Great Kings*, 232–236; F. J. Giles, *The Amarna Age: Western Asia* (Warminster: Aris & Phillips, 1997); Liverani, *International Relations*; William Moran, *Amarna Studies: Collected Writings*, ed. J. Huehnergard and S. Izre'el (Winona Lake, Ind.: Eisenbrauns, 2003); Redford, *Egypt, Canaan, and Israel*, 166–177. All translations of the Amarna Letters are quotes from Moran, *Amarna Letters*. For analysis of the tablets' clay, see Yuval Goren, Israel Finkelstein, and Nadav Na'aman, *Inscribed in Clay: Provenance Study of the Amarna Tablets and Other Ancient Near Eastern Texts* (Tel Aviv: Emery and Claire Yass Publications in Archaeology, 2004).

62. The Records Office is building Q42.21 at Amarna; for its context in the Central City, see Kemp and Garfi, *El-'Amarna*, 61–62; Lacovara, *Royal City*, 43–44.

63. Moran, *Amarna Letters*, xix.

64. EA 27, in which Tushratta requests solid gold statues rather than the gold-plated wooden objects he has been sent by Akhenaten, has an Egyptian docket whose most likely reading is "year two"; see Walter Fritz, "Bemerkungen zum Datierungsvermerk auf der Amarnatafel KN 27," *SAK* 18 (1991): 207–214.

65. Bryce, *Letters of the Great Kings*, 57–63; the Akkadian scribal tradition at Amarna might have originated in Hatti—see Gary Beckman, "Mesopotamians at Hattusa," *Journal of Cuneiform Studies* 35 (1983): 112–114 (reference courtesy of Benjamin Foster). For evidence that Egyptian scribes of the Ramesside Period learned cuneiform, compare the shabti of Tjuro, which incorporates a cuneiform sign into the hieroglyphic text; see Kenneth Kitchen, "High Society and Lower Ranks in Ramesside Egypt at Home and Abroad," *British Museum Studies in Ancient Egypt and Sudan* 6 (2006): 31, http://www.thebritishmuseum.ac.uk/bmsaes/issue6/kitchen.html.

66. In addition to the Asiatics in the royal bodyguard, compare the stela of an Asiatic soldier and his wife (Freed, Markowitz, and D'Auria, *Pharaohs of the Sun*, 239; Petschel and von Falck, eds., *Pharao siegt immer*, 96–97).

67. EA 65 (Moran, *Amarna Letters*, 136); compare also the "hymn to the Pharaoh" in EA 147, written by Abimilku, king of Tyre (ibid., 233).

68. Martin, *Memphite Tomb*, 94–98, pl. 111–115, 117.

69. Ellen F. Morris, "Bowing and Scraping in the Ancient Near East: An Investigation into Obsequiousness in the Amarna Letters," *JNES* 65 (2006): 179–195.

70. Roth, *Gebieterin*, 68–84.

71. EA 28 and EA 29, Moran, *Amarna Letters*, 91–99.

72. EA 26, Moran, *Amarna Letters*, 85.

73. Moran, *Amarna Studies*, 235.

74. Freu, *Histoire du Mitanni*, 32–53.

75. Klengel, *Syria*, 84–97.

76. S. Smith, *The Statue of Idrimi* (London: British Institute of Archaeology in Ankara, 1949); Klengel, *Syria*, 86–89.

77. For overviews of the Hittite Empire, see Kuhrt, *Ancient Near East*, 225–282; J. G. Macqueen, "The History of Anatolia and of the Hittite Empire: An Overview," in *Civilizations of the Ancient Near East*; Trevor Bryce, *Life and Society in the Hittite World* (Oxford, U.K.: Oxford University Press, 2002); Bryce, *The Kingdom of the Hittites*, 2nd ed. (Oxford: Oxford University Press, 2005); Horst Klengel, *Geschichte des hethitischen Reiches* (Leiden: Brill, 1999). For the Hittite's military capabilities, see Richard Beal, *Hittite Military*; Beal, "Hittite Military Organization," in *Civilizations of the Ancient Near East*; Bryce, *Hittite World*, 98–118.

78. Darnell, *SAK* 18 (1991): 113–140.

79. Kuhrt, *Ancient Near East*, 332–348; Walter Sommerfield, "The Kassites of Ancient Mesopotamia: Origins, Politics, and Culture," in *Civilizations of the Ancient Near East*.

80. Moran, *Amarna Letters*, 12–16.

81. Kuhrt, *Ancient Near East*, 348–355.

82. Karol Myśliwiec, *The Twilight of Ancient Egypt* (Ithaca, N.Y.: Cornell University Press, 2000), 105–109.

83. According to EA 16, his predecessor Ashurnadinahhe had already written to Egypt (Moran, *Amarna Letters*, 39).

84. Moran, *Amarna Letters*, 39.

85. Ibid., 18.

86. Kuhrt, *Ancient Near East*, 254–257.

87. D. Fabre, *Le destin maritime de l'Égypte ancienne* (London: Periplus, 2005), 29–30; Goren, Finkelstein, and Na'aman, *Inscribed in Clay*, 70–75; the earlier name *Izy* appears in the topographical lists of Amunhotep III—see Elmar Edel and Manfred Görg, *Die Ortsnamenlisten im nördlichen Säulenhof des Totentempels Amenophis' III* (Wiesbaden: Harrassowitz, 2005), 28, 42–43.

88. EA 31–32 (Moran, *Amarna Letters*, 101–103).

89. The ruler of Alashiya might have been particularly diligent after being reproached for not dispatching a courier in time for an important event in Egypt, possibly a festival,

such as the year twelve durbar, or even the coronation of Akhenaten (EA 34, Moran, *Amarna Letters*, 105–107).

90. E.g., EA 35–37 (Moran, *Amarna Letters*, 107–111); Vassis Karageorghis, "Relations between Egypt and Cyprus: Second Intermediate Period and XVIII Dynasty," *Ä&L* 5 (1995): 73–79; Hikade, *Expeditionswesen*, 123–129.

91. EA 38, Moran, *Amarna Letters*, 111–112.

92. Moran, *Amarna Letters*, 112–113.

93. For the history of Amurru, see Itamar Singer, "A Concise History of Amurru," in Shlomo Isre'el, *Ammuru Akkadian: A Linguistic Study*, vol. 2 (Atlanta: Scholars Press, 1991), vol. 2, 135–195.

94. See inter alia Redford, *Egypt, Canaan, and Israel*, 195; Nadav Na'aman, "Ḥabiru and Hebrews: The Transfer of a Social Term to the Literary Sphere," *JNES* 45 (1986): 271–288; Michael B. Rowton, "Dimorphic Structure and the Problem of the 'Apirû-'Ibrîm*," *JNES* 35 (1976): 13–20; Giorgio Buccellati, "'Apirū and Munnabtūtu: The Stateless of the First Cosmopolitan Age," *JNES* 36 (1977): 145–147.

95. P. Horden and N. Purcell, *The Corrupting Sea: A Study of Mediterranean History* (Malden, U.K.: Blackwell, 2000), 54–59 and 546; Marfoe, *Between Qadesh and Kumidi*; Marfoe, *BASOR* 234 (1979): 1–42.

96. Angus Fraser, *The Gypsies* (Oxford: Oxford University Press, 1992); Mozes Heinschink and Ursula Hemetek, eds., *Roma: das unbekannte Volk, Schicksal und Kultur* (Vienna: Böhlau, 1994). During the Roman imperial period, people known as the Ituraeans appear to have been at least the spiritural if not direct descendants of the Apiru and were well known for their audacious acts of brigandage within the old area of Amurru, their attacks even reaching into the cities of Byblos and Beirut (Isaac, *Limits of Empire*, 60–62, citing Strabo, xvi 2.18).

97. See the discussions listed in Cohen, *Canaanites, Chronologies, and Connections*, 159 (index page); Samuel Mark, *From Egypt to Mesopotamia: A Study of Predynastic Trade Routes* (London: Chatham, 1998): 122–131.

98. A. D. Espinel, "The Role of the Temple of Ba'alat Gebel as Intermediary between Egypt and Byblos during the Old Kingdom," *SAK* 30 (2002): 103–119.

99. Mario Liverani, "Pharaoh's Letters to Rib-Adda," in *Three Amarna Essays* (Malibu, Calif.: Undena, 1979), 75–85; for an interesting character study of Ribaddi, see W. L. Moran, "Rib-Hadda: Job at Byblos?" in A. Kort and S. Morschauser, eds., *Biblical and Related Studies Presented to Samuel Iwry* (Winona Lake, Ind.: Eisenbrauns, 1985), 173–181.

100. EA 106, Moran, *Amarna Letters*, 179.

101. Compare EA 124, Moran, *Amarna Letters*, 203.

102. For the identification of many cities mentioned in the *Amarna Letters*, see Gabolde, *D'Akhenaton à Toutânkhamon*, 43–57; Bryce, *Letters of the Great Kings*, 131–144.

103. Mario Liverani, "A Seasonal Pattern for the Amarna Letters," in *Lingering over Words*, ed. T. Abusch et al. (Atlanta: Scholars Press, 1990).

104. Moran, *Amarna Letters*, 365.

105. The following discussion follows the divisions of James, in *Amarna Diplomacy*, 114–119.

106. Moran, *Amarna Letters*, 307.

107. Compare EA 151, Moran, *Amarna Letters*, 238–239.

108. For other overviews of the Amorite kingdom under the leadership of Abdiashirta and Aziru, see Shlomo Izre'el and Itamar Singer, *The General's Letter from Ugarit: A Linguistic and Historical Reevaluation of RS 20.33* (Tel Aviv: Tel Aviv University, 1990), 122–154; Bryce, *Letters of the Great Kings*, 145–165, presents some similar conclusions about the careers of Abdiashirta and Aziru.

109. The accusations of Pahhanate are recorded in the fragmentary beginning of EA 62, restored by Moran, *Amarna Letters*, 133, followed by Bryce, *Letters of the Great Kings*, 166, n. 7.

110. Compare EA 84, where Ribaddi reports that Abdiashirta even had the gall to sleep in the Egyptian palace in Sumur (Moran, *Amarna Letters*, 154–156).

111. Moran, *Amarna Letters*, 131–132.

112. Compare EA 71 and EA 73 (Moran, *Amarna Letters*, 140–142).

113. EA 74, Moran, *Amarna Letters*, 142–143.

114. Moran, *Amarna Letters*, 145.

115. Following the interpretation of Murnane, *Road to Kadesh*, 6–7.

116. EA 85 (Moran, *Amarna Letters*, 157): "Moreover, the king of [Mi]tanni came out as far as Sumur, and though wanting to march as far as Byblos, he returned to his own land, as there was no water for him to drink." EA 95 (Moran, *Amarna Letters*, 169): "The king of Mitanni visited the land of Amurru itself." See also the fragmentary mention of Mitanni in EA 58 and EA 84, which might refer to the same events; an obscure passage in EA 100 may suggest that the pharaoh disapproved of Irqata dispatching gifts to a Mittanian vassal (Moran, *Amarna Letters*, 172–173). For Amurru's relationship with Mitanni and exploitation of those ties when allying with the Hittites, see Murnane, *Road to Kadesh*, 139–142.

117. Singer, in *Amurru Akkadian*, vol. 2, 146–147, and Bryce, *Letters of the Great Kings*, 141–149, doubt reports about Mitanni's incursions into Egyptian territory, both from Abdiashirta and Ribaddi, but offer no independent evidence for their position.

118. Moran, *Amarna Letters*, 163: "Moreover, that [do]g (Abdiashirta) is in Mitanni, but his eye is on Byblos."

119. Moran, *Amarna Letters*, 152.

120. Ibid., 162–163; see also Bryce, *Letters of the Great Kings*, 151.

121. Moran, *Amarna Letters*, 152.

122. Bryce, *Letters of the Great Kings*, 152, citing EA 83 and 91.

123. Compare among the many examples EA 74 (Moran, *Amarna Letters*, 142) and EA 79.

124. Bryce, *Letters of the Great Kings*, 153 and 167, n. 33; Moran, *Amarna Studies*, 227–236. For a different interpretation of EA 101, see Mario Liverani, "How to Kill Abdi-Ashirta Once Again," *Israel Oriental Studies* 18 (1998): 387–394.

125. Moran, *Amarna Letters*, 141; similar statements are made in EA 93 (ibid., 167).

126. For overviews of Aziru's career, see Isre'el and Singer, *The General's Letter*, 134–159; Bryce, *Letters of the Great Kings*, 156–165.

127. Moran, *Amarna Letters*, 243; see also EA 171 and the discussion of Bryce, *Letters of the Great Kings*, 156–157.

128. Aziru's epithet "dog" used in Ribaddi's correspondence is not derogatory, but rather emphasizes the Amorite's subordinate status vis-à-vis Egypt; see Galán, *Ugarit-Forschungen* 25 (1993): 173–180.

129. Moran, *Amarna Letters*, 177; see also EA 102.

130. See the description in EA 105.

131. The following discussion of Mediterranean travel relies on a number of sources. See in particular J. H. Pryor, *Geography, Technology, and War: Studies in the Maritime History of the Mediterranean, 649–1571* (Cambridge, U.K.: Cambridge University Press, 1988), 94–95, 114–134; Pryor, "The Geographical Conditions of Galley Navigation in the Mediterranean," in R. Gardiner and J. Morrison, eds., *The Age of the Galley* (Annapolis, Md.: Naval Institute Press, 1995), 206–216; S. Wachsmann, *Seagoing Ships and Seamanship in the Bronze Age Levant* (College Station: Texas A & M University Press, 1998), 295–299;

S. D. Goitein, *A Mediterranean Society: The Jewish Communities of the Arab World as Portrayed in the Documents of the Cairo Geniza* (Berkeley: University of California Press, 1967), vol. 1, 212–214, 316–317, 320–326; Horden and Purcell, *The Corrupting Sea*, 137–143.

132. Pryor, *Geography, Technology, and War*, 114–115.

133. For the limitations of Hittite sea power, see Bryce, *The Kingdom of the Hittites*, 2nd ed., 332–333.

134. Fabre, *Le destin maritime*, 20–23 and 27–35; note that during his journeys, Wenamun stopped at Dor, Tyre, Sidon, and Byblos, then sailed to Cyprus.

135. Engels, *Logistics of the Macedonian Army*, 54–55.

136. For the Great Syrian Campaign, also known as the "First Syrian War," see Bryce, *The Kingdom of the Hittites*, 2nd ed., 161–175; Murnane, *Road to Kadesh*, 8–11, 115–124 (for chronology); Klengel, *Geschichte des hethitischen Reiches*, 155–167.

137. Nadav Na'aman, "Tushratta's Murder in Shuppiluliluma's Letter to Akhenaten (EA 43)," *Abr-Nahrain* 33 (1995): 116–118; Freu, *Histoire du Mitanni*, 123–124, 133–138.

138. The treaties between Suppiluliuma I and Shattiwaza recount these events; see Gary Beckman, *Hittite Diplomatic Texts*, 2nd ed. (Atlanta: Scholars Press, 1999), 41–54.

139. Kuhrt, *Ancient Near East*, vol. 1, 292–293; Klengel, *Geschichte des hethitischen Reiches*, 165–166.

140. Michael Astour, "Ugarit and the Great Powers," in *Ugarit in Retrospect*, ed. G. D. Young (Winona Lake, Ind.: Eisenbrauns, 1981), 15–20; for the treaty between Suppiluliuma and Niqmaddu, see Beckman, *Hittite Diplomatic Texts*, 34–36.

141. Murnane, *Road to Kadesh*, 142–143.

142. Moran, *Amarna Letters*, 249. For the date of this letter before Aziru's journey to Egypt, see Murnane, *Road to Kadesh*, 17–18; an alternate chronology is offered by Isre'el and Singer, *The General's Letter*, 130–134.

143. Akhenaten's preparations for a strike against Kadesh may explain Aziru's willingness to travel to Egypt; see Nadav Na'aman, "Praises to Pharaoh in response to his plans for a campaign to Canaan," in *Lingering over Words*, 404–405.

144. EA 169, Moran, *Amarna Letters*, 256.

145. Murnane, *Road to Kadesh*, 20–21.

146. According to petrographic analysis, this letter was sent from Irqata, which may have been Aziru's base of operations; see Goren, Finkelstein, and Na'aman, *Inscribed in Clay*, 101–125. For the region of Amki, see Marfoe, *Between Qadesh and Kumidi*, 501–502.

147. Murnane, *Road to Kadesh*, 15–18.

148. Moran, *Amarna Letters*, 247; the date of this letter is somewhat uncertain, but Murnane, *Road to Kadesh*, 119–120, suggests that it was sent some time after the Great Syrian War. The mention of Hani, the Egyptian commissioner, further indicates that EA 161 was written after Aziru's return from Egypt; see also Isre'el and Singer, *The General's Letter*, 130–134.

149. Bryce, *Letters of the Great Kings*, 161–162.

150. Nuhasse, as a confederation of rulers, could act both for and against Egypt; for the complexity of Nuhasse's relations with Egypt and the Hittites during the Amarna Period, see Klengel, *Syria*, 152–154.

151. Moran, *Amarna Letters*, 247.

152. EA 106 (Moran, *Amarna Letters*, 179).

153. EA 131 (Moran, *Amarna Letters*, 212–213).

154. Moran, *Amarna Letters*, 237.

155. Philip Warner, *Dervish* (Hertfordshire, U.K.: Wordsworth Editions, 2000), 109–113.

156. Compare Ribaddi's description of his peasantry "turning Apiru" when he was assaulted by Abdiashirta (EA 74).

157. For Ribaddi's fate after Aziru's takeover of Byblos, see EA 136, 137, and 138.

158. Described in EA 142 (Moran, *Amarna Letters*, 228–229).

159. Bryce, *Letters of the Great Kings*, 163–164.

160. Summary of Stephen R. David, "Realism, Constructivism, and the Amarna Letters," in *Amarna Diplomacy*, 55–57.

161. For another application of realism to the Amarna Letters, see David, in *Amarna Diplomacy*, and compare the other theoretically based articles in the same volume.

162. Luttwak, *Grand Strategy*, 111–116.

163. Following Murnane, *Road to Kadesh*, 21.

164. For a second campaign against Kadesh between years 29 and 31, see Redford, *Wars in Syria*, 217–219.

165. Murnane, *Road to Kadesh*, 142–143.

166. Moran, *Amarna Letters*, 125.

167. Similar events late in the reign of Akhenaten probably constitute the historical setting for the "General's Letter" from Ugarit (Isre'el and Singer, *The General's Letter*); the date of this letter remains a topic of debate. See also Bryce, *Letters of the Great Kings*, 181–184; Spalinger, *War in Ancient Egypt*, 160–164.

168. Murnane, *Road to Kadesh*, 18–19. Isre'el and Singer, *The General's Letter*, 162–165, date the preparations slightly later, after Aziru has returned to Amurru.

169. In addition to the two letters quoted, see also those written by Ammunira of Beirut (EA 141, 143). For the letters during Akhenaten's preparations for his Kadesh campaign and the reality of the event, see Na'aman, in *Lingering over Words*, 397–405.

170. Moran, *Amarna Letters*, 230.

171. Ibid., 242.

172. See Gabolde, *D'Akhenaton à Toutânkhamon*, 195–207, and pl. 25 for a reconstruction of the army's itinerary.

173. Compare the comments of Engels regarding the supply of the Macedonian army during Alexander the Great's movement through Syria-Palestine (*Logistics of Macedonian Army*, 57–58).

174. For Tjaru in the Eighteenth Dynasty, see Morris, *Imperialism*, 45–47, 56–60, 276–294; Mohamed Abd el-Maksoud, "Tjarou, porte de l'Orient," in *Le Sinai durant l'antiquité et le moyen age*, ed. D. Valbelle and C. Bonnet (Paris: Éditions Errance, 1998).

175. James Hoffmeier, "A New Military Site on 'The Ways of Horus'—Tell el-Borg 1999–2001: A Preliminary Report," *JEA* 89 (2003): 179–182.

176. Elizer Oren, "The Establishment of Egyptian Imperial Administration on the 'Ways of Horus': An Archaeologicval Perspective from North Sinai," in *Timelines*, ed. Czerny et al.; Alan Gardiner, "The Ancient Military Road between Egypt and Palestine," *JEA* 6 (1920): 99–116.

177. Morris, *Imperialism*, 295–299.

178. For travel across the Sinai, see Murnane, *Road to Kadesh*, 47; Engels, *Logistics of the Macedonian Army*, 59–60; Redford, *Wars in Syria*, 202–204.

179. For the logistics of maritime travel between Egypt and the Syro-Palestinian coast, see Spalinger, *War in Ancient Egypt*, 52–55; Redford, *Wars in Syria*, 203–205.

180. Spalinger, *War in Ancient Egypt*, 56–58.

181. The map of Gabolde, *D'Akhenaton à Toutânkhamon*, pl. 25, showing the Egyptian army potentially going to Byblos, should be amended.

182. Murnane, *Road to Kadesh*, 19–20.

183. *Urk.* IV 2027, l. 13–14.

184. Garth Fowden, *Qusayr 'Amra: Art and the Umayyad Elite in Late Antique Syria* (Berkeley: University of California Press, 2004), 31–33, 155–156.

185. Compare the map in D. Nicolle, *The Crusades* (Oxford: Oxford University Press, 2001), 34; a narrative summary of Amalric's attempts to control Egypt appears in S. Runci-

man, A History of the Crusades, vol. 2 The Kingdom of Jerusalem and the Frankish East 1100–1187 (Cambridge, U.K.: Cambridge University Press, 1962), 362–400. For Muslim forces also going south around the Kingdom of Jerusalem, through the desert, to reach Egypt from Syria, see R. Röhricht, Geschichte des Königreichs Jerusalem (1100–1291) (Amsterdam: Verlag Adolf M. Hakkert, 1966), 322–323.

186. For the campaigns of Seti I, see Murnane, Road to Kadesh; Spalinger, War in Ancient Egypt, 187–208.

187. Murnane, Road to Kadesh, 51–58.

188. Ibid., 31–35; Itmar Singer, "The Kurustama Treaty Revisited," in Sarnikzel, Hethitologische Studien zum Gedenken an Emil Orgetorix Forrer, ed. D. Groddek and S. Rößle (Dresden: Technische Universität, 2004); Dietrich Sürenhagen, "Forerunners of the Hattusili-Ramesses Treaty," British Museum Studies in Ancient Egypt and Sudan 6 (2006): 59–67, http://www.thebritishmuseum.ac.uk/bmsaes/issuer/suerenhagen.html. For an overview of treaties in the ancient Near East, see Westbrook in Amarna Diplomacy, 36–40.

189. The second Egyptian attack on Kadesh at the end of Tutankhamun's reign might also be related to treatymaking activities, since another treaty between Egypt and Hatti might have been sealed by Horemhab or Ramesses I (Murnane, Road to Kadesh, 37–38).

190. Discussions of the Battle of Kadesh abound; a summary of the events, references, and insightful analysis of the limited Egyptian victory appears in Spalinger, War in Ancient Egypt, 209–234.

191. R. C. Smail, Crusading Warfare 1097–1193 (Cambridge, U.K.: Cambridge University Press, 1956), 148–152.

192. John Coleman Darnell and Richard Jasnow, "On the Moabite Inscriptions of Ramesses II at Luxor Temple," JNES 52 (1993): 263–274.

193. Bryce, The Kingdom of the Hittites, 2nd ed., 175–178.

194. Freu, Histoire du Mitanni, 146–155.

195. Johnson, Asiatic War; Heinz, Feldzugdarstellungen, 237–239.

196. Johnson, Asiatic War, 59–60; Spalinger, War in Ancient Egypt, 181–182.

197. Davies, The Tomb of Rekh-mi-Re, pl. 22; Carter and Newberry, Thoutmosis IV, pl. 9, 10; Epigraphic Survey, Battle Reliefs of King Sety I, pl. 107. For Hittite chariots, see also Beal, Hittite Military, 141–190.

198. Epigraphic Survey, Battle Reliefs of King Sety I.

199. Spalinger, Ä&L 13 (2003): 185–190, passim.

200. The Hittite chariots are not always depicted with consistency in the various versions of the Kadesh scenes, but those with details of the Hittite chariots show those vehicles with axles mounted under the center of the cab, not under the rear, as on the chariots of the Egyptians; compare Christiane Desroches-Noblecourt et al., Grand temple d'Abou Simbel: La Bataille de Qadesh (Cairo: Centre d'études et de documentation sur l'ancienne Egypte, 1971) pl. 3; Wreszinski, Atlas, vol. 2, pl. 84.

201. In the Kadesh battle poem, Ramesses himself refers to the arrows of the Hittites not being able to hit him (KRI II 65, sec. 203–204), which suggests that there were Hittite archers, possibly even chariot archers, at Kadesh; for Hittite chariots lacking quivers, see Spalinger, Ä&L 13 (2003): 180–181.

202. Drews, End of the Bronze Age; Eliezer Oren, ed., Sea Peoples and Their World: A Reassessment (Philadelphia: University Museum, 2000). Both diplomacy and warfare were part of Hittite interactions with the Ahhiyawa; see Trevor Bryce, "Relations between Hatti and Ahhiyawa in the Last Decades of the Bronze Age," in Hittite Studies in Honor of Harry A. Hoffner, ed. G. Beckman et al. (Winona Lake, Ind.: Eisenbrauns, 2003). See also chap. 6, 197–198.

203. Johnson, Asiatic Battle Scene, 116–124, 172–176.

204. An inscription on a stone bowl, likely a forgery, has an oddly written cartouche of Horemhab and mentions a campaign in year sixteen "beginning at Byblos and ending at Carchemish" (Donald Redford, "New Light on the Asiatic Campaigning of Horemheb," *BASOR* 211 [1973]: 36–49); for arguments against the authenticity of this object, see Murnane, *Road to Kadesh*, 30–31.

205. The word for fortress in this label is *dmi*, for which see Dominique Valbelle, "Précisions apportées par l'iconographie à l'un des emplois du mot *dmj*," in *Mélanges Mokhtar*.

206. Alfred Grimm, "Ein Käfig für einen Gefangenen in einem Riual zur Vernichtung von Feinden," *JEA* 73 (1987): 202–206; Grimm, "Der Tod im Wasser: Rituelle Feindvernichtung und Hinrichtung durch Ertränken," *SAK* 16 (1989): 111–119.

207. More specifically, the relief and its counterpart showing the tribute from Punt are on either side of a doorway on the interior of the east wall of the court, between the bark shrine of Amunhotep II and the east tower of the tenth pylon. For photographs, see R. A. Schwaller de Lubicz, *The Temples of Karnak* (Rochester, Vt.: Inner Traditions, 1999), pl. 407 and 408. On these reliefs, see also W. Hovestreydt, "Secret Doors and Hidden Treasures: Some Aspects of Egyptian Temple Treasuries from the New Kingdom," in *Essays in Honour of Herman Te Velde*.

208. Martin, *Memphite Tomb*, pl. 91; on this so-called Zizinia relief and its implications for the career of Horemhab, see also Gnirs, *Militär*, 46–50. For the single Hittite depicted in the tomb of Horemhab and the nonexistence of such depictions in other Amarna sources, see Darnell, *SAK* 18 (1991): 113–140.

209. Martin, *Memphite Tomb*, 87–92, pls. 99–108.

210. Ibid., 58.

211. Carter, *Tut.Ankh.Amen*, vol. 2, 52–53 and pl. 67.

212. Translation of Hans Gustav Güterbock, "The Deeds of Suppiluliuma as Told by His Son, Mursili II," *Journal of Cuneiform Studies* 10 (1956): 94–95 (slightly altered).

213. Trevor Bryce, "The Death of Niphururiya and Its Aftermath," *JEA* 76 (1990): 97–105; Bryce, *Letters of the Great Kings*, 188–189 (with references to the debate); Isre'el and Singer, *The General's Letter*, 165–169. For other interpretations, compare inter alia Gabolde, *D'Akhenaton à Toutânkhamon*, 194–212; Helck, *Grab Nr. 55*, 39–51.

214. For a chronology of the visit and its relation to the burial rites of Tutankhamun, see Bryce, *Letters of the Great Kings*, 189–195.

215. Murnane, *Road to Kadesh*, 25–27.

216. Güterbock, *Journal of Cuneiform Studies* 10 (1956): 96–97.

217. Ibid., 97.

218. Ibid., 97–98.

219. Ibid., 107–108. For the highly unlikely proposition that Zannanza actually becomes pharaoh (under the name Smenkhkare) before dying, see Gabolde, *D'Akhenaton à Toutânkhamon*, 221–224.

220. Itamar Singer, *Hittite Prayers* (Leiden: Brill, 2002), 58–59.

221. P. E. Newberry, "King Ay: The Successor to Tutankhamen," *JEA* 18 (1932): 50–53.

Chapter 6. Uniting the Two Lands: Domestic Security and the Army in Peacetime

1. Jean–Marie Kruchten, *Le Décret d'Horemheb* (Brussels: Université Libre de Bruxelles, 1981), 80, 91–95, for an examination of the more precise legal ramifications of this section of the decree; for the stealing of hides, see A. Nibbi, "A Note on the Value of Animal Skins in Ancient Egypt" in *La dépendance rurale*, 103–106.

2. See chap. 3, n. 67.

3. Kruchten, *Le Décret d'Horemheb*; Andres Gnirs, "Haremhab—ein Staatsreformator?" *SAK* 16 (1989): 83–110. See also Kruchten, "Nouveaux fragments du 'Décret d'Horemheb,'" *Cahiers de Karnak* XI (2003): 487–502.

4. Ronald Leprohon, "The Reign of Akhenaten Seen through the Later Royal Decrees," in *Mélanges Mokhtar*.

5. Compare among many possible citations, the statement of Panehesy in his tomb (Davies, *Rock Tombs* II, pl. 7; Murnane, *Amarna Period*, 171): "Adoration to you . . . the ruler who made me from among humankind . . . who caused me to be powerful when I had been poor."

6. R. B. Parkinson, *Poetry and Culture in Middle Kingdom Egypt* (London: Continuum, 2002), 204–216.

7. For Horemhab as the founder of a new dynasty, see Philips, *Orientalia* 46 (1977): 116–121.

8. E. Blumenthal, *Untersuchungen zum ägyptischen Königtum des Mittleren Reiches* (Berlin: Akademie, 1970); Grimal, *Les Termes de la Propagande*.

9. Davies, *Rock Tombs* V, pl. 27, ll. 2–3, 8–10.

10. The promotion of a western Asiatic, Aper-el, to the post of vizier during the reigns of Amunhotep III and Akhenaten may be a further feature the cosmpolitanism of the late Eighteenth Dynasty; see Alain Zivie, *Découverte à Saqqarah: Le Vizir Oublié* (Paris: Éditions du Seuil, 1990).

11. Murnane and Van Siclen, *Boundary Stelae*, 41.

12. Ibid., 166–168.

13. Erik Hornung, *Das Buch von den Pforten des Jenseits* (Geneva: Éditions de Belles-Lettres, 1979), vol. 2, 260–263.

14. Assmann, *Sonnenpriester*.

15. For the "dictatorship" of Akhenaten, compare Sandman, *Texts*, 86, l. 15–16: "When he rises, he exercises his might against him who is ignorant of his teachings, and his favors towards him the one who knows him."

16. Alan Gardiner, "Davies's Copy of the Great Speos Artemidos Inscription," *JEA* 32 (1946): 43–56.

17. Redford, *Pharaonic King-Lists*, 259ff.; Manassa, *Merneptah*, 110–113.

18. Alan Gardiner, "The Graffito from the Tomb of Pere," *JEA* 14 (1928): pl. V, l. 6–12, 19–21.

19. On the graffito of Pawah, see pages 46–47 and n. 175.

20. Davies, *Rock Tombs* III, pl. 31.

21. Two members from each of the four races—Egyptians, Nubians, Asiatics, and Libyans—appear in the royal bodyguard in the tomb of Meryre; see Davies, *Rock Tombs* I, pl. 10, 15, 20, and 26 (including Nubian fan-bearers); for other foreign auxiliaries, see Davies, *Rock Tombs* II, pls. 10, 13, and 17; Davies, *Rock Tombs* IV, pls. 10, 13, 22, and 40; Davies, *Rock Tombs* V, pls. 20, and 29; Martin, *Royal Tomb*, 35.

22. Kemp and Garfi, *El-'Amarna*, 62–63; Lacovara, *Royal City*, 45.

23. Davies, *Rock Tombs* IV, pls. 24, 25, and 26; for a similar depiction on a talatat, see Aldred, *Akhenaten and Nefertiti*, 145.

24. D. J. Woolliscroft, *Roman Military Signalling* (Charleston, S.C.: Tempus Publishing, 2001).

25. Davies, *Rock Tombs* VI, pl. 30.

26. Similar raised platforms were constructed during the Roman Period in the Eastern Desert of Egypt; see R. E. Zitterkopf and S. E. Sidebotham, "Stations and Towers on the Quseir-Nile Road," *JEA* 75 (1989): 155–189; Van't Dack, "Postes et Telecommunications Ptolémaïques," *CdE* 37 (1962) 338–341. One might also compare the "milecastles" along Hadrian's Wall (Woolliscroft, *Roman Military Signalling*, 58–78). For a different interpreta-

tion of the raised platforms in the tomb of Mahu, see David O'Connor, "Demarcating the Boundaries: An Interpretation of a Scene in the Tomb of Mahu, El-Amarna," *Bulletin of the Egyptological Seminar* 9 (1987/88): 41–52.

27. Davies, *Rock Tombs* IV, pls. 21–25 and pl. 28 for the interrelationship of some of the scenes on the south wall.

28. Davies, *Rock Tombs* IV, pl. 26. The Theban Desert Road Survey discovered similar outposts on the west bank of Thebes at a site called Gebel Antef. Nubian Pan-Grave ceramic remains were discovered around cairns and dry-stone huts, which suggests that Medjoy patrolmen were stationed on this promontory during the Second Intermediate Period (J. C. Darnell, in *Egypt and Nubia*, 132).

29. Compare the patrol system that protected the northern border of the Theban nome during the Second Intermediate Period (see chap. 3, n. 253), and the patrol routes connecting the Nubian fortresses (see page 96).

30. Davies, *Rock Tombs* IV, pl. 26, lower register, and pl. 41 (photograph of a portion of the scene).

31. Contra translation of Murnane, *Amarna Period*, 149–50.

32. Kemp and Garfi, *El-'Amarna*, 39 and map pl. 1.

33. Kemp and Garfi, *El-'Amarna*, map pl. 1.

34. Kemp, *Ancient Egypt*, 1st ed., 273 and 344, n. 23.

35. O'Connor, in *Libya and Egypt*. For Libyan settlements, see ibid., 63–66, and Manassa, *Merneptah*, 87.

36. For the scope of these terms and the possible linguistic associations of the term Tjemehu, see Manassa, *Merneptah*, 82–85. The Libyans who appear in Egyptian representations, wearing their long cloaks and penis sheaths, also have left depictions of themselves in the same costume deep in the Sahara, at the modern border between Libya and Algeria; see Malika Hachid, *Le Tassili des Ajjer* (Paris: Éditions Paris-Méditerranée, 2000), 249.

37. Anthony Spalinger, "Some Notes on the Libyans of the Old Kingdom and Later Historical Reflexes," *JSSEA* 9 (1979): 125–160 and references therein; Jean Leclant, "La 'famille libyenne' au temple haut de Pépi I," *Livre du centenaire* (Cairo: Institut Français de'Archéologie Orientale, 1980).

38. For the existence of Libyan envoys operating in Nubia, note a stela of Thutmose III at Buhen (Caminos, *The New Kingdom Temples of Buhen*, 50).

39. Amunhotep III also appears to have built a fortress to combat the Libyans (*Urk.* IV, 1656, l. 15–17).

40. Kenneth Kitchen, "The Arrival of the Libyans in Late New Kingdom Egypt," in *Libya and Egypt*; Manassa, *Merneptah*; Murnane, *Road to Kadesh*, 99–100; Stephen Snape, "The Emergence of Libya on the Horizon of Egypt," in *Mysterious Lands*.

41. Jacke Phillips, "Ostrich Eggshells," in *Ancient Egyptian Materials and Technology*.

42. G. Kopcke, *Handel, Archaeologica Homerica Kapitel* M (Göttingen: Vandenhoeck & Ruprecht, 1990), 34–35.

43. O'Connor, in *Libya and Egypt*, 96–97. For "fat bulls of the Meshwesh" being used during the celebrations of Amunhotep III's second jubilee at Malqata, see W. C. Hayes, "Inscriptions from the Palace of Amenhotep III," *JNES* 10 (1951): 91.

44. Richardson, "Libya Domestica: Libyan Trade and Society on the Eve of the Invasions of Egypt," *JARCE* 36 (1999): 149–164; E. Fabbricotti, "Silphium in Ancient Art," *Libyan Studies* 24 (1993): 27–33.

45. Manassa, *Merneptah*, 85–88; Richardson, *JARCE* 36 (1999): 149–164. For later versions of the trans-Saharan itineraries, see Edward William Bovill, *The Golden Trade of the Moors: West African Kingdoms in the Fourteenth Century* (Princeton, N.J.: Markus Wiener Publishers Bovill, 1995), 28–44; E. M. Ruprechtsberger, *Die Garamanten, Geschichte*

und Kultur eines Libyschen Volkes in der Sahara (Mainz: Philipp von Zabern, 1997), 26–28; J. Thiry, *Le Sahara Libyen dans l'Afrique du Nord Medievale* (Leuven: Uitgeverij Peeters, 1995), 432ff.

46. Davies, *Rock Tombs* II, pl. 37 and 40; note also the potential Libyan delegation on a talatat from Hermopolis discussed in Petschel and von Falck, eds., *Pharao siegt immer*, 192.

47. Davies, *Rock Tombs* III, pls. 14–15. The depiction of the Libyans is somewhat ambiguous; the bulk of the scene is occupied by feather-wearing men, at least some of whom carry Egyptian axes and officers' batons. In the second row these apparent Libyans carry metal (copper?) ingots on their shoulders, while below, several offering bringers carry large metal vessels. Farther down in the same series of offering bringers is a group that finds close parallels in depictions of Nubian tribute. A number of men in the register, however, wear feathers identical to those of the Libyans above, and the exact point of origin of the different groups is unclear, and one might best term the entire ensemble "Libo-Nubian." Libo-Nubian groups might also be behind the inscription on the obelisk base of Hatshepsut, which lists Nubian tribute being presented by Libyans (*Urk.* IV 373, l. 6–11).

48. O'Connor, in *Libya and Egypt*; Manassa, *Merneptah*, 85–88.

49. Manassa, *Merneptah*, 88–90.

50. A. P. White and D. White, "Coastal Sites of Northeast Africa: The Case against Bronze Age Ports," *JARCE* 33 (1996): 11–30; D. White, *Marsa Martruh* (Philadelphia: Institute for Aegean Prehistory Academic Press, 2002). Imported Levantine pottery and stirrup jars excavated in the coastal Rammesside fortress of Zawiyet Umm el-Rakham further demonstrate the importance of the Libyan coast for eastern Mediterranean trade; see Stephen Snape, "Imported Pottery at Zawiyet Umm el-Rakham: Preliminary Report," *Bulletin de Liaison du Groupe International d'Étude de la Céramique Égyptienne* 21 (2000): 17–22. Lucien Basch, "Une représentation de navire de type égéen dans l'oasis de Dakhleh (Égypte) vers 1200 av. J.-C.," in *Res Maritimae: Cyprus and the Eastern Mediterranean from Prehistory to Late Antiquity*, ed. Stuart Swiny, Robert Hohlfelder, and Helena Swiny (Atlanta: Scholars Press, 1997) interprets a graffito of a ship in Dakhla Oasis as an Aegean vessel manned by Libyans, but the inscription was most likely made during the post-pharaonic period.

51. See, among the many possible references on the Sea Peoples, Drews, *End of the Bronze Age*; Oren, ed., *The Sea Peoples*; David O'Connor and Eric Cline, "The Mystery of the Sea Peoples," in *Mysterious Lands*.

52. O'Connor, in *Libya and Egypt*, 88–89.

53. For publications and discussions of papyrus British Museum EA 74100, see Richard Parkinson and Louise Schofield, "Images of Mycenaeans: A Recently Acquired Painted Papyrus from el Amarna," in *Egypt, the Aegean, and the Levant: Interconnections in the Second Millennium B.C.*, ed. V. W. Davies and L. Schofield (London: British Museum Press, 1995); Schofield and Parkinson, "Of Helmets and Heretics: A Possible Egyptian Representation of Mycenaean Warriors on a Papyrus from El-Amarna," *Annual of the British School at Athens* 89 (1994): 157–170; Kemp and Garfi, *El-'Amarna*, 61, suggest that the papyrus fragments might have originally come from the "House of Life," to the north. For the shrine of the king's statue see Kemp, *Ancient Egypt*, 1st ed., 283–285.

54. Schofield and Parkinson, *The Annual of the British School at Athens* 89 (1994): 163–169; N. Grguric, *The Mycenaeans c. 1650–1100 B.C.* (Oxford: Osprey, 2005), 11–14.

55. Vronwy Hankey, "Stirrup Jars at el-Amarna," in *Egypt, the Aegean and the Levant*.

56. The blocks were originally part of Horemhab's mortuary temple and later reused for Khonsu Temple (Johnson, *Asiatic Battle Scene*, 113–120, 166, 172, catalog nos. 57, 58, and 65).

57. Snape, in *Mysterious Lands*, 100–105; Manassa, *Merneptah*, 48–50, 57–58; Morris, *Imperialism*, 611–644. For a depiction of a Ramesside fortress named "Ramesses III Drives

Back the Tjemehu-Libyans," see Epigraphic Survey, *Medinet Habu* 1, pl. 21, and *Medinet Habu* 2, pl. 69.

58. A Middle Kingdom fortress in the Wadi Natrun, Qaret el-Dahr, may be a much earlier precursor to the Ramesside western frontier fortresses; see Ahmed Fakhry, "Wâdi-el-Natrûn," *ASAE* 40 (1940): 837–848.

59. Colin Hope, "Oasis Amphorae of the New Kingdom," in *Egypt and Nubia*, ed. Friedman; Giddy, *Egyptian Oases*, 62–63, 75, 78–80, 84, 89, and 156–157. Basketry was another important export of the oasis region; see Lisa Giddy, "Some Exports from the Oases of the Libyan Desert into the Nile Valley—Tomb 131 at Thebes," *Livre du centenaire*.

60. Sylvie Marchand and Pierre Tallet, "Ayn Asil et l'oasis de Dakhla au Nouvel Empire," *BIFAO* 99 (1999): 307–352; D. Darnell, in *Egypt and Nubia*, ed. Friedman, 173; Hayes, *JNES* 10 (1951): 89.

61. Manassa, *Merneptah*, 94–107.

62. For the conflicts of the early Twelfth Dynasty caused by the militarization of the preceding period, see Darnell, *ZÄS* 131 (2004): 31–37; Grajetzki, *Middle Kingdom*, 29–30.

63. Eyre, in *Labor in the Ancient Near East*, 187–188; Gnirs, *Militär*, 36–37, 141–158; Darnell, *Theban Desert Road Survey* 1, 60; Grajetzki, *Die höchsten Beamten*, 128. For paramilitary troops participating in the construction of fortresses, compare a stela from the reign of Amenemhat III, where the "sheriff Antef" lists the number of bricks delivered for a fortification; see Ronald Leprohon, *Corpus Antiquitatum Aegyptiacarum, Museum of Fine Arts Boston, Stelae I: The Early Dynastic Period to the Late Middle Kingdom* (Mainz: Philipp von Zabern, 1985), 2, 90. For the large military involvement in a quarry expedition to the Wadi Hammamat during the reign of Ramesses IV, see Hikade, *Expeditionswesen*, 38–46.

64. Klemm and Klemm, *Steine und Steinbrüche*, 362; Donald Redford and Susan Redford, "Graffiti and Petroglyphs Old and New from the Eastern Desert," *JARCE* 26 (1989): 44–46; 3–49; Murnane, *Amarna Period*, 68–69; Hikade, *Expeditionswesen*, 195.

65. *Urk.* IV, 1962; see also the translation of Murnane, *Amarna Period*, 29–30.

66. Cemal Pulack, "The Uluburun Shipwreck: An Overview," *International Journal of Nautical Archaeology* 27, no. 3 (1998): 188–224; see Wachsmann, *Seagoing Ships*, 303–314, for Uluburun in the context of Mediterranean trade.

67. Wachsmann, *Seagoing Ships*, 42–47.

68. Ibid., 295–301; Eric Cline, *Sailing the Wine-Dark Sea: International Trade and the Late Bronze Age Aegean* (Oxford: Tempvs Reparatvm, 1994), 91–94.

69. Susanne Bickel, "Commerçants et bateliers au Nouvel Empire," in *Le commerce en Égypte ancienne*, ed. N. Grimal and B. Menu (Cairo: Institut Français d'Archéologie Orientale, 1998).

70. Darnell, in *Ägypten im Afro-orientalischen Kontext*, 121–123; Michal Artzy, "Nomads of the Sea," in *Res Maritimae*.

71. See n. 50 above.

72. Compare Norman de Garis Davies and Raymond Faulkner, "A Syrian Trading Venture to Egypt," *JEA* 33 (1947): 40–46.

73. Bickel, in *Le commerce en Égypte ancienne*, 159; Alan Schulman, "Mhr and Mškb: Two Egyptian Military Titles of Semitic Origin," *ZÄS* 93 (1996): 123–132; Chevereau, *Nouvel Empire*, 169–171. For the economic functions of policeman, see also Darnell, *Theban Desert Road Survey* I, 60.

74. Davies, *Rock Tombs* I, pl. 29.

75. Norman de Garis Davies, *The Tomb of Nefer-hotep at Thebes* (New York: Arno Press, 1973), pl. 63. For this one might compare the "place of examination" near the riverbank at Deir el-Medina; see Andrea McDowell, *Jurisdiction in the Workmen's Community of Deir el-Medina* (Leiden: Nederlands Instituut voor het Nabije Oosten, 1990), 219–222.

The tradition of justice taking place on ships goes back at least to the Middle Kingdom—in the story of the Eloquent Peasant, the official Rensi deliberates on his "court-vessel"; see Dieter Kurth, *Der Oasenmann* (Mainz: Philipp von Zabern, 2003), 113.

76. Darnell, *SAK* 18 (1991): 122–123; for more peaceful relations between Egyptians and Aegeans, see Shelly Wachsmann, *Aegeans in the Theban Tombs* (Leuven: Peeters, 1987); Lyla Pinch Brock, "Art, Industry, and the Aegeans in the Tomb of Amenmose," *Ä&L* 10 (2000): 129–137.

77. *Urk.* IV, 1821, l. 13ff.; Wolfgang Helck, *Die Beziehungen Ägyptens und Vorderasiens zur Ägäis bis ins 7. Jahrhundert v. Chr.* (Darmstadt: Wissenschaftliche Buchgesellschaft, 1979), 133 and n. 5–7; Darnell, *SAK* 18 (1991): 122. Joos van Ghistele, *Le Voyage en Égypte de Joos van Ghistele 1482–1483*, ed. R. Bauwens-Préaux (Cairo: Institut Français d'Archéologie Orientale, 1976), 8 describes the construction of similar lookout posts along the Egyptian coast to protect pilgrims.

78. See pages 152–153.

79. H. Ormerod, *Piracy in the Ancient World* (Liverpool: Liverpool University Press, 1978), 81–83.

80. Kenneth Kitchen, *Pharaoh Triumphant: The Life and Times of Ramesses II* (Cairo: American University in Cairo Press, 1997), 40–41; Manassa, *Merneptah*, 79–81.

81. For foreigners in the *heb-sed* festival, see Gunlach, *Die Zwangsumsiedlung*, 177–184.

82. Williams and Logan, *JNES* 46 (1987): 245–285.

83. Serrano, *Royal Festivals*, 80–91; Gilbert, *Early Warfare*, 85–86.

84. Do. Arnold et al., *Egyptian Art in the Age of the Pyramids*, 318–321.

85. E.g., Edouard Naville, *The Temple of Deir el-Bahari*, part 4 (London: Egypt Exploration Fund, 1901), pl. 90–91; Epigraphic Survey, *Luxor Temple* 1.

86. William Murnane, "Opetfest," in *LÄ* 4; Lanny Bell, "Luxor Temple and the Cult of the Royal *Ka*," *JNES* 44 (1985): 251–294.

87. See page 103.

88. Pierre-Marie Chevereau, "Le porte-étendard Maienheqau," *RdÉ* 47 (1996): 9–28.

89. Epigraphic Survey, *Luxor Temple* 1, pl. 91, l. 2; translation follows that in the commentary volume, 35; for an additional parallel, see Manassa, *Merneptah*, 127.

90. Darnell, *SAK* 22 (1995): 47–94; Renée Friedman, "Pots, Pebbles, and Petroglyphs, Part II: 1996 Excavations at Hierakonpolis Locality Hk64," in *Studies on Ancient Egypt in Honour of H. S. Smith*, 101–108. On the goddess of the eye of the sun in general, see Christiane Desroches-Noblecourt, *Amours et fureurs de La Lointaine* (Paris: Sock/Pernoud, 1997); Geraldine Pinch, *Votive Offerings to Hathor* (Oxford, U.K.: Griffith Institute, 1993), 190–196; Danielle Inconnu-Bocquillon, *Le mythe de la Déesse Lointaine à Philae* (Paris: Impr. Nationale, 2001).

91. Epigraphic Survey, *Luxor Temple* 1, pl. 28 and 32; for Nubian dancers in general, see Emma Brunner-Traut, *Der Tanz im alten Ägypten* (Glückstadt: J. J. Augustin, 1938), 54–56; Henri Wild, "Une danse nubienne d'époque pharaonique," *Kush* 7 (1959): 76–90.

92. Hans Hickmann, "Die altägyptische Rassel," *ZÄS* 79 (1954): 116–125.

93. Wreszinski, *Atlas*, vol. 2, pl. 161–162; for dance scenes at Beit el-Wali, see Ricke, Hughes, and Wente, *Beit el-Wali Temple*, pl. 9.

94. Hermann Te Velde, "Some Remarks on the Mysterious Language of the Baboons," in *Funerary Symbols and Religion*, ed. J. H. Kamstra et al. (Kampen: J. H. Kok, 1988). The positive associations of Nubians and baboons are overlooked in Smith, *Wretched Kush*, 27.

95. Victor Davis Hansen, "The Ideology of Hoplite Battle, Ancient and Modern," in *Hoplites: The Classical Greek Battle Experience*, ed. V. D. Hansen (London: Routledge, 1991), 28–30; Pritchett, *The Greek State at War*, part 2, 216–217.

96. Knight, *Zulu Army*, 83–84.

97. Epigraphic Survey, *Luxor Temple* 1, pl. 20.

98. Schulman, *Ceremonial Execution*, 116–148; Kemp, *JEA* 62 (1976): 81–99.

99. Davies, *Nefer-hotep*, pl. 14.

100. Compare the description of the presentation of tribute before the Window of Appearances in the Late Egyptian Miscellanies (Caminos, *Miscellanies*, 64, 200–201, 438–439). A group of Asiatic and Nubian rulers are present at the reward of Meryre II (Davies, *Rock Tombs* II, pl. 33 and 35).

101. Other pieces of royal statuary incorporated heads of enemies to create the same effect—Petschel and von Falck, eds., *Pharao siegt immer*, 50–51.

102. Wolfgang Decker, *Sports and Games of Ancient Egypt* (Cairo: American University in Cairo Press, 1992), 82; Rosemarie Drenkhahn, "Darstellungen von Negern in Ägypten," Ph.D. diss., Universität Hamburg, 1967, 82–86 and 166; Epigraphic Survey, *Kheruef*, pl. 61 and 63. Note also the depiction of Nubian wrestlers from Sesebi, Blackman, *JEA* 23 (1937): pl. 12.

103. Epigraphic Survey, *Medinet Habu* 2, pl. 111.

104. For fencing in ancient Egypt, see Peter Piccione, "Sportive Fencing as a Ritual for Destroying the Enemies of Horus," in *Gold of Praise*; Decker, *Sports and Games*, 82–87.

105. See pages 109–110 and 145.

106. Davies, *Rock Tombs* II, pl. 37. A parallel to the poses of the wrestlers appears on a talatat in the Metropolitan Museum of New York, L.1996.74; although labeled as a "melée," the scene is probably a depiction of ritual rather than actual combat.

107. Ritual combat was also part of Amunhotep III's third jubilee celebration (Epigraphic Survey, *Kheruef*, pl. 47 and 60–63). Some of the armed participants in religious processions, such as the club-wielding Nubians in the Opet scenes, might themselves at some point during the festivities have engaged in ritual combat, as we see stick fighters fencing atop the cabin of a vessel in the riverine procession of Montu (Decker, *Sports and Games*, 87).

FURTHER READING

The following list contains publications for readers wishing to learn more about the history, culture, and religion of Amarna Period Egypt as well as overviews of Egyptian military history.

Aldred, Cyril. *Akhenaten: King of Egypt*. London: Thames & Hudson, 1991.

Arnold, Dorothea. *The Royal Women of Amarna: Images of Beauty from Ancient Egypt*. New York: Metropolitan Museum of Art, 1996.

Assmann, Jan. *Egyptian Solar Religion in the New Kingdom: Re, Amun, and the Crisis of Polytheism*. Translated by A. Alcock. London: Kegan Paul International, 1995.

Bryce, Trevor R. *Letters of the Great Kings of the Ancient Near East: The Royal Correspondence of the Late Bronze Age*. London: Routledge, 2003.

Carter, Howard. *The Tomb of Tut.Ankh.Amen*. 3 vols. 1928–1933. Reprint, London: Gerald Duckworth, 2000–2003.

Cohen, Raymond, and Raymond Westbrook, eds. *Amarna Diplomacy: The Beginnings of International Relations*. Baltimore: Johns Hopkins University Press, 2000.

Desroches-Noblecourt, Christiane. *Tutankhamen*. New York: New York Graphic Society, 1963.

Epigraphic Survey. *Reliefs and Inscriptions at Luxor Temple*. Vol. 1, *The Festival Procession of Opet in the Colonnade Hall: Translation and Commentary*. Chicago: University of Chicago, Oriental Institute, 1994.

Freed, Rita E., Yvonne J. Markowitz, and Sue H. D'Auria, eds. *Pharaohs of the Sun*. Boston: Museum of Fine Arts, 1999.

Gabolde, Marc. *D'Akhenaton à Toutânkhamon*. Lyons: Institut d'Archéologie et d'Histoire de l'Antiquité, 1998.

Gnirs, Andrea. *Militär und Gesellschaft: Ein Beitrag zur Sozialgeschichte des Neuen Reiches*. Heidelberg: Heidelberger Orientverlag, 1996.

Hawass, Zahi. *Tutankhamun and the Golden Age of the Pharaohs*. Washington, D.C.: National Geographic Society, 2005.

Healy, Mark. *Armies of the Pharaohs*. Oxford, U.K.: Osprey Publishing, 1992.

Heinz, Susanna. *Die Feldzugsdarstellungen des Neuen Reiches: Eine Bildanalyse*. Vienna: Verlag der Österreichischen Akademie der Wissenschaften, 2001.

Hornung, Erik. *Akhenaten and the Religion of Light*. Translated by David Lorton. Ithaca, N.Y.: Cornell University Press, 1999.

———. *Conceptions of God in Ancient Egypt: The One and the Many*. Translated by J. Baines. Ithaca, N.Y.: Cornell University Press, 1996.

James, T. G. H. *Tutankhamun: The Eternal Splendour of the Boy Pharaoh*. London: Tauris Parke, 2000.

Johnson, W. Raymond. "An Asiatic Battle Scene of Tutankhamun from Thebes: A Late Amarna Antecedent of the Ramesside Battle-Narrative Tradition." Ph.D. diss., University of Chicago, 1992.

Kozloff, Arielle P., and Betsy M. Bryan, eds. *Egypt's Dazzling Sun: Amenhotep III and His World*. Cleveland: Cleveland Museum of Art, 1992.

Liverani, Mario. *International Relations in the Ancient Near East, 1600-1100 B.C.* New York: St. Martin's Press, Palgrave, 2001.

Martin, Geoffrey T. *The Hidden Tombs of Memphis*. London: Thames & Hudson, 1992.

Moran, William. *The Amarna Letters*. Baltimore: Johns Hopkins University Press, 1992.

Murnane, William J. *The Road to Kadesh: A Historical Interpretation of the Battle Reliefs of King Sety I at Karnak*. Chicago: University of Chicago, Oriental Institute, 1990.

O'Connor, David, and Eric H. Cline, eds. *Amenhotep III: Perspectives on His Reign*. Ann Arbor: University of Michigan Press, 1997.

Petschel, Susanne, and Martin von Falck, eds. *Pharao siegt immer: Krieg und Frieden im Alten Ägypten*. Bönen: Kettler, 2004.

Redford, Donald. *Akhenaten: The Heretic King*. Princeton, N.J.: Princeton University Press, 1984.

Reeves, Nicholas. *Akhenaten: Egypt's False Prophet*. London: Thames & Hudson, 2001.

———. *The Complete Tutankhamun*. London: Thames & Hudson, 1990.

Roth, Silke. *Gebieterin aller Länder: Die Rolle der königlichen Frauen in der fiktiven und realen Aussenpolitik des ägyptischen Neuen Reiches*. Freiburg: Universitätsverlag, 2002.

Shaw, Ian. *Egyptian Warfare and Weapons*. Buckinghamshire, U.K.: Shire, 1991.

Spalinger, Anthony. *War in Ancient Egypt*. Oxford, U.K.: Blackwell, 2005.

INDEX

NOTE: Page references in *italics* indicate illustrations and/or art.